Recording Broadway

Recording Broadway

A LIFE IN CAST ALBUMS

THOMAS Z. SHEPARD
GAYDEN WREN

APPLAUSE
THEATRE & CINEMA BOOKS

APPLAUSE

Bloomsbury Publishing Group, Inc.
ApplauseBooks.com

Distributed by NATIONAL BOOK NETWORK

Copyright © 2025 by Thomas Z. Shepard

All rights reserved. No part of this book may be reproduced in any form or by any electronic or mechanical means, including information storage and retrieval systems, without written permission from the publisher, except by a reviewer who may quote passages in a review. British Library Cataloguing in Publication Information available

Library of Congress Cataloging-in-Publication Data

Names: Shepard, Thomas Z. (Thomas Zachary), 1936- author. | Wren, Gayden, 1961- author.
Title: Recording Broadway : a life in cast albums / Thomas Z. Shepard, Gayden Wren.
Description: Essex, Connecticut : Applause Theatre & Cinema, 2024. | Includes bibliographical references and index. | Summary: "If your alley is Shubert, then Recording Broadway: A Life in Cast Albums is definitely for you, as it will be for every Broadway fan. For the first time, the alchemy behind the production of 'The Original Cast Album' is told – and no one is better positioned to do so than Tom Shepard" —Provided by publisher.
Identifiers: LCCN 2024014125 (print) | LCCN 2024014126 (ebook) | ISBN 9781493081257 (cloth) | ISBN 9781493081264 (epub)
Subjects: LCSH: Shepard, Thomas Z. (Thomas Zachary), 1936- author. | Sound recording executives and producers—United States—Biography. | Musicals—New York (State)—New York—History and criticism. | Original cast recordings—History. | LCGFT: Autobiographies.
Classification: LCC ML429.S463 A3 2024 (print) | LCC ML429.S463 (ebook) | DDC 782.1/4092 [B]—dc23/eng/20240329
LC record available at https://lccn.loc.gov/2024014125
LC ebook record available at https://lccn.loc.gov/2024014126

♾™ The paper used in this publication meets the minimum requirements of American National Standard for Information Sciences—Permanence of Paper for Printed Library Materials, ANSI/NISO Z39.48-1992.

CONTENTS

	Acknowledgments	ix
	Author's Note	xi
	Foreword by John Kander	xiii
	Introduction: Sound in a Box	xv
PART I	**Early Years (1936–1960)**	**1**
1	Jersey Boy	2
2	Music and Me	9
3	The Right Place at the Right Time	13
4	Ready to be Lucky	16
PART II	**Columbia (1960–1974)**	**21**
5	Goddard	22
6	Making Records	29
7	The Making of a Producer	33
8	The Word Is "Stereophonic"	44
9	The Sixth Record Is Free	48
10	Not the Original Cast	52
	Show Boat (1962); *The Merry Widow* (1962); *Annie Get Your Gun* (1963); *Lady in the Dark* (1963); *The Student Prince* (1963)	
11	Of Cattlemen and Kings	65
	Oklahoma! (1964); *The King and I* (1964)	
12	The Original Cast	74
	O Say Can You See! (1963); *To Broadway with Love* (1964); *The Secret Life of Walter Mitty* (1964); *Bajour* (1964); *The Decline and Fall of the Entire World as Seen Through the Eyes of Cole Porter* (1965); *The Zulu and the Zayda* (1965)	
13	My Name Is . . . Friend	87
	Harold Sings Arlen (with Friend) (1966); *The Megilla of Itzik Manger* (1968)	
14	Yankee Doodle Dandies	95
	George M! (1968); *Dear World* (1969); *1776* (1969); *Dames at Sea* (1969)	

| | 15 | Annus Mirabilis | 108 |

The Sesame Street Book and Record (1970);
The Year of Roosevelt Franklin (1971);
Bob and Ray: The Two and Only (1970);
The Rothschilds (1970); *Two by Two* (1970)

| | 16 | "Mr. Shepard, Mr. Sondheim" | 123 |

Company (1970); *Company: The London Cast Recording* (1970)

| | 17 | The Movies and Me | 135 |

The Reivers (1960); *M.A.S.H.* (1970); *Tell Me that You Love Me, Junie Moon* (1970); *Such Good Friends* (1971)

| | 18 | Nanette, Irene, and Friends | 140 |

No, No, Nanette (1971/1973); *70, Girls, 70* (1971);
Man of La Mancha (1972); *Of Thee I Sing* (1972);
Dr. Selavy's Magic Theatre (1972); *Elephant Steps* (1974);
A Little Night Music (1973); *Irene* (1973); *Shelter* (1973);
Raisin (1973); *Candide* (1974)

| | 19 | All Good Things Must End | 157 |

| PART III | | **RCA (1974–1986)** | **163** |
| | 20 | Sondheim Times Three | 164 |

A Little Night Music (1975); *Goodtime Charley* (1975);
Pacific Overtures (1976); *Side by Side by Sondheim* (1976)

| | 21 | Richard Rodgers and Me | 172 |

Rex (1976); *The King and I* (1977)

| | 22 | The High-Water Mark | 178 |

Porgy and Bess (1977)

| | 23 | A Man Named Sweeney Todd | 187 |

Sweeney Todd: The Demon Barber of Fleet Street (1979);
The Ballad of Sweeney Todd (1979)

| | 24 | Everything Old Is New Again | 198 |

Ain't Misbehavin' (1978); *Oklahoma!* (1979);
42nd Street (1980); *Sophisticated Ladies* (1981)

| | 25 | Sondheim Times Three, Again | 207 |

Marry Me a Little (1981); *Merrily We Roll Along* (1981);
A Stephen Sondheim Evening (1983)

| | 26 | Trips to Greece and France | 217 |

Zorba (1983); *La Cage aux Folles* (1983)

| | 27 | Sunday in the Park with Steve | 225 |

Sunday in the Park with George (1984);
A Collector's Sondheim (1985)

| | 28 | Two Nights at Avery Fisher Hall | 232 |

Follies in Concert (1985)

| | 29 | Sondheim and Me | 251 |
| | 30 | Interlude: "Song and Dance" | 261 |

Song and Dance (1985)

PART IV	**MCA (1986–1989)**	263
31	Parting Ways with RCA *Me and My Girl* (1986); *Carousel* (1987); *Romance/Romance* (1988)	264
32	Parting Ways with MCA	273
PART V	**Free Agent (1989–Present)**	277
33	Hired Gun *John Williams Conducts John Williams: The Star Wars Trilogy* (1990); *Kismet* (1991); *Man of La Mancha* (1996); *Catch Me If I Fall* (1995); *The Secret Garden* (1991); *Love in Two Countries* (1991)	278
34	A Jukebox, a Revamp, a Sequel, and a Revival *Jelly's Last Jam* (1992); *Crazy for You* (1992); *Annie Warbucks* (1993); *Damn Yankees* (1994)	286
35	A Solo, a Replacement, a Revue, and Julie *Wings* (1995); *Kiss of the Spider Woman* (1995); *Swinging on a Star* (1996); *Victor/Victoria* (1995)	295
36	Trips to Chicago and Alaska *Chicago* (1998); *King Island Christmas* (1999)	304
37	Lerner & Loewe, Live *My Fair Lady* (2007); *Camelot* (2008)	310
38	Yesterday, Today, and "Tomorrow" *Beauty and the Beast* (2007); *The Little Mermaid* (2008); *Thespis* (2008); *Annie* (2013)	316
	Epilogue : Still Putting Sound into Boxes *Anna Christie* (2019)	325
	Appendix: Discography	327
	Index	331

ACKNOWLEDGMENTS

MANY PEOPLE HAVE CONTRIBUTED to the creation of this book, beginning with my parents and my family and extending through all the people I've known and worked with throughout a career that began in 1960 and continues to this day. But certain individuals have contributed directly to the book, and I'd like to acknowledge them here.

I began writing my memoirs on my own, back in the 2000s, and Naomi Graffman and Gary Marmorstein provided advice and assistance that kept me going. Other projects led me to put the book aside for some years, until my friend and eventual coauthor, Gayden Wren, took an interest in it. He suggested a new focus for the book and certain new ideas for its content, and in 2019 we set to work on what became the book you hold in your hands.

Two women, both graduates of Oberlin College, were invaluable to our writing process: Sayer Elliott Holliday was our first reader and contributed immeasurably to the shaping of each chapter as it emerged. Later in the process, Stephanie M. Muntone read the entire manuscript, and her passion for Broadway musicals, her love of Broadway cast albums, and her keen editorial eye led to the correction of innumerable details, large and small, along the way. (Any surviving errors, of course, are entirely our fault.) Christopher Cerf also read some advance chapters and offered useful suggestions.

Peter Sawyer, our agent, offered us invaluable advice and counsel, besides bringing us together with Applause Books.

John Cerullo, our acquisitions editor at Applause, brought a marketplace eye to what is and isn't in the book and had many valuable suggestions that have improved it markedly. Production ace Barbara Claire kept the wheels turning and made sure all of the chapters, photos, captions, and other pieces of the project came together on schedule—or at any rate, not so off schedule as to keep the book from coming out. Emily Burr also made important behind-the-scenes contributions, as did Raymond Lang, my friend who did so much to help keep me in focus. Thanks also to project editor Ashleigh Cooke.

My professional archives are at Yale University, where Jane Meditz was helpful above and beyond the call of duty in locating the right photos to illustrate my story. Thanks also to Miranda Moore, senior director of clearances at The Recording Academy, and Ken Grossi at the Oberlin College Archives, for generously providing two specific photos.

Austin John McLean of ProQuest helped us track down an arcane detail about *Follies in Concert*, and Terry Hochler helped us with an arcane detail about *Leading Man: The Best of Broadway*. The New York Society Library provided useful research resources. On the internet, the Internet Broadway Database (IBDB), CastAlbums.org, Discogs.com, and MasterworksBroadway.com, while not infallible, have been valuable references.

Finally I'd like to dedicate this book, at the footlights, to my wife, Irene Clark; my daughter, Elizabeth Shepard; my brother, Lewis Shepard; and my most special relative, Madeleine Green Kalb.

And upstage, I dedicate it to my parents, Dorothy and Seymour Shepard, without whom this story could not have happened.

AUTHOR'S NOTE

DUE TO LENGTH LIMITATIONS, significant portions of the original manuscript for this book had to be deleted, totaling roughly 10 percent of the original. These portions can be read on www.ThomasZShepard.com. In addition to extended versions of two chapters, there is also a chapter on my remastering work and coverage of such theater-adjacent albums as *Barbara Cook: The Disney Album, Sarah Brightman: The Songs that Got Away, Placido Domingo: The Broadway I Love,* Thomas Hampson's *Leading Man: The Best of Broadway, Betty Buckley: An Evening at Carnegie Hall, With a Song in My Heart: The Great Songs of Richard Rodgers,* and more.

FOREWORD
BY JOHN KANDER

IF SOMEONE CALLS HIMSELF A "RECORD PRODUCER" . . . well . . . that obviously calls to mind someone who records music . . . songs for us to hum . . . symphonies for us to experience. But if a record producer specializes in recording musical theatre, that, I believe, is something quite different. Yes of course he's making a permanent recording of songs from the show and often performances by cast members, but the great ones . . . and Tom Shepard is a great one . . . can make you feel while you're listening that you are actually there in the theatre witnessing a live performance. You can almost see the stage through your ears.

My first experience with this kind of genius was in 1966. We were recording the original cast album of *Cabaret* and Goddard Lieberson (one of Tom's heroes and an early employer) was producing the record. We were recording the dance music at the Kit Kat Club . . . a noisy, funny piece accompanying a wildly frenetic choreography. The orchestra played it well . . . we listened . . . and for some reason it just felt dull. We tried again . . . the orchestra played perfectly what they played in the theatre but . . . again . . . it made no impact. So we considered cutting it out of the record when Goddard said. "Try doubling the tempo." I thought that was pretty ridiculous but he was the boss here so we doubled the tempo. Suddenly the excitement was back and you could literally see in your mind a stage full of dancers wildly knocking themselves out in a nightclub in Weimar Germany. That was when I first understood the job of the record producer. He is, in some magical technical way, supposed to bring us back into the theatre every time we play that recording.

Nobody knows more about how to do that than Tom Shepard! It seems to me that in each recording we hear an attempt to create that "opening night" excitement. In *Porgy and Bess*, I feel that I am sitting in the opera house. In *Zorba*, I am in Row H at the Broadway Theatre. Talk about Magical Realism!

A glance at the list of musicals he has "recreated" is dazzling. And the list of star performers and composers involved includes pretty much an entire generation of music theatre notables. His observations and recollections of working with them are quite fascinating . . . sometimes surprising . . . but always honest . . . and respectful. My own experiences of working with him are all too few but all memorable. We were happily in synch about the goal . . . raising the curtain every time you listened. . . . The judicious addition of dialogue, various sound perspectives, and occasional sound effects . . . particularly in *Chicago* and *Spider Woman*, are, I think, successful examples of this.

In the interest of full disclosure . . . I went to Oberlin College . . . a full decade before Tom did. But Oberlin grads tend to find each other in New York . . . sooner or later.

And we did!

—John Kander, 2024

INTRODUCTION

Sound in a Box

FOR AS LONG AS I CAN REMEMBER, I've been fascinated by the idea of recorded sound. Long before it ever occurred to me that I might make my living doing it, the notion that sound could be captured in a physical object—sound in a box—captivated me.

As a small boy growing up in East Orange, New Jersey, the possession I longed for most in the world was my very own phonograph. I wanted to own the magical mechanism that could convert those hard, black, silent discs into glorious sound.

I grew up and became accustomed to record players as household furniture, and as an adult I've recorded many of the world's greatest musicians. You might think I'd lose my fascination with recorded sound, but it has only grown. To this day, the mere fact of sound recording amazes and awes me.

Of all the sensory stimuli in the world, sound is the most evanescent. If you look away from a beautiful painting, step away from a fragrant flower, put down a physical object, or set aside a bite of food untasted, you can return in a few minutes and resume the experience. With sound, though, if you don't hear it the first time, it's gone. The most beautiful song in the world lasts only until the last note has faded.

How is it possible, then, that today we can hear the voices of legendary singers who have been dead for a century or more?

As it turns out, it isn't really that hard. Modern recording technology dates only from the late nineteenth century—Edison's phonograph was invented in 1877—but nothing about it was intrinsic to that century. Unlike CDs, movies, television, radio, and the computer, the phonograph doesn't depend on electricity, fossil fuels, or any other modern technology. Like the grandfather clock or the sewing machine, the phonograph operates on such basic technologies as levers, cranks, and spools. Leonardo da Vinci could have built a working phonograph; so could Archimedes, probably.

All you need to create an Edison phonograph—a device that in the nineteenth century made recordings we can still listen to in the twenty-first century—is a big horn similar to a megaphone; a sensitive diaphragm at the narrow end of the horn to capture the air vibrations that constitute sound and a needle connected to that diaphragm. You'll also need a three-dimensional medium on which to record the needle's vibrations (Edison started with wax cylinders, then wax discs, and then shellac; later vinyl became the medium of choice). To play it back, you simply reverse the process.

There have been many improvements in recording technology since the phonograph, and I've worked with them all: mikes, two-sided records, long-playing records, tape recording, stereo recording, quadraphonic recording, cassettes, CDs, and now digital recording. They're nothing more than increasingly sophisticated versions of the original idea—richer, more versatile forms of that original magic.

When I was still a boy, maybe ten or eleven, I had a fantasy that Mozart came by and visited our apartment in East Orange. I was the only one home, so I showed him around. He was impressed by the electric lights, the indoor plumbing, all the modern conveniences—but what really wowed him was our shelf of phonograph records. I showed him how the phonograph worked, and he said that my family in East Orange had more music at our disposal than the emperor of Austria had had in his day. He couldn't get over it.

I'm with Mozart. It's easy to take the magic of recorded sound for granted, and I suppose I do sometimes, but I don't always. It's too amazing to me, even after all these years. I stood in a room with Elaine Stritch in 1970 and heard her sing Stephen Sondheim's "The Ladies Who Lunch." Today, whenever I want to, I can walk into my studio, pick up a piece of plastic, and hear that very same performance, every note, every inflection, every breath, half a century later. It's a miracle.

I've been privileged to spend my life recording the greatest musicians of the twentieth and twenty-first centuries. It's been a long life and an interesting one, and it isn't over yet. I hope you'll find it as interesting to read about as it's been for me to live it. And I hope you'll come away appreciating that underlying miracle a little more.

Sound in a box. It still knocks me out.

Thomas Z. Shepard
West Gilgo Beach, New York 2024

PART I
Early Years (1936–1960)

1

Jersey Boy

ON A CLEAR DAY IN THE 1940S, from the roof of 67 South Munn Avenue in East Orange, New Jersey, you could see the Manhattan skyline, towering almost due east some ten or twelve miles away, over the roofs of Newark and Hoboken. Among the skyscrapers was the Empire State Building, from which radio and television signals were transmitted to East Orange and all other points of the compass.

My path in life would take me to many of New York's most storied buildings, including the Metropolitan Opera, Carnegie Hall, and the great theaters of Broadway, but that still lay far ahead. For the first eighteen years of my life, Manhattan was a long way away and East Orange was home.

That isn't to say that plenty of people didn't commute from East Orange to Manhattan, or that my family never went there. It took two trains—the Lackawanna train from East Orange to Hoboken and then the Hudson tubes to 33rd Street—to get to Midtown, but we could and did attend theater and concerts in the city occasionally. (The first Broadway show I ever saw, I believe, was the original production of *Oklahoma!*, when I was nine.) Indeed, I made that trip every Saturday from when I was eleven to when I was thirteen and added an additional train: the Broadway local to 125th Street for music studies at the Juilliard School, which in those days was on Claremont Avenue at 123rd Street.

But my life was in East Orange, which was a suburb not of New York but of Newark. When my family took me to see a play or hear a concert, it was most often in Newark or elsewhere in New Jersey, not in New York.

I was not born in East Orange: When I entered the world on June 26, 1936, it was in Orange, New Jersey, which then had a population of between 35,000 and 36,000 people, my parents included. I was their first child, and their only one for the next nine years, until my brother was born in 1945. The first eighteen years of my life were spent in New Jersey—all but the first three of them in East Orange, where my parents settled in 1939.

Originally a part of Newark, East Orange was once an affluent community, but by the 1930s it wasn't what it had been. There were still some stately homes on tree-lined streets, but not in the part of town where we lived. Neither, though, did we live in the small, working-class rental homes that made up much of the city's housing stock. We spent almost all my childhood on South Munn Avenue, a street lined with high-rise apartment buildings whose tenants ranged from middle-class to upper-middle-class.

Some of these apartments were quite luxurious, and many executives working in Manhattan lived in those apartments.

In those days East Orange was a mix of races and religions, peopled by hardworking men and women who did their jobs, raised their families, and didn't make a big deal of it. In certain respects the town is still like that today, but its ethnic makeup changed substantially in the 1960s, as highly publicized rioting in nearby Newark led to white flight to further-outlying suburbs. Today the town's population is overwhelmingly Black, but when I was growing up most of its people were white.

In later years East Orange would become something of a hotbed for musical talent: Dionne Warwick would be born there in 1940, Janis Ian in 1951, Whitney Houston in 1963, Queen Latifah in 1970, and Lauryn Hill in 1975. But in 1936, as the Great Depression dragged on, that was all still in the future. East Orange was not an artistic enclave, and as a musically inclined boy from early childhood, I often felt more than a little out of place in my own hometown.

I haven't lived in New Jersey for many years, but I'm told there's still a Jersey-boy edge to me, in my lack of interest in small talk, in my occasionally volatile temper, and in the colorful language that's sometimes an awkward fit in the corporate conference rooms and classical-music recording studios in which I've spent much of my life.

(I was producing the recording of *Victor/Victoria* with Julie Andrews, and at one point she asked me if we were hearing enough piano. I said, "Julie, we've got a shitload of piano." She laughed and said, "Oh, you sound just like André Previn!" I didn't know André as well as Julie did, but apparently he was a witty, insightful man with a flair for the *mot juste*.)

My parents, Seymour and Dorothy Shapiro (the family name changed to Shepard when I was four years old), married in 1935—on February 12, Lincoln's birthday—and after living with her parents in Orange for four years, they moved to East Orange, where my father worked as a lawyer.

A graduate of Rutgers Law School, he was the counsel for a real-estate firm called Frank H. Taylor & Son. Under their logo, for some reason, appeared the words "Note First Name," which I did but never understood why I should. The company was run by Harry A. Taylor Sr., the "Son" of the name. My father also had a private law practice, but his primary income came from his work for the real-estate company. It was didactic and dry—basically the nuts and bolts of closings, mortgages, and so forth.

My father was a very intelligent man, and he had a gift for words: he and my mother, who had graduated from New York's Harriette Melissa Mills Teachers College (later absorbed into the New School), gave me many things, but prominent among them is a love of the English language. I'm fascinated by words: where they come from, how they fit together, all the things people can do with them. I've had many friends who were song lyricists, and that shouldn't surprise anyone who knows me. I learned to talk and to read earlier than most of my peers, and I've never lost that initial love of the language.

In many ways my father was a generous parent. He recognized my musical talent very early and did everything he could to support it—buying recordings for me and signing up for the concert series at the Mosque Theater in Newark (today it's the Sarah Vaughan Concert Hall), where every year four great pianists would appear.

In other ways, though, he and I were very different. He was far more athletic than I ever was: despite being very short, like everyone in my family, he was an excellent horseback rider and a good swimmer. He was also gregarious, more comfortable in large groups of people than I've ever been. As an only child, I learned to appreciate solitude, and to this day would rather spend time with one or two close friends than in a big party of people I don't know well.

He, on the other hand, was the middle of five surviving children, with a brother and sister before him and a brother and sister after him. Two others, the two immediately before him, had died as infants, so he was the prized child, in a way: after two deaths, Seymour had lived.

My father and his brothers and sisters were close, metaphorically but also literally: they all lived nearby—if not in East Orange, then in South Orange or West Orange—and they got together a lot, quite casually. They were all relatively successful, and four of the five were college graduates. Two of them taught school, and one of them sold insurance—that was my Uncle Bill, the eldest, who had gone to Wharton, the only one of the five to go away to college.

We saw my uncles and aunts a lot because my father's parents lived in the apartment building next door to us. His mother, my Grandma Bertha, would come over just to hear me practice on the piano.

It wasn't always easy to be my father's son. He was short-tempered and very judgmental.

To his credit, he supported me in the choices I made in my life, though often they disappointed him. For example, he would very much have liked me to go to prep school as a teenager, specifically to Andover or Exeter. They would have accepted me if I had been willing to repeat a year because their academic standards were higher than those at East Orange High School, but I wasn't willing to do that. I wasn't a scholar by nature, and I didn't get very good grades. Also, I didn't want to spend an extra year in high school, so I refused.

One of his real pleasures was shopping with my brother and me, taking us to Brooks Brothers several times a year to outfit us for the coming season. He had a flair for style, another way in which he and I were different: he was a natty dresser who loved fine clothes, loved neckties, and loved cars. I love cars and neckties but have no interest in fashion and never have any idea whether what I have on is or isn't in style.

Although we didn't have a great deal in common, there were things we shared: we both loved Gilbert & Sullivan, for instance. He remembered with great pleasure the Winthrop Ames productions in the late 1920s, which he said were quite lavish.

Toward the end of his life, my father became a part-time civil-court judge in Essex County, a job which he very much enjoyed, although he felt the police often lied, and he tended to be lenient toward those who were brought before him.

I think about him often because he was such an influence on my path. He died in 1997, a little past his ninetieth birthday, so he lived to see me achieve success in what I do. He was proud of that, which makes me happy. He never tried to take any credit for my success; in fact, I think I was a little inconsiderate in refusing to share the spotlight, not giving my parents enough credit for the way my life evolved.

My mother, Dorothy Kahn Shepard, was five years younger than my father—she'd been born in 1912, he in 1907. She was a schoolteacher and a dedicated volunteer. In later years she was the head of the Essex County Community Chest. I remember that during the Second World War, when there was such poverty in Newark (especially in the Black community) owing to so many families' breadwinners having been sent overseas, she worked as a volunteer teacher there, teaching kids who sometimes came to school in pajamas because their mothers couldn't afford proper clothes.

In 1961, after her mother (my Grandma Gus) had died and Irene and I had gotten married, my mother decided she wanted to go back to work, so she became a real-estate agent and took to it immediately. She was an extraordinary success. She loved dealing with people, driving them around in her car and helping them make one of the most important decisions people make in life.

One of her clients was the great singer Marilyn Horne, with whom I later made some wonderful recordings. It turned out that, when Marilyn and her husband (conductor Henry Lewis) were buying a house in Orange, it was my mother who sold it to them and my father who was the attorney at the closing. So Marilyn had history with the Shepard family before we ever met.

That was my family until 1945, when my brother Lewis was born. He was named after my grandfather, Louis Kahn, but my parents spelled it "Lewis" because my mother was adamant that she didn't want him being called "Louie." Lewis' childhood was basically the mirror of mine: I was an only child until I was nine, and when he was nine, I went off to college and he effectively became an only child.

My brother is a wonderful person. In the nine years since my birth, my parents had become more economically comfortable and (thanks to me) they were more experienced in child-rearing. So Lewis really had the best of it. We've always gotten along extremely well, and I think our nine-year age difference is the reason we've never fought.

For some years after my parents got married, money was very tight as the Great Depression, which had been starting to ease in the mid-1930s, took a severe downturn in 1937 and 1938. They started out living with my mother's parents and brother (my Uncle Teddy) at 186 Park View Terrace in Orange. My first few years were spent in that house, where I had a room on the second floor and my parents had the attic room. It was not a large house, but it was certainly a pleasant one. It's still there—I drove by it once, some years ago, to see what it looked like after so long.

Our next-door neighbors were the Scavones, and on the same day I was born, Joan Scavone was also born. Her mother and my mother became friends—they gave birth at the same hospital (St. Mary's in Orange) and on the same day. I don't remember Joan terribly well, but I recall she had a cousin named Sharon, on whom I had a toddler's crush.

We lived there until shortly after my grandfather died, which was in 1939, and then Grandma Gus and Uncle Teddy moved up to Providence, Rhode Island, where they had relatives. My parents and I moved to East Orange, which ironically was a bigger city than Orange, with almost twice the population. It had five movie theaters, two high schools and a college, Upsala College, and its shopping district housed Best & Co., Woolworth's, B. Altman, Bamberger's, and many others.

We didn't move into one of the working-class, wood-frame homes that housed most of the population of East Orange, however. My parents had their eyes on South Munn Avenue and Harrison Street, the two elegant apartment-house streets, which mostly housed commuters, people working either in Newark or in Manhattan. We moved into an apartment at 61 South Munn Avenue.

My parents had let their aspirations outstrip their practicality, however: money was still tight, and my father's practice was struggling, so after a year we had to leave South Munn Avenue, moving to a far-less-nice apartment on Harrison Street where the rent was lower. About a year later—when things were going a little better financially—we moved back to South Munn Avenue.

Our new home was No. 67, the building next door to where we'd lived before. No. 67 was quite a luxurious building, with actual gold trim on the roof line, and it had a doorman, two elevator operators and a heated parking garage. It was only ten stories high, but it had a garden on the roof of the building and another garden on the garage. The latter featured a tennis court and a few benches. When my mother was pregnant with Lewis in 1945, she would lug our large Philco portable radio up to the garage roof to listen to the Dodgers broadcasts. (She had been born in Brooklyn, not far from Ebbets Field.)

There were many prominent business executives who lived at 67 South Munn, including Helen Meyer, president of Dell Publishing. Not all of them were on the side of the angels, though: a prominent New Jersey gangster named Abner "Longie" Zwillman, an associate of Lucky Luciano and Meyer Lansky, lived there for several years, and there was a longstanding rumor that during the war a Nazi spy operated from the building.

Many of the upper-story apartments were quite elegant, but we weren't in one of those apartments. Ours was what they called a studio apartment, which meant a ground-floor apartment, at sidewalk level. It was the apartment you didn't need the elevator to get to, so it always felt a little bit like the poor-relations apartment. It was a very nice apartment, though, with large rooms.

I was five when Pearl Harbor was attacked. Everybody's lives changed, and so did ours: for six months, while my Uncle Teddy was waiting to go into the Glider Corps, he and Grandma Gus lived with us in our four-room apartment. That was among the happiest times of my life.

Fred Kahn, whom I called Uncle Teddy, was my mother's only brother. Grandma Gus (it stood for "Gertrude") lived alternately with us and (in later years) with Teddy's family until her death in 1961, and she wasn't an easy person to deal with, but I loved my Uncle Teddy.

Uncle Teddy was a wonderfully even-tempered and generous man, who was twenty-four when he moved in with us. He had wanted to be a pilot, but the Army Air Corps wouldn't take him because he was color-blind. That probably should have kept him out of the Glider Corps, too, but I think by the time he was re-tested he'd memorized the color charts and got in that way. It was dangerous work: he flew into France in the D-Day invasion—among the first ashore, landing troops from the 82nd Airborne Division behind enemy lines in the first phase of the attack, in order to hit the Germans from the rear—and earned the Bronze Star for his bravery.

(He lived into his mid-eighties. I gave a piano recital at Carnegie Hall in 2001, and that's the last time I saw him: he and one of his sons drove up from Annapolis, Maryland, for the concert, and three or four months later he died.)

We lived at 67 South Munn Avenue until I was thirteen. By that time my brother had been born and the family's finances had markedly improved, enabling us to move to an even nicer apartment in a building at 32 South Munn. They stayed there until I left for college, when they moved to 158 South Harrison Street.

I wasn't destined to be a great student, but I started out well. I was always verbal, and I learned to read very early, which was a source of pride for my mother, because she was a teacher. Before I ever went to kindergarten, I was reading fluently.

I attended Mrs. Tisdale's nursery school in South Orange, where my mother taught. She and Mrs. Tisdale had made a deal: my mother taught without pay, and in exchange I was able to go to nursery school gratis.

That school is one of the first places I remember, outside of my home. I remember the way the bathroom smelled—whatever cleansing agent they used, it had a distinctive smell and all these years later, whenever I smell it, it takes me back to Mrs. Tisdale's—and I can still sing the song we sang at our graduation.

I was master of ceremonies at that graduation when I was four years old. They made a platform out of a couple of sawhorses and some planks, and I was up there with a fake microphone. I remember that, but what I don't remember—I only know it because for years my parents got a kick out of telling me about it—is that, when some other kid climbed up onto the platform with me, I just shoved him right off. There was only going to be one star that day!

I remember kindergarten well. That was when I met my oldest friend. His name was Richard Feder, but I knew him as "Winkie," because apparently, as a baby, he winked at people. He was very bright and super-achieving. He got into Yale from East Orange High School, which was no easy feat, and went on to Harvard Business School, after which he joined the Marines. He lived in Greenwich, Connecticut, and worked in marketing for many years. Winkie and I stayed very close friends until his death in 2020.

In first grade I had a wonderful teacher, Mrs. Lehman. Because of the war, I think, they were doubling up certain classes, and I was in a class that was first and second grade together. She was an excellent teacher, and by the time I finished what was officially first grade, I'd really learned the second-grade material as well. Predictably, I paid the price for that the next year when I had to go into real second grade. It was a complete waste of time because I already knew everything they had to teach, and my new teacher was a monster.

There were a few monster teachers. But in fourth grade I had the most wonderful teacher, Mrs. (Hester) Switzer. Her husband was very short but nevertheless had played basketball, and she told me this while trying to coax me out of the mindset that to be short was to be inadequate.

Looking back at the Tommy Shepard I remember, as my childhood came to an end, I'm not surprised that many of my teachers—and many of my fellow students—didn't warm to me. I had a sense of superiority founded in my musical gifts and fostered by my parents, in particular by my mother.

I got better at this as my life went on, obviously—we all have to grow up and take stock, and you can't run a successful recording session without being sensitive to the needs of the people around you. I feel tremendous loyalty and gratitude to those who put up with me and who encouraged me along the way—people like Mrs. Switzer.

What I did care about was music, and that gave me a sense of purpose. While other kids dreamt about being cowboys, soldiers, firemen, or ball players, I dreamt about playing the piano, about writing music, about orchestrating—I wasn't sure what I'd end up doing or how I'd get there, but I always knew it would involve music.

2

Music and Me

I AM TOLD I COULD HUM "THE BLUE DANUBE" with all its numerous variations and permutations before I was three years old; that apparently was my parents' first real clue I had a musical bent. I don't remember that, but I literally can't recall a time when I wasn't obsessed with music—listening to it, playing it, thinking about it, writing it and eventually recording it.

People who know me and my work as a pianist, composer, orchestrator, and record producer often assume I come from a musical family, especially if they know my brother and several Shepards in the next two generations all have musical talent.

The funny thing is, I can't trace those musical proclivities back any further than myself. My mother played the piano a bit by ear, and her mother loved to play the piano—but she wasn't any good at all. My father's eldest brother played the piano, but in a most eccentric way with peculiar, crazy fingerings. So if my own passion for music has roots in my family, it must descend from people of earlier generations whose talents were hidden and never got the chance to be expressed.

One of my earliest memories dates from when I was three and revolves around my burning desire for a phonograph of my very own.

We were still living with my grandparents in Orange, and they had a phonograph. I was fascinated by this strange machine that could take those big, black, heavy "dinner platter" discs and squeeze music out of them at the turn of a crank. The trouble was, it was a towering piece of furniture, much taller than I was, and I couldn't operate it for myself. I wanted one that was scaled to me, one that I could carry around with me.

Eight decades later I can still remember with crystal clarity the day my grandfather, Louis Kahn, took me shopping to buy me a phonograph of my own. The store was packed with phonographs of all shapes and sizes, but Grandpa Lou knew what we were looking for and took me to a section offering portable phonographs. After we'd looked through the available options, my grandfather picked one from the Plaza Music Company and flipped open the lid to reveal its prominently stamped brand name: "Pal."

"This is the one for us, Tommy," he said to me, "because you're my pal."

My grandfather died later that year at fifty, from colon cancer. I don't have many memories of him, but I've never forgotten that day. That Pal portable was hand-cranked and so small that it could play only 10-inch discs. Its sound quality must have been horrible, but it became my favorite possession, and I carried it around with me like Linus carrying his blanket. I played it so much, the needles kept wearing down and needed to be sharpened—which was OK because a neighbor had a sharpener, and my father would walk me down to her house to have the needles sharpened.

The first records I had are also crystal-clear in my memory: Raymond Scott's "In an Eighteenth-Century Drawing Room" (1939), the Frankie Masters Orchestra playing "Scatterbrain" (1940), the Andrews Sisters singing "Beer Barrel Polka" (1939), Kay Kyser playing "Three Little Fishies" (1939), Judy Garland singing "Over the Rainbow" (1939), and Dinah Shore singing "Yes, My Darling Daughter" (1940). I can hear them in my head to this day. ("Over the Rainbow" is particularly resonant for me because more than a quarter-century later I made a record with its composer, Harold Arlen.)

I'd heard many other songs, of course, but these were the first ones I'd been able to play for myself, and that sense of accomplishment, of power and of wonder, has never left me. (It's also worth noting that of those first six only "Three Little Fishies" is really a children's song. My tastes ran in more sophisticated directions, even when I was a toddler.)

Three years later, when I was six and had grown tall enough to work the new family phonograph on South Munn Avenue, I was given some records of my own for Christmas/Chanukah in 1942. Those records also linger in my memory: Prokofiev's "Peter and the Wolf," Enescu's "Roumanian Rhapsodies," Artur Rubinstein playing Chopin nocturnes, Mozart's "Eine Kleine Nachtmusik," Victor's "Gems from Gilbert & Sullivan." Again, not the usual six-year-old's taste in music. It's no coincidence, though, that those records embody my favorite music to this day—especially the Gilbert & Sullivan, a thread which has run through my life ever since.

That same year, I started piano lessons and got my first piano. Grandma Gus bought it for me. It was a Wissner, which I looked up recently: it was actually a very good American piano made by a company that went out of business during the Second World War. It was called an upright grand, which means that it was an upright but unusually high, which allowed it to take up no more floor space than an upright, but it had longer strings and a larger soundboard for a richer, fuller sound.

I had that piano until I was eleven. That year my father was representing a man who had gone bankrupt. He had no money to pay my father, but what he did have was a ticket for a piano that he had in hock at the Griffith Piano Company in Newark. The piano could be retrieved for that ticket and five hundred dollars, and that's what my father did.

It was an 1879 Steinway, which, curiously, was three notes short at the top—it stopped at A instead of C. It was in a rosewood case, and it had special hexagonal, tapered legs. The piano was six-feet-ten-and-a-half-inches long, just short of a concert grand, with long, resonant strings and a rich bass. It was a magnificent relic, but it needed a great deal of work. It had been to some degree restored, but not well—the ivory had been removed and replaced with plastic, and they'd tried to repair the sounding board, but unsuccessfully: it was a wonderful piano, but it got out of tune in a matter of hours because the pin block had stretched so much that the pins wouldn't hold.

I had the piano for many years. When Irene and I got married, we moved into a one-bedroom apartment in Forest Hills; it was pleasant, but the living room wasn't large. Even so, my parents immediately offered to give me the piano. They said, "What good is it going to do us, when you're not here?" I know it was an emotional wrench for them, with everything that that piano represented. Sometime afterward I said to my mother, "It must have been hard for you to do," and she teared up, so obviously it was.

About four years after Irene and I were married, we were living in a larger apartment in Manhattan, and I'd gotten to know people, both at Steinway and privately, who restored pianos. I had some of the work done by A. C. Pianocraft, and I had become friendly with David Rubin, who was running Steinway, so the rest of the work was done in the same factory in Queens where the piano had been made almost a century before. I had the piano rebuilt top to bottom. It had the same glorious rosewood case, but now the insides lived up to the outsides. They even happened to have an old set of ivories from another piano, so they took off all the plastic keys and put ivories back on.

I wish I still had that piano. But in 2009 there was a fire in the apartment next door to us, and it left our apartment with an odor we couldn't get rid of. Irene and I had a summer home in West Gilgo Beach on Long Island, and we decided to move there full time.

There was really no way to bring that piano with us. It probably would have crashed through the upper floor, and the weather here is too variable: between the different seasons the house has to endure, not to mention the extraordinary amount of salt in the air, which rots out automobiles and everything, I knew I couldn't have the piano here. That's when I decided to sell it, and I used some of the money to buy what was then a state-of-the-art Yamaha Clavinova, which came in a case that looked like a piece of furniture. I was fond of that piano, which served me well for a decade and which I replaced only recently.

But I have some home recordings of Sheldon Harnick and me playing Mozart and Brahms violin-and-piano sonatas. When I listen to them, it's so great to hear that piano again. Sheldon was a good violinist, and he loved playing. It was one of the things that tied us together over so many years. We wrote two comic operas together, but we also made music together.

When I was seven years old, I began studying with a wonderful piano teacher named Mark Nevin. Mark wrote and published many children's instructional piano folios, which were so good that you can still buy them eighty years later. I was with him for several years. He not only taught me piano, but he spent a year teaching me music theory. He did it so well that when I got a scholarship to the Juilliard School of Music four years later, I was put in a theory class that was at high-school level, though I was only eleven.

I played local piano recitals—I'd get fifteen dollars or, if I was really lucky, a recording for my efforts. If I could trade a piano recital for Isaac Stern playing the Tchaikovsky violin concerto, it was a good deal for me. I also entered a lot of local competitions and did pretty well.

Music has never let me down. No matter what else was going on in my life, I could sit down at a keyboard, put on a record, or even turn on the radio and be transported, the same way I had been in 1939, with my little Pal phonograph.

When I was in high school, my love of music was my greatest joy but perhaps my biggest social problem.

I wasn't going to be happy until I found a place where people felt about music the same way I did, where I could find new friends with similar backgrounds. As it turned out, that place would be amid the cornfields of northern Ohio, thirty miles outside of Cleveland.

3

The Right Place at the Right Time

WHEN I WAS ELEVEN, my father wanted very much for me to spend my summer at the camp he'd gone to when he was my age. Located in upstate New York, it was called Schroon Lake Camp, and God, I hated it. It was a place where all my abilities were wasted and all my limitations were highlighted.

The most unhappy times in my childhood were the summers I spent at camps that were athletically oriented, and some of the best times were the two summers I spent at New England Music Camp, in 1948 and 1951. I loved it there because for the first time in my life I was among people who cared about the things I cared about and shared some of the same gifts I had.

Best of all was when I was seventeen and I went to Norfolk, Connecticut, where the Yale Music School had a six-week summer program. Those may have been the happiest six weeks of my life up to that point. There were no counselors, and we weren't campers—we boarded in private homes in the area, and all we did every day was learn about and make music. Also, I had a huge, largely unrequited crush on one of the girls there. It was a great summer.

I got to know many of the Yale Music School professors then, and after high school I could have gone to Yale Music School, which was then an undergraduate school, not just a graduate program. It was sort of my ace in the hole. I knew I could do it, but one night I was at a party in South Orange, New Jersey, and I ran into a girl I hardly knew, a harpist named Toni Chanko.

She said, "What are you doing next year?" I said, "I'm not sure, maybe I'll go to Yale Music School." And she said, "Tommy, look at Oberlin. I just got back from there." And she kept raving about it.

So I went out to Oberlin, Ohio, to check it out. I got on the Nickel Plate Railroad train, and it took me thirteen hours—it made every whistle stop you could imagine. I auditioned for a piano-faculty member named Edward Mattos. The one piece I remember playing was the Beethoven "Waldstein" sonata.

I asked him at the end of the audition, "When do I find out if I get in?" And he said, "You're in, you're in." And that was that.

We later had a quarrel: he was teaching me the Schumann Symphonic Etudes, and I became so enraptured with them that I kept bringing it into each lesson week after week. I finally wore him out with it, and he refused to ever let me play it for him again. I got frustrated and angry, and so did he. He said, "You're acting like a child." And I replied, "That's so I can meet you on equal terms." He then said, "Freshman bastard!" And he kicked me out of the room.

Edward Mattos was maybe thirty-five when I met him, looked like Al Franken, and was incredibly smart. He was a terrific pianist, but he was typical of the people you meet at Oberlin, talented not just in one way, but in many ways. In 1963 he joined the US Information Agency and became a cultural-affairs officer in the Philippines, Spain, Malaysia, and Canada, before becoming director of the agency's Arts and Humanities Program in the 1970s. He then became executive director of the Wolf Trap Foundation and died in 1985. (His daughter worked for Harold Prince, the legendary Broadway producer/director with whom I worked so often through the years.)

Founded in 1833, Oberlin is unique. It's unique today in different ways from when I was there, but it's as unique now as it ever was. Its combination of a world-class musical conservatory and a highly regarded liberal-arts college is like nowhere else I know of, and its liberal political consciousness make it a remarkably stimulating place to be.

Oberlin comes naturally by its liberal politics: the Oberlin Collegiate Institute was originally founded to educate ministers and missionaries and drew the core of its early faculty from rebels who left the Lane Theological Seminary in Cincinnati because they were passionate advocates of the immediate abolition of slavery, which the Lane leadership viewed as premature. It is because of their commitment to that cause that Oberlin became the first still-existing American college to admit Black and white students alike without reference to race, and why, in 1837, Oberlin because the first place in the United States where a woman could get a four-year degree. It was also a central hub for the Underground Railroad.

The Oberlin of the 1950s was not the Oberlin of the 1960s and 1970s, nor of the 2000s and 2010s: we dressed more formally, our dorms were not coed, and we treated our professors with more deference. Our opposition to McCarthyism and Jim Crow was as heartfelt as former students' opposition to slavery, or as future students' opposition to the Vietnam War, apartheid, or the war in Iraq would be.

I entered the Conservatory in the fall of 1954, and then two years later switched to the College as a music major. During my two years in the Conservatory, I'd grown dissatisfied with the education I was getting. It was exhilarating to be among such gifted musicians—and I include both students and faculty in that—but my interests were more broad, less confined.

I didn't fit in with the music students as well as I'd expected. After growing up in East Orange as practically the only serious music student I knew, I'd adored my music-camp experiences and thought all I needed was to surround myself with other people who cared as much as I did about music. I did appreciate that experience, but it turned out there was more to it than that.

I wanted a broader education, and most of my friends were in the College, not the Conservatory. Their conversations were richer, what they were reading was more interesting, and their views of the world were many and varied.

So in the spring of 1957 I switched to the College, where I mainly took basic college classes—math, physics, that sort of thing—which I could do because I'd basically finished my major, which was kind of doing things backward, but which worked for me.

My time at Oberlin had some ups and downs—I was even on academic probation for a while—but it remains a formative influence on my life. I had some wonderful teachers and formed some friendships that have lasted throughout my life. There are moral assumptions that come with an Oberlin education, assumptions that go back to those professors in 1833. It's hard not to be influenced by an atmosphere that stresses you should do good, rather than simply do well. That ethos has stayed with me.

The idea of doing good, of giving something back—I don't want to sound sanctimonious, but I do believe in it. If you can in some way make the world a slightly richer place, go for it!

I've been honored to work with some of the world's greatest musicians, and even when the job has been difficult, I've tried hard to remember it is an honor. I have enormous respect for other people's gifts, even when I'm jealous of them. (Especially when I'm jealous of them.)

For example, I might never write a show as brilliant as Stephen Sondheim, but if I could help get his shows out to the world, that was the contribution I would make.

Our culture is richer because *Merrily We Roll Along* isn't a lost show. I can't reverse climate change or eliminate racism, but there are many ways we can benefit other people and people in future generations. I like to think that a few of the recordings I've made have fallen into that category.

For a while I stayed active in Oberlin affairs, serving on outreach committees and that sort of thing. I'd be there a couple times a year. I got to be very friendly with S. Frederick Starr, the college's president from 1983 to 1994. We got along especially well. He was a musician—he played the saxophone—and he was an authority on early jazz.

My biggest memory of being on those committees is getting to meet Artie Shaw, the 1940s clarinetist and band leader, who as a young man had been dazzlingly handsome and an enormous star. He was married eight times, and among his wives were Ava Gardner and Lana Turner. But I met him when he was in his eighties and was a conspicuously old man—short and bald, yet highly energetic. I don't know how he was recruited to serve on our planning committee, but he had an abundance of good ideas and I very much enjoyed spending those few hours with him.

Fred Starr talked to me about becoming dean of the conservatory. It was a tempting idea because it came at a time when I was feeling disenchanted with the record business. It wasn't the records—I've never tired of making recordings—it was the business, which is a whole separate thing. Far too often people in the record business lose sight of the fact that, without the artists, they wouldn't exist at all.

As a conservatory dean, I'm sure I would have failed within the first twelve months, but I was tempted. However, the lives of my wife and daughter were anchored in New York, and I couldn't uproot them and move us all to the Midwest.

4

Ready to Be Lucky

MY EXPERIENCE AT OBERLIN HAD BEEN SO GOOD on so many levels that it was almost inevitable that my next experience would be a disappointment. It certainly was.

After graduating from Oberlin, I moved on to Yale Music School to major in composition. I was studying with an academically rigorous composer named Quincy Porter, who was very talented—he had won the 1954 Pulitzer Prize in Music—but we were on different wavelengths.

I wanted to write for Broadway. I needed Cole Porter, not Quincy Porter. The only thing Porter could teach me was how to be a serious classical composer, and I'd never wanted that. In retrospect, the real question was, what the hell was I doing there?

The problem was that at that time there wasn't really a school for what I wanted to do. By that time UCLA had some courses in film composition, but nobody was preparing composers for Broadway. The people who were writing on Broadway hadn't gotten there by going to college, and few of those who were going to college were interested in Broadway.

One of my Quincy Porter classmates was the extraordinarily gifted David Shire, an incredible composer who, with Richard Maltby Jr., has gone on to write the music for *Starting Here, Starting Now* (1977), *Baby* (1983), *Big* (1996), and (on his own) God knows how many film scores. He won a Best Song Oscar for "It Goes Like It Goes" from *Norma Rae* (1979). So I was not only floundering with Porter, but I was being totally outshone by David.

I lasted a year at Yale, but by the end of that year it was clear to me—maybe to everybody—that this wasn't where I needed to be. When I returned for my second year, in September 1959, I stayed about four days and then said, "I can't handle this anymore." So I left.

As it turned out, the year and four days I spent at Yale weren't what mattered to my future. What mattered was the summer between those years, the summer of 1959.

I'd gotten a job as a waiter at Yale Law School. The Law School served eighteen meals a week, and if you signed on to be a waiter, you would serve one meal a day, six days a week, and you got all your meals for nothing. That was a savings of almost five hundred dollars, so it was a good deal. I actually liked the work, and at that time, the Law School had the only good food in any of the colleges at Yale.

There was an extra bonus, too. After I'd finished waiting on tables and cleaning up, I'd go into the large commons room next to the dining hall, which had a piano. I'd sit down and play, just for my own amusement. And occasionally a law student named David Rosen would sit down with me, and we'd play four-hands piano.

So one day toward the end of the term, more or less out of the blue, he asked me, "What are you doing this summer?"

I had auditioned for the Tanglewood Music Center and gotten an acceptance letter and a five-hundred-dollar fellowship toward the fees. I explained this to him, and he said, "So you're not making any money." Which, of course, I wouldn't be—I, or rather my parents, would be paying for me to be there.

Then he asked if, instead of spending some money, I'd like to make some money. I said, "Well, yes I would."

He then told me he was going to spend the summer with a theater company, touring the East Coast with either *Bells Are Ringing* or *Li'l Abner*, both of which were being produced and directed by Stanley Prager. (Prager had been a stage and movie actor: his biggest stage credit was *The Pajama Game* (1954), in which he was the original Prez, and his biggest movie was Billy Wilder's *A Foreign Affair* (1948). Then he got blacklisted in Hollywood and switched to stage and television work as a director and producer.) These shows were touring without an orchestra, with the accompaniment limited to two pianos. David would be one, and he invited me to be the other.

I was torn. To anyone involved in classical music, Tanglewood was a big deal. But David said, "Don't be a schmuck, take the money." And it sounded like fun, so I did.

Everyone gets the occasional stroke of good luck—but when you get that stroke of luck, you have to be ready for it. I don't suppose I'm any luckier than anybody else, but I've managed to take advantage of my luck when I've had it. That's what had happened when Toni Chanko pitched me on going to Oberlin, and that's what happened when David Rosen offered me a job touring with a show that summer. I didn't do anything to bring about those opportunities, but I was at least smart enough to grab them when they came along. That decision changed my life.

The show we were doing turned out to be *Li'l Abner*, the 1956 musical with lyrics by Johnny Mercer and music by Gene De Paul, based on the famous comic strip by Al Capp, which at the time was very popular. It was a terrific company full of talented performers, and one of them was a young dancer and actress named Irene Clark, who was assisting the choreographer and playing the role of Moonbeam McSwine. I can't say that, right then, I saw that she and I would end up married for more than sixty years, but we did click right from the start.

That wasn't the only thing, though. I can't express how much I enjoyed that summer because for the first time since junior high I had no homework, no studying. When you're on the road with a show, you're playing eight performances a week, but for at least four or five of those days there's only one show per day. You work for two or three hours a day, and except for brush-up rehearsals, the rest of your time is your own. And I was in a new place every week, with an exciting bunch of people who loved Broadway as much as I did. It was a great adventure.

It made it even harder for me to go back to Yale in September because, after twelve weeks when I really felt I was where I should be, doing what I should be doing, suddenly I wasn't. I missed the days, I missed the nights, and I missed the people in the company, who were terrific. Bud Maggart and Renee Taylor, Kitty Dolan—they were wonderful in the lead roles, and it was a great company. And yes, I missed Irene.

It wasn't immediately apparent, though, that I was in the midst of the luckiest year I'd ever have. It looked pretty much like I was screwing up my entire life. Seventeen years of devotion to classical music had ended with me dropping out of Yale Music School, leaving me with no obvious future, no job, and no real idea of how to get one.

When I left Yale, I didn't have anywhere else to go, so I packed up my Fiat 600 and went back to East Orange, where I moved back in with my parents, who were really very good about the whole thing.

I got a few jobs playing the piano, accompanying for a chorus at the Elisabeth Irwin High School in Manhattan and for an amateur theater group in Montclair or maybe West Orange. They were doing *Lady in the Dark*, the 1941 musical by Moss Hart, Ira Gershwin, and Kurt Weill. That's how I learned that show, which has remained a personal favorite and would be, a few years later, one of the first shows I ever recorded.

You couldn't make a living accompanying school choruses and amateur shows, though. I needed a real job.

It had never been clear to my parents or me what I was going to do with my life. I knew I loved to play the piano and to compose music, but I wasn't crazy enough to think I could make a living doing either one. I played the piano very well, but my time at Oberlin had shown me there were people who could play it better. I loved writing music, but my year with Quincy Porter had shown me writing classical music wasn't for me—and anyway, even Porter, who had won the Pulitzer Prize, couldn't live off composing, and the idea of ending up teaching a bunch of arrogant kids like me didn't appeal to me at all.

So if I wasn't going to be the next Rubinstein or the next Mozart, who was I going to be?

There had been some strange possibilities along the way. My mother had an uncle named Harry Kahne. He wrote a couple books and billed himself as "a business consultant," but what he mostly did was to tour in vaudeville, billed as "The Incomparable Mentalist" or "The Man with the Multiple Mind."

The idea was that, whereas most of us use only 10 percent of our brains, my great-uncle Harry had trained himself to use much more of his. He could perform at least six different mental activities at once. He would come out on stage and, bending over a big chalkboard held in front of him, would write out a poem while reciting a different poem, and he'd write it upside down and backward, starting at the end of the sentence and writing forward. He'd talk about one subject while writing about something entirely different or listen to a randomly selected reading while writing something different, and then answer questions about what he'd just heard. It was amazing. There's still some footage of him on YouTube, and people still read his books.

After World War II the old vaudevillians found new life on television, a medium still in its infancy and looking for talent of all kinds. A lot of jugglers, comedians, and magicians were on television in those years, and my great-uncle Harry thought he and I could do a show together. I couldn't write backward, but I could play on cue any song I'd ever heard and do various stunts and improvisations at the piano. I was fourteen, and Harry was getting old by then, and he thought an old-and-young duo could be a successful act.

He may have been right. We auditioned at CBS, and they offered us a sixteen-week engagement—but my parents put their foot down. Whatever my future might be, as far as they were concerned, it wouldn't be televised vaudeville.

Another could-have-been came about because of the head of the Oberlin Conservatory of Music, David Robertson. He was friends with Alan Schulman, a freelance cellist and a professional working musician on Broadway. Schulman was very cordial and helpful, and he got me an appointment to talk to Robert Russell Bennett, the great Broadway orchestrator.

Orchestrators don't get as much attention as composers and lyricists, but anybody who really knows anything about Broadway understands a great orchestrator is at least as hard to find as a great songwriter, and just as important for a successful show. And Bennett was a superstar. He was sixty-five at this point, and he had composed some beautiful music and was a fine conductor, but he was and is best known as an orchestrator. He'd been an assistant to George Gershwin for the last couple years of Gershwin's life and had orchestrated pretty much every Broadway composer there was, including Irving Berlin, Jerome Kern, Cole Porter, and Richard Rodgers. His list of credits included *Show Boat* (1927), *Of Thee I Sing* (1931), *Oklahoma!* (1943), *Annie Get Your Gun* (1946), *Kiss Me, Kate* (1948), *South Pacific* (1949), *The King and I* (1951), *My Fair Lady* (1956) and *The Sound of Music* (1959).

I brought him a lot of the music I had composed for *Haircut*, a musical I'd written at Oberlin, based on the Ring Lardner story. Robert Russell Bennett was soft-spoken and generous to take time out of his busy schedule to sit down with a complete stranger and look at his music.

He said something to me that at the time I took to be very flattering, but which, in retrospect, may have had a double meaning: "You have as much talent as anyone who has ever walked into this office." Coming from a guy who worked with Berlin and Porter and Rodgers, that was quite a compliment. Later I realized he might have been comparing me only to other wannabes who'd sought him out. At the time, though, it was very encouraging.

It didn't lead to anything, though, and in retrospect, I'm not sure what I thought it could lead to. At most, I guess, I was hoping for a little push in the right direction, whatever that direction might be. But it was great to have met him, however briefly.

So I did what many Oberlin graduates do: I came up with a few places I'd like to work and applied for jobs there, even though I couldn't explain exactly why I was exactly the right person for them.

That meant RCA and Columbia, two of the major record companies in New York. Recorded music had fascinated me for as long as I could remember, and record companies had pianists, composers, and other musicians on their payrolls. Why not one more?

My first stop was at RCA. I had expected to go to the RCA Building at Rockefeller Center, but the record company was downtown, somewhere around 23rd Street. I headed into the personnel office ready to explain to them why they should add to have me to their payroll—and got nowhere.

Fourteen years later I'd be in charge of RCA Red Seal, a vice president responsible for all the company's classical and Broadway recordings, but in 1960 I couldn't get past its personnel department.

I left RCA feeling discouraged; but as it turned out, another one of those inexplicable strokes of luck was about to happen to me. My next stop took me uptown to 799 Seventh Avenue, at 52nd Street—headquarters of the only other name on my list of places to apply: Columbia Records.

PART II
Columbia (1960–1974)

5

Goddard

BACK IN 1951 I HAD ENCOUNTERED A RECORDING like none I'd ever heard before. If there's one particular recording that set me on the path to what I ended up doing with my life, that was the one.

It was a complete studio recording of *Porgy and Bess*, the 1935 opera (and it is an opera, not a Broadway show) with music by George Gershwin and lyrics by DuBose Heyward and Ira Gershwin. It was the first-ever complete recording of *Porgy and Bess*. Previous recordings had offered only selected songs, dispensing with most of the opera's recitatives.

It was the first recording I'd ever heard that let you experience a show almost as if you were watching it with your eyes closed, using your ears to follow the story. It included the judicious use of sound effects: at the crap game, you could hear the dice bounce and the winners picking up the money; when the hurricane hit, you could hear its power and devastation.

It was like sitting in the theater. No, it was like being there on Catfish Row.

Today there are plenty of recordings that produce this kind of effect (many of them produced by me). In the early 1950s, though, it was a revelation.

This isn't to say the people who produced Broadway cast albums in the 1930s and 1940s were bad producers, and that we're all good producers today. They were battling daunting technical limitations that precluded anything like the *Porgy and Bess* recording that dazzled me.

The idea that Broadway songs would be a good source for recorded music—especially if sung by the same people who sang them onstage—was an old one. The earliest original-cast album (using the term loosely) may be the one for the West End hit *Florodora* (1899). The modern Broadway original-cast album dates from Musicraft's recording of *The Cradle Will Rock* (1938), with Decca's recording of *Oklahoma!* (1943) the genre's first big hit.

But these recordings were called "cast albums" for a reason: the groundbreaking *Oklahoma!* recording, produced by Jack Kapp, was a literal album, like a photo album. The "pages" were paper sleeves that held six 10-inch, 78-rpm records, each of which held only one song per side. All twelve sides added up to a grand total of less than an hour of music.

Under those circumstances, there was no way to record a musical scene involving a couple songs sandwiching some underscored dialogue—a couple disc-flips would break the continuity. If a song was longer than the disc space allowed, verses had to be cut. Overtures and other instrumentals were routinely omitted, as were reprises and the songs that the record producer deemed least appealing. Two generations of musical-theater fans grew up not realizing there was a song in *Oklahoma!* called "Lonely Room," and the element of the show that was most remarked upon by critics, Agnes De Mille's innovative dream-sequence ballet "Laurey Makes Up Her Mind," wasn't heard on the album, though it was released a couple of years later as an addition to the original-cast recording and seen in the 1955 film.

Kapp's album was rightly titled *Selections from Oklahoma!*, but the same could be said of every cast album at that time. They weren't recordings of the show, they were recordings of songs from the show. Some were less incomplete than others, but none was in any sense complete. It wasn't the recording producers' fault—completeness simply wasn't feasible.

The 33⅓ rpm long-playing record, which in its soon-dominant 12-inch version could accommodate twenty-three minutes of music per side, changed the calculus of recording. It was introduced by Columbia Records in 1948, only three years before the *Porgy and Bess* recording that so captivated me, and both events bore the fingerprints of the same man: Columbia executive Goddard Lieberson, who oversaw the introduction of the LP in 1948 and was the recording producer of the 1951 *Porgy and Bess*.

Each of us has a few people outside our families who exercise an outsized influence on our lives—teachers, mentors, friends, or colleagues. I've had a handful of them, and Goddard Lieberson is among them.

By the time I met him in 1960, Goddard was forty-nine and had been a legend in the recording industry for many years. In certain ways his career paralleled mine: raised in the United States (though born in England), he was a classically trained pianist and composer who graduated from the Eastman School of Music. After a few years teaching, writing music reviews, and trying to make a living as a composer, he landed a job with Columbia Records as an artists-and-repertory executive in 1938.

That same year Columbia was acquired by CBS, the giant radio company run by the legendary William S. Paley, and Goddard prospered under the new regime. He immediately proved to have a flair for record producing and, though an ambitious man who climbed the corporate ladder quickly, he always kept one foot in the studio. Even after he became the president of Columbia Records in 1956, he remained the producer of the company's most important Broadway recordings.

(Goddard was a man of cosmopolitan taste who appreciated almost any kind of music, from classical and opera to Broadway and swing to folk and jazz. His only blind spot was an important one, though: he neither liked nor understood rock 'n' roll, which during the 1960s caused Columbia to fall behind its rivals in the most commercially important sector of pop music. He appreciated the softer sound of Simon & Garfunkel, whom he signed to Columbia, but missed the potential in the harder-rock bands in the wake of the "British Invasion." When Goddard was finally replaced at the helm of Columbia, it would be by Clive Davis, a lawyer who had infinitely less musical experience but a sharp ear for rock talent.)

Goddard was a brilliant producer because he understood the difference between a live performance and a recording, between a performance for all the senses and one for sound alone.

We make some sacrifices in immediacy to make a cast album, but it is always—not usually, but always—better than any specific performance you could ever see in the theater. It's better because we can focus only on the sound, only on the music. A stage performance can never be entirely about the sound, whereas a recorded performance is about nothing else.

Though he came of age in the era before the LP, when cast albums were basically collections of songs, Goddard understood the difference between live and recorded performance on a deep level. I learned many things in the decade-plus I spent working for him, and especially watching him at work in the studio, but that's the lesson that made the greatest impact on me.

The obvious difference between live performance and a recording is the absence of sets, lights, and costumes, but there's more to it than that.

Broadway theaters are big barns that may hold upward of a thousand people, and even in the age of amplification, Broadway singers are trained to belt out their songs with a boldness of expression and a broadness of gesture that communicate their performance to the balcony as well as to the orchestra seats. On the other hand, people listen to Broadway cast albums in their living rooms, their bedrooms, or their cars. A performance that's perfect for the Gershwin Theater at 10:45 p.m. may be way too much for someone's living room at 10:45 a.m.

The magic word is "intimacy," and that's what Goddard brought to his work as a producer. He'd grown up in the age before theaters were amplified, so he understood the perspective of singers who were trained in that tradition, and he helped them to rework their performances for the different world of recording.

Many years ago I saw a documentary that included footage of Goddard working with Judy Holliday on "The Party's Over," her great solo from *Bells Are Ringing* (1956). He works with her one on one, slowly, tactfully, even seductively, to shape the song into something more intimate, more personal than it was onstage. By the time he finishes, the song has become an interior monologue, sung more to herself than to an audience. She wouldn't have sung it that way in the theater, but on the record its intimacy works in a way that the original performance wouldn't have.

Mondays through Fridays, Goddard wore custom-tailored suits and sat in conference rooms with the top executives at CBS and other companies. On many a Sunday, though, fifty or sixty Broadway singers and orchestra musicians would assemble in Columbia's large, windowless recording studio on 30th Street, and Goddard would take off his jacket and loosen his tie to spend the next ten hours or so guiding them in an audio-only re-creation of their show.

I attended as often as I could, as a fly on the wall, to watch him ply his craft. He worked with Broadway's greatest talents and helped them see their work in a new way—his way—by suggesting subtle alterations in characterization and interpretation, pausing to make occasional tweaks to the orchestrations and make imaginative use of the technological possibilities in the recording process, many still very new, that could add perspective and depth to the final mix.

The final album would bear on its jacket the words "Produced for records by Goddard Lieberson." It might as well have said, "Re-directed for audio by Goddard Lieberson." No other record company's Broadway cast albums had the drama and excitement of Columbia's, and the reason was Lieberson. There was a brightness, a sheen to the recordings he produced—"the sizzle," I call it—that nobody else's work had.

But Goddard was more than a brilliant producer. He was a brilliant man with terrific judgment and taste, and he brought a tremendous amount to Columbia.

He had seen the potential in long-playing records when Peter Goldmark, Columbia's chief research scientist, first presented the idea to him in the mid-1940s, and he committed a lot of Columbia's money to the idea—in part because he knew it would be a particularly good format for classical and Broadway, the kinds of music he loved best.

It was because of Goddard that—in an arrangement that at the time was unique in the American record industry—Columbia put Broadway recordings into their classical department, Columbia Masterworks, rather than under the pop department. Classical and Broadway were Goddard's babies, and he wanted to keep them together.

(Partly this was because he wanted Broadway's sales revenues for Masterworks. The income from Broadway cast albums had everything to do with the division's ability to keep a classical-artist roster that included Glenn Gould, Vladimir Horowitz, the Juilliard String Quartet, the Mormon Tabernacle Choir, Leonard Bernstein and the New York Philharmonic, Eugene Ormandy and the Philadelphia Orchestra, Isaac Stern, and many more.)

It was Goddard who in 1955, when he was pitched on the original-cast album for a new musical called *My Fair Lady*, recognized the show as a potential gold mine. The story of the show was problematic—it was about phonetics and didn't include a love story—and it was struggling to find financial backing. The people behind it desperately wanted an advance on album sales to help make the show happen. Goddard not only agreed to make the album but also talked his boss, William Paley, into coming up with a then-staggering four hundred thousand dollars to make CBS the sole investor in the show.

That investment was repaid many times over. Beyond the profits churned out by the original production, the national tour, the London production, and any number of revivals, the original-cast album made a fortune in 1956, topping the Billboard Top 200 for fifteen straight weeks. That recording was in mono, but in 1959, a stereo recording with the London cast made another fortune. In 1964 Columbia made yet another fortune with the soundtrack for the movie—and of course, CBS had a piece of the movie as well. The sheet music, the published script, covers of the songs by pop singers—*My Fair Lady* was a money machine, and one consequence of this was that, for the next fifteen years, Paley let Goddard do pretty much whatever he wanted to.

There wasn't much Goddard couldn't do. He had been a music critic, a caricaturist, a raconteur, a novelist, a screenwriter, the head of CBS's Cinema Center Films, as well as the president of the Recording Industry Association of America for thirteen years. In an industry dominated by pop music, it was perhaps remarkable that a man with such highly refined, eclectic tastes would be calling the shots for a major entertainment company.

It was all very impressive, but the Lieberson decision that mattered most to me was a smaller-scale one. With his own background in mind, Goddard encouraged Columbia's personnel department to set up a special training program for young people with musical backgrounds who wanted to learn the record business.

He believed strongly that Columbia's creative decisions had to be made by men and women who were musically knowledgeable. He didn't want those decisions made by marketing people who could be enthusiastic about a new artist or project only if it closely resembled something they already knew to be a salable commodity.

"We can turn a musician into a businessman," he explained, "but we can't turn a businessman into a musician."

When I walked into Columbia's personnel office that October 1959, I gave them my résumé and said, "Look, I can arrange, I can conduct, I can play the piano. Can you use me?" (Which wasn't entirely true—I could only arrange a little bit, and I couldn't conduct at all—but I figured I could learn it.)

They tactfully reminded me that they already had "Percy Faith, André Previn, Leonard Bernstein, Glenn Gould. . . . We're really not looking for new recording artists right now."

But as I started to walk out the door, a secretary named Bobbie called after me and said, "Young man, we're reactivating a training program for A&R men. Would you like to apply?"

I said, "What's A&R?"

She said, "Artists and repertoire."

I had no idea what that meant, but it sounded like something with a salary, so I said "OK."

She told me they'd give me some tests, and if I did all right, I'd start the job in February—a long time to wait, but I didn't have anything else going on, so I said "OK."

They gave me a whole battery of tests, personal and psychological, most of which had nothing to do with the record business: "If you had a day off, would you rather go fishing or read a book?" I don't remember all the questions, but I do remember the results: they told me that my ambition curve ran off the chart, that I was slightly oversexed, and that I was relatively honest.

I can't speak to the accuracy of any of that, but they said, "You're hired," so it was fine with me.

(It has subsequently occurred to me that maybe my résumé played a part in their decision after all. Goddard's passions were classical and Broadway, and after classical work at Oberlin and Yale, I'd spent the preceding summer playing in a touring Broadway show. If I'd gone to Tanglewood, would I have gotten the job? I'll never know.)

So on February 1, 1960, I went to work at Columbia Records. I was reporting to a man named Schuyler Chapin, who reported to Goddard Lieberson, who reported to William Paley. But I owed the job, at least indirectly, to Goddard, for whom I would work, directly or indirectly, for the next fourteen years.

I can't say I was ever friends with Goddard—frankly, I was in awe of him. He was my boss's boss, and I didn't interact directly with him very often.

In my eyes he was larger than life, handsome, witty, impeccably dressed, urbane, and charming. Virtually everything he said was clever and unexpected. I remember once running into him in the lobby of Columbia's headquarters, as we both waited for the elevator (Goddard had walked to work from his home on the Upper East Side, as he always did). We got in, and as he was getting off, Oscar the elevator operator said to him, "Have a good day, Mr. Lieberson."

"Thanks," Goddard replied, "but I have other plans."

All in all, he was more like the leading man in a Noel Coward comedy of manners than any business executive I'd ever heard of. Coward was a friend of his, as were a Who's Who of the twentieth century's most glamorous names, among them Leonard Bernstein, Dick Cavett, Aaron Copland, Duke Ellington, John Gielgud, Benny Goodman, Oscar Levant, Groucho Marx, W. Somerset Maugham, Jacqueline Kennedy Onassis, Richard Rodgers, Stephen Sondheim, and Igor Stravinsky.

He wasn't a perfect man to work for. He hired well—the people he brought to Columbia were an all-star team of sorts—and he gave the people who worked for him the freedom to bring their ideas to life, but he didn't like firing people. He rarely could bear to do it face to face, so people at Columbia got nervous only when Goddard was in Europe or Japan. If the axe was going to fall, that was when it would fall, so the victim could be told the bad news and be out of the building, bag and baggage, by the time Goddard got back into town. (I would subsequently work with people who were far less squeamish about firing people.)

He also wasn't a ready man with a compliment. If you were looking for a pat on the back, it wasn't going to come from Goddard. The two or three times in my life he ever told me I did a good job on something stick out because they were so rare.

With the passage of time, I've come to realize that, even though he rarely if ever complimented me, he selected me for projects that had personal meaning for him. That has to mean he appreciated my work.

In 1967, for example, when his wife, former ballerina and Broadway star Vera Zorina, was narrating a recording of Honegger's *Joan of Arc at the Stake* in an English-language version, with Seiji Ozawa conducting the London Symphony, Goddard sent me to London to produce the record. This wasn't the highest-profile project in the world, but it was important to Goddard because his wife was involved. He could have sent anyone, and of course there were plenty of good producers already in London, but he sent me. To me, looking back, that's proof he trusted me.

In 1968 he was going to be honored by the music-industry division of the United Jewish Appeal at a dinner/dance at the New York Hilton. Dick Cavett was the emcee, and Jerry Vale was going to be singing songs by Rodgers & Hart and Rodgers & Hammerstein, in recognition of Goddard's long association with Richard Rodgers. And Goddard said to me, "I'd like you to please oversee this." The event went well, but to me the real point was that Goddard wanted me to do that—to be his surrogate, as it were—making sure this dinner honoring him went smoothly.

And I did please him at least once that I remember: on one of my trips to London, I found in some store, God knows where, a very, very old souvenir program from the 1937 London production of *On Your Toes*, in which Vera Zorina—long before she married him—had starred in England, in the movie, and on Broadway. I bought it, and when I came back to New York, I gave it to Goddard. He was very happy to have it.

If it weren't for Lieberson, my life as I know it might not have happened, and I'd never have made my 1976 *Porgy & Bess* recording on RCA, which is probably my favorite of all my recordings. But that was a bittersweet thing because to get the recording rights RCA had to beat out several competing bids, one of which came from Goddard, who by this time had retired from Columbia and was producing on a freelance basis. We won and I was glad we did, but it hurt me that Goddard lost out on it. I know he loved that opera as much as I did.

And only a few months afterward, I was at a concert at the New York Philharmonic and went backstage afterward to see Pierre Boulez, with whom I had a long working relationship. I had to wait outside Boulez's dressing room, and right there, standing not 15 feet away from me, were Goddard and his wife, also waiting to see Boulez. And we did not say hello to each other. I should have, and I didn't.

As it turned out he died of cancer in less than a year. He was only sixty-six, and I hadn't realized how sick he was.

I never told Goddard how much his *Porgy and Bess* recording meant to me, and that's another thing I wish I'd done. It was hard to talk to him about personal things, and of course I was in awe of him. Maybe it wouldn't have meant that much to him, but it would have to me.

One of the things that motivates me is that I know, firsthand, the difference one producer's work on one recording can make. I've had people tell me that about recordings I've made, and I wish I'd told Goddard that. I wish I'd said, "Goddard, if it weren't for you, and if it weren't for that *Porgy and Bess*, I wouldn't be here."

6

Making Records

I'VE DESCRIBED RECORDED MUSIC AS "SOUND IN A BOX," and my career has been spent largely concentrating on the sound. It began, however, with close attention to the box—the physical object in which the sound is almost mystically captured and contained.

I arrived at Columbia Records on February 15, 1960, without much sense of exactly what my job would involve—though I knew it would pay me the princely sum of eighty dollars a week. The offices were at 799 Seventh Avenue, a very old building (its history in recording went back to the early 1920s, when it had been owned by Brunswick Records) that no longer exists today. Its six floors contained virtually all of Columbia's New York operations, everything from legal affairs to tape storage. The decisions made in those six floors ranged from international contracts to album liner notes. There were a dozen editing rooms, five disc-master cutting rooms and a recording studio (though most of the sessions on which I was to work would be held in other, larger facilities). It also housed the Columbia Record Club, which was to loom large in my future.

Home base for me would be the second floor, which housed the Artists & Repertoire departments (usually called A&R) for Columbia's three divisions: pop, Masterworks (which encompassed classical and Broadway), and international. This was the creative center of Columbia Records, where the decisions were made about who should record for Columbia and what they should record.

For my first two months, the question of what I would do and for whom I would do it—pop or classical—remained up in the air. I spent those months as a wandering trainee, visiting nearly every office in the building, attending recording sessions, and watching the producers and engineers as they took the tapes from those sessions and assembled them into highly polished masters ready to be committed to vinyl.

I learned a great deal during those months, and at the end of them I was ready for bigger things, so they told me—to get out of town. I would work for three weeks in Bridgeport, Connecticut.

Bridgeport was the home of Columbia's major manufacturing plant. It was important to Goddard that his A&R men, in addition to possessing musical training and taste, be grounded in the physical reality of the product we were manufacturing.

I spent those three weeks seeing how discs were manufactured, watching as they were pressed, processed, and packaged. I spent time in the listening rooms in which specially trained staff played each thousandth pressing of a record, listening for any kind of electronic aberration. Their job was to ignore the content of the record, and instead to focus on the sound quality alone. Pressing records is like printing anything else: as the stamping process goes on, the sharpness of the results diminishes and small, subtle imperfections will creep into the finished product. Those employees in the listening rooms were there to spot deterioration and let the factory know when it was time to replace the stamper.

Perhaps it was an omen, and perhaps it wasn't, but during the time I was there, they were listening to a Broadway original-cast album: Rodgers & Hammerstein's immense hit *The Sound of Music* (1959), starring Mary Martin. The iconic movie was still five years in the future, but the show was a runaway hit on Broadway, and Columbia couldn't crank out the albums fast enough.

I loved those weeks looking behind the curtain at the magic of recorded sound. I came away from my weeks in Bridgeport with a thorough understanding of the process by which records were created. I understood the technology, its capabilities, and its limitations in a way that I never had before, despite two decades of fascination with recorded music. The technology has changed and grown in the ensuing sixty years, but that understanding has stood me in good stead ever since.

When I arrived back in New York, in May 1960, my days as a wandering trainee were behind me, but a crucial question awaited me, one whose answer lay completely beyond my control: Would I be placed in the pop department or in Masterworks? My background would seem to argue for the latter, but there was an overriding issue: Which department needed another guy?

It was my great good fortune that Schuyler Chapin, the head of Masterworks, happened to need another warm body to help with editing and mixing, so I was assigned to classical. I'd be working on the music I loved best, meaning Broadway and classical.

In retrospect, in the early 1960s, Columbia Records was Camelot. I didn't appreciate it at the time because I didn't have anything to compare it to, but Columbia Records—and especially, Columbia Masterworks—was an almost unbelievably good place to start a career.

Not only was Columbia run by the brilliant Goddard Lieberson, but he saw to it that the key people on his staff were musicians. Right down the hall from me was Mitch Miller, who would soon be making fortunes on his television program *Sing Along with Mitch* (1961–1964) but was also the head of pop music for Columbia, for whom he signed Johnny Cash and Aretha Franklin, among others. I saw Mitch almost every day. He was incidentally a gifted oboist who, like Goddard, had attended the Eastman School of Music. He can be heard on a Masterworks recording of Mozart's "Oboe Quartet in F Major" with members of the Budapest String Quartet.

The executives, the producers, the engineers, the artists, the music we were recording—it was magical, and it's only in later years that I've fully realized how fortunate I was to begin my career at Columbia Masterworks.

At the time Columbia Records was owned by CBS, the huge radio and television network founded and then still headed by William Paley. Goddard was the head of Columbia Records, reporting directly to Paley; Schuyler Chapin and Mitch Miller both reported to Goddard. Reporting to Schuyler was a team of producers (the most notable ones were Thomas Frost, John McClure, Paul Myers, and Howard Scott), as well as assorted business operations—marketing, publicity, finance, personnel, and so forth—and me.

Schuyler was in his early forties at the time, and in his own way he was as memorable as Goddard. A patrician of the old school whose ancestral roots extended back to colonial America, he was handsome and strikingly debonaire, with an erudite presence that led people to think he was an Ivy League graduate, even a professor. And yet he was a high-school dropout, but no ordinary dropout: he later served as dean of Columbia University's School of the Arts. He was intelligent, well-read, and knowledgeable on pretty much any subject you could think of. He had spent four years as a pilot in the Army Air Corps during World War II, flying regular flights in the dangerous China-Burma-India theater.

With his aristocratic air, Schuyler was an odd fit for the music business, which is heavily populated with egotistical self-promoters. The great *New York Times* music critic Harold Schonberg once called Schuyler "a gentleman in an ocean of sharks."

Schuyler's great passion was music, and the tragedy of his life was he never became the composer he had longed to be. (He had studied with the legendary teacher Nadia Boulanger, who famously told him, "It's very simple: you have no talent.") After the war he married Elizabeth Steinway, of the piano-making family, and became an artist's manager and agent for such stars as Jascha Heifetz, Vladimir Horowitz, Van Cliburn, and Gary Graffman, before Goddard hired him as vice president in charge of Masterworks in 1959.

He would be my boss for only a few years—he left Columbia in 1964 to become Lincoln Center's first vice president for programming, then general manager of the Metropolitan Opera and New York City's commissioner for cultural affairs—but he made an enduring impression.

Schuyler was a man of taste and refinement, but in one sense he was the odd man out in the Masterworks hierarchy: he led a team of record producers, and his boss was one of the world's greatest record producers, but he himself had no experience in the making of records. His primary job was to manage Masterworks and to recruit and develop a broad, deep roster of classical artists for the label, in both of which he excelled.

The roster was at least as good as any other label could boast and included major orchestras like the New York Philharmonic, the Cleveland Orchestra, the Philadelphia Orchestra, the Mormon Tabernacle Choir, small ensembles like the Juilliard String Quartet, and countless individual artists, among them soprano Eileen Farrell, pianist Glenn Gould, pianist Vladimir Horowitz, violinist Isaac Stern, and tenor Richard Tucker.

The first time I walked into Schuyler's office (like most Columbia executives, he encouraged a certain degree of informality; his door was often open, and he preferred to be on a first-name basis with his staff) after being assigned to Masterworks, he shook hands, wished me well, and advised me to introduce myself to the rest of his department.

This involved a walk down a single hallway, where all the Masterworks producers had their offices. These men all had been groomed by Goddard and chosen with an eye for musical taste and insight. Masterworks's superb engineers included Buddy

Graham, Roy Hallee, Frank Laico, Fred Plaut, and Stanley Tonkel. Their technical skill was so great that they could—and did—rescue a producer from an occasional lapse of judgment or lack of foresight with ease and discretion.

The people I met that day included John McClure, who as music director was Schuyler's second in command, and Howard Scott, a top classical-music producer who would be my first mentor at Columbia. That day I also met associate producer Joe Scianni. It would be several more weeks before I met Thomas Frost, who was in Los Angeles producing the final recordings of conductor Bruno Walter. Tom was and is an unusually gifted musician and producer who set an industry standard for careful and creative production, and we were to become lifelong friends.

In terms of its leadership, its administrative structure, and its key personnel, Columbia Masterworks was a remarkable place to be.

7
The Making of a Producer

I HAD BEEN TOLD I WAS COMING TO COLUMBIA to train to be an A&R executive—basically, someone who decides which musicians perform on records and what music they sing or play. This sounded good, and I did become an A&R executive; however, I also became a producer, and while I stopped being an A&R executive in 1989, I hope to be a producer until the day I die.

One of the worst things about my job is what it's called, because "producer" is an all-purpose word that means different things depending on what business you're in. Even restricting it to entertainment, a movie producer, a Broadway producer, a television producer, and a record producer are all very different things.

In the record business it depends on the genre of music in which a producer is involved. The job of a classical producer—and I've been a classical producer since before I was a producer of Broadway recordings—is to coordinate and facilitate the work of the artist and the engineer, maximizing the talents of each and resolving any difficulties that may arise in the recording session or in editing and mixing.

A producer of Broadway recordings does everything a classical producer does but a good bit more, because usually the material is original music and the composer (and the lyricist, as well as—often—the book writer, the director, and the orchestrator) is involved in the making of the recording. A show recording almost never includes every note of music that is heard in the stage performance, so deciding what not to include is important—and often those choices create new issues. It's not unusual for me to ask the creative team to revise their work specifically for the recording.

The best Broadway creators are happy to do that. Stephen Sondheim, with whom I collaborated for fifteen years, was probably the best Broadway composer with whom I've ever worked in this respect: he embraced the fact that the recording was not a record of the stage production but a separate work of art, and he was willing—even eager—to revisit his own artistic choices for this new medium.

The most obvious difference between a Broadway show and a Broadway recording is the absence of sets, costumes, and lighting, but there's more to it than that. Almost every creative choice made in a Broadway show is made in full awareness that the results will be seen by the audience. None of this will be seen by the listening audience, so all those choices need to be reassessed.

A particularly extreme case, and one of the biggest challenges I've faced in my career, came with *1776* (1969), the finale of which builds to a crowning coup d'théâtre, the onstage re-creation of a famous painting, John Trumbull's "Declaration of Independence" (1817). Virtually everything in the show, from set and costume design to casting to staging to the very unusual decision not to end the show on a song, is keyed to this final image, and the listener at home won't see that image. (Sondheim's brilliant show *Sunday in the Park with George* [1984] posed a similar problem.)

The creative team knows the audience will see the show and chooses accordingly; I know the audience won't see it, so it's my job to come up with new ways to convey to a listening audience what could be seen in the theater. (This isn't the case with classical performances, as a rule: they have a visual component, to be sure, but the concert audience's focus is almost entirely on listening.)

Most shows don't re-create famous paintings, but all of them utilize the visual faculties of their audience in a variety of ways. In Sondheim's *Company* (1970), for example, the song "The Little Things You Do Together" is sung simultaneously with an onstage karate match, which provides an ironic counterpoint, physicalizing the conflicts that are brought out in the lyrics of the song. When I recorded the original production of *Company*, I decided to include the sound of the karate match. Most Broadway recording producers would have omitted it. And this perhaps explains why I feel that a record producer should be called a recording director.

What I—and other producers of Broadway recordings who share my perspective—do is more analogous to what the director does with the stage production. We combine and balance the various creative elements (singers, orchestra musicians, sound effects, engineers, and even the liner notes and the design of the package) in an effort to tell the story effectively and with emotional power. The stage director is combining and balancing different elements, but he or she is trying to tell the same story we are.

I don't get to decide what my job is called, though, and in 1960 I had only the most shadowy sense of what that job would turn out to be. But the assignment to Masterworks meant I would be trained to be a producer, and within my first week there, I was assigned to assist Howard Scott, one of Columbia's top producers of classical recordings.

Howard was thirty-nine when I arrived, and he was a fourteen-year veteran at Columbia. Like Goddard and Mitch, Howard was a graduate of Eastman; he was a pianist, and I've been told, a good one, though I never heard him play. He had been studying at Juilliard when he was drafted into the army in 1942. He returned to civilian life in 1946 and was hired at Columbia Records, much as I would be fourteen years later.

His first major job at Columbia was overseeing the transfer of old classical recordings from lacquer onto the newly invented LP; in a strange coincidence, after leaving Columbia in 1961, he would return to the label in 1986 to oversee the transfer of old classical recordings from LPs to the newly invented CD.

In between, however, he became a gifted record producer, overseeing hundreds of recordings for Masterworks. He made many recordings of legendary artists, including Leonard Bernstein and the New York Philharmonic, and was particularly noted for his collaboration with the pianist Glenn Gould. When Howard left Columbia, only a year after I arrived, John McClure took over some of his artists, and a few fell to me as well.

Only a couple days into my working with Howard, we met in front of the office, and he hailed a taxi. We were off to the St. George Hotel on Clark Street in Brooklyn to attend my first-ever recording session. His instructions were, "Keep your eyes open and your mouth shut"—words to which I wish I'd paid more attention through the years.

The St. George, which closed as a hotel in 1995 and today serves as student housing for area colleges, was then one of the most glamorous hotels in New York and had once been the city's largest. Its Grand Ballroom had exceptionally good acoustics, so it was used frequently by Columbia to record the New York Philharmonic, and that's why we were there that day.

It was my initiation into classical recording: Bernstein and the New York Philharmonic. I couldn't believe my luck. It's fair to say I was mesmerized from beginning to end.

The session was scheduled to run from 10 a.m. until late afternoon. Bernstein was conducting Tchaikovsky's "Capriccio Italien," Prokofiev's *Peter and the Wolf* (only the music—Bernstein's narration would be added later), and Mahler's *Kindertotenlieder* (*Songs on the Death of Children*) sung by Jennie Tourel. Howard and I got there by 9 a.m., and by 9:30 the orchestra was assembling in the ballroom. We were down the hall, set up in a comfortable, much smaller room that would serve as our control room.

There Howard introduced me to the chief recording engineer, Fred Plaut, and to engineers Buddy Graham and Frank Bruno. They were longtime Columbia veterans and gifted engineers—the Philharmonic got Columbia's best. They'd arrived at the hotel several hours before the session, setting up the mikes and cables that would link the ballroom to the recording equipment in the control room, while the Philharmonic's librarians and their assistants, along with the hotel's crew, set up the music stands, chairs, and other necessary orchestral paraphernalia.

And then the door of our control room opened, and Leonard Bernstein swept in. He was impeccably dressed in medium-gray slacks, a turtleneck shirt, and a russet-colored, cashmere sports jacket. He looked like a matinee idol—trim and impeccably groomed, with a great crop of lightly graying hair—and was accompanied by a cloud of tobacco smoke, which I would learn was all but inevitable with Bernstein, who was a chain smoker.

At this point Bernstein was forty-two and probably the most famous conductor in America. He was also the toast of Broadway as the composer of *Candide* (1956) and *West Side Story* (1957), the latter of which had run for almost two years and was about to reopen at the Winter Garden Theatre for another run after a national tour; a movie was in the works and would open in 1961. Having become the youngest conductor ever to lead the Philharmonic, in 1943, he had become its youngest-ever music director in 1957 and was a television star, thanks to his enormously influential "Young People's Concerts" that aired on CBS. I knew all about Leonard Bernstein—as did anyone in America who was interested in either classical music or Broadway.

I was surprised to see that he was fairly short in stature, because in every other respect he was larger than life. He was relaxed and smiled easily, but he exuded incredible enthusiasm, charisma, and energy, and he galvanized his players.

Accompanying Bernstein into our control room was a squat old lady (well, she was almost sixty, a formidable age from the perspective of a twenty-three-year-old) who snuggled and cooed with him in a maternal fashion. She was introduced to me as Jennie Tourel. I barely knew who she was and had never heard the Mahler song cycle she was about to record (what does a twenty-three-year-old care about songs about dead children?), but I found it hard to believe that such an old lady could still be able to sing.

Howard and I sat at a long folding table in the control room, the score open in front of us, as Bernstein and Tourel went into the ballroom and began to record. We listened through the monitor loudspeakers—huge Macintosh amplifiers powering enormous Altec-Lansing speakers arranged stereophonically to the left, center, and right of the producer's table—which provided the richest and most beautiful electronic reproduction I'd ever heard.

But it wasn't only the sound quality that held me rapt. This "little old lady" began singing about dead children, and time stopped. Mahler's five songs are so compelling, and Tourel's performance was so powerful that they created a mood and a space all their own. The songs range from sad to tender, regretful to angry, frustrated to resigned, running the gamut of emotional, psychological, and musical moods experienced by parents of dead children. As I sat with Howard at that table at the St. George Hotel, the songs pierced my soul.

Magic was happening in the next room. I couldn't see it—there was no closed-circuit television in those days—but I could hear it, and it possessed me.

After the Mahler came the Tchaikovsky and then the Prokofiev, a piece I had known and loved since I was six years old. But the recording I had cherished as a boy, with Serge Koussevitsky conducting the Boston Symphony, was on a stack of Victor 78s, and I was listening to it on a typical family phonograph; I had never heard the piece played at a concert. Koussevitsky's wasn't a bad recording, but as I sat in the control room and listened, I realized I had never really heard the piece at all. I became aware of so many beautiful details I'd never noticed. When a rush of French horns came up during Peter's final, triumphant march, I was astounded.

I was there in a professional capacity and perhaps should have played it cool, but I couldn't contain my enthusiasm. I began sputtering to Scott—and later to Bernstein—that I had never heard anything like this before, and how wonderful everything sounded. I suppose they smiled indulgently, but I was too swept away to notice.

It was a fabulous day—such an unexpected and powerful experience: an abundance of beautiful music, meeting Bernstein, watching a recording session take place, observing the interaction between Scott and Bernstein, Bernstein and Tourel, Scott and the engineers, and Bernstein and the orchestra.

This last observation was a splash of cold water, however. While Bernstein was intense and inspiring, the men (at that time there were no women) who comprised the orchestra seemed remarkably casual, even business-as-usual in their attitude. And they were noisy. Bernstein had to ask for quiet many times. Even while they played, someone always seemed to nudge something or drop something. As the session tapes would subsequently confirm, their performance of Mahler's poignantly beautiful music was riddled with scrapes and creaks, some of it perhaps the fault of the room's heating system, but most of it due to the players' seeming indifference to it. Bernstein either didn't notice or chose not to.

To Howard it was just another day's work. He spent the session in a state of total concentration, following the music, keeping track of errors, calling breaks, calling for retakes, ordering adjustments in microphone placements and balances, as well as noting musical issues he wanted to bring to Bernstein's attention. If either the beauty of the music or the frustration of the extraneous noise affected him, he didn't show it.

I rode back to Manhattan with him in a taxi, however, and during that ride he vented his rage and frustration at the orchestra's behavior. One of the reasons the sessions had dragged on so long, he said, and cost more money than he was budgeted for, was the players' disrespectful attitude. He called them slobs and added that Bernstein was just as much of a slob for letting them get away with such lousy decorum.

For me, a green twenty-three-year-old, to hear this blunt criticism of Bernstein and the Philharmonic was jarring. It was fun to listen to Howard's frankness and his iconoclasm, but it disoriented me. When I'd gotten into that cab, I was still coming down from my stay in an almost-perfect world. When I got out, I was back in the real world.

I did more than simply listen to the music, of course. I was there to observe the session, with nothing in particular I was supposed to be doing, so I did my best to keep my eyes open and my mouth shut. Between the orchestra, the Philharmonic staffers, Columbia's people, and the hotel people, the place was a hive of activity, and I tried to take it all in.

I was particularly fascinated by the relationship between Howard and Bernstein because it was collegial and not master-and-servant. This clearly was Bernstein's ballgame, but he respected Howard. If Howard felt something should be redone or altered, Bernstein listened to him and gave him what he needed.

The producer and the conductor have the same goal—to produce the best possible recording—but they have different means to that end. For the conductor, it's about directing a great performance of the music; for the producer, it's getting the raw material—the session tapes—from which a great recording will be constructed. It's vital that nothing be overlooked, and a big part of that is a ferocious sense of concentration during the session: even the smallest mistake that is overlooked in the session may pose serious problems in the editing cubicle.

Howard and Bernstein (I would call him "Lenny" before too long, but not that first day) had a long-standing working relationship, and they appeared very comfortable with each other. Howard's years of experience working with temperamental, volatile artists had equipped him with the tact to point out things Bernstein might have overlooked, but to do it in such a way as to spare Bernstein's ego.

It could be a small, very specific detail: Howard might mention, for example, that a given instrument in a particular passage was too prominent, and that perhaps he should play more softly or the mikes ought to be readjusted—or it might be a sweeping overview: Howard might ask if the tempos were starting to drag—he wouldn't say they were dragging, which could be taken as an aspersion on Bernstein's conducting, but would ask if this might be the case.

A good partnership between the producer and the artist (or between the producer and the engineer) can make the difference between a routine recording and a great one. Issues of articulation and balance that might be let go for a live performance can be fine-tuned for a recording—which will, of course, ultimately be heard by a far larger audience for years to come.

It wasn't too long after that session that Howard produced another one with Lenny, for a children's opera called *The Second Hurricane*, by Aaron Copland. That session was done at Columbia's 30th Street studio because it called for a reduced orchestra, not the full Philharmonic. Howard produced the session, and what I recall most is that the time was running out. We were running close to the wire, and as the clock struck 11 p.m., Howard said, "I'm sorry, Lenny, but we're out of time."

Bernstein said, "Howard, you can't do this to me. You can't leave it like this. You have to give me the time."

It cost Columbia a lot of money, I'm sure, because overtime with a union orchestra is ferociously expensive, but Howard relented, and gave him the time. He knew that, in the big picture of Columbia's relationship with Bernstein and the Philharmonic, preventing Bernstein from getting the results he was aiming for would have been ill-advised.

When Howard died in 2012, his family asked me to say a few words at his memorial celebration. I said that perhaps the biggest compliment I could pay Howard is that, when an artist said to him, "Howard, are we covered?" and Howard said, "Yes," they really were covered. Whatever had to be fixed or repaired had been taken care of, and everything that needed to be recorded had been. The artist knew he or she had nothing to worry about.

Howard could be firm, even stubborn when he needed to be, but he was innately a good man and a good producer. Preparation was the foundation of his work. I never saw him walk into a recording session with less than a perfect knowledge of the score, and his copy was always marked up in advance with places to watch out for, based on the trickiness of the music or its likely problems with balance and volume.

He wasn't the first person to teach me about the importance of preparation, or the last, but he may have been the one who had the most impact. He taught me that one of a producer's most valuable skills on any recording session is time management. He begins with a limited amount of time and can get more only at tremendous cost. On a major orchestral recording, you may be dealing with as many as a hundred union musicians, and thirty or more on a typical Broadway recording; any time lost unnecessarily will result in staggering cost overruns. Anything you can do before a session, when you have time to think things through carefully, you should do; there are too many things that can be done only within the session to burden yourself with anything you could have done beforehand.

Running a session is not for the faint of heart. There's a lot of pressure involved, as you juggle a complicated schedule and neurotic, sensitive artists, all in the face of a ticking clock, but Howard was almost unfailingly cool and tactful. I immediately picked up his habit of beginning every take not with some dramatic announcement, but rather with a low-key "OK, here we go." It was many, many years before I could begin a take any other way.

The most immediate thing Howard was teaching me is how tapes are edited and mixed. The recording session is only the beginning of the process. It provides the raw material from which the final recording will be assembled. It's in the editing cubicle that the producer and the engineer, working in tandem, put those pieces together into what will become the final recording.

The producer is ultimately responsible to see to it that all errors have been accounted for, and that the best moments of each take are assembled to create the final edited master.

Mixing is subtler. Levels and balances can be controlled. The quality of sound can be altered and enhanced. Balancing the elements perfectly can create a recording that can be more refined than the performance of which it is a record.

In today's multi-track recording, it isn't difficult to electronically move a singer or an instrument from one spot to another, to alter the sound quality, to adjust the perspective, to create a different aural atmosphere. The degree of control we have today is truly extraordinary.

In my earlier days, when all the engineers were unionized, there were strict rules that no non-union person, that is to say, the producers, could turn any knob or touch any recording console.

These days the rules are looser, especially since I'm not always working at a union facility, but nonetheless I rarely touch the board. The engineer is my partner in the recording session, and in the editing cubicle.

So I listen and I talk. I talk to the singers, to the conductor, to the musicians, exploring and explaining what we need to get the most our of our combined efforts. I work with the engineers as well, explaining what we're trying to achieve so they can inform me what is needed to achieve it.

When I am recording a Broadway show, one of my tricks is never to watch actors as they sing. A talented musical-theater actor learns a thousand little ways to use expressions, attitudes, flickers of the eyes, body language, and so forth to heighten their performances. But none of those little tricks will come through on the recording. If you are watching them while they record, you can be drawn in and think you're hearing a great performance, when what you're really doing is *seeing* a great performance and perhaps *hearing* only an adequate one. So I just gaze at my score, or at the engineer, or at the conductor—at anything except the person at the microphone. I make my living with my brain and my ears; my eyes have nothing to offer but pitfalls.

Let me cite an example: In 1983 RCA made a deal to make the cast album for the revival of *Zorba* (1968), the stage musical based on the film *Zorba the Greek* (1964). I hadn't been involved in the original-cast album, which was made by Capitol and starred Herschel Bernardi in the title role, and I didn't really know the show. This revival was on a pre-Broadway tour, and I had to fly out to California to make the recording there, with scant time to familiarize myself with the script and score and no time at all to get to know this production or its cast before we were in the studio at work.

The star of the show was Anthony Quinn. We met for the first time in the recording studio. Quinn was an intimidating guy. He'd won two Oscars and been nominated for *Zorba the Greek* and one other film. He was sixteen years older than I was; he stood six feet two inches, and I stood, well, quite a bit less. And he may well have figured that, considering his history with the role of Zorba, he knew what he should do with the part better than some guy from New Jersey who had no history with the show at all.

If that was how he figured it, he was wrong. Playing the part onscreen was one thing, but playing the part onstage was another thing, and playing it on record was a third thing altogether. Quinn was no stranger to the recording studio—he'd done some pop records for Capitol—but he'd never made a cast album. There were things he could teach me about playing Zorba, but there were things I could teach him about making a cast album.

There's a number in the show called "Goodbye, Canavaro." It's a duet between Zorba and Madame Hortense, played by Lila Kedrova, who had also been in the movie and had won an Oscar for it. The song calls for him to get progressively angrier at her, until by the end he's bathed in fury and frustration. As I listened to—but didn't watch—their first take, I realized Kedrova was coming through exactly as needed, but Quinn was getting too mad, too soon. Onstage his performance escalated through the end, but onstage he communicated that with visible gestures and expressions. On this first take of our recording, with only his voice to work with, his anger and frustration hit their maximum vocal intensity much too soon and had nowhere to go. So I had to tell Anthony Quinn how he should be playing Zorba the Greek.

Quinn heard me out. "Let me hear it." I played it for him, he listened. When the playback was over, he nodded to me and said, "I know what to do." He did: on his next take the emotional arc of the song was expressed entirely audially, with Zorba's anger and frustration building to a climax exactly when it needed to. It was far more dramatic.

In my early years, Columbia Records had too much going on to be able to accomplish all its editing and mixing during daylight hours, so these chores often continued into the night. All too often, because I was the new kid in town, those late-night jobs fell to me. But in 1960, I was dating Irene, and she and her mother happened to live only a couple of blocks from Columbia Records. When I worked late, they would let me sleep over on their couch, saving me the trip back to New Jersey. I would begin the next day a little more rumpled than the day before, but that was OK.

After several months of easing into these responsibilities under Howard's eye, my first editing project was the song cycle Jennie Tourel had sung on that first recording session—the Mahler *Kindertotenlieder*. Thus the tapes from the first recording session I had ever attended were to be the first ones I ever edited on my own, not to mention my first Bernstein project.

I wasn't entirely on my own, of course. Howard gave me his orchestra score and the job sheets that included all his editing instructions for *Kindertotenlieder*. These instructions formed the rough skeleton of a final recording, indicating which parts of which takes had been judged best (by Howard and by Bernstein) during the session.

And of course, I had the session tapes themselves, lots of music on lots of pieces of tape, large and small. My job was to listen to all of them and then, guided by Howard's notes and my own judgment, sit down with an engineer and put them together into a record that lived up to the standards and the reputations of Bernstein, the Philharmonic and Columbia itself.

This process took place in one of the editing cubicles at Columbia's headquarters on Seventh Avenue. This was a windowless, acoustically padded room measuring about 12 by 18 feet—the antithesis of the spacious, ornately decorated ballroom of the St. George Hotel. At the far end of the room from me sat the tape machines and the splicing equipment; between them sat the engineer, with the editing and mixing console in front of him, positioned so he could turn either back to look at the machines and editing equipment or forward to look at me as I sat facing him. At my end of the room were two sets of monitor speakers near the left and right corners.

I have said that I was flying solo on this mission, but of course I wasn't: my ace in the hole was Buddy Graham, a gifted engineer of proven skills and judgment. Howard trusted me to handle the editing but I was working with a veteran hand at the console.

Buddy was particularly adept at editing, at splicing pieces of takes together. His splices were quick and accurate, and he was remarkable at making a precise edit point very quickly. (These days engineers work with digital files and razor-blade-and-splicing-tape editing is a thing of the past, but in those days it was an art form, and Buddy Graham was a master of that art.)

We began by listening again to all the takes, following along in Howard's score, with his editing notes. I had been dazzled by Tourel's performance as I listened to it in the studio. As I listened to the tapes, however, free of the adrenaline and electricity of the live session and with the time to go back and listen to a given take as many times as was necessary, I realized that Buddy and I had a big job ahead of us.

Tourel had been fifty-nine when we'd made the recordings. She still sang well—well enough to dazzle a twenty-three-year-old studio novice—but she was past her prime, and her voice was uneven. Some notes were rich and beautiful, others fuzzy and poorly focused. A few were off pitch, and all too often the orchestra lost precision and intonation. I'd begun to learn how to listen hyper-critically, and once I applied those lessons to the *Kindertotenlieder* tapes, I was amazed how much there was that could be improved.

Then there was that infuriating background noise, coming most often from the orchestral players. It had been vexing during the session, but listening now to the tapes revealed it to be far worse and more pervasive than initially realized. Furthermore, Howard's markings, while invariably precise and accurate, didn't reflect all the tiny flaws that would be discovered when the tapes were listened to very carefully at this later time.

All in all, we had a Herculean task before us. We got it done, though. Buddy and I must have spent more than a week on those tapes, and we edited those five songs to within an inch of their lives. I was trying not only to get the best of every phrase out of Tourel's voice, but to do that while simultaneously working around the background noises.

The mixing was still to come, however. That would wait until Bernstein had approved the edited version.

A week or so later, it was time to play the recording for him. It was one thing to have been a fly on the wall while Bernstein was recording the songs in a room full of people, but it was a whole other thing to be in a small room with only him and Buddy. I knew this was a crucial moment in my young career—and of course, so did Bernstein, who was fully conscious of the effect he had on people and enjoyed it.

He arrived punctually at 7 p.m., and he and I sat down, each opening our own copy of the score. We listened carefully to all five songs, and—to my delight, since I'd been watching his face as carefully as he'd been listening to the music—he couldn't find a thing he wanted to improve or correct.

In those days, if you watched the tape advance through the machine (which Bernstein was doing), you could see where each edit was because the white editing tape was clearly visible. So he was very much aware, as these little white things flew by, that this tape sustained seriously heavy editing.

"Christ, look at all those splices," he said not far into the tape, and he probably said it several more times as we played through all five of the edited songs. We finished very early—a session scheduled for three hours ran roughly an hour—and as we wrapped up, Bernstein said, "I'd like it if you could do all my editing from now on."

(John McClure agreed, so for the next several years I was the editor and often the mixer on most of Lenny's recordings.)

Best of all, because we had time to spare, Bernstein said, "Come on, let's go over to the Winter Garden"—which was just a block away. *West Side Story* was back in town and playing there, where it had originally opened. I couldn't believe what was happening, Leonard Bernstein and Tom Shepard backstage at *West Side Story*.

We got there toward the end of the first act, and of course, at intermission, the cast came over and mobbed him. I went out into the house and stayed for the whole second act—I don't know if he did or not—but this was my reward for a job well done: to be in his company, to go backstage at *West Side Story*. These were the early perks of the business.

Another one came later that year, when I was assigned to produce a session during which Lenny was going to record a narration and add some piano tracks for an upcoming album called *Humor in Music*, based on the script from one of his Young People's Concerts.

One musical example was from Darius Milhaud's "Le Boeuf Sur le Toit," and the score Lenny had brought with him was a four-hand piano version. He decided he would play the left side of the brief phrase he wanted to demonstrate and he asked me if I would play the top. It wasn't an easy passage for me, but it wasn't a killer either, and I pretty well nailed it on the first take.

I was relieved, and now that the pressure was off, I was also thrilled: "I'm a performing partner of Leonard Bernstein on a commercial recording! Wait till I tell my parents—who will then tell every relative and friend they have in the world!"

At that time Lenny was in his early forties and was really a lot of fun to be around, most of the time. As he got older, he got less and less pleasant to be with, but in the early 1960s he still had the fire and generosity of youth.

During that year, I attended many Berstein/New York Philharmonic sessions,, some with Howard and others with John McClure. Between Howard and John—who also asked me to do a lot of his editing—I attended a great many Bernstein sessions during those first couple of years. This was in 1960 and 1961, when Columbia was re-recording so many stereo remakes of classical-music warhorses. So there was a lot going on almost every week.

My first recording session as the actual producer came only eight or nine months after I'd started with Columbia. It was in the fall of 1960, and I was recording a young violinist named Joseph Silverstein, who was performing Bach's "Sonatas and Partitas for Solo Violin." Silverstein had just won the Naumburg Award, a major honor, and was shortly to become the concertmaster of the Boston Symphony.

It was no accident, I'm sure, that an unaccompanied soloist was to be my first session. Schuyler probably figured, "How badly could he screw it up, with only one guy and one violin?" But I got on well with Silverstein, and it was a very pleasant experience.

Schuyler then assigned me to a newly-signed pianist named Ivan Davis, and after Howard left Columbia early in 1961, some of his artists were assigned to me. I was now officially an associate producer at Columbia Masterworks—still the junior with no chance yet of running Bernstein's sessions or Horowitz's, but a producer at a prestigious record company in its most prestigious department. Not bad for a guy who'd been unemployed at the beginning of the previous year!

By then, though, I also had my eye on something else, something unconnected to classical music. My eye was on Broadway.

8

The Word Is "Stereophonic"

HISTORICALLY THE INDUSTRY HAS BEEN SHAPED by waves of technological innovation, and those waves have offered opportunities to young arrivals who are comfortable with the new technology. Howard Scott had begun his career on the crest of the previous wave, the arrival of the LP in 1948, as had another guy I'd get to know better pretty soon, a Columbia pop producer named Jim Foglesong. Now my career was to be shaped by the arrival, in the late 1950s, of a new technology called stereophonic sound.

The evolution of recording technology had brought huge improvements in the quality of the sound. Particularly after the development of the microphone in the mid-1920s, the sound you heard through a phonograph had become more and more like the original sound you'd have heard in the recording studio. By the mid-1950s it was possible to hear singing in the next room and mistake high-fidelity recorded sound for live sound.

In one aspect, however, the realism of recorded sound was still lacking. The human ear is a remarkable mechanism, and Edison's invention had deftly imitated its capabilities by using an artificial diaphragm to replace the membranes of the inner ear. However, he had left the human brain out of the equation. (Although not very well known, it is also a fact that Edison was seriously deaf!)

Most people understand the concept of binocular vision, whereby the input from each of our eyes is received by the brain, which combines and interprets the two to produce depth perception. The brain's capabilities in this area are astounding: most of the time our two eyes—placed as they are only an inch or so apart—seem to be seeing exactly the same thing: you have to be very close to something before covering one eye and then the other results in a noticeable difference in what you see, but the brain is so finely tuned that it can process the incredible amount of information perceived by each eye, combine it and give us a reliable sense of depth—and do it all unconsciously!

The ears work on the same principle. Placed six or seven inches apart, each of your ears receives mostly the same sonic information at minutely different moments in time and in intensity, and processes that information to produce a three-dimensional aural version of the visual landscape created in your mind through the information once provided by your eyes. Both ears hear a fly buzzing, but it's the brain that compares the information received from your left and right ears and leads you—without even thinking about it—to turn your head in the correct direction and set your eyes to work at spotting the fly.

This happens in a theater or concert hall as well. If you see two people on a stage holding guitars and close your eyes before one of them starts playing, you'll probably be able to tell which one is playing. Because you have two ears, your mind will use the two different inputs to triangulate the sources and locate where each sound is coming from. And it will do the same thing, even if both guitarists are playing at once, separating their sounds subtly even if your eyes can't distinguish the fingering to tell you who's playing which part.

This is one reason why hearing a monaural recording of a Broadway show or a symphony concert isn't like hearing the event in person. The power of your brain to absorb and synthesize all that sound is what makes the experience of hearing twenty or thirty professional musicians performing a Broadway show (or seventy or ninety playing a classical symphony), so powerful. There's a richness and a breadth to the sound that can't be replicated if all sound is channeled through a single source.

This was fully understood by acousticians, and there had been attempts at stereo as early as 1881, when Clément Ader demonstrated the idea by mounting twin telephones at opposite sides of the hall at the Paris Opera, with a separate line connecting each telephone to a room at the Paris Electrical Exhibition. By putting one receiver to each ear, the listener could hear a tinny approximation of what he'd hear sitting in the hall.

Ader wasn't making a recording, of course, but his successful experiment demonstrated the basic principle that multiple devices, situated some distance apart, could simulate the same result as a pair of human ears. They could produce different variants of the same sound experience—and a listener's brain could synthesize this into a richer soundscape than monaural recording could produce. In recording, the challenge was to find a way to store those separate sound perspectives and then feed them into a delivery system that could be used in a home setting.

The first movie to use stereophonic was Walt Disney's *Fantasia*, in 1940, in a handful of specially equipped theaters. Movies wouldn't be routinely made in stereo until the 1970s, but the basic methodology had been established.

As far as home audio was concerned, it took another quarter-century to work out the kinks in the process and to devise an affordable way to make it available to the mass market. This was greatly accelerated by the development of magnetic recording tape, which was first used in Nazi Germany in the early 1940s. It made its way to the United States and the rest of the world.

The first commercial stereo recordings were released in 1954 on magnetic tape, but initially the expense of the tapes, and of the equipment necessary to play them, limited them to high-end audiophiles. I heard my first stereo (then known as "binaural") recording at Oberlin, when a fellow student played one for me as I listened through his headphones; I was impressed, but I didn't necessarily see it as the wave of the future.

But in 1958, the vinyl stereo disc came along. It was an immediate hit, and by 1960, the major labels had begun manufacturing stereo discs. Many records were still sold in both mono and stereo versions, and there were various methods of "processing" tapes from monaural sessions to produce imitation stereo of one sort or another—with results that were, frankly, awful. But all the biggest records, whether in classical, pop, jazz, or Broadway, were being recorded in stereo, and by February 1960, when I entered the record-business, stereo was the wave of the present.

Stereo was to be foundational in my career, both as a producer and, at the risk of sounding pretentious, as an artist.

I could see that there was more to stereo than the simple ability to distinguish left from right. As soon as you can do that, I realized, you can also convey movement. A singer who starts at the left side of the stage and moves to the right side, still singing, will pass from an area in which she's picked up only by the stage-left microphone toward one in which she registers only on the stage-right microphone; she'll pass through areas in which both mikes pick her up, to a degree that varies as she moves further from one and closer to the other. Particularly if there are a series of mikes between stage left and stage right, it's possible to create an audial equivalent of seeing her cross the stage, one that "reads" to the listener's ears as if he were seeing her walk across the stage.

The implications of this were enormous—more so, of course, in Broadway recordings (because actors often move while singing) than in classical, in which the musicians typically remain stationary. Opera singers do move, to some extent, but rarely as often or as extensively as musical-theater actors, and few opera recordings are meant to capture the audience experience of seeing a particular production.

Stereo opened a whole new area of endeavor for me as a producer, enabling me to re-create not only the sound of the show (the work of the show's music director) but also important aspects of the look of the show (the work of the stage director). To some degree, I could re-create, in the listener's mind, what the staging looked like: hearing footsteps traveling across the stage, right to left, the listener could imagine that space and place it in his mental soundscape.

As I've said, the reason early cast-album producers couldn't tell the story of the show on their records (they relied on liner notes to fill that gap) wasn't necessarily a lack of artistic imagination, but the physical limitations of the 78-rpm format. That format could provide only four or five minutes of continuous music before the listener's experience was disrupted by the need to change discs. Producers were forced to cut verses, whole songs, and instrumental numbers. Until the introduction of magnetic recording tape, they were unable to edit as such—any mistake on a song, and they had to start over. Given these limitations, they reasonably chose to record *selections* of songs from a show, rather than the essence of the show itself. (That was one of the reasons that Goddard's *Porgy and Bess* hit me with such impact.)

But I arrived in the age of the LP and magnetic tape (and have worked into the age of the CD and of digital recording) and I got there just as the age of stereo was dawning. There was a new world of sound afforded by stereo, and it sparked my imagination in ways I never could have predicted.

I should hasten to add I'm not talking about a one-size-fits-all approach to recording a show, whether in 1927, 1961, or 2024. Stereo, multitrack recording, and digital editing put a vast array of new tools into my metaphorical toolbox, but no producer uses all his tools on any given job any more than a carpenter does. He looks at the show he's recording and uses the tools he needs for that particular project.

For example, when I produce a Jerry Herman show, I largely put together a collection of its songs, the way Goddard might have done with a show in 1940. Jerry was a throwback, a guy who wrote his shows the same way that Rodgers & Hart or Cole Porter had, with the songs standing pretty much on their own, not necessarily integrated with the story or the characters. Working with a creator like him, the approach is to serve the songs, more than to serve the show dramatically.

Stephen Sondheim, on the other hand, wrote tightly integrated shows, ones in which the songs were very character-specific, dialogue wove in and out of songs, and there were often two things going on at once on different parts of the stage—or even three or four things at once. Working on Steve's shows, I needed to dig deep into the toolbox, and I'm profoundly grateful that in the 1970s and 1980s, when I was making those recordings, I had such a lot in my toolbox.

The biggest challenge I face in adapting an audio-visual experience into an audio-only one is how to convey those elements necessary to tell the story. Sometimes the clatter of a sheathed sword or the clank of armor, or the tolling of a bell or the shot of a gun, is useful to paint a picture in the listener's mind. It depends on the dramatic moment whether or not I elect to add these effects.

As I said at the beginning of this chapter, I arrived at Columbia in the middle of a recording boom. Stereo was trendy, and people were scrambling to buy the new players—and new records to play on them.

This had happened before, of course. In the late 1940s and early 1950s, earlier recordings of Beethoven's Fifth and of *Oklahoma!* that originally had been recorded as a stack of 78s had been re-released on vinyl LPs, and aficionados could now appreciate their favorite recordings in uninterrupted flow by rebuying them on LP. It would happen again in the 1980s, as Broadway devotees who had bought the original *Oklahoma!* on 78s in 1943, and on LP in 1949, lined up to buy it again on CD.

9

The Sixth Record Is Free

THE COLUMBIA RECORD CLUB WAS ITS OWN LITTLE KINGDOM within the larger empire of Columbia Records. Originally launched in 1955 as a mail-order marketing arm of Columbia, it had aggressively pursued agreements that would allow it to market records from other labels as well. Most of Columbia's top rivals, such as RCA and Capitol, ran their own record clubs and weren't interested, but by 1958 Columbia had signed licensing deals with Kapp, Liberty, Mercury, United Artists, Vanguard, Verve, and Warner Bros., among others.

(Though few people realized it at the time, the Record Club wasn't literally selling records manufactured by other labels: Instead, the master tapes and all the artwork would be sent from the other label to Columbia, and then the discs to be sold by the club would actually be manufactured by Columbia at its own factories. The label may have said "Mercury" or "Warner Bros.," but the record itself was pressed by Columbia.)

The club worked on a membership basis, using what's known in the trade as "negative-option billing." Once you became a member, you remained a member until you chose to cancel; if you did nothing, the records kept coming, and so did the bills.

Negative-option billing has been controversial since it was created because some see it as exploitative, but most members of the Columbia Record Club weren't complaining. Drawing not only on Columbia's extensive catalog (almost all of which was available through the Record Club as of six months after its release) but also on products from all those other labels, the club offered a wide range of choices in pop, classical, Broadway, country, jazz, spoken word, and more.

The deal was simple: members got a new catalog each month and could choose any six records they wanted. The order form came with a sheet of stamps depicting the album covers of the club's offerings. Members would stick the stamps onto the order form and send it back, and the records would arrive in due course. The customer was billed for five, but the sixth record was free. There was also a magazine, hyping upcoming releases from the club.

The club sold a substantial volume of records each month, and its profit margins were high because it didn't have to give a piece of the pie to record-store owners. So the people running it were given a lot of leeway by the management of Columbia—most of the time, they got what they wanted. And what they wanted most was product: the Record Club needed a steady flow of records to sell, and while its leaders couldn't control what records Mercury or Warner Bros. made, they could influence what Columbia made.

Broadway musicals were big sellers in the Record Club catalog, and the club was always happy to see them on the Columbia schedule. But there were only so many new Broadway musicals, and some of them had been made by labels like Decca or RCA, where the Record Club wouldn't have access to them.

The advent of stereo opened new vistas, however, and somebody at the Record Club—I don't know who—came up with a good idea: the Club offered the Masterworks division $35,000 per project to make new studio recordings of classic Broadway shows from the past, almost all of them previously unavailable in stereo. In the early 1960s that was enough money to sign a cast of well-known singers and make a top-quality recording—and it was guaranteed money, which you don't often get in the record business. So it was a great idea as far as Masterworks was concerned.

And it was a great idea as far as I was concerned—I desperately wanted to get in on this project because I loved Broadway, I loved Broadway recordings, and this would be the way I could get my foot in that door. I went to Schuyler sometime in the summer of 1961, and I said, "You know how much I love Broadway. I very much want to be involved in these recordings for the Record Club."

And Schuyler told me, "It would be OK with me, but I've already assigned these projects to Jim Foglesong. Talk to him, and if it's OK with him, it's OK with me."

I didn't know Jim very well because he did most of his work for the pop department. He was fourteen years older than I was and had been with Columbia since 1951, when he'd been hired to help work on transferring old 78s to new LPs. I knew only that he was a veteran producer (he'd started in the business as a singer), that he was a gentleman and a good judge of talent, and that he was the man who would decide whether I'd be involved in the studio-cast albums for the Record Club.

(A few years after this, he'd move to RCA and then, in 1970, to Nashville, where he became president of Dot Records and switched the label from pop to country. This led to great success, as the label was acquired first by ABC and then by MCA, with Jim heading the Nashville offices of the combined companies, along the way signing people like Barbara Mandrell, Reba McEntire, the Oak Ridge Boys, George Strait, and Tanya Tucker. In 1985 he became president of Capitol Records Nashville, where he discovered Garth Brooks. He was inducted into the Country Music Hall of Fame in 2004 and was ninety when he died in 2013.)

So I went to Jim, and I said, "Schuyler says I can work with you on this if you can agree to it. If you'll agree, I'll do all the editing and mixing for you."

This was a good offer because by then I was already known around Columbia as a very good editor and mixer, the one Leonard Bernstein wanted on his recordings. And I don't know where I came up with the chutzpah to also say to Jim, "And I'd like a coproducer credit."

This would mean that the album would be labeled "Produced by James Foglesong and Thomas Z. Shepard." It was a big thing to ask! We producers are jealous of our billing, as I'll be the first to admit, and I was asking him to share credit with a guy who, a couple of years before, had to ask what "A&R" stood for.

Jim sat there looking at me, and I don't know what he was thinking, but finally he said, "OK. But here's the rule: on actual recording sessions, only one person deals directly with the performers—and that's not you."

So I had the job, and I was as happy as perhaps I've ever been in my professional life. For the past year or so, I'd been living out my classical-music dreams; now maybe I could do the same with Broadway.

To people outside the business, a studio album of a show—one whose cast is recruited solely for the recording, made up of people who may not have ever played their roles onstage—may seem like a poor step-cousin to the original-cast album, in which the cast of a Broadway show goes to a recording studio, usually in the week after opening, to recreate their roles for posterity. Like a baseball player's rookie card, the original-cast album gets all the glamour. Replacement casts, revival casts, studio casts—they're all destined to be "and also" in official histories of the show.

And I'll agree, there's an excitement to an original-cast album that you rarely get with a studio-cast album. It's rare to do a studio album for a show that isn't already a confirmed hit. So the excitement that comes with the gamble of an opening night isn't there. For all these reasons, there's an electricity to an original-cast album, with the buzz of the opening night still fresh in everybody's ears, that a studio album can rarely match.

There are compensations, however. The ability to work on an album for as long as needed is one: when I was hired to remaster some classic old original-cast albums for CD release in the 1990s, I realized afresh that the rush in which those albums had been recorded and released may have forced some artistic compromises, and inevitably, some small mistakes had to be overlooked.

In a word, though, the real glory of the studio album is casting.

It's a dirty little secret of Broadway that even a hit show isn't always ideally cast. Sometimes, by the time a problem becomes clear, it's too late to do anything about it: if you realize, in the last week before opening, that your star doesn't quite have what your show needs. So you do the best you can to work around the problem. The show, as they say, must go on.

There are also some performers who are brilliant onstage but less suited to the different demands of a recording. People who know the 1981 Broadway production of *The Pirates of Penzance* only from the original-cast album may think of Tony Azito, who was not an exceptional singer, as a poor choice for the role of the Sergeant of Police. But we who saw the show remember Azito as a sensational comic dancer whose amazing performance has been imitated (to no avail) by actors ever since. In a movie, his singing voice might have been dubbed; on stage, his physicality made him an audience favorite; on a record, though, what he did best simply couldn't be communicated.

Be that as it may, in almost every case the producer of the original-cast album is obliged to use the original cast, whether he likes it or not. There have been some exceptions, when an actor was seriously ill when the session took place (as would be the case with my recording of *1776*) or under exclusive contract to another record label, but they're vanishingly rare.

On a studio album, by contrast, every singer has been chosen because he or she is deemed to be right for the part, and right for a recording. Because the record producer doesn't have to live with the choices made by the production team of the stage show and doesn't have the cost of a huge stage production to take into consideration, he's free to cast with more imagination, trusting his own judgment and taking risks that a stage director might avoid.

Finally, there's a reasonable chance that the dream cast for a show will be the one that makes the studio album, not the original-cast album. Putting together the perfect people for a few days is easier than signing them for the entire production process of a show, which usually involves several months of rehearsal followed by eight shows a week for months thereafter. To be in the original cast of a show requires the commitment of a year, at least, out of an artist's life.

Many great productions that are announced never happen, and it's often because the stars' availability has changed in midstream. So if you want to hear your ideal cast, you should probably think about a studio album, not a stage production.

When Jim and I did *Annie Get Your Gun*, we had Doris Day in the lead role as Western sharpshooter Annie Oakley. This was perfect casting, and I'm quite sure we weren't the first people to think of casting Day—who had played a similar role as the star of the film *Calamity Jane* (1953). Any Broadway producer with her signature on a contract could have mounted that revival in a matter of weeks.

But in the early 1960s, Day was one of the world's biggest movie stars, earning millions of dollars in sunny California. There was no way she was going to spend a year or more on the other side of the country, savoring a New York winter while doing eight shows a week for a fraction of the money. That people can hear her sing songs from *Annie Get Your Gun* today is due to the magic of the studio album—she'd never have done it any other way.

Working with Jim Foglesong was a pleasure. He was a truly sweet-natured man and very easy to get along with. Though we worked together for only a couple of years, I'm happy to say we remained friends until his death in 2013. Sometime in the last ten years of his life, before he retired, he was in New York on business, and we had lunch together. I hadn't seen him in a long time, and he had visibly aged quite a lot.

Some of the best times we had during the years we were working together took place not in the studio, the rehearsal room, or the editing cubicle, but just the two of us sitting in his office, throwing out casting ideas for a show that would never exist except as a record. It was particularly fun because, with Jim coming from a pop background and me coming from the classical world, we loved to mix and match, taking a Broadway star, an opera star, and a pop singer and throwing them together in combinations that could never have existed on a stage.

10

Not the Original Cast

Show Boat (1962)

The first of these shows was the classic Jerome Kern/Oscar Hammerstein II musical *Show Boat*. We recorded it in December 1961, and it was released in July 1962.

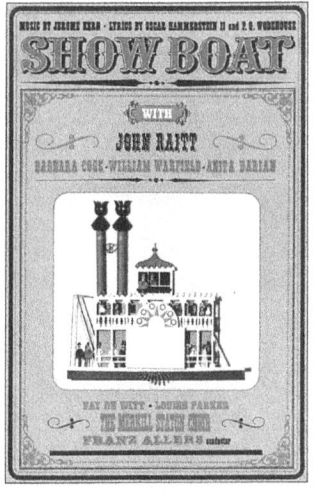

It was entirely appropriate to begin with *Show Boat* because in many ways it was the first modern Broadway musical. It was based on Edna Ferber's best-selling novel of the same name, with book and lyrics by Hammerstein (except for the song "Bill," with lyrics by P. G. Wodehouse) and music by Kern, and the interpolation of "After the Ball" by Charles K. Harris. *Show Boat* was a monster hit when it opened in 1927, produced by the legendary Flo Ziegfeld. Its appeal has never faded: as it nears its one hundredth anniversary, *Show Boat* has been filmed in 1936 and 1951 (the 1929 movie, not a musical, was based on Ferber's novel) and has enjoyed more Broadway revivals (and more record albums) than I can count.

The first problem we faced is unique to *Show Boat*: there's no other show that has so much material that can reasonably be considered authentic, including multiple songs occupying the same slots in the show. There were three different versions of the Kern/Hammerstein score: the opening-night version (in 1927), the first Broadway revival (in 1932), and the first movie (1936). In addition, there are numerous songs that were written for the original production but cut before opening night.

We had long discussions about whether to attempt a "complete" *Show Boat*. Arguing strongly for it was Miles Kreuger, a musical-theater maven who was working at Columbia at the time. Miles knew more about *Show Boat* than everyone else at Columbia put together. And I sympathized with him. I loved *Show Boat*, and even that early in my career, I had always thought show records should include as much of the score as possible.

The trouble was, to do a complete *Show Boat* would have taken at least three LPs, which wouldn't fit with either the Record Club's pricing structure or Masterworks' budget. Although it was a disappointment to Miles, we had to pick and choose what we would record from *Show Boat*.

Looking back at the record today, I'm comfortable with the choices we made. There are things I'd have liked to include—"I Might Fall Back on You," for example, or "I Have the Room Above Her," which was written for the film and is a beautiful ballad—but not at the expense of anything we did.

As far as casting was concerned, Jim and I would take some real chances as we moved along with this series, but for the first one we cast it very traditionally. That I was pleased with how our choices worked out can be judged by the fact that, in later years, I often came back to our three primary *Show Boat* stars for other projects.

Barbara Cook had won a Tony Award only four years before for her career-making performance as Marian the librarian in *The Music Man* (1957) and was fresh from a 1960 revival of *The King and I* at City Center. As Magnolia, she brought a freshness and life to songs that had been sung by a generation of great singers before her.

I would work with Barbara again and again and only wish I'd been able to do so more often. When I do lecture programs and take audience questions, one of the ones I get most often is, "Of all the stars you've worked with, who's your favorite?" My answer is always the same: I don't have a favorite as such, but the one whose performances have moved me the most is Barbara Cook. She was always a pleasure to work with, and her voice always makes me smile, no matter what she's singing.

Not many singers ever managed to keep pace with Barbara, but John Raitt, who played Gaylord Ravenal for us, was one who did. By 1960 Raitt already had a string of Broadway triumphs behind him, having been the original Billy Bigelow in *Carousel* (1945) and the original Sid in *The Pajama Game* (1954), a role he also played in the movie opposite Doris Day. Anita Darian was an excellent Julie.

To anybody who'd ever seen the 1951 movie of *Show Boat*, it was impossible to imagine "Ol' Man River" sung by anyone but William Warfield, the great African American bass-baritone who was then at the peak of his career. We were lucky that he was available for our recording.

The orchestra was led by Franz Allers, a remarkably gifted Austrian conductor who was to become a good friend of mine for many years. He was born in Carlsbad, which was then part of the Austro-Hungarian Empire, and he grew up in Vienna. Franz was a fine violinist and spent the 1920s playing with the Berlin Philharmonic and becoming an excellent conductor as well. He was Jewish, so when the Nazis seized Austria, he moved to the United States and established himself as a conductor. He was particularly linked with Frederick Loewe, five of whose musicals—including *My Fair Lady* (1957)—he had conducted in their original productions.

I loved Franz Allers. He was the most decent, friendly, affectionate, warm man you could imagine, the opposite of the cliché of the imperious conductor. Years later, when Charlie Burr and I wrote a musical based on *The Snow Queen*, it was Franz who arranged for us to pitch the show to the Dallas State Theater. (They didn't take it, but it was such a generous thing for him to do.)

One of the great thrills for me came while making this recording, and it was thanks to Franz and his busy schedule. He was conducting *Camelot*, which was a big and demanding show and took up a lot of his time. He had to be at the Majestic

Theater for eight shows a week, and it was hard for him to get away to rehearse *Show Boat*. So we brought the rehearsals to him. At that time the Majestic had an upright spinet piano in its lower lounge, right next to the bar.

We did three recording sessions for *Show Boat*, December 14, 17, and 18—and they went very smoothly. I stuck to my deal with Jim and didn't talk (much) to the singers. Mostly I kept out of the way and watched Jim at work; if I had any ideas, I'd mention them to him, and he'd pass them on if he agreed with them.

I do remember one of my ideas that made it onto the record, though. We were always looking for ways to take advantage of stereo, which was the big new thing, and the show opens with a song called "Cotton Blossom," for a chorus of men and women, in which they trade lines. And I thought, "Just for the hell of it, wouldn't it be interesting if, as the girls were singing to the men, they sounded like they walked over to them and then walked back?"

It was possible, even without physically marching the girls across the studio. There's a knob on the control panel called a pan pot—it's short for "panoramic potentiometer"—that lets you take the signal from a given microphone and place it anywhere in the stereo spectrum from left to right, and then bring up that microphone and another one down by the same degree, creating the illusion that the singer is actually moving.

Fred Plaut—who was one of Columbia's best—fed the output from the girls's mike through the pan pot so that we could direct that signal left, right, center, and anywhere in between. I was performing a sort of acrobatics in the studio, pantomiming for Fred where I wanted the girls to be, creating the illusion that they were walking to the left where the men were, and then walking back to the right, their original position.

Except for that one piece of gimmickry, the recording is very straightforward.

One strange little offshoot of *Show Boat* involved my first published song. One of our supporting players was Fay DeWitt as Ellie, whose big song is "Life Upon the Wicked Stage." I hadn't known Fay, but she was a pop artist for Columbia, and her producer was Jim Foglesong. During the time we were working on *Show Boat*, she was also recording an album of novelty songs called *Through Sick and Sin*, all comedy songs, and her producer commissioned me and my writing partner, Charlie Burr, to write one for her. We did—it was called "I'm the Girl Representing Brand X," and Jim placed it as the first song on the album.

And it was "published" by Leeds. Never printed, so far as I know, and I never saw a penny from it, but yes, it was my first published song.

The Merry Widow (1962)

The next one in our series of studio-cast albums was a totally different kind of show. The American musical theater descends from two ancestors: the popular-song and minstrel revues of the late nineteenth and early twentieth centuries and the operettas that were also popular at that time, some of them Viennese (notably those of Franz Lehar and Johann Strauss Jr.) and some by Americans such as Rudolph Friml, Victor Herbert, and Sigmund Romberg working in the same style.

Of these, the acknowledged masterpiece is Lehar's *The Merry Widow*, which premiered in Vienna in 1905 and immediately became an enduring American favorite, in various English translations. Set in Paris, it's a light romantic comedy with one terrific song after another.

Most translations of the opera's lyrics are not as good as the music, though. Translating song lyrics, especially humorous ones, is a very tricky business—the translator needs to balance the needs of the rhythm, the needs of the humor, and of course, faithfulness to the content of the original, while still producing lyrics that are easy to sing. There were a good number of *Merry Widow* translations, but Jim and I agreed that we wanted something fresh and new.

Jim had known a married couple, Merle Puffer and Deena Cavalieri, who were excellent translators and lyricists. He hired them to make a whole new English version of *The Merry Widow*.

Thanks to Schuyler we had acquired a star for our recording: Lisa Della Casa, a forty-three-year-old Swiss soprano who specialized in lighter works such as those of Mozart and Richard Strauss. She'd made her Metropolitan Opera debut in 1953, so having her for our recording gave it an extra touch of class.

The only problem was that Della Casa's native language was Italian, and she'd spent most of her career singing German. She had a very hard time speaking English and an even harder time being understood.

Now, it so happened that she and her husband—a man who came to every rehearsal like he was afraid to let her out of his sight—were living in New York in 1962 because she was singing at the Met that season. They had rented a house in Forest Hills, which was two blocks from where Irene and I were living, so I was designated as the person to work with Lisa on her English pronunciation.

I've taught some music in my time, but I'm not Henry Higgins, and I think the only reason I was assigned this job was that I happened to live nearby. I was a miserable failure. When Lisa sang the song "Vilya, the Witch of the Wood," it came out "Willya, da Vitch a da Vood." But she was a very gracious woman, and she worked hard on it with me, even though the end results weren't so good. Anyhow, it was a treat to meet her and work with her. And she sang the music beautifully. She was a lovely woman and very glamorous, very beautiful.

We paired her with John Reardon, a strong-voiced baritone, as Danilo, and Franz Allers—who was again our conductor—brought in a few singers from the Met, where he was just beginning to be known as a conductor of lighter works, to take the supporting roles. One of them was Paul Franke, who was midway through a forty-year career at the Met, and another was Laurel Hurley. One of her roles at the Met was Gretel in Humperdinck's Christmas favorite *Hansel and Gretel*, for which Franz was the Met's conductor.

Given the size of the chorus and the number of leading roles, this was a bigger company than you'd typically have for a Broadway recording, I recall that we were literally running out of mikes. Fred Plaut, again our engineer, didn't have enough mikes to cover orchestral sections individually, so instead of miking them up more closely, he miked them collectively, only three mikes, from above and at something of a distance, which gave it a symphonic sound that turned out wonderfully well for this recording.

We had our share of problems at the recording session, though, because of the microphone situation. I remember one point at which I needed the girls to come in at a fresh location for only a single phrase—"Ladies' choice, ladies' choice!"—but we couldn't free up a microphone to cover them. Finally we sent the women into the orchestra itself to stand right by the violins and sing, so they'd come in on the left. Another thing I'd already learned about studio work: when in doubt, improvise.

It was a difficult album to edit and mix, chiefly because of the large number of people and the microphone issues, and it took a while, but I was very proud of it. Most of these studio-cast albums have been released on CD, and I got the chance to oversee the remastering myself, but for whatever reason this *Merry Widow* has never come out on CD, which is too bad. I did remix a couple of the songs from it for a Sony CD of Viennese favorites, but I'm sorry that I wasn't offered the chance to remix the whole show.

Annie Get Your Gun (1963)

This was an interesting one, with a terrific cast that featured Doris Day as Annie Oakley and Robert Goulet—red hot after his triumph as Sir Lancelot in Lerner & Loewe's *Camelot*—as Frank Butler, the ace sharpshooter. (Both were conveniently already Columbia artists, so there wouldn't be any need to negotiate their availability with some rival company.) The show was a 1946 hit for Irving Berlin, who wrote the songs, and Dorothy and Herbert Fields, who wrote the book.

To anyone who appreciates brilliant songwriting, Berlin was an icon, as towering a figure in Broadway and Tin Pan Alley songwriting as Mozart was in classical, as Hank Williams was in country, or as Bob Dylan is in folk.

(I actually got to be in a room with Berlin once, when I attended Lieberson's recording session of *Mr. President* [1962]. He was seventy-four at the time, and *Mr. President* would be his last show.)

I had less to do with our studio-cast recording of *Annie Get Your Gun* than with any of the others; I was more a bystander than an active participant and half the time not even that. This was primarily because Day—who I think was first suggested to us by Schuyler—agreed to do the show on one condition: she did not want to come to New York.

Normally, wherever they might be, the singers on these studio-cast albums came to us, recording their songs in a session where we'd all be in the room together. It wasn't a big deal to set up a couple of different sessions, when everybody's schedules simply didn't fit together—even if the show called for two singers who couldn't be in the studio together to sing a duet. By that stage the technology was there to combine the tracks seamlessly.

This wasn't a normal session for us at this time. Day would be the first person recorded for our project, but she would be doing her singing on the West Coast, accompanied by a pianist whose name, I believe, was Jim Harburg, who may have been one of our producers on the West Coast. The orchestra would be recorded later, in New York, with Robert Goulet and the rest of the cast.

The recorded piano would later be removed and replaced by the orchestra, in complete isolation from Doris. She was in another room and had headphones on so she could hear Jim, and he had headphones on so he could hear her.

At that time this was an unusual way to do a recording, but it wasn't a problem. The difficulties came for us later were when we tried to put a live orchestra on top of her very free-flowing performances. This was no problem for Harburg, an experienced accompanist who could adapt on the fly to whatever she did, slowing down or speeding up to match her, but it was one hell of a task for a whole orchestra to do that after the fact.

On the more rhythmic numbers with steady tempos, such as "Doin' What Comes Naturally," it was no big deal—she stuck close to the beat. But when she got to a ballad like "I Got Lost in His Arms," she sang very, very freely. Even if we had the conductor or even the entire orchestra listening on headphones, there was no way they'd be able to predict what she would do next.

The answer was for Phil Lang, who was doing the new orchestrations for our recording, to listen to her performance, bar by bar, and tailor those orchestrations to match whatever she was doing. If the amount of rubato she used turned a four-beat bar into five-and-a-half beats, Phil would write a five-and-a-half-beat bar into his orchestration.

Even then, this posed a big chore for Franz Allers, once again our conductor in New York. Show orchestras are made up of very gifted musicians, but they aren't usually confronted by scores that are so erratic, so unpredictable, and so outside their usual way of working. Franz was, of course, listening to her on headphones while he was rehearsing with the orchestra, leading them through the songs in what was at best a phrase-by-phrase slog.

All this would be much easier to accomplish in today's digital world. I was present during the New York sessions, with Goulet as the headliner; I don't know for sure if he did anything live with Day—it's possible he went out to the West Coast to do the big duet, "Anything You Can Do," but my best memory is he didn't. This recording was very much a tale of two coasts, and he was the East, and she was the West.

He was in good voice and didn't seem put out by the need to shape his performance to what Doris had already done on their duet numbers. The only problem I remember him having was, in "Bad, Bad Man," he kept singing the word "hours" as a single syllable as if it rhymed with "bars." He got it right on our final take.

So I wasn't there for the Doris Day sessions and didn't have a lot to do in the Robert Goulet sessions. I didn't even do the editing and mixing because in the end, despite my deal with Jim, I didn't get a coproducer credit when the album was originally released. Irving Townsend, a Columbia vice president on the West Coast, wanted to share the credit with Jim. I think he was involved in the negotiations to snare Doris Day, but I'm not aware of anything else he may have done for the recording. But because the West Coast office was involved in this, office politics prevailed. And Jim felt very bad about that, so he said, "Look, you don't have to edit and mix this one." So I didn't.

More than thirty years later, though, I was asked to remaster it by Sony, which meant I had to go back and re-synchronize Doris with the orchestra. I had to deal with those five-and-a-half-beat-bars all over again. This time around, I added my name to the producer credits.

Lady in the Dark (1963)

Of the seven studio-cast albums I worked on for Columbia in the early 1960s, the one that meant the most to me was *Lady in the Dark*. This was in part because it posed the most challenges to me as the editor and mixer, but it's also because it's a fascinating show that had been a favorite of mine since I first encountered it many years before.

In many respects *Lady in the Dark* was an odd choice for this series of studio albums. The other six shows in the series—*Show Boat*, *The Merry Widow*, *Annie Get Your Gun*, *The Student Prince*, *The King and I*, and *Oklahoma!*—were acknowledged classics, smashes from the day the curtain went up, and subsequently staples of community theater, school shows, and repertory theater. They'd each had at least one Broadway revival and at least one movie adaptation.

Written by Moss Hart with songs by Kurt Weill and Ira Gershwin, *Lady in the Dark* was by no means a flop: it ran for a healthy 467 performances after opening on Broadway in 1941, with a cast headed by Gertrude Lawrence. Its reviews were respectable, though they focused more on the performers—especially Lawrence and a newcomer named Danny Kaye—than on the show. However, it has had no subsequent Broadway revivals, never had an original-cast album, and when it was made into a movie in 1944, starring Ginger Rogers, the filmmakers cut most of the songs. The show never entirely vanished from the scene—the people who loved it (including me) *really* loved it—but it was a cult favorite, not a Broadway classic.

I can't speak for others who love the show, but what I love about *Lady in the Dark* are the very things that kept it from becoming a success on the level of *Annie Get Your Gun* or *Oklahoma!*. In many ways it was a pioneering show that looked forward to the musicals of the next generation, shows by people such as Stephen Sondheim or Kander & Ebb. Its subject matter was deeper than anything that had been seen on the musical stage previously, it was profoundly infused with Freudian psychology, and its structure was experimental, doing things that would be common in the Broadway of the 1970s and1980s but were unheard of in 1941. It foreshadowed elements of such shows as *Oklahoma!* (1943) and *Company* (1970) to an extent that isn't widely appreciated today, simply because those shows are so much better known than *Lady in the Dark*.

I know it continued to be performed at least occasionally because, during the months between my departure from Yale and my arrival at Columbia Records, I served as the rehearsal pianist for an amateur production of *Lady in the Dark* in New Jersey. Nobody knows a show better than the rehearsal pianist! Because of that experience, I knew *Lady in the Dark* far better than I'd known *Show Boat*, *The Merry Widow*, or *Annie Get Your Gun*.

Franz Allers wasn't available for this one, so Jim had lined up veteran conductor and musical-theater expert Lehman Engel. Lehman would later become an important person in my life, but at this time I didn't know him well. He was twenty-five years older than I was and was a very accomplished musician at a time when I was still only starting out.

Even so, I knew *Lady in the Dark* so well that when Lehman came to us with a version of the show he had cut down to fit onto one LP, I had enough chutzpah to push back. I wanted him to expand it, reinstating some things he'd cut. I said, "Let's put this back, let's put that back." He was agreeable. I think he was surprised but quite happy to find somebody who wanted more rather than less.

We came out with a carefully planned recording. It still fit on one LP, so there were obviously cuts, but they did not interfere with the flow of the show. *Lady in the Dark* tells its story in its music and lyrics, and our record does, too. You can pretty well understand what it's all about just by listening to it. That's important because this wasn't the easiest show for people to understand.

Lady in the Dark happened because Moss Hart, who wrote the book, had been in analysis for many years—and probably was up until the day he died. He was heavily invested in it, so he wrote the first musical that dealt with psychoanalysis. When I say *Lady in the Dark* is like *Company*, I mean it's not so much about the plot—what there is of it—as it is a study of the psychology of the central character, someone who on the face of it is happy and successful, but who on the inside is frightened and insecure.

Liza Elliott, the character played by Gertrude Lawrence on Broadway and by Risë Stevens on our recording, feels she needs professional help. And she gets it and is cured in three hours, which is not quite the way it works in real life!

But when we first see her, it's not at all obvious she needs anybody's help. Liza is a very efficient, very successful, very smart woman, the editor-in-chief of a fashion magazine, kind of like the character Meryl Streep plays in *The Devil Wears Prada* (2006). She runs a big operation with a whole team of men and women working for her, she makes a lot of money, and she lives a very glamorous life. She's involved with a rich and handsome man—who, OK, is married to somebody else—but there are plenty of other men who are interested in her. She's on top of the world.

The only trouble is, she's having disturbing dreams she doesn't understand. They involve the people in her life, both past and present, often transmogrified in ways that frighten and worry her. There's a tune that recurs in all her dreams; she knows it should have words, but she can't remember what they are. So she goes to see an analyst, and the story of the musical is him trying to help her understand her dreams—and use them to make sense of what's really going on in her life.

Now, for Broadway in 1941, a story that's entirely internal was bold. As the title implies, there's only one leading character in *Lady in the Dark*, and that's Liza herself. The story isn't about what she does, it's about how she understands what she does.

But there's more about the show that's pioneering because it presents the story in a way that's strikingly different from the traditional Broadway musical.

In a normal Broadway musical, people talk to each other the way we do in real life—but they also break into song and dance, which most of us don't ever do. On

Broadway, what Coleridge called "suspension of disbelief" asks audiences to accept that in the world on the stage, people do sing and dance, and nobody thinks it's unusual. The audience understands the rules of Broadway musicals, so they don't think it's unusual either.

Lady in the Dark doesn't work that way. The dialogue scenes are played entirely realistically, at least by the standards of the fashion world, which can get unrealistic. People talk or don't talk, but they don't burst into song. All the songs occur in four separate dream sequences in which many of the same characters appear but in bizarre, heightened versions of themselves, as they appear in Liza's subconscious. Liza is the only one who sees the world this way—to all the other characters in the play, they're not in a musical at all.

Weill's score is a gorgeous one, using unusual rhythms and harmonies to capture the dream state in which the songs occur. Gershwin's lyrics are deliberately fragmented, strong images that don't necessarily fit together. Songs shatter, flow together, double back on themselves, and reappear in different guises in different dream sequences. Liza's dreams are strange, heightened experiences that, even when they're funny, have a scary undertone to them, a sense of desperation and need. (Only two years later, in *Oklahoma!*, Agnes de Mille's psychologically charged dream ballet, "Laurey Makes Up Her Mind," would draw heavily on similar ideas.)

All in all, *Lady in the Dark* is a highly unusual show and by no means a popular favorite. I believe the idea of our recording it originated not from the Record Club but from Schuyler. He very much wanted to make the recording with Anna Moffo, and I believe she was interested. But she was an exclusive RCA artist, and she couldn't get clearance from them to make a recording for Columbia. This wasn't uncommon in those days, though a record company might give the OK if the artist put up enough of a fuss or if the project was high-profile enough that it seemed likely to boost the artist's appeal.

Risë Stevens wasn't our first choice, in short; I think we ended up with her because Schuyler was good friends with her husband and manager, Walter Surovy. Walter knew that we'd missed out on Anna Moffo and said to Schuyler, "You know, Risë's available," and Schuyler couldn't really say no.

Risë may have been past her prime, but she did a really fine job. A wonderful job, except for one spoken line, on which I didn't like her reading but I didn't have the courage to try to get her to change it. There's a place where she screams, "What is all this?" And to my mind she was too hysterical. Liza Elliott could certainly be angry or confused, but I didn't think she should ever sound out of control. That was my opinion in the early 1960s, anyway; at this stage I've gotten so used to the way Risë did it that I probably wouldn't change it if I could.

By this time Jim and I were functioning as true coproducers, instead of as a producer and his sidekick, so I didn't hesitate to offer suggestions about the casting.

The role of fashion photographer Russell Paxton, who's the ringmaster in the "Circus Dream," isn't a huge part, but it had made a star out of Danny Kaye, who sang the patter song "Tchaikovsky," which is nothing but a rhyming list of fifty Russian composers. It hadn't been written for the show—the lyric was a nonsense poem that Gershwin had written for his college newspaper decades before—but they stuck it into the "Circus Dream" because, well, Kaye was a great patter singer (he, Ira Gershwin, and I were all devotees of Gilbert & Sullivan), and anyway, it was a dream, so it didn't have to make sense.

We never considered asking Danny Kaye to do our record—but anyone else who played this relatively small part would inevitably be compared to Kaye, because he'd become so identified with "Tchaikovsky." It was as if we'd decided to do a studio album of *The Wizard of Oz* and had to find someone besides Judy Garland to sing "Over the Rainbow."

But I had an idea. I said to Jim, "Let's ask Adolph Green." Green was best known as a writer—he and his writing partner, Betty Comden, had written the book and/or lyrics for three of MGM's most successful musical films and four hit Broadway shows. The first of these, *On the Town* (1949), had proven he and Betty were also excellent performers. I knew Adolph slightly, having met him when Goddard produced a studio album of *On the Town* and again when he arrived with his wife, Phyllis Newman, at Goddard's recording session for *Subways Are for Sleeping*. He had the chops and charm to sing "Tchaikovsky," along with enough self-confidence not to give a damn about the inevitable comparisons to Kaye.

I also knew the choice would please Schuyler, who was friendly with Betty, Adolph, Bernstein, and their whole circle. I didn't pick Adolph to make Schuyler happy, but it didn't hurt.

Adolph was fun to work with, and my sense that he'd be great on "Tchaikovsky" was right on the money. In fact, I also had the idea to do the song twice in a row on the recording. Like the rest of the world, I'd known it only from the Danny Kaye recording, in which he sings it once, very quickly. My idea was to have Adolph do it the first time at a reasonably fast tempo and then do it a second time at breakneck speed. It came out very well.

It also stuck because, years later, Mandy Patinkin put "Tchaikovsky" into his solo act, and he also sings it twice. When I saw the show and talked to him afterward, I said, "You know, it wasn't written that way." But I was very glad to see my idea continuing to be effective. (In the 1980s, when *The Pirates of Penzance* was produced on Broadway, George Rose sang the last verse of "I Am the Very Model of a Modern Major-General" twice, the same way. I have no idea if there's any connection.)

Lady in the Dark offers challenges like no other show of its era, and we were going to be the first people ever to make a full-scale album of the show. And I ate it up. Having the four different dream worlds to play with, to put each in a whole different sonic perspective from a conventional musical, getting to play around with different levels of reverberation, things that were on-mike and things that faded off—for me this was a dream come true. (As it were.)

The first problem we faced was an obvious one. We were recording a show defined by its multiple layers, but one of the layers—the realistic one that existed only in the dialogue sequences—wasn't going to be on our album at all. Even if we added some snatches of dialogue, there was no way we could recreate the audience's awareness of how realistic all the dialogue scenes were; we also couldn't recreate the cues in scenery, costumes, and lighting that helped the audience understand the nature of the dream scenes. We would have to figure out how to do that with sound.

Most of the responsibility for this fell to me as editor and mixer. The singers and orchestra made a conventional recording, using the customary studio techniques we'd used for, say, *Show Boat*. Beyond the usual job of picking the right takes, editing out errors, and making sure the sound was properly balanced, I wanted to create the other-worldly feeling that defines *Lady in the Dark*.

The first thing I did involved something we'd had the ability to do for years but almost never did. As I've described before, you can use stereo and volume levels to create a sense of movement, as if a singer is coming toward the audience or another character or moving away from them. The effect is called "walking somebody in" (or out), and normally you use this on a single person or, at most, on a small group, as I had with the female chorus in *Show Boat*'s "Cotton Blossom."

In this case, though, I also used it on the entire orchestra, walking them toward the listener at the beginning of each dream sequence, as if the orchestra was on a boat pulling into shore and the listener was on the dock. Or—because Einstein tells us that, from within a system of relative motion (like, say, people on two different moving trains), it's impossible to tell whether you're moving, the other person is moving, or both—it sounded like the orchestra was on the pier and the listener was on the boat.

The listener is pulled into the dream like Liza herself, with a sense of motion that is vaguely unsettling. It's the opposite of opening a traditional Broadway recording with a stationary orchestra and singers clearly located at left, right, or center, allowing the listener to construct a mental soundscape that approximates the stage. This opening sense of movement tells us right off that we're going to be in a shifting, unstable soundscape. Throughout the dreams, characters suddenly appear without warning, popping into the soundscape unexpectedly, or fade off into the distance, as though they're on a boat being swept off by a strong current.

At the end of each dream sequence, a similar device moves the orchestra away from the listener (or the listener away from the orchestra), providing an inflection point, a means of telling us that the next track, in which we walk the music back in, is a new and different dream, one in which the earlier rules don't necessarily apply.

There are a lot of spooky voices that come into *Lady in the Dark* out of nowhere. There are these "ghost reminiscences," you might call them, individual voices that come out of Liza's past—like a chorus of cheerleaders chanting "Mapleton High, Mapleton High!" or the glee club doing the high-school song. Because they're all part of her dreams, I had them coming from different places and with different perspectives, violating some of my own basic rules of stereo recording. If you have a singer at left at point A in the music and then at right at point B, for example, I need you to hear the singer cross somewhere between those points. But in this case, I didn't do that at all, in order to give the whole thing an unpredictable, unsettling quality.

This recording had my name on it before we even knew we'd be doing it. Nothing could have been dearer to my heart.

There's an insignificant orchestral passage in "Girl of the Moment," the song which closes the first fantasy sequence, the "Glamour Dream." It's leading up to a chorus entrance, and it sticks in my mind because, after we'd recorded that passage, Jim called "cut," Lehman lowered his baton, and we all went home for four months with the record still unfinished.

That was at the end of our session on January 23, 1963, and we had no idea that we wouldn't reconvene until May 22. It turned out that the project had run out of money. It was seriously considered—not by me, God knows—that we might not finish the recording at all. You can be sure that this possibility made me very, very unhappy. But in the fullness of time, a new fiscal quarter dawned, more money was available, and we finished the show, for which I am forever grateful.

I can only speculate about the reasons we ran out of money. My guess is that, because this was a lower-profile show with less of an assured audience than its predecessors, it was given a tighter budget, and whatever modest overruns we may have had led to a financial crunch that put us on the brink of cancellation.

I returned to this album in 1997, when Sony—which by then had acquired Columbia—hired me to remaster it for CD release. Revisiting this project was a real joy, and that we finished it, and that it's now available to new generations of listeners, brings me great pleasure.

The Student Prince (1963)

Recorded after the first sessions for *Lady in the Dark*, our recording of *The Student Prince* caught up with it and passed it in the production process, making it into the stores a few days ahead of *Lady in the Dark*.

After the relatively risky *Lady in the Dark*, *The Student Prince* was a return to safer ground for Columbia and for the Record Club. Unlike *The Merry Widow*, which was an Austrian import that found success on the American stage, *The Student Prince* was an American product, written in English, that had scored an immense hit on Broadway in 1924. The music was by Sigmund Romberg and the book and lyrics by Dorothy Donnelly, and the show ran for longer than any other show of the 1920s. It had had two Broadway revivals by 1963 and two movie adaptations. Several of its songs, notably "Serenade (Overhead the Moon Is Beaming)" and "Drink! Drink! Drink!" had become standards.

I was quite familiar with *The Student Prince*. When I was a kid, one of the recordings my father brought home was Richard Crooks's recording of the "Serenade" from *The Student Prince*, so I knew that one aria from very early on. And then the Paper Mill Playhouse, in Milburn, New Jersey, did *The Student Prince*—I can't remember any cast names, except that Kathie was played by Rosemarie Brancato. I was probably around ten years old, and so I went to see it with my mother, and I cried and cried because the lovers had to part at the end, and it all seemed so unfair. They revived it a few years later, with the same Kathie but with a different Karl Franz, and we saw it again.

It's a beautiful, moving show for me. The score is, to me, a perfect intersection of Broadway and opera, even more so than Gilbert & Sullivan. It's very, very beautiful.

Franz Allers was back for this one, and the cast was built around a package deal Schuyler made with Columbia Artists Management, which represented both Roberta Peters and Jan Peerce, our Kathie and Karl Franz. Peerce was past his prime—he was fifty-nine at the time—but he was an interesting guy, and he was very funny. There's a line in *The Student Prince* where he says, "I'll go back to Heidelberg!" and during a rehearsal he added, "Yeah, I'm going to open up a Jewish delicatessen." We all laughed. It's not that good a joke, but it was so surprising coming out of a legendary Met star like Jan Peerce.

One day, after we'd finished recording, Peerce came into my office to listen to the editing and mix. We sat down, and I played it for him, and when we were done, he said, "You want to have lunch?" I wasn't going to turn down a chance to have lunch with Jan Peerce, so we went up to the Stage Delicatessen, which was a block and a half away.

We ordered our food—he paid—and there was Henny Youngman. Peerce knew Youngman, so he invited him to sit with us at our table. It turned out that in their prior lives they both played the violin in a club orchestra together, probably somewhere in the Catskills. It was a fun lunch. Youngman got off most of the jokes, but Peerce got in his share. Me, I ate my sandwich and wondered if Irene would believe me when I told her about my day.

I also enjoyed working with Roberta. You can tell because, despite my agreement with Jim that I wouldn't be talking to the stars, there's a really nice picture in my collection of Roberta and me in the studio going over something. This was in 1963, however, and I was Jim's full partner by then, though he was still the lead producer.

Roberta was in her early thirties at the time, much closer to my age than Peerce was, and she was adorable. Just a lovely woman, and a fantastic singer. She and Peerce were very close. Her first marriage, which lasted maybe a month, was to Robert Merrill, and it was Jan Peerce who gave the bride away. Peerce was a generation older than she was, and they had a father/daughter vibe.

Jim and I had hired Hershy Kay to do new orchestrations for *The Student Prince* that would be more tailored to the greater capabilities of stereophonic sound. In hindsight I think maybe that was unnecessary. The originals had a certain cobwebby charm that could have been worth preserving.

But it was worth it to me because this was how I met Hershy, and how we became friends for life. And there was nothing wrong with the new orchestrations—Hershy was a great orchestrator, and his work had contributed greatly to *On the Town*, *Peter Pan*, *Candide*, and *110 in the Shade*. Later he would orchestrate *Barnum* and *Evita*. He was also a fine composer who wrote several ballets for George Balanchine.

Jim cast Giorgio Tozzi to play Dr. Engel, and we also had Anita Darian back to play Princess Margaret, who sings the famous duet "Just We Two" with Captain Tarnitz, played by Lawrence Avery. And what I remember about that is another ad-lib during rehearsal: in their duet they sing "Just we two/if they knew/how in the waltz we woo"—but Anita changed it to "how in the world we screw!"

There was a very relaxed atmosphere to this recording. Peerce and Roberta were such good friends, and they both knew Giorgio Tozzi very well, and by this time we had our own little repertory company—Jim and me, Franz, Anita, and even the Merrill Staton Choir. It was a lot of fun to make, and it turned out very well.

11

Of Cattlemen and Kings

IN 1964 JIM FOGLESONG LEFT COLUMBIA RECORDS FOR RCA, the first step on a path that would lead him to Nashville and iconic status in the field of country music. With his departure, the final two releases in our series of studio albums of classic Broadway shows fell entirely to me.

If he had left in, say, 1962, this probably would have been daunting. At that point I had been producing records for less than a year and had never been personally responsible for anything on the scale of what we were doing with *The Merry Widow* or *Annie Get Your Gun*.

By 1964, though, I wasn't Jim's trusty sidekick any more, and his departure didn't really change things for me. I kept doing what I had been doing—and of course, the Broadway records were only one piece of a job that also included a great deal of work on classical recordings. The decisions fell more on my shoulders than before, but I was ready for that responsibility.

I was sorry to see Jim go because I liked him and had enjoyed working with him. He was a very impressive guy. He didn't self-advertise at all, and he didn't talk a lot, but he knew exactly what he was doing. That said, I honestly don't recall being in the least intimidated by the prospect of handling things on my own. Thanks to people like Schuyler, Howard Scott, and Jim himself, I also knew what I was doing.

Besides, the two shows that would wrap up the series were by the great Rodgers & Hammerstein—one groundbreaking hit and one masterpiece written at the peak of their abilities. It would be hard to go wrong working with such rich material.

Oklahoma! (1964)

Oklahoma! will always occupy a special place in my heart because it was the first Broadway show I ever saw. I was seven or eight at the time, and my Aunt Florence took me to see it at the St. James Theatre in 1944, I think. There are many wonderful things about *Oklahoma!*, but at that age I was just overwhelmed by the scenery—I have a clear memory of this beautiful blue sky with white clouds That's all I remember of that performance, actually, but it made a big impression on me. (Four years later I'd see *Finian's Rainbow*, which I enjoyed very much—and at twelve years old, not just for the set.)

I'm far from the only person who thinks of *Oklahoma!* as a special show. It's the only classic show in the history of Broadway that rivals *Show Boat* for its impact on the shape and style of the musical theater.

Broadway was never the same after *Show Boat*—musicals like *Pal Joey* (1940) and *Lady in the Dark* (1941), ambitious shows that explored adult themes with believable, flawed characters, wouldn't have happened without the immense success of *Show Boat* to show the way.

The same was true of *Oklahoma!*, though more in terms of structure and style than of subject matter. The way its songs, its dialogue, and its dances were woven together was unprecedented and forced those people who still thought of musicals as glorified revues to rethink their stance. *Oklahoma!* earned Rodgers & Hammerstein a special Pulitzer Prize in 1944—the first such prize ever awarded in the arts. It was a special, one-of-a-kind prize because the Pulitzer jury recognized this was a Pulitzer-worthy event, even if it didn't quite fit the established prize categories of drama and music.

Equally important, *Oklahoma!* was a massive success. *Pal Joey* and *Lady in the Dark* had been ambitious productions that were lauded by critics, but they'd run for 374 and 467 performances, respectively—nothing to be ashamed of but well short of *Show Boat's* 572 performances. In Broadway as in everything else, nothing succeeds like success—and running for a year wasn't going to change the way people thought of Broadway, or Broadway thought of itself.

When *Oklahoma!* ran for a record-shattering 2,212 performances, however, that was a game-changer. Most people date the so-called "Golden Age of the Broadway Musical" from March 31, 1943, the night *Oklahoma!* opened.

Arguably the most important aspect of the show, however, was that it launched a new creative team, Rodgers & Hammerstein. They were not a song-writing team, but a show-writing team: Oscar Hammerstein II wrote not only the lyrics but also the book, with substantial input from composer Richard Rodgers, and in their heyday, they controlled virtually every aspect of their shows, from casting to design and production. They didn't do everything on their shows, but every creative element required their consent. Except for George M. Cohan in the 1900s and 1910s, only Gilbert & Sullivan had exercised such comprehensive control over their own works in the musical theater.

Rodgers & Hammerstein were able to accomplish so much because each came to their partnership as an established creative force with a proven track record and a veteran's knowledge of Broadway. Most of the great Broadway teams—George & Ira Gershwin, Lerner & Loewe, Bock & Harnick, Kander & Ebb, and yes, Hammerstein & Kern, and Rodgers & Hart—came to Broadway as bright-eyed novices. If Rodgers & Hammerstein had been a band, though, they'd have been a supergroup, a new fusion of established stars. That's why, unlike the teams mentioned above, they were able to hit a home run on their first swing.

Most of the attention paid to the partnership seems to focus on Rodgers, and maybe that's inevitable. I would work with Rodgers on several occasions later in my career, and his musical gifts awed me. Still do, really. It was particularly impressive that, despite the end of a twenty-four-year partnership that had made Rodgers & Hart musical-theater legends, Rodgers survived and emerged in an even more successful partnership with Hammerstein.

Most amazing of all, perhaps, he changed his working process in midstream: with Hart, Rodgers had always written the music first, with Hart setting words to the existing music; with Hammerstein he reversed the process, writing his music to Hammerstein's existing words.

At the same time, it's no coincidence that, when Columbia Records decided to do a series of studio recreations of Broadway classics, three of the seven featured librettos by Oscar Hammerstein II: two with Rodgers, and *Show Boat* with Jerome Kern. Like Rodgers, Hammerstein came to the partnership with nothing to prove—and he, too, changed his process in midstream, having always written his lyrics to Kern's existing tunes.

As with Gilbert & Sullivan, Rodgers & Hammerstein was a partnership of equals, one in which each man made the other better. In one respect they even exceeded the Victorian masters: while neither W. S. Gilbert nor Arthur Sullivan produced much that has lasted outside of their collaboration, Rodgers and Hammerstein both produced great works with other collaborators. Had they never written a single song together, Rodgers would still be remembered for "Bewitched, Bothered and Bewildered" and a host of other wonderful songs with Lorenz Hart, and Hammerstein for *Show Boat* and for his other songs with Jerome Kern, notably the gorgeous "All the Things You Are."

By the time we came to *Oklahoma!*, in short, the show was thoroughly familiar to anybody who cared at all about Broadway. This wasn't *Lady in the Dark*, in which we were introducing a new generation to an overlooked classic. *Oklahoma!* was a constant presence in community and school productions, professional revivals, and of course, the 1955 film. Its songs were performed by nightclub singers across America and recorded on innumerable albums.

All the same, we thought we had something to add. In my first solo effort as a producer of show albums, my goal was neither to produce an all-star recording of a classic nor to offer a radical new vision of an old show, but rather to mingle the expected and the unexpected to produce a new way of looking at (or rather, listening to) a classic.

Some choices were obvious. Our *Show Boat* star John Raitt had been associated with *Oklahoma!* since its original production, in which he had first played Curly on the national tour and then succeeded to the role originally created by Alfred Drake on Broadway. Rodgers & Hammerstein loved him—he went on to create the leading role of Billy Bigelow in their next show, *Carousel* (1945)—but while he had recorded some individual songs from the show, he'd never done a full recording of *Oklahoma!*.

And of course, one of the advantages of a studio album was that we could cast people who were too old to play their roles onstage. At forty-eight, Raitt was never going to play Curly again onstage—but his voice was still strong and youthful, and I'm proud of the fact that our album gave him a chance to immortalize one of the key performances in his career.

Our choice to play Laurey may seem whimsical to a present-day audience because Florence Henderson is remembered today mainly as the ever-present mother on *The Brady Bunch* (1969–1974). That was still in the future, however, when I chose her for *Oklahoma!*. I knew her for what she was then, which was a veteran of the Broadway musical stage, most notably as the originator of the title role in *Fanny* (1954), with a particular gift for comedy.

She also came with the Rodgers & Hammerstein seal of approval, having played Laurey in the touring version of the original production and then in a 1954 Broadway revival. Here again was somebody who had played the part hundreds of times but had never yet had a chance to record it.

With Raitt and Henderson in place, we could afford to be a little more adventurous in casting the supporting roles. If there was a difference in philosophy between Jim and me, it may have been that, with my greater grounding in Broadway and in classical music, I was able to cast a wider net for talent. Either way, I've always enjoyed finding the offbeat casting choice that works out.

My first thought for Ado Annie was Helen Gallagher, but that didn't get far: I spoke to her manager, and he said, "How much are you paying?" I said, "$350," and he said, "Forget it." He never even told Helen I'd asked (I worked with her years later, and she told me she'd had no idea of any of this. Which was stupid of him.) No, $350 wasn't a lot even then (it's a little less than $3,500 today), but an agent's job isn't to not get his client work. It's to be imaginative and work something out. I learned that with my second choice for the role, which was Phyllis Newman.

I didn't know Phyllis well, but she'd charmed me when I met her during the sessions for *Lady in the Dark*. I called her manager, Leo Bookman, and I said, "I'd like Phyllis to do Ado Annie." He said, "How much can you pay?" I said, "$350." Leo thought it over for a minute, and then he said, "OK, but will you put her name in a box on the front cover? Will you say, 'Phyllis Newman as Ado Annie?'" I said, "Yes."

That's a smart agent. He found a way to get more value for his client—something it didn't cost me anything to give away but would help Phyllis in the long run.

And she was great. We even had some of our rehearsals at her apartment in the Beresford on Central Park West, where she and Adolph lived for so many years. Phyllis had recently given birth to their daughter, Amanda, so she wanted to stick close to home, and she invited us all over.

Phyllis was already a star, though. The guy I picked to play opposite her, as Will Parker, was a much bigger shot in the dark. At this stage of my producing career, I was intent upon doing unusual yet appropriate creative casting.

As it happened, Goddard was producing a series of Columbia recordings called "The Legacy Series." These were elegantly packaged book-and-record collections of what I'd guess you'd call Americana today—old-time music from American history. There was one set called *The Confederacy* and another called *The Union*, all Civil War songs performed with something that at least attempted to be historical authenticity. It was a prestige thing: they didn't make any money, but they won awards and boosted Columbia's image, and Goddard liked that.

Well, one of these "Legacy Series" albums was a double record of western music, outlaw songs, called *The Badmen* (1963). I went to one of the sessions, and I heard this guy whose name was Ramblin' Jack Elliott. He was a folk singer, an old partner of Woody Guthrie, and he came across as every inch a cowboy.

When I found out who he was, I was quite amazed: he looked like a cowboy, but actually he was from Brooklyn, and his real name was Elliot Charles Adnopoz. This was in 1963, but I already knew we'd be doing *Oklahoma!*, and—not knowing he was Adnopoz from Brooklyn—I said to myself, "Wouldn't he be perfect to do that hick role, Will Parker?"

Now, I'm quite sure Ramblin' Jack had never done a Broadway recording and never did another one, but he did a very good job. He was very funny singing "Kansas City," and he and Phyllis were great on their duet together, "All Er Nuthin'," despite being from different worlds. Or maybe because of it. I remember rehearsing with them at Phyllis' apartment, and Phyllis got such a kick out of this guy. You know, because he really wasn't acting; he sang the stuff just like he regularly sang, and he sounded perfect. Their one duet is absolutely charming.

Then there was the villain, Jud Fry. He has the duet with Curly, "Poor Jud Is Dead," but especially the solo "Lonely Room," which was cut out of the original-cast recording for space reasons but restored for ours. It gives a whole different picture of Jud. Hammerstein didn't really like obvious or cardboard villains any more than he liked perfect heroes. As soon as he created a bad guy like Jud, he'd start wondering what made him the way he was, and he'd try to show this to the audience.

He did the same with his heroes and heroines. Nellie Forbush in *South Pacific* is a heroine who has been brought up to think along racist lines. The King of Siam is a despotic ruler who practices polygamy. Billy Bigelow is truculent, sullen, and violent—more an antihero than a hero—but we see a whole new side to his character in the wonderful "Soliloquy," as he looks ahead to the birth of his first child. We may not like everything these characters say or do, but we do understand it, and we cheer for them when they grow and change for the better. Jud Fry remains a villain, but "Lonely Room" helps us understand him. It makes him a believable human being.

In the summer of 1963 I had been playing chamber music at Marlboro, Vermont, where Rudolf Serkin had his music festival. One of the musicians there was Ara Berberian, a bass/baritone who was just beginning his career at the Metropolitan Opera. He was going to give a recital in Old Lyme, Connecticut, and he needed an accompanist. He asked me, and I said sure, and so we rehearsed for about two weeks and then went to Old Lyme. I liked Ara, and I loved his voice. So when it came time to cast Jud, later that same year, I thought of Ara, and I asked him to do it. It turned out he couldn't have been more perfect as Jud.

Technically, his songs were not challenging to him from a musical point of view. Rodgers was a composer with great technique and great discipline, and because he was involved in casting his shows, he always knew exactly what he had to work with. Sometimes he got a great singer like Alfred Drake, and he could be bold in his writing, but sometimes the person who was best for the part (in this case, the actor Howard da Silva) had a very limited range. In *The King and I*, for example, Anna's songs all have a very narrow range because they were tailored to Gertrude Lawrence. "Lonely Room" is an incredibly poignant song, but it spans only a single octave.

Franz Allers was back on the podium, which was an added pleasure, and Phil Lang wrote the new orchestrations. With a little help from me, which—at least as I see it now—made things worse.

One of the most distinctive aspects of *Oklahoma!* is its opening. The curtain rises on Aunt Eller sitting alone onstage, churning milk. Curly's voice is heard from offstage singing the opening words of the show: "There's a bright, golden haze on the meadow." He enters as the song goes on, but it's already something new and different, a signal that this is no ordinary Broadway show. I remember telling Phil Lang that I'd love to hear just a single high-string note accompanying Curly to be held, as I had planned to use stereo to walk Curly in from the distance. And Phil said to me, "I don't know why we need any accompaniment at all."

Phil was right. I should have left it alone. In 1980 I did the show again with Laurence Guittard as Curly, and I had nothing to do with the arrangements. Curly sings unaccompanied at the beginning, and it's just the way it ought to be.

But you learn as you go along. It's smart to hire good people to work for you, but you've also got to be smart enough to listen to them.

The King and I (1964)

By the time *The King and I* premiered in 1951, Rodgers & Hammerstein were a partnership with a track record rivaled only by that of Gilbert & Sullivan in the 1870s and 1880s. Their only rivals were themselves. Their fifth show together, *The King and I* followed in the footsteps of four spectacular hits: *Oklahoma!*, *Carousel*, the film *State Fair* (1945), and *South Pacific*. With each success it seemed more and more unlikely that Rodgers & Hammerstein could live up to their previous glory, and with each new show they did.

The King and I, adapted from Margaret Landon's historical novel *Anna and the King of Siam* (1944), found the two at the peak of their powers and was recognized as a classic from the moment it opened. It was the last triumph of the great Gertrude Lawrence, who played Anna and died from liver cancer during the original run. It launched the career of an unknown actor named Yul Brynner, who had achieved more success as a television director until he was cast as the King, a role he would return to, onstage, in the movies and on television, for the next three decades—eventually performing it live more than forty-six hundred times.

As for the show itself, it ran for three years, was a hit in London, and has had four Broadway revivals and four West End revivals; it has been made into two films, one starring Brynner and the other an animated version from 1999. The show also had enjoyed several revivals at City Center in Manhattan, the most recent in 1963.

When we came to it in 1964, in short, our challenge once again was not how to spur popular interest in *The King and I*, but rather how to live up to listeners' expectations. The original-cast album had been a hit for Decca in 1951, as were the London original-cast album in 1953 and the movie soundtrack in 1956. We had stereo, yes, but what else could we bring to the table?

We needed an answer to that question because ours wasn't going to be the only stereo recording of *The King and I* issued in the summer of 1964: barely two weeks after our album was released on July 13, RCA issued the cast album for the Music Theater of Lincoln Center's revival of the show, starring Darren McGavin and our old friend Risë Stevens. Our *King and I* had been recorded on June 1, 5, and 11; I don't remember for sure, but I think we accelerated our production process in order to beat RCA to the punch, if only by a couple weeks.

I was certain we had an album that would rank with the best of them. To begin with, I knew it would sound wonderful. By this point our studio-album operation resembled a repertory company of sorts, and I brought back two of my favorites from *Show Boat*: Barbara Cook, who had been a terrific Magnolia, now became Anna; and the wonderful Anita Darian, previously Julie, became Lady Thiang. An added plus was that both were intimately familiar with their parts, thanks to the City Center revivals: Barbara had played Anna there in 1960, and Anita had been Lady Thiang in both 1960 and 1963.

Barbara was wonderful as Anna, just wonderful. Whether it was something angry, like "Shall I Tell You What I Think of You?" or something beautifully lyrical, like "Hello, Young Lovers," she made the songs her own.

Gertrude Lawrence, a great actress but only an adequate singer, created the role of Anna. Since then it's been sung by Marni Nixon (singing for Deborah Kerr) in the movie, by Julie Andrews in a studio album, and in assorted revivals, by Constance Towers, Angela Lansbury, Kelli O'Hara, and Marin Mazzie. They're all great—but when I hear the songs in my head, the voice I hear is Barbara's. She got under my skin somehow, in the best possible way. I just loved the sounds she made; I loved what she brought to things. I did at least five albums with her, and I wish I'd done more.

Casting the King was tricky because the role had become strongly associated with Yul Brynner, thanks to his originating the role, winning a Tony Award for his performance, and then re-creating it in the movie and winning the Oscar as Best Actor—a rare honor for a performance in a musical.

It was my fellow Masterworks producer Paul Myers who suggested Theodore Bikel for the role. This was a bit of a stretch. Bikel was an Austrian-born Jew who was famous as an actor, but arguably, even more famous as a folk singer: he cofounded the Newport Folk Festival, sang frequently with Pete Seeger, and was an early mentor to Bob Dylan. When he created the role of Captain von Trapp in *The Sound of Music* (1959) or appeared as the pompous Hungarian linguist Zoltan Karpathy in the movie version of *My Fair Lady* (1964), he was very much playing to his strengths. As an Asian absolute monarch, he would be going thoroughly against type.

But when Paul suggested him, I saw immediately what a good idea it was. His performance in *The Sound of Music* had proven he could handle Rodgers & Hammerstein but hadn't given him the chance to sing as much as he deserved. And he was more than just a singer: when Laurence Olivier directed the London production of Tennessee Williams's *A Streetcar Named Desire* in 1948, with Vivien Leigh (then Olivier's wife) playing Blanche, he chose Bikel to understudy both Stanley (the Marlon Brando role) and Mitch (the Karl Malden role).

Doing *The King and I* would give Bikel a chance to bring together several aspects of his artistic persona, and indeed it did. His King isn't as showy as Brynner's, not as much a temperamental child in a man's body; but Bikel was a more sensitive musician and brought an intense humanity to the part that I think has held up well as the years have passed. (He also told me, during the sessions, his favorite Arab curse . . . which, unfortunately, isn't even close to printable.)

Another treat was being able to cast Daniel Ferro, an opera singer and teacher who had never done a recording before, as Lun Tha. I first met him when he was the singing teacher of my wife, Irene. He was on the faculty of the Juilliard School for thirty-four years, but he made few if any other recordings. And he was very good, singing opposite Jeanette Scovotti as Tuptim.

One regular on our team couldn't join us for this one: Franz Allers was music director for the Lincoln Center *King and I* and was at work on his own recording of the show. Fortunately, our other regular, Lehman Engel, was available. He had done outstanding work for us on *Lady in the Dark*, and he knew Rodgers & Hammerstein well, having conducted studio recordings of *Oklahoma!* (1952) and *Carousel* (1955). This was his first *King and I*, and he did a masterful job.

I wanted to round out the recording, to get in more of the original music. We restored the dance that Sir Edward and Anna do—it's an instrumental, and usually instrumentals are the first thing to go when you're making cuts to fit a show onto an album, but that dance is lovely and was largely unknown. With Anita on board, we restored "Western People Funny," which hadn't been on any of the previous recordings. It's a great character song, and Anita was great.

Maybe the most important change we made was not an addition, but an expansion. On the original-cast album, "Shall I Tell You What I Think of You?" is truncated. It plays like a song rather than what it is in the show, which is basically an interior monologue during which Anna's mood changes back and forth as she goes along—what in opera is called a "scena." I included the whole song, and I think it helps a lot in making the character of Anna more understandable. And of course Barbara had a field day with it.

Phil Lang was back to do new orchestrations. Again, I don't know if this was necessary—the new arrangements were great, but now I believe that it would have been fine if we'd stayed with the Robert Russell Bennett originals—but it was nice to work with Phil again.

(I did, in fact, second-guess this decision in one respect—three decades later: I'd never been very happy with Phil's orchestration for "March of the Siamese Children," another important instrumental in the show. It was fine, of course, but it was abbreviated. When I was remastering the show for Sony in the 1990s, I discovered the Columbia archives included a recording of the march by Louis Lane and the Cleveland Pops Orchestra. They had used the original Bennett arrangement, so I substituted this performance and used that for the CD instead of the orchestration we had done in 1963.)

Speaking of Siamese children, one of the real inspirations I had for *The King and I* concerned casting the King's many sons and daughters. They have one of the show's most popular songs, "Getting to Know You," so I needed a chorus of children. Somehow, I'd heard or read there was a school associated with the United Nations, for the children of diplomats posted there, and that the school had a choir. So I reached out to the United Nations International School, and we managed to get them to sing "Getting to Know You." It was an unusual day in the recording studio—they weren't professional singers, they were real little kids, and a great many of them were Asian—but it was a lot of fun, and it turned out very well. Obviously, I could have rounded up a professional children's chorus, but there was a naturalness to these kids that appealed to me and that comes through on the recording.

It's the sort of off-the-wall thing I like to do. Today it would probably be hard to manage—each kid's parents would come in with a separate lawyer—but in those days it was something you could put together on the fly, and it adds something unique to the album.

Everything about this recording was fun to do. I even hired a good friend of mine, Al Simon, to write the liner notes. Al was director of light music at the classical-music station WQXR, and he came from a gifted family: his brother was Richard Simon, who cofounded the book publishers Simon & Schuster. Al was a gifted pianist and his nieces were Carly Simon, the pop singer/songwriter; Joanna Simon, the opera singer; and Lucy Simon, the composer with whom I would work decades later recording her musical *The Secret Garden* (1991). Al was roughly the same age as my father, and he had known George Gershwin—I think he was the rehearsal pianist for one of Gershwin's shows.

So *The King and I* was a very warm experience for me, working with a familiar team on a show I'd always loved. It was a good way to wrap up our Columbia Record Club Broadway series.

And it was exactly the right time for me to wrap it up because that same year I'd been assigned a project called *To Broadway with Love*. It wouldn't be my first Broadway original-cast album because the show was playing a couple of miles off Broadway, but it would be my first original-cast album—but not, of course, my last.

12

The Original Cast

BY EARLY 1964 I HAD BEEN WITH COLUMBIA FOR FOUR YEARS, and I was no longer a record-business novice. I had served key apprenticeships under Howard Scott and Jim Foglesong and had proven myself, first, as an editor and mixer and then as a producer. I had produced classical albums in my own right and worked with Jim on a successful series of Broadway studio albums. What I hadn't done was make an original-cast album. And for all the advantages of a studio-cast album, I very much wanted to get into the original-cast business.

In certain ways, making an original-cast album isn't too different from making a studio album. The actual recording process is the same, and the preproduction is easier because—as the term "original-cast album" suggests—the record producer almost never has to recruit anybody for the cast. For better or worse, it will be the same group that's playing at the theater.

The stakes, however, are much higher.

Most obviously, the original-cast album is a historical document. A hit show may lead to any number of additional recordings—a London cast recording, a movie soundtrack, revival-cast albums, studio albums, and more—but the original-cast album will always hold the place of honor. Since 1956 there have been many recordings of *My Fair Lady* (including one by me), but the "real" recording will always be Goddard Lieberson's original-cast album with Rex Harrison and Julie Andrews. Our studio-cast recording of *Oklahoma!* was in many respects superior to the original-cast recording from 1943 (it offered stereo sound, improved recording technology, and substantially more of the score), but we never fooled ourselves into thinking it would become the new standard reference for this iconic show.

Not every original-cast album captures a masterpiece, of course, and not every one lives up to the show it captures (we'll talk about the disastrous original-cast recording of *Follies* later!), but to make an original-cast album is to contribute to musical-theater history. There's not a Broadway record producer who doesn't realize that and savor it.

Because the stage cast is a given, the original-cast album also presents unique challenges. These actors have been living in a world of unrelenting pressure, with daily deadlines and constant changes to the script, score and staging for months before the opening. Sometimes the show is a hit, and they come into the studio feeling like they've survived a battle, more ready to relax than to tackle a whole new challenge;

sometimes the show is a flop, and they come into the studio despondent and wondering whether the whole thing has been worth it.

Notwithstanding, it's an original-cast recording, so you've got to work with the original cast. It's fun to put together a dream cast for a studio recording, but the real test of a producer's mettle comes in playing the hand he's dealt. It's a tightrope walk with a rigid deadline.

A studio album may well have a target date for completion. However, there's no great price to be paid for missing that date. When we made our studio album of *Lady in the Dark*, we began recording and then had to go on hiatus in midstream for several months; if this vexed the record-buying public, I never heard about it.

But you really do want to release the original-cast album as quickly as possible after opening night. The most obvious market base for a cast album is the audience in the theater—people who loved seeing the show and may want to pick up the cast album on their way out. Eight times a week between when the show opens and when the album hits the stores, the record company misses out on hundreds more prospective customers. I've worked for three major record labels and with God knows how many record executives, but I've never known one who liked the idea of missing out on prime customers.

In the early 1960s the pressure not to miss out on those customers was a defining force in the production process. Every original-cast recording was made within a few days of the opening—typically on the first Sunday after opening night, beginning at 10 a.m.—and had to be recorded in a single day or, very often, a single day and night. Anything you didn't get in that first day's sessions, however minor, was logistically difficult to redo (the cast had an ironclad schedule onstage, of course) and also staggeringly expensive.

Nor did the recording producer's workday end with the final note of the evening session. Throughout the day, as material was completed, the tapes were sent by courier uptown to Columbia's editing cubicles, where an engineer and a designated assistant from the A&R staff began the process of editing them. As soon as the evening session concluded, the producer left the studio and rushed uptown to join in the editing and begin the mixing. How long he and the engineer worked that night depended only on how long they could keep their eyes (and ears) open.

For the next few days, the producer and engineer would edit and mix the recording, trying to fight the ticking clock in the background. As soon as humanly possible, the masters would be finished and on their way to Bridgeport (or in later years, Terre Haute).

This intensity produced both triumphs and failures. People with talent and training can accomplish great things under pressure, and Goddard made sure his show recordings were in the hands of such people; but inevitably, there were missed opportunities and oversights. In the 1990s, when Sony hired me to remaster for CDs not only my own earlier recordings, but classic shows by other producers, I had the chance to listen to the original unedited tracks and—working without any real deadline pressure—found many opportunities for improvement.

O Say Can You See! (1962)

Predictably, Columbia brought me along slowly, starting out on low-stakes projects rather than on high-profile Broadway hits. The first original-cast album I ever produced, back in 1962, was hardly released at all.

O Say Can You See! was an Off-Broadway revue that opened on October 8, 1962, at the Provincetown Playhouse in Greenwich Village. It ran for less than a month and was dismissed by *The New York Times* as "glib and facile" and as "a rickety excuse for a musical." It certainly wasn't the kind of hit an Off-Broadway revue needed to be to get an original-cast album from a major label like Columbia.

As it happened, though, the publisher was a friend of Schuyler's, and as a favor to him, Schuyler agreed to make them a record of the show. It was never intended to be commercially released, and when it was, it was in a limited edition. But that made it an ideal project for a young producer who hadn't yet finished his second year with Masterworks to get his feet wet in the cast-album business.

It helped that *O Say Can You See!* was a cute show, with lyrics by Bob Conklin and Bill Miller, and music by Jack Holmes in a 1940s style. Most of the songs spoofed World War II tunes, which in 1962 were still familiar to New York audiences. There was a big song, for example, called "Buy Bonds, Buster, Buy Bonds." Holmes was a very talented guy who knew musical theater well, having spent many years working in the Rodgers & Hammerstein office. The cast was young and enthusiastic—and with nine men and seven women, larger than most Off-Broadway shows could muster—and the songs were fun. The whole thing had a bright, upbeat feel to it.

I'm pretty sure all Schuyler expected me to do was to let the singers go through their numbers and then send them home. But this was my big chance, and I had no sense of proportion—I took this as seriously as if it had been *My Fair Lady*, and I worked very, very hard on it.

The real challenge of this show was that the actual World War II songs had been accompanied by big bands, whereas *O Say Can You See!* had only two pianos. So I had to go about it a different way, trying to get a more 1940s sound out of the existing company and piano players. I had a great time, too—I remember trying to make the female trio, a kind of ersatz Andrews Sisters, sound even more mindless than they did onstage by telling them, "Just pretend you're chewing gum."

It was a nice opportunity, and I ran with it. Why not? The show came with a large cast, a fun score, and absolutely no expectations. If the recording was great, there'd be no payoff; but if it was terrible, there'd be no recrimination.

Was it good? I can't be objective about it. All I can say is we made the recording, Schuyler's friend was happy with it, and I guess Schuyler was happy with it, too, because he let me do some more originals a year or two later.

To Broadway with Love (1964)

I spent my youth in New Jersey, my middle years in Manhattan, and the past couple of decades on Long Island. For three and a half years, however, from December 1960 to June 1964, Irene and I lived in Queens. In the years immediately following our marriage, we occupied a small but pleasant apartment at 102–40 67th Road in Forest Hills.

(For those familiar with the code of Queens street names, this means we lived on 67th Road off 102nd Street; you might also expect 67th Road was between 66th Road and 68th Road, but instead it was (and is) between 67th Drive and 67th Avenue. Finding one's way around in Queens is famously difficult, even for locals, let alone outsiders!)

Lying to the northeast of Manhattan, Queens is the largest of the five boroughs that make up New York City, and the most populous, with nearly two million inhabitants when we arrived. Traditionally Queens is a borough of strivers, young couples, and families attracted—as we were—by its proximity to Manhattan and its much lower rents. Many people in Queens dream of "making it" and crossing the bridge into Manhattan, as Irene and I would after a few years.

Forest Hills was an ethnically mixed neighborhood with a substantial Jewish population. It was the home of the US National tennis championships (which became the US Open in 1968), at the fabled Forest Hills Tennis Club. It would soon have other claims to fame. We got there two years after Paul Simon and Art Garfunkel graduated from Forest Hills High School, and two years before comic-book creators Stan Lee and Steve Ditko made Forest Hills the home of Peter Parker, a.k.a. Spider-Man, who attended the same school.

(We liked our new apartment in part for its location: it was only a block away from the subway, where I could get the RR train to 63rd Drive and then the E to West 53rd Street and Seventh Avenue, handy to Columbia's office at 799 Seventh Avenue.)

Queens was more than a transition point in the early 1960s, however. It had been the site of the 1939 World's Fair, which was followed by a second in 1964, both held on the same grounds in Flushing Meadow, only a couple miles from our apartment. The World's Fair lived up to its name, with eighty nations participating in a massive series of displays covering 646 acres. More than fifty million people visited the fair between April 1964 and October 1965, and Irene and I were among them. I came back several times, though, on business.

The display pavilions were glorified Chamber of Commerce exhibits, promoting the sponsoring nation or state as a tourist destination, a great place to do business, a leader in industry or culture or athletics or whatever else its political leaders thought made them look good. As the host nation, the United States had a bigger presence than any other nation; the host state and city were also lavishly represented. And when New York City tells the world about itself, it never forgets to mention Broadway.

To Broadway with Love was presented at the Texas Pavilion, only because the Texans had built a huge theater called the Music Hall, which could accommodate as many as twenty-four-hundred people. Essentially the show was a revue encapsulating the history of Broadway, from nineteenth-century minstrel shows and the days of George M. Cohan and Flo Ziegfeld, up to what was then the present day of Rodgers & Hammerstein, Leonard Bernstein, and Lerner & Loewe. A huge cast—eighty-five singers and dancers, plus a big orchestra—was featured in an opulent production that included newsreel films projected on a backdrop as well as live performers. It was bigger and splashier than even the biggest Broadway shows, but clearly the producers hoped it would inspire the millions of out-of-town visitors, once they were back on the other side of the East River, to take in a show. No doubt it did, for at least some of them.

The songs were mostly medleys of hits from each era. As a brief tour of Broadway's past, it was an impressive job! In the opening number, songs by Daniel Decatur Emmet and Stephen Foster represented the nineteenth century. The second number took us from 1904 into World War I, with songs by Cohan, Victor Herbert and Henry Blossom, and Jerome Kern. Later numbers featured hits and standards by Cole Porter, Irving Berlin, Rodgers & Hammerstein, Kurt Weill, and Jule Styne and Sammy Cahn.

To Broadway with Love was more than a greatest-hits collection, however. No currently running shows were represented, probably to avoid sparking rivalries, but one of the hottest current creative teams was hired to write several songs representing Broadway's present and future: the show's golden oldies were woven together with original songs by Jerry Bock and Sheldon Harnick, who had had major hits with *Fiorello!* (1959) and *She Loves Me* (1963). To do *To Broadway with Love*, they had taken time out from work on their next show: as our 1964 liner notes observed, "Bock and Harnick are currently working on the score for *Fiddler on the Roof*, a musical version of Sholom Aleichem's *Tevye's Daughters*, scheduled for Broadway."

I didn't know Bock, Harnick, or any of the actors, but the conductor was my old friend Franz Allers, who must have been one of the busiest musicians in New York. The actors were all new to me, fresh faces who didn't cost much, after all the money the producers had spent on production values, but they were very good.

The show had two casts, working on alternating days because, unlike a Broadway show, *To Broadway with Love* played several shows a day and never had a day off. The day we recorded the show, a second cast was out in Queens, performing for the audiences there.

I had been to see the show a few times, and I got to know it pretty well. I liked all the cast members so much that I don't even remember how we chose which ones to use for the recording. I imagine either Franz cherrypicked from the casts for the recording, based on his intimate familiarity with their performances, or—as we would do in the case of *Porgy and Bess* years later—we just said, "The designated cast is the opening-night cast." Anyway, however we ended up with them, they were very, very good. One who particularly impressed me was Millie Slavin, who was delightful.

We did the whole thing in a single day, the way almost everything was done in those days. Besides the drive to get the record out as soon as possible, the economics were a big factor because the cast were all members of Actor's Equity—the union for performers and stage managers. Under Equity rules, each singer got a week of his or her salary for a single day of recording—but that day was defined as eight hours of work plus an hour for a meal; if they worked one minute over that, you owed them an entire second week's salary. So we arranged our schedules very efficiently to try to make sure that as few people as possible, ideally none, worked more than the artificially defined "one day."

Now, this wasn't technically a Broadway original-cast album—the show was performed several miles from Broadway, at the World's Fair—but it was my first shot at recording a Broadway-size production that was still playing and that had a score that was at least partly original.

I wasn't nervous at all. I'd familiarized myself with the show, and because it was basically a revue, it didn't have storytelling elements to deal with. In a way it was easier than the studio albums we'd been doing because we didn't have a John Raitt, a Bob Goulet, or a Risë Stevens, let alone a Doris Day. The whole cast were newcomers, eager to make a good recording and prove themselves—which probably describes me as well.

The funniest thing about this recording, in retrospect, is that it was the first show I ever did with Sheldon Harnick, who was to become one of my closest friends in the world. He and Jerry came to the recording session, and I'm sure I was introduced to them, but I don't recall either one having anything to say during the session, most of which was, of course, focused on music they had nothing to do with. It would be another six years before we got to know each other.

The Secret Life of Walter Mitty (1964)

James Thurber's "The Secret Life of Walter Mitty" (1939) is one of the great American short stories and is pretty much the only one of Thurber's works that is widely known today. It's been made into two movies and at least two plays—including a 1964 Off-Broadway musical whose cast album I was assigned to produce.

The two movies and two plays have almost nothing in common with one another, except that they all extrapolate wildly beyond Thurber's plot. Which is understandable because in the original story Walter Mitty doesn't do anything except drive his wife into Waterbury, Connecticut, to do their Saturday-morning errands. Along the way, of course, he has fantastic daydreams of being a pilot braving a raging storm, a brilliant surgeon performing a life-or-death operation, a master assassin on trial for his life, and a Royal Air Force pilot on a suicide mission to destroy a Nazi ammunition dump.

So, since nobody wants to see a movie, play, or musical about someone running errands in the suburbs, all the adaptations use the short story as a jumping-off point for . . . other things. In the musical Mitty is tempted to leave his wife and their suburban existence and become the man of action he's always dreamed of being.

Walter Mitty was a much tougher album to record than *To Broadway with Love* because it had a plot and characters that the audience needed to believe in. It also offered some technical challenges: there were places in the show where the melodic line was being passed back and forth by five different people. I set the scenes up in stereo so that it came out left, left-center, center, center-right and right, an instance of really making use of stereo.

It was a fine show. It was a small show, as all Off-Broadway shows are, but the cast was wonderful, and the songs were great. Earl Shuman did a beautiful job on the lyrics, and Leon Carr's music was very, very good. I had a wonderful time doing it.

Bajour (1964)

My first official Broadway original-cast album—well, let's just say it didn't achieve immortality as the next *Oklahoma!* or *My Fair Lady*. *Bajour*, which opened at the Schubert Theatre on November 23, 1964, notched a respectable but not exceptional 232 performances and has never been revived on Broadway.

It probably never will be, despite having three strong lead roles and some very good songs by lyricist/composer Walter Marks. Its subject matter would almost certainly rule it out because the plot (based on a couple of New Yorker stories by Joseph Mitchell) is built on ethnic stereotypes that could never play on Broadway today.

The original liner notes begin: "The highest of all arts, to gypsies, is the bajour—a confidence game in which they swindle lonely and unhappy women out of their life savings." Even with a substantially rewritten book, I can't imagine *Bajour* playing to twenty-first-century audiences, and it wasn't enough of a hit that anyone is likely to try.

Nonetheless, it made for a good recording. Walter Marks was a very talented guy. He went on to write *Golden Rainbow* (1968), a show for Steve Lawrence and Eydie Gorme, based on the Frank Capra movie *A Hole in the Head* (1959). That show also ran for less than a year, but it included the big song "I've Got to Be Me," which was a hit for both Lawrence and later Sammy Davis Jr., who changed the title to "I've Gotta Be Me."

As with *To Broadway with Love*, I started out with an ace in the hole: a conductor with whom I was already thoroughly simpatico. *Bajour* was being conducted by Lehman Engel, literally a friend of the family: he lived across the street from Irene and me, and he'd known Irene's father, the actor Harry Clark. As already mentioned, I had worked with Lehman on a couple of studio albums by then, and I'd also been a student in his famous BMI workshop for aspiring Broadway composers and lyricists.

Lehman's presence made *Bajour* a very comfortable experience for me. There are lots of people involved in a Broadway recording, and many of them are important voices in the session, including the writers and the orchestrator (on one occasion even the choreographer!). But the only ones the producer works with directly on every song are the engineer and the conductor. The engineer is always a known quantity, somebody I've chosen or at least been involved in selecting, but the conductor comes with the show. When it turns out to be somebody with whom I have the kind of track record I did with Lehman or Franz Allers, it makes everything easier.

The director of the show was someone else I knew, Lawrence Kasha. He'd been the stage manager of the Broadway musical *Lil' Abner* and had then held a similar position on the summer tour of that show for which I'd been one of the pianists. As the road-company stage manager, Larry was effectively our director. He knew every line and exactly how it should be read; he never had to look at his notes.

In *Bajour*, Herschel Bernardi had the male lead as Cockeye Johnny, "the Gypsy King," and he was easygoing and terrific, as he always was. Chita Rivera, a bought-but-not-yet-paid-for Roma bride intended for Johnny's son, played a woman who is also a gifted pickpocket and con artist.

Chita was then what she is now: an amazing talent who can sing, dance, and act with the best of them, a true triple-threat performer who can and has gotten work doing any or all the three and has always excelled. She's been nominated for ten Tony Awards, won three, and could easily have won a half-dozen more.

She's a force of nature, funny and dynamic offstage as well as on, and very down-to-earth, with a bawdy sense of humor that makes her a lot of fun to be with. I remember once talking with Chita backstage during a break in rehearsals at the theater. (I spent a lot of time backstage, getting to know the cast and the production team ahead of the session.) On the wall next to us was one of those great big canvas fire hoses that you see backstage in theaters, a huge hose wound around a wheel. And out of nowhere, Chita picked up the big, brass nozzle and held it up to her mouth and sang, "Someday he'll come along, the man I love."

The show's other leading lady was Nancy Dussault, who played a New York University anthropology student who's studying the city's Roma community for her Ph.D. dissertation. I remember she was having some vocal trouble on the recording session. This isn't unusual because often actors strain their voices in the high-pressure runup to opening night, and Nancy soldiered through it very well. But on one of her big songs, "Must It be Love?" she couldn't get her high notes out for the final phrase, "I just mustn't let it be love." It simply wasn't there, and hammering away at it wasn't going to make it any better.

As it happened, a soprano, Urylee Leonardos, was in the ensemble. She was Black, I think of Jamaican heritage. She was a very large woman with a beautiful voice and wasn't just an anonymous chorus woman—she'd played the title character in the 1946 revival of Oscar Hammerstein's Bizet adaptation, *Carmen Jones* (1943). Lehman asked her to sing that final phrase, and during the editing we spliced it in, with Nancy singing the whole song and then Urylee singing the last line. If you listened to it, and I didn't tell you what we'd done, I don't think you would ever notice that it goes from one voice to another. It really worked miraculously well. Lehman called it "black magic!"

Now, you have to realize that, even though I was a novice, I was already very sure of myself, perhaps arrogant. About halfway through the overture, there was a point at which one tempo finished and then a short solo violin cadenza, in a Roma style, segued into a faster tempo that continued for the rest of the overture. The violinist playing that solo passage didn't play it very well, and after several attempts, I said to music director Mort Lindsay, "Let's knock out the cadenza and just go from Part 1 into Part 2."

He didn't want to do it, and we had an argument about it, but I held my ground, and we ended up doing it my way. Now, this wasn't a big thing—I had lunch with Walter Marks fairly recently, and he had no recollection of this whatsoever—but when I listened to this recording again, not terribly long ago, I recalled that moment where everything stops short and then goes into a new tempo. And I think it's very effective.

The editing and mixing went smoothly. It was my first actual on-Broadway cast recording, and I was trying to do it in the Goddard Lieberson tradition, so overall sound quality tended to be very bright and sparkling, with a fair amount of reverberation. Toward the end of my mixing, as I listened afresh to what I had done, I got cold feet, I really was afraid I'd gone overboard and that the whole thing was just too brittle. I asked engineer Fred Plaut, who was the engineer on Goddard's cast albums, "Do you think I went overboard?" And he said, "No, no, no, no, no!"

Listening to it again, all these years later, it's a good recording. It's an entertaining show, with very talented principals, and the recording works well. I remixed it for its CD release in 1992, and I'm glad people can still hear it.

The Decline and Fall of the Entire World as Seen Through the Eyes of Cole Porter (1965)

One of my regrets is that, in a long career, I've gotten only one chance to record a Cole Porter show—and it turned out to be an unfortunate experience for me.

I don't think there's anyone who loves Broadway who doesn't love Cole Porter. His flair for melody and especially the urbane sophistication of his lyrics have held up remarkably well for more than half a century. To this day, when people want to say that a songwriter is clever and writes with a certain witty flair, they compare him or her to Cole Porter.

Porter wasn't in any sense a pioneer, at least when it came to the shows he wrote. He helped bring Latin rhythms into the Broadway scene, but Porter was a songwriter, not a writer of integrated musicals. Part of his appeal in the 1940s and 1950s was that, even after the innovations of *Show Boat*, *Lady in the Dark*, and *Oklahoma!*, all of which occurred after he'd established himself on Broadway, Porter still did it the old way: his shows were light, frothy comedies with no connection to the real world, and his songs weren't integrated into the story and didn't provide deep insights into the characters. As Broadway kept growing around him, Porter kept doing what he'd always done—and it worked because his songs were funnier, catchier, more tuneful, and more romantic than almost anybody else could write. And we still extol *Anything Goes* and *Kiss Me, Kate*, two of his greatest musicals.

I'd always loved Cole Porter, so I was pleased when I got the chance to produce the original-cast album of the Off-Broadway revue *The Decline and Fall of the Entire World as Seen Through the Eyes of Cole Porter*. This was a clever revue with a terrific cast, put together by Ben Bagley, who'd mounted his first show when he was only twenty-two and quickly proven himself a master of the sophisticated revue and of spotting up-and-coming stars. His three previous revues, *Shoestring Revue* (1955), *The Littlest Revue* (1956), and *Shoestring '57* (1957), had featured early performances by Bea Arthur, Joel Grey, Tammy Grimes, and Chita Rivera, among others. After a stretch of inactivity due to tuberculosis, *Decline and Fall* was his comeback to Off-Broadway.

It was a new approach for Bagley, whose previous shows had featured songs by assorted different songwriters, exploiting his knack for finding overlooked gems from past shows while offering early work to such promising young songwriters as Sheldon

Harnick, Lee Adams, and Charles Strouse. Devoting a whole show to a single songwriter was a different tack, but with Porter's enormous catalog to choose from, Bagley had plenty to work with.

And the show was a lot of fun. Bagley was a clever guy who knew how to put together these revues, a mix of some familiar songs and some wonderful ones that you'd probably never heard of, accompanied only by piano and drums. He always got very talented casts—Carmen Alvarez, Kaye Ballard, and Harold Lang are the three I remember who were in this one—and he would have them very sharp and polished. He really understood this kind of material, and it was a great show.

The trouble was, he wanted to run the recording session. This show was his baby, and he had very specific ideas about how to make the record. Maybe I should have just let him have his way, but I was very proprietary. It may have been his show, but it was my record. I did my version of Jim Foglesong, "Only one person talks to the cast, and that's not you."

So it was an uncomfortable day. That doesn't mean the record ended up being bad—the cast was very, very good and the material was fun, and it came out very well. But there was almost no pleasure in it for me.

In a way this was a very forward-looking show because it was basically a miniature version of what today we call the jukebox musical. A couple of decades later, I'd be involved in two of the first ones to hit Broadway, with *Ain't Misbehavin'* (1978) and *Sophisticated Ladies* (1981). These shows tend to be song revues, not book musicals, so a lot of the things a producer tries to do in recording a more traditional musical don't apply. In the case of *Decline and Fall* with no story or characters, the recording producer isn't called upon to build dramatic tension or help the audience understand the story.

It's a very interesting show, with some wonderful Cole Porter songs that I don't think many people had heard before, and it was a great cast. But it was the first of only three or four unhappy experiences I've had in my whole career, which is more than sixty years now. And every time I've had a bad experience it's been centered on things like this, a situation where somehow I felt that things were getting away from me and I couldn't let that happen.

That's usually not a problem. Of course, everybody present at a session may have their own ideas of what the record should be like, but usually civilized behavior and rational minds prevail. I guard my territory, probably both out of good judgment and rampant ego, but I don't go crazy about it. I'll always listen when other people ask me questions or make suggestions. I wouldn't be much good at my job if I didn't.

Musical theater is maybe the most collaborative art form there is, and the recording is part of that. But I think when anybody—the director, the composer, occasionally the orchestrator—has something they want to contribute, their first step should be to talk to the record producer instead of going straight to the cast or the conductor.

In the long term, maybe what I got most out of *Decline and Fall* was an awareness of the scope of Cole Porter that I otherwise wouldn't have had. Most of the songs Ben had come up with were ones I never knew, and that came in handy many, many years later, when another Porter project came my way. My friend Robert Kimball, a noted Cole Porter scholar, had acquired many 1930s master recordings of Porter singing his own songs, accompanying himself on the piano. I agreed that we would release these commercially. I worked with Bob on choosing the selections and remastering them. It wasn't a creative project for me, but I suppose my experience with Ben's show helped. Certainly I came away from *Decline and Fall* with a sense of perspective on Porter's work that I hadn't had before.

The Zulu and the Zayda (1965)

By 1965 Harold Rome was a living legend of Broadway. He'd made his debut with the famous revue *Pins and Needles* (1937), a pro-union show produced by the International Ladies Garment Workers Union. Rome had always been associated with left-wing politics—he wrote a 1939 song called "Who's Gonna Investigate the Man Who Investigates Me?" sung by Zero Mostel—but his gifts reached far beyond that. His biggest hits were *Call Me Mister* (1946), *Wish You Were Here* (1952), *Fanny* (1954), and *I Can Get It for You Wholesale* (1962), which introduced the young Barbra Streisand. He was fifty-seven in 1965, and if anyone had told me *The Zulu and the Zayda* would be his last Broadway show, I wouldn't have believed it. As it turned out, though, it was, so I'm glad to have gotten in on it. He went on to write a musical based on *Gone with the Wind* but it didn't make it to New York.

The Zulu and the Zayda wasn't a typical Broadway musical. It was billed as "a comedy with music," meaning that proportionally it had less music and more dialogue than most musicals, and it dealt with a controversial subject: the apartheid regime in South Africa.

The great Yiddish actor Menasha Skulnik played a Jewish grandfather ("zayda" means "grandfather" in Yiddish) whose family hires a very meek, withdrawn Black man (a member of the Zulu tribe, played by Louis Gossett Jr.) as his caregiver. The elderly man, originally a refugee from Czarist Russia, and the young man who has grown up under apartheid get to know each other and find they have surprising things in common.

This story probably appealed to Harold Rome, who wrote both the music and the lyrics. Rome was a Jewish man who had a lifelong fascination with Africa and with African art, of which he had a magnificent collection. I was lucky enough to see it, beautifully displayed, at the Rome family's spacious and elegant apartment. He was also a student of African music, and combined elements of Jewish and African music in his score for *The Zulu and the Zayda*.

The book was written by Felix Leon and the actor Howard Da Silva, and besides Gossett, the cast also included two other remarkable Black actors, Ossie Davis and Yaphet Kotto, young men who would go on to long careers on stage and screen.

The show was produced and directed by Dore Schary, who is best known as a film producer. Curiously enough, Schary had been a high-school fraternity brother of my father's in Newark, New Jersey. They were both members of Sigma Phi Delta but by this time had completely lost touch.

Not long ago, I heard from Jill Schary Robinson, Dore's daughter. She was looking for a recording of *The Zulu and the Zayda*, which she'd never heard. She contacted me online, and I said, "You're in luck. I have two copies; I'll give you one of them."

The original orchestrations were for a very small group—I believe only three players—and they had been written by Meyer Kupferman. He was both a talented musician and an incredibly generous person, because I had prevailed upon him to redo them, expand them, all from scratch for our upcoming recording. Meyer then re-orchestrated the entire show for an orchestra of ten or twelve musicians. Perhaps he thought it would pay off in the long run, because these were his orchestrations and he owned them. But he did them over, and he did them beautifully.

Not that the sound of this show was typical for Broadway. Between them, Rome and Kupferman had used a tremendous amount of what you might call musical dialogue between various African drums. That was the case in the original orchestrations and even more so in the revised ones.

It's a very, very good score but not one that sounds like a typical good Broadway score. It uses indigenous instruments, rather than the typical Broadway orchestration, to tell its story about an indigenous people. It doesn't have breakout songs the way most shows do—its songs are tightly rooted in the show they came from, and they aren't the kind of tunes you leave the theater humming, though they were very effective in their own context.

Lou Gossett, who sang well, was the lead, but I recall that Ossie Davis's character did more of the singing. Davis had a wonderful voice, singing or speaking, and he carried a lot of the music.

Menasha Skulnik, essentially a character actor, didn't have much of a voice, but he was charming singing these cute little Jewish songs Rome wrote for him. He was immensely charismatic and very active for an old man. The recording session was in one of Columbia's smaller studios because this was a smaller group. Skulnik was prancing around the room like a kid during the session. I think he was about seventy-four at the time, which to me was older than God, and I was worried he was literally going to drop dead right there in the middle of the session. He obviously didn't, in fact he lived to be eighty. From my perspective today, he really wasn't very old at all.

In 1967 I worked again with Harold on an album called *Harold Rome's Gallery*, which was a very unusual project: a collection of twelve new songs, each of which had been inspired by a painting he'd done. It was a very handsome package, which opened to reveal reproductions of the twelve paintings. The songs were sung by a talented quartet, mostly people who had worked with Harold previously, consisting of Betty Garrett, Jack Haskell, Rose Marie Jun, and Harold himself. Some of those songs are quite clever, with titles like "Stop Waltzing Around in My Mind" and "The Wolf that Swallowed Red Riding Hood," but this type of recording was never destined to sell a lot of copies.

Harold was a diversely talented man. He graduated from Yale and went on to Yale Law School but then changed gears and earned a degree in architecture. In the 1930s he worked as an architect while trying to make it as a songwriter, which he did with *Pins and Needles* and *Sing Out the News* (1938), another socially conscious revue he did with George S. Kaufman and Moss Hart. He was also a painter and sold some of his work professionally. A very impressive man, very sophisticated, and apparently an avid poker player—he, Lehman Engel, and a few other friends had a regular game.

He had also been a good friend to Harry Clark, who would have been my father-in-law. Harry died suddenly when he was only forty-five—that was in 1956, before I met Irene. He was a widely respected actor, and Harold Rome must have loved him because he cast him in at least three of his shows: *Pins and Needles*, *Wish You Were Here* (1952), and *Fanny*.

Harry was one of the two gunmen who sang "Brush Up Your Shakespeare" in *Kiss Me, Kate*.

My last encounter with Harold Rome was in the 1970s, when I was at RCA. He had written a new show which was first staged in Tokyo under the title *Scarlett*, and then retitled *Gone with the Wind* for its London production two years later. He wanted to get it staged in New York, and he hoped RCA would commit to an original-cast recording.

But, to my regret, I had to turn it down. That was a hard decision because I liked Harold so much. He was a legendary figure, and I respected everything he'd accomplished. But I didn't think this show was going to be successful. It was almost four hours long, there wasn't much humor in it, and it would be hugely expensive to mount. There have been times when I thought a show wasn't going to work and yet it did, but this wasn't one of them: *Gone with the Wind* got done regionally in places like Los Angeles and Dallas but wasn't well received, and, as I feared, it never made it to New York.

It can be tremendously expensive for a record company to commit to a Broadway show, depending on how much they need or want from you. Even without investing in the show, which at RCA we did our damnedest not to, it's still a huge commitment. Orchestrations alone are a substantial expense: virtually all Broadway shows have orchestrations written especially for them. There is a significant re-use fee charged to the record company that goes to the orchestrators and copyists, even though they were initially hired and paid by the show's producer. Everybody who's associated with the show has got their hand in on the recording somehow, so it gets very expensive very fast. Recording Harold's show probably would have cost at least half a million in today's dollars.

Listening to *The Zulu and the Zayda* today, you can tell what a great songwriter Harold was. But the album, like *Harold Rome's Gallery*, probably would not have come to us if it hadn't been for the friendship he had with Goddard Lieberson.

By the end of 1965, I'd been in the record business for almost five years. I'd been a producer for four years, I'd produced studio albums of classic shows with big stars and original-cast albums of small shows with casts of young unknowns, and I'd learned a lot. The bigger shows were about to come my way, and I was ready for them. Or I thought I was, anyway.

13

My Name Is ... Friend

Harold Sings Arlen (with Friend) (1966)

Not every record I made with Columbia was either a classical album or a cast album. Technically *Harold Sings Arlen (with Friend)* was probably a pop album—the bulk of its sales surely went to pop fans, not Broadway aficionados—but it was under the umbrella of Masterworks because of who the artists were and how the project came to the company. I think I'm safe in saying that it was and remains unlike any other album I've ever made.

In 1966 Barbra Streisand was a star by anybody's definition, but it never occurred to me that I'd ever work with her. I'd missed my chance to record her first two Broadway shows, *I Can Get It for You Wholesale* (1962) and *Funny Girl* (1964), and the success of *The Barbra Streisand Album* (1964), her debut record and winner of the Grammy as Album of the Year, had established her as a major pop star. She had signed to make her film debut in a big-screen version of *Funny Girl*, which two years later would earn her an Oscar as Best Actress, and her first television special, *My Name Is Barbra* (1965), had been a ratings bonanza and earned five Emmys and a Peabody Award. It was clear she wouldn't be doing another Broadway musical any time soon. (She never has.)

And while she and I were both signed to Columbia Records, there wasn't much chance we'd ever cross paths. I worked for Masterworks, and she was in the pop department, and those departments rarely intersected.

We weren't hostile to one another, mind you, at least not most of the time. My friend and mentor Jim Foglesong was from the pop department, of course, and I had a lot of respect for Mitch Miller and many of the people who worked for him. It was simply that members of the two departments didn't have much occasion to work together.

That I ended up recording Barbra Streisand was, therefore, a remarkable fluke, and it came about because of another legend in the music business, Harold Arlen.

If Arlen isn't as well-known as Barbra Streisand, it's not because he wasn't a genius—lots of people knew that, including Streisand herself. Arlen was arguably the greatest twentieth-century songwriter never to have a lasting Broadway hit. With a variety of lyricists, he wrote "Ac-cen-tchu-ate the Positive," "Any Place I Hang My Hat Is Home," "Come Rain or Come Shine," "Down with Love," "Get Happy," "It's Only a Paper Moon," "The Man that Got Away," "One for My Baby (and One More for the Road")," "Stormy Weather," "That Old Black Magic," and even "Lydia the Tattooed Lady." He had a particular bond with Judy Garland, who returned to his music again and again and immortalized his greatest hit, "Over the Rainbow."

His catalog is studded with songs that Irving Berlin, George Gershwin, Frank Loesser, or Cole Porter would have been proud to have written, but his best songs overwhelmingly represent his work in Hollywood. Only a handful, such as "Come Rain or Come Shine," from *St. Louis Woman* (1946), come from his Broadway shows, where his track record was mixed. Of his seven Broadway musicals, only *Bloomer Girl* (1944) and *Jamaica* (1957) were hits. None of the other five—*You Said It* (1931), *Hooray for What!* (1937), *St. Louis Woman*, *House of Flowers* (1954), and *Saratoga* (1959)—ran for more than two hundred performances, and none has ever been revived on Broadway.

This doesn't mean they aren't good shows; the issue is more likely their subject matter. Arlen was one of America's great proponents of Black music and was drawn to stories about Black life in America or the Caribbean. *Bloomer Girl*, *St. Louis Woman*, *House of Flowers*, *Jamaica*, and *Saratoga* all treated Black subject matter, and—while Arlen's politics and racial attitudes were strikingly progressive for his era—1940s and 1950s stories on Black themes are sometimes problematic for contemporary audiences. Even *Bloomer Girl* and *Jamaica* were only modest hits.

By 1966 Arlen was sixty-one, and his glory days were behind him. Hollywood wasn't making many musicals anymore, Broadway was moving away from his kind of songs, and assorted other projects weren't panning out.

It so happened there was a record label called Monmouth-Evergreen Records, which had been struggling in the early 1960s and was closing down. One of the people affiliated with this label was my old friend Stanley Green, who had written some liner notes for me and would later ghostwrite Richard Rodgers's autobiography and, under his own name, publish *The Rodgers and Hammerstein Story* in 1980. When Monmouth-Evergreen was closing, Stanley brought a lot of their masters to Goddard Lieberson, to see if Columbia would like to re-release these records. Goddard wasn't interested.

But one of those recordings stuck in his mind. It was a two-volume collection called *The Music of Harold Arlen* from 1955, with the legendary songwriter singing his own material. I wasn't there for these conversations, but afterward Goddard told me about the Harold Arlen album. He said, "I think we could do it better ourselves." And then he asked me to do it, to make a new recording of Harold Arlen singing his own songs.

I was thrilled, but I wasn't really prepared for a job like this. I knew all the famous Harold Arlen songs. I knew *The Wizard of Oz*, of course, and I knew a lot of the songs from *Jamaica* and *Bloomer Girl*. I wasn't ignorant about Arlen, in short, but I wasn't an expert, either. And because I don't necessarily like to do things in the traditional way, I knew that if I were going to do an album with him, I'd want it to be not only the obvious hits, but also the sleepers. And I knew only the obvious hits.

I think it was from Stanley Green that I learned about Bill Sweigert, a New Yorker who had assembled a definitive taped collection of Arlen songs. I reached out to him, and he was willing to lend me his entire collection, which Columbia's engineering department copied for me on 7.5-inch-per-second open-reel tapes.

When I say, "definitive collection," I mean it. We aren't talking about a few reels of tape, we're talking about many, many linear feet of boxes of reels. I started to immerse myself in them. I didn't have time to listen to any song more than once, except when something really struck me, but the whole thing was a wonderful learning experience because I'd never heard the vast majority of this material before. And there were several very obscure songs I very much wanted to be on our new recording.

After I'd spent as much time as I could listening to the songs, and I had some real perspective on the material, I went to visit Harold. He lived in a beautiful apartment on Central Park West. On his wall was an oil painting of Jerome Kern by George Gershwin.

We clicked almost immediately, probably because I didn't expect him to sing only the songs everyone knew and loved. Instead I said to him, "There's one song I hope very much you'll do, and that's 'In the Shade of the New Apple Tree.'" This is a wonderful song with lyrics by Yip Harburg, from *Hooray for What!*, that practically nobody had ever heard since then.

And he said, "Well, that's the audition song that got Yipper and me *The Wizard of Oz*."

So I happened to have picked a song because I loved it, which had a great story behind it. And because it wasn't one of his hugely popular songs, it told him I'd prepared for this, I knew his work well, and he could work with me and trust me.

The arrangements for the Arlen album were done by Peter Matz, a man Harold had worked with for years. He had, in fact, been the orchestra conductor on *The Music of Harold Arlen*, back in 1955. Peter was a joy to work with because he was so gifted and knew the material so well. He was youngish, somewhere between my age and Harold's, who turned sixty-one within our recording period. (His birthday was on February 15.)

The whole concept of the album was that Harold would be singing his own songs. This isn't always a good idea, of course, because not every songwriter is a good ambassador for his own songs.

Harold was different, though. He was the son of a cantor—he was born in 1905 as Hyman Arluck in Buffalo, where he grew up in a two-family house. The family in the upper half of the house was Black. So Harold got the cantorial germs from his father and the idiomatic Black music through the ceiling. It's all in his music.

He had started in show business while still a teenager, forming a vocal group called the Snappy Trio when he was only fifteen. He later sang with a big touring band called the Buffalodians and made records singing with well-known bands led by such people as Red Nichols and Eddie Duchin. It was only when he started making too much money with his songwriting to be able to afford to go on the road as a singer that he became a full-time songwriter. He went on to write four years' worth of revues for the Cotton Club, two shows a year, and wrote many songs for Black singers such as Adelaide Hall, Lena Horne, and Ethel Waters.

Many songwriters perform their own works in a simple, straightforward way, conveying the words and the tune as clearly and unaffectedly as they can; they leave interpretation to the professional singers. Harold wasn't afraid to put a lot of personality into his recordings. He didn't have the voice of a Bing Crosby or an Al Jolson, but when he sang "Ac-cen-tchu-ate the Positive" on our album, he brought a flair to it that was his own. Harold was indeed a singer.

Having said that, somewhere along the line it occurred to us—maybe to me, maybe to Peter—there should be somebody else on the recording, to make it a little different—extra special—from the composer alone doing his own stuff.

And while Peter Matz had worked with Harold ever since he'd been a rehearsal accompanist on *House of Flowers* a decade earlier, he'd worked with a lot of other people as well. Major artists, including Noel Coward, Marlene Dietrich, and yes, Barbra Streisand. Only a year or two before this, he'd worked with her on *My Name Is Barbra*, and they'd gotten along so well that he conducted and arranged her next four albums, including *People* (1964), the title song of which won him a Grammy for Best Arrangement.

So he had a great relationship with Barbra, and he thought she'd like to be involved. Barbra was a student of songwriters even then and knew all about Harold because she was a huge fan of Judy Garland. She'd already recorded several of his songs, in fact, and Harold had even written the liner notes for her first album.

In one respect it was easy to approach her because she was a Columbia artist—if she'd been with another label, they wouldn't have let her anywhere near this recording.

At Columbia, Barbra was produced by Mike Berniker, who was my friend and colleague from the pop department. He told me how to get to her manager, Marty Erlichman (who at this writing is ninety-three and is *still* her manager), and so I called him.

Pop managers don't get paid to make life easy for record labels, and Marty didn't make it easy for us. Marty agreed to her participation only if she'd have almost all of the available royalty income which would leave Harold with a token share.

Of course, Harold owned all the copyrights, so he could make money on the back end. And it was still a good deal, if you look at the big picture: Harold was one of the songwriting greats (and sang better than any other songwriter I've ever worked with), but his name alone on the album cover wasn't going to sell a lot of records. In those days there was no Internet on which to stream songs, and there would be no singles released from this album, so the only way Barbra's fans could get her two songs was to buy the album.

I remember saying to Harold, "She's taking all the royalties!" And he said, "It's OK, Tom, she's the queen." He was so delighted, so grateful to have her.

She and Harold chose the material they wanted to do, which was a duet on "Ding Dong, the Witch Is Dead," from *The Wizard of Oz*. They did it with a whole introduction I had never heard before—apparently written for the movie and then cut, the same way the introduction to "White Christmas" (1942), which hardly anybody knows, was cut. And then Barbra was going to do one song on her own: "House of Flowers," a beautiful song with lyrics by Harold and Truman Capote.

I had an idea for the album title and cover that I liked very much. I called it *Harold Sings Arlen (with Friend)*, without ever identifying the friend; but we added a small, cameo-style picture of her in profile.

The cover had a rarefied, sophisticated look. Harold's name was in big letters, with a big picture; Barbra had a tiny picture, and she wasn't named—she was just a "friend."

After all that, I got into trouble with Bill Gallagher, head of sales and marketing for the pop department. Unbeknown to me, they were negotiating a new contract for Barbra, and somehow, he thought my making this one-off deal would make things harder for them to leverage in a new negotiation. Gallagher was a hard-headed guy who could be very tough, and he was angry at me. He said, "How could you just go ahead and do this without checking with us?"

And maybe he thought the lesson I'd learn from his displeasure was that in the future I would always check with him before I instigated a new project. But I was pretty sure that if I'd checked with him, getting Barbra's participation would never have happened. So what I really learned was, if you check in with too many people, you're never going to get the job done.

I think Gallagher's objections were entirely based on protecting his own turf—they had nothing to do with Barbra's contract, which she duly signed. She remains an exclusive Columbia artist (or now, a Sony artist) to this day.

Barbra came to the recording session in jeans, sneakers, and a mink coat. In later years she would develop a reputation as a perfectionist who could be difficult to deal with, but I found her very down-to-earth and easy. I remember a photograph of her in the recording studio along with Jonathan Schwartz, the radio host, and Edward Jablonski, the author who had written a biography of Arlen a few years before. In the photograph, there they were: Schwartz, Jablonski, Matz, Barbra and me. She's listening to a playback and enjoying listening to herself.

I remember Harold, during the session, telephoning his wife, Anya, who had serious emotional issues, and who rarely left the house. He was holding the telephone near the loudspeaker so she could hear what was probably the playback of his duet with Barbra, "Ding Dong, the Witch Is Dead."

My most striking memory of Barbra at that session was after our second take on "Ding Dong, the Witch Is Dead." It was a great take, the one we would wind up using. Barbra said to me, "The coda is better on the first take." I said, "What do you mean?" She said, "The orchestra, the band, they played it better on the first take at the end."

At this point I was still young and had limited experience in the studio, compared to what I have now, but she was even younger and had even less experience. And she was right. I listened again to take one, and it had indeed a stronger finish. She had heard it better than I did! She knew what she was talking about, even then. At twenty-four, she had as canny an ear as any veteran I've ever worked with.

We had at least two recording sessions for the album, maybe three, each lasting three hours, but Barbra was only at the one. All of them went well. Harold had recorded a few of these songs, including "In the Shade of the New Apple Tree," as a young man, with a band. He sang better then, but he didn't sing badly three decades later. He had a kind of Southern take on things, with a flavor of Black music to it that still came through well. I was very pleased with this recording, and so was he.

One day Irene and I had an idea involving Harold. She was studying with a vocal coach who was also a fine actor, Ludwig Donath. Among his many film roles, he played the father of Al Jolson (Larry Parks) in *The Jolson Story*. Donath had been blacklisted and had come to New York to restart his career. At this time he was in his sixties and was playing Mr. Maraczek in the hit Bock & Harnick show *She Loves Me* (1963).

Donath was Jewish as well as being of the same generation as Richard Tucker and Harold Arlen. Tucker was in his prime a great Metropolitan Opera tenor, and I knew him well after years of having produced his recordings, so all three of them had come to have important places in our lives but they had never met one another before. At this time, four years before our daughter Elizabeth was born, Irene and I had a one-bedroom apartment in Manhattan, and we decided to have a Sunday brunch and invite the three couples: Harold and Anya Arlen, Ludwig and Jean Donath, and Richard and Sarah Tucker.

In retrospect I don't know where we found the chutzpah to ask these three legendary men and their wives over to our modest apartment, but it was a great afternoon. These were three highly creative and successful men with long careers in show business. It was an afternoon of history, of anecdotes, one after another. I wished I had tape-recorded it.

Anya Arlen, whom I had never met before, was a beautiful woman in her early fifties. After about an hour and a half, during which time she had said almost nothing, she began looking uncomfortable, restless, twitching a little bit around the eyes. Harold said, "It's time for us to go home," and they left.

That's the only time I ever saw her. She died in 1970 of a brain tumor, and Harold was riddled with guilt, convinced that all her problems were somehow his fault. I remember running into him in 1976 at the cast party for the first Broadway revival of *Fiddler on the Roof* with Zero Mostel. Irene and I were there because we were friendly with the Harnicks. Harold was there by himself and obviously just wallowing in depression, six years after Anya's death. I remember Mostel saying to him, "Harold, life is for the living." Mostel was trying to connect with him. It was a very human, very poignant moment.

But prior to his wife's death, when I first met him, when life was good, Harold was very debonair. He looked like the stage version of a Mississippi riverboat gambler: he dressed in beautifully tailored clothes and always had a fresh boutonniere and a pencil-thin mustache. At that time, I remember playing for him a song I'd written with Charlie Burr, and he said, "You've got a really gifted lyricist. Gifted lyricists are hard to find. You hold onto him." He was speaking from experience.

That party for the *Fiddler* revival was the last time I saw him, though he lived another ten years.

The Megilla of Itzik Manger (1968)

Most times, when a Broadway cast album gets made, it begins with the producers of the show pitching it to the record company, hoping to get some advance funding for their production in return for the recording rights. That isn't always the way it works, of course. If a show is a high-profile affair, the record label may come to the producers. And sometimes a producer has a long-standing relationship with a given record company, the way David Merrick had with RCA, and it's generally assumed his shows will end up with that label.

None of these was the case with *The Megilla of Itzik Manger*. As I recall, one of the producers phoned me to say a Columbia representative who was affiliated with Eastronics, the Israeli record label that distributed Columbia's recordings there, had committed us to making an American recording of the show, which had been a big hit in Israel and was about to open on Broadway. He wanted me to make the Broadway premiere. Maybe I ought to have dug deeper into it and found out to what extent Columbia had been committed to this project, but I went to see the show, and I liked what I saw.

Itzik Manger was a Yiddish writer born in 1901 in Czernowitz, a city which at the time was part of the Austro-Hungarian Empire; later it was part of Romania, and currently it's in Ukraine. Manger had bounced around a lot, establishing himself in Warsaw, fleeing the Nazis to Paris and then on to Marseilles, Tunis, Liverpool, London, and finally, Israel.

In 1936, while he was still in Warsaw, he'd published a modernist poem in Yiddish called *Songs of the Megillah*, in which he retold the Purim story from the Book of Esther, setting it in the Eastern Europe of his day. It was written in semi-dramatic form, and after Manger had settled in Israel and earned acclaim there, an Israeli composer, Dov Seltzer, staged a musical version of it called *The Megilla of Itzik Manger*. Seltzer wrote the music and collaborated with Manger and a couple of other writers on the book and lyrics, both in Yiddish. Yiddish theater had rarely succeeded in Israel, but Seltzer's production ran for more than four hundred performances and an American version was planned, with Joe Darion (who'd written the lyrics for *Man of La Mancha* three years before) working on English narrations to tie the Yiddish-language songs together.

I liked it. It was a modest, charming production with a homespun feel, in large part because the six-person cast featured, besides Susan Walters as Esther, the Burstein family: Pesach Burstein, his wife Lillian Lux, and their son, Mike Burstyn. Except for Walters, I think they'd all been doing the show in Israel as well, and it had an all-in-the-family feel to it.

And it was on Broadway, even though, with Yiddish songs and a small cast, maybe it really belonged Off-Broadway. It wasn't a hit—it ran for 78 performances at the Golden Theatre in 1968 and 12 more at the Longacre Theatre in 1969. But the show was appealing, so I wrote a short note to Goddard saying, "It's a very cute show, and we have a commitment from Eastronics to go forward with it," and he said, "All right, go ahead."

In the panoply of shows that come and go on Broadway, this kind of show is really a blip on the radar screen. It wasn't set up to be a smash hit, and nobody expected it to be, but it was very entertaining.

Things were about to change for me. I had spent the early 1960s learning the record business, and the mid-1960s learning the cast-album business. In both cases Columbia—where Goddard Lieberson focused on the development of young executives—brought me along carefully, making sure I took my first flights under the watchful eye of veterans like Howard Scott and Jim Foglesong.

Now, though, I was going to be entrusted with shows whose Broadway profile was much higher, Tony winners (including one Best Musical winner that was shortly thereafter made into a successful movie) whose cast albums were widely anticipated, and whose sales figures would be of considerable interest to Columbia's accounting department. I was in the major leagues.

In baseball they apparently call being promoted to the major leagues "going to the show." In their case it's a metaphor, but in my case, it was literal. I would spend a substantial part of the next few decades going to shows—and then meeting up with the cast, down the line, to make a recording.

14

Yankee Doodle Dandies

George M! (1968)

Like anything else, Broadway has its trends. Operettas ruled the Great White Way in the 1900s and early 1910s, giving way to musical revues for the 1920s. Then came the golden age of Broadway drama, with Katharine Cornell, Alfred Lunt, and Lynne Fontanne ruling the stage in the 1930s and 1940s. In turn, drama gave way to the great era of book musicals, with Rodgers & Hammerstein leading the way in the 1940s and 1950s.

The big trend of the past few decades has been what's known as the jukebox musical, defined as a show built around existing songs, usually those associated with a particular songwriter or performer. Sometimes the show is in a revue format, as was the case with *Ain't Misbehavin'* (1978) and *Sophisticated Ladies* (1981), showcasing the songs of Fats Waller and Duke Ellington, respectively. Sometimes it's biographical, tracing the story of the central figures through their songs, as *The Boy from Oz* (1998) and *Jersey Boys* (2005) did for Peter Allen and for the Four Seasons. And sometimes, as with the ABBA show *Mamma Mia!* (1999) or the Bob Dylan show *Girl from the North Country* (2020), fictional plots are built around the existing songs.

In all three cases, the unifying element is that the songs were not written for this or any other show, but are familiar tunes that have been gathered for a "greatest hits" score. In the great musicals of the 1950s, the goal was to have the audience come out of the theater humming the songs; in the jukebox musicals of the 1980s to the present, the goal is to have the audience come *into* the theater humming the songs.

All trends take time to develop, of course. The 1950s may have seen the blossoming of book musicals, for example, but that trend was built on earlier hits such as *Show Boat* and *Oklahoma!*, which established the basic form that would be exploited by Rodgers & Hammerstein and such later artists as Lerner & Loewe, Bock & Harnick, Jerry Herman, Stephen Sondheim, and Kander & Ebb.

This is true of jukebox musicals as well. The idea of building an autobiographical story around a songwriter's existing songs originated in Hollywood, with such films as *Night and Day* (1946) and *Three Little Words* (1950); the same was true of building a fictional story around a songwriter's catalogue, as was done for *An American in Paris* (1951) and *Singin' in the Rain* (1952). It may have taken until the 1980s and 1990s for the idea to gain real traction on Broadway, but it was there for the taking all along. I know because I recorded one of the first jukebox musicals to make it to Broadway, *George M!*, back in 1968.

That I ended up recording the show was quite surprising. A 1966 management reorganization at Columbia had changed things considerably. Schuyler Chapin had left Masterworks in 1963 and left Columbia one year later to become vice president for programming at Lincoln Center, where he helped create the immensely popular "Mostly Mozart" summer festival. Now Goddard Lieberson was also gone, kicked upstairs, with an office next to William Paley's on the 52nd floor, where he would handle a broader portfolio of CBS interests, including the new Cinema Center Films, a theatrical-film distributor.

In Goddard's place as president of Columbia Records, Paley appointed Clive Davis, a thirty-five-year-old attorney from Brooklyn who had been with Columbia since 1960 as its general counsel and later as Goddard's administrative vice president and general manager.

Paley could no longer overlook Goddard's one blind spot as a record-company president: his general lack of interest in rock 'n' roll. By the mid-1960s, rock was the driving force behind the record industry, with bands like the Beatles, the Beach Boys, and the Rolling Stones each selling more records than many whole companies did. None of those bands were on Columbia, and Paley was determined to change that. He wanted somebody younger and more attuned to the interests of younger record buyers, and Clive—twenty-one years younger than Goddard—looked like the man for the job. Clive had Paley's ear, and Paley liked his ideas about putting Columbia back onto the Billboard sales charts.

Clive was going to live or die by the performance of the pop department, so already that was bad news for Masterworks. We were used to having one of our own running the company, and having a pop guy in charge would mean we'd have to fight harder for our projects and goals.

Moreover, while Clive was by no means disliked, he wasn't one of us. He wasn't a musician, so his appointment flew in the face of Goddard's old maxim that you could teach a musician about business, but you couldn't teach a businessman about music. It wasn't only Masterworks that had doubts about the reorganization—the pop department surely wasn't wild about having a lawyer in charge, either.

As it turned out, we were selling Clive short. That he was a smart guy nobody doubted, but we didn't realize he had ears—not necessarily taste, but certainly ears. He signed Aerosmith, Chicago, Billy Joel, Santana, Bruce Springsteen, and many others, and in three years doubled the company's market share. And while there was never any question his heart was with the pop department, he left Masterworks pretty much alone, recognizing we were already among the leaders in our market sector.

When Clive took over, he met with each of the company's producers, and I told him I wanted to keep doing the Broadway recordings. He didn't say anything to the contrary, but it was a couple of years before I was back on the Broadway side again.

Most of the work in this area went to two other producers, Ed Kleban and Mike Berniker, and I spent those years working largely on classical albums.

So it was a surprise when Clive called me in to see if I was interested in producing the original-cast album for a new show called *George M!*.

A jukebox musical before the term was invented, *George M!* was something out of the ordinary in 1968. Most musicals since *Show Boat* had been written on the same basic template: book, music, and lyrics were created to bring a specific story to life onstage, whether it was based on real-life events, as with *The King and I* and *Fiorello!*, or on a novel or a play, like *Cabaret* and *She Loves Me*.

George M! didn't fit this template because it didn't have an original score. As *Night and Day* had done with Cole Porter's songs or as *Three Little Words* had done with the songs of Kalmar & Ruby, this new musical was a showcase for the songs of George M. Cohan. Despite a modest amount of tweaking by Cohan's daughter Mary, these songs were a half-century old, and most of them had long since become part of America's musical heritage. As for the book by Michael Stewart and John and Francine Pascal, it told Cohan's life story from the 1880s until 1937, from his beginnings as a born-in-a-trunk child of vaudeville performers to his emergence as a singing, dancing, songwriting, playwriting star so successful he became known, to quote the title of one of his own shows, as "The Man Who Owns Broadway."

He was unique in being a performer as well as a writer, and a powerhouse performer at that. Cohan's final Broadway show, *The Return of the Vagabond*, opened in 1940, two years before he died, and audiences in 1968 included many people who remembered him in his glory days. Nor was Cohan's the only ghost with which *George M!* star Joel Grey had to contend: in 1942 James Cagney had delivered an Oscar-winning performance as Cohan in *Yankee Doodle Dandy*, an instant classic that was familiar to anyone who loved musical films—including, of course, myself. (I was particularly taken by its re-creation of a number from Rodgers & Hart's *I'd Rather Be Right* (1937), in which Cohan had starred as a singing, tap-dancing President Franklin Delano Roosevelt.)

It was February 1968, and I'd done only one Broadway cast album in the past three years—and *The Megilla of Itzik Manger* wasn't much of a warm-up for a big, brassy musical like *George M!*. Clive, who knew me basically as a classical producer, wanted to make sure I was up to it. I assured him I was, so they put me on a plane to Detroit, where the show was in previews at the Fisher Theatre.

I'm too young to have seen Cohan on the stage (I doubt anyone is alive who remembers him), but *Yankee Doodle Dandy* is one of my favorite films. I remember seeing it when it first came out. My mother, my grandmother, and I went to see it and Cagney's performance as Cohan, singing, dancing, and bringing his own incandescent charisma to the role, is one that's stayed with me since I first saw the movie, eighty years ago now. It's one of the greatest movie performances ever.

Even to a big Cagney fan like me, Joel Grey's performance in *George M!* was a revelation. We all knew how good Grey was in supporting roles—he'd just won a Tony for his performance as the sardonic Master of Ceremonies in *Cabaret* (1966)—but *George M!* was his first starring role, and it was one of those shows where the lead actor is onstage almost continuously. Grey needed to act as well as Cohan, sing as well as

Cohan, and thanks to Joe Layton's outstanding choreography (which earned him a Tony), dance better than Cohan. In addition, he needed industrial-strength doses of that mysterious commodity known as star quality.

Joel lived up to those challenges in every respect. He lost the Tony for Best Actor in a Musical to Jerry Orbach in *Promises, Promises*—and while Orbach was outstanding in the role, I'd have a hard time convincing myself he was any better than Joel was as George M. Cohan.

Also in the cast, playing Cohan's big sister Josie, was a young actress with whom I would cross paths for many years to come, the delightful Bernadette Peters.

The show ran for slightly more than a year and was criticized for its book, which depicted Cohan as a headstrong, domineering, self-obsessed force of nature whom some critics found hard to sympathize with. That's true, I suppose, but by all accounts, it's accurate to Cohan as he was. His daughter was involved in the making of the show, and so far as I ever heard, raised no objections to its portrayal of her famous dad. In 1968 most musicals still focused on plucky ingenues, and maybe George M. Cohan was a tough nut to crack in those days; since then, of course, we've seen hit musicals built around murderous opera coaches, Argentinian dictators, homicidal barbers, and presidential assassins.

Making the album exhausted me. Reflecting the subject material, it was a recording very much in the Lieberson tradition, meaning things were generally bright, flashy, brassy, and recorded with a good deal of reverberation. We were probably in the studio for about ten hours, and I was "on" for pretty much that entire time, without any backup; and when I was finished recording, with very little sleep, I had to plunge into editing it and then mixing it. Everything had to be done very, very quickly, and I made it through, but barely.

The album came out fine, and I was very happy with it. The one thing that continued to trouble me was that Joe Layton, who was both the choreographer and the director, had asked me to include one extra spoken line, and I simply forgot to do it. It was an audition scene, and at the end of the audition, he wanted the director to say something like, "Very good, miss. Next!" Which wasn't necessary in the stage production, but on the record, it would have helped make it clear that we were listening to a stage audition. In my exhaustion, I just forgot it.

I apologized to Joe afterward, and he was very gracious about it: "Oh, that's all right, it wasn't that important." But it bothered me. And yes, it would have made the record just a little bit better.

Michael Stewart, the main writer of the book, didn't like the recording. He said that it was too brittle, meaning it was too bright and mixed with too much high end. That didn't please me but I have to say that, if I were doing the show today, I'd probably mix it more conservatively.

And I told him so, years and years later, when we happened to meet at a dinner at Steve Sondheim's. This was many years after *George M!*, and I remember saying to Michael, "You know, you were right, it is too bright." And he said, "No, no, I was wrong, it's fine as it is."

George M! was the first time I ever worked with Joel Grey, and I've worked with him twice since then. He asked me to record his club act when he was in Florida doing a one-man show called *Joel Grey Live 1973*. Years later, I was very taken with a show called *Goodtime Charley*, in which Joel played the Dauphin to Ann Reinking's Joan of Arc. That show was a total flop, which surprised and disappointed me, but I don't regret having recorded it.

I like Joel very much. He's a very decent and sweet-natured person. Irene came with me to Florida when I was making *Joel Grey Live*—Columbia paid for us both—and Joel was the one who told us where to get stone crabs and the best key-lime pie in Miami. His business manager happened to be a friend of Irene's, so the whole experience was very upbeat.

I recorded his live show several times. When the tapes got back to New York, though, Joel wanted to redo some of it. At that point I had so much other stuff to do that I assigned it to a staff assistant I had just hired, a young and aspiring composer named John Corigliano. The first assignment I gave him was to complete the overdubbing, editing, and mixing of Joel Grey's act. John did it; but as soon as the job was finished, he said, "You know, I'm really a composer, I don't belong being a producer. Thanks for the opportunity, but this is not for me." I said "OK." He made the right choice, as he's proven many times in the intervening years with two symphonies, the opera *The Ghosts of Versailles*, and a beautiful clarinet concerto. And maybe he owes it all to Joel Grey!

Dear World (1969)

This show, which was adapted from Giraudoux's classic satire *The Madwoman of Chaillot*, gave songwriter Jerry Herman a rare trifecta, with the original productions of three shows running on Broadway at the same time: *Hello, Dolly!* (1964) and *Mame* (1966) were both still running when *Dear World* opened on February 6, 1969. Only Rodgers & Hammerstein had achieved this previously, and only Frank Wildhorn (very briefly) and Andrew Lloyd Webber have matched it since.

Unfortunately, Jerry's luck had run out. *Dear World* barely made it to the end of May. By the end of 1970, *Hello, Dolly!* and *Mame* had both closed. *Dear World* was the beginning of a fourteen-year string of disappointments for Jerry.

By the time we did our session on February 9, it was clear *Dear World* was in trouble. The show had endured a long and stressful period of tryouts and previews, during which it had gone through three directors and two choreographers. The problems, as usual in such cases, involved the book: initially conceived of as a chamber musical, *Dear World*—perhaps due to the tremendous success of Herman's two previous musicals, both of which were large-scale extravaganzas—had been inflated into a Broadway spectacular, and the book had collapsed under the strain. In later years Herman and book writers Jerome Lawrence and Robert E. Lee took the show back to its roots, with several successive revisions, including new songs and significant book alterations, first by Lawrence & Lee and later by David Thompson. Regional productions have achieved some success, but the show has never returned to Broadway.

I have a hard time criticizing *Dear World* because I've hardly ever come out of any show I've been deeply involved with without ending up liking it. You become attached, even to the ones that don't quite work.

Besides, this resulted in a very good recording that was also memorable for a couple of specific reasons unrelated to the show itself: this was my first time working with Jerry Herman and my first time working with Angela Lansbury.

Jerry was something of a throwback, a 1920s Broadway songwriter somehow transported to the 1960s. He didn't write musical scenes or deeply character-specific songs the way Bock & Harnick, Steve Sondheim, or Kander & Ebb did. Jerry was out of a tradition even older than Rodgers & Hammerstein, a tradition of songs that might have been plot-inspired but weren't plot-driven. He wrote songs the way Porter, Berlin, or the Gershwins did, not necessarily anchored in the character or story, but relying on clever lyrics and catchy, deceptively simple tunes that stayed with you.

I found Jerry to be a very sweet-natured guy, a man who didn't talk very much about himself. He was soft-spoken, polite, very kindly, obviously very proud of his work, and yet never boastful.

Early on, Charlie Burr (who was writing the liner notes for *Dear World*) and I had lunch with Jerry in the restaurant on the ground floor of the CBS building. It was an enjoyable lunch, friendly and relaxed. The only thing Jerry wanted from us was that we should make sure his picture appeared somewhere on the album—because, he said, "It would help with my sex life."

I can't say I ever really got to know Jerry because I never spent time with him just schmoozing, the way I did with, say, Sheldon Harnick, John Kander, or Steve Sondheim. I have no idea what Jerry's cultural interests were. I don't know if he liked classical music, what kind of theater or opera he liked, what books he read. All I know about Jerry is he was a kind of latter-day Irving Berlin, writing his own lyrics and music, and doing everything he could to write songs that would grab you instantly. He very consciously set out to write anthems like "Hello, Dolly" or "The Best of Times," from *La Cage aux Folles*, which will be sung forever in revues and at weddings or bar mitzvahs.

And when he came up with a great song, he knew what to do with it. Jerry was as savvy about show business as anyone I've ever worked with. He placed those potential hit songs very skillfully in his shows and was the king of reprises. If you heard a song more than once in a Jerry Herman show, it was always the most commercially promising one. Often, you'd hear it again in the finale.

And we shared perhaps the most unlikely bond of all: Jerry's grandmother and my Grandma Bertha, my father's mother, were roommates at a retirement home in New Jersey. They both loved to brag about their grandsons, but my Grandma Bertha, well, she was enormously proud of me, but she was constantly being outgunned by Jerry's grandma.

I also had a familial connection with Angela Lansbury, who was the loveliest person in the world. Her younger brother, producer Edgar Lansbury, was almost my producer! He and his producing partner, Joseph Beruh, wanted to produce a show Charlie Burr and I had written. It didn't work out . . . no fault of Edgar's.

And Angela was just a wonderful person. She'd made her film debut at age nineteen in *Gaslight* (1944); by 1945 she'd earned two Oscar nominations and was on her way to a long and triumphant career. Neither movie stardom nor being the toast of Broadway had affected her graciousness.

Angela played Countess Aurelia, the Madwoman of Chaillot, playing opposite two other wonderful actresses: Jane Connell, another Jerry Herman veteran (the original Agnes Gooch in *Mame*) as the Madwoman of Montmarte, and Carmen Mathews as the Madwoman of the Flea Market. They were terrific and very funny together. There's a "Tea Party Trio" in which these three nutty ladies are all talking at once, reminiscing and talking about their lives, and they're like three Mad Hatters.

(The song is slightly different on the recording than in the theater because originally there was a lot of space between the end of each verse and the beginning of the next; in the theater they presumably covered the gaps with business, but it was too much space for a recording. I asked Jerry, on the session, if he'd mind if we closed it up. And he was very willing to let us do so.)

It wasn't Jerry's best score, but it was a very good score, and I did my best not to get in its way. People know me as a producer who uses a lot of dialogue, sound effects, and interstitial material when I record a show, but that's only when it's appropriate. I recorded two Jerry Herman shows, and I made little or no effort to tie the material together with anything of that nature. It just didn't feel appropriate. I would always approach a Jerry Herman show differently from a Stephen Sondheim show because I wanted to be faithful to each songwriter's concept of what makes a good theatrical experience.

Things went very smoothly on the recording session, although the entire atmosphere was a bit depressed because everybody realized the show wouldn't last long. It had opened only a few days before, and the reviews were mixed at best. Angela got very good notices, but Jerry's songs didn't get a lot of praise, and nobody liked the book.

I felt bad for Alexander Cohen, a friend of mine who was the lead producer. Alex was a very smart man and was successful in many other areas of his life, including as a producer of dramas, revues, and concerts, but somehow never of musicals. He always seemed to latch onto the wrong properties or to do the right show at the wrong time.

It just may be that certain projects don't translate well into musicals, irrespective of the talents of the people involved. With Jerry Herman, Angela Lansbury, and Jane Connell, you'd think you couldn't miss, but the Giraudoux play has a certain tone of its own, an evanescent sort of charm that somehow doesn't carry over into the musical version. It just didn't really hang together.

I wish I'd gotten the chance to record more Jerry Herman shows. But I do have the consolation of knowing that, while I was there to kick off Jerry's epic run of bad luck, I would also be there to end it when, in 1983, we got back together again to record *La Cage aux Folles*.

1776 (1969)

Looking back from a Broadway dominated by *Hamilton* (2015), the idea of building a musical around the politics of Revolutionary-era America doesn't seem as outlandish as it did in 1969, nor does the idea of turning America's Founding Fathers into singing, dancing musical-comedy stars seem as outrageous.

In 1969, though, it was a different story. Rodgers & Hart had looked in that direction with *Dearest Enemy* (1925)—their first book musical— but had set their action in wartime New York, kept the politics safely offstage, and avoided depicting any of the iconic Founding Fathers except for a brief appearance by George Washington (who, ironically, does not appear onstage in *1776*, though his presence is certainly felt); *Arms and the Girl* (1950), with songs by Dorothy Fields and Morton Gould, was a flat-out farce involving entirely fictional characters.

No Broadway expert would have thought the deliberations of the Continental Congress in Philadelphia during the summer of 1776 had the makings of a musical, and indeed no Broadway expert did. It was a pianist and pop songwriter named Sherman Edwards, best known for Johnny Mathis's "Wonderful! Wonderful!" (1956) and Elvis Presley's "Flaming Star" (1960), who came up with the idea and saw it through to fruition. Edwards's only previous Broadway experience had been writing the incidental music for a comedy called *A Mighty Man Is He* (1960), which ran for a grand total of five performances.

Sherman Edwards had majored in history at New York University and briefly worked as a high-school history teacher before becoming a full-time songwriter. He saw the story of the Founding Fathers and their disagreements and compromises as both entertaining and inspiring—especially, perhaps, in an era when the country was riven by conflicts over civil rights and the Vietnam War. He spent years working on the songs and libretto for the show and was able to convince producer Stuart Ostrow that he was onto something. Ostrow brought in the more experienced Peter Stone to work with Edwards on the book, and the show was off and running.

Its fundamental conceit was to humanize the men of Independence Hall, bringing out their prickly pride, their personal crotchets, their diverse political perspectives, and above all, the seriousness with which all of them take the idea of their nascent country. William Daniels played an "obnoxious and disliked" John Adams, hectoring his reluctant colleagues to press forward with independence; Howard Da Silva played a cagey, humorous, and Machiavellian Ben Franklin, with Ken Howard as an idealistic Thomas Jefferson who wants nothing more than to go home to his lovely young wife. The songs didn't shy away from such realities of the era as the colonies' military weakness, their difficulty in getting along with each other, and the fact their economy was built on slavery—but nonetheless most of the songs were light, funny, charming, and genuinely moving.

Nobody saw it coming, but *1776* became a runaway hit, earning some of the best reviews in Broadway history and running for three years. In 1972 it became a hit movie, with most of the Broadway cast recreating their roles.

Among the so-called experts who gave the show no chance was me. When Edwards brought the show to audition it for Columbia Records, I had absolutely no confidence in it. I thought, "This'll never make it." Goddard was the one who saw the potential and decided we were going to go forward with it.

I've never been happier to be wrong. This was such fun, from beginning to end. It's a show that, because of the nature of the performances, the beautiful orchestrations, and everything else about it, was almost made to be a wonderful cast album. And I get more compliments about it than almost any other thing I've done. People tell me this is a recording that really made a difference to them.

The show was still in flux when we signed on for it, and songs kept being added, dropped, and replaced until shortly before opening. There was originally a song in it called "Doxey, Honey," which was about the prostitutes in the Revolutionary War, for example. "Mama Look Sharp" was one of the last things written, I think because they thought it might have some commercial life as a single outside of the show. I never thought so, but I do remember Tommy Valando, the publisher, trying to get other singers to record "Mama, Look Sharp." I don't believe that any of them did.

"The Egg" was the last thing added to the show. That wasn't in several of the previews—I think it may not have been added until they were previewing in New York. It was put in, as I recall, because Howard Da Silva, whose performance as Ben Franklin was a highlight of the show, had a lot of dialogue but no real songs, and had asked for more.

This was my first experience working with Betty Buckley, who played Mrs. Jefferson. I thought she was great. We've worked together in the intervening years, and we always hark back to the fact we were both so young—not much more than kids when this was done. It was her first show, and her big number was "He Plays the Violin." She was just delightful. And we've stayed in touch.

Virginia Vestoff played Abigail Adams, and she was wonderful. Irene and I got to know her because she was dating a friend of ours, a stage director named Ben. We used to play poker with them, along with Herb and Cookie Grossman—Herb was a conductor, and Cookie was a writer. Virginia died only a few years later, of breast cancer; she was only forty-two. Virginia was also in the film *Such Good Friends* (1971), for which I composed the score.

William Daniels was the star, of course, no matter what it said on the poster, where his name wasn't above the title (and so they refused to nominate him for a Tony as Best Actor in a Musical). He was nominated instead as Best Featured Actor, but that he turned down the nomination was crazy. Anyone who saw the show knew he was the star.

He was fantastic as John Adams, strutting and demanding the floor in that obnoxious and piercing voice. What a gifted actor. And whenever I think of John Adams, I think of William Daniels. I included lots of his dialogue in the recording because one of the iconic motifs of that show is Adams talking (and talking and talking!). They may not be listening, but he's not going to shut up until he gets what he wants.

And *1776* had wonderful orchestrations by Eddie Sauter. The first thing you hear in the show is a fife-and-drum introduction, and for the recording I started playing around with stereo movement right from the beginning. If you listen to the recording, I'm moving this fife and drum around like a parade march, as if the characters from the famous Archibald Willard painting "The Spirit of 76" were marching around the stage.

The recording session was a joy, but it had an interesting problem: This is one of the rare instances in which the original-cast album doesn't feature the entire original cast because during the final previews, four days before the show was to open, Howard Da Silva had a mild heart attack. His doctors wanted him in the hospital, but Da Silva thought he was playing the role of his life and wanted it to be seen. He returned to the stage for the final three previews and opening night—and immediately thereafter, his glowing reviews safely in the bank, he was rushed to the hospital in an ambulance. He didn't rejoin the cast for several months.

Our recording session was, of course, a week after the opening, which had been on a Sunday. Da Silva was out of the question, so his understudy—Rex Everhart, who was now playing Ben Franklin onstage—recorded the session. He did a perfectly fine job, but he didn't have the bite or charisma Da Silva has when you see the film.

The biggest problem with that recording was always going to be the end of the show, which is a powerful moment whose impact is entirely visual. After the show has taken these iconic men and turned them into living, breathing, fallible people like the rest of us, in the final scene they step up to sign the Declaration, and they move into the pose familiar from John Trumbull's classic painting "Declaration of Independence," and the curtain comes down on that tableau. It's a spine-tingling moment, as if they're turning into immortals before our eyes—but there's no way, listening to a recording, that you can have any idea of what it looks like, where they're standing, and in what attitudes. It's simply impossible.

I kept wrestling in my mind, trying to figure out how we could possibly make it come off. The script calls for the bell in the tower—the Liberty Bell—to be ringing during the final signatures. What I came up with was the idea that, as the secretary of Congress (Ralston Hill) reads the name of each signer, the orchestra gets louder and louder—first a high-strings chord, then cymbals, finally crashing brass—until it threatens to drown out his voice and leaves the listener with the impression that this historic ceremony is going on forever.

There was one aspect of this recording I didn't get right until about thirty years later, when I got the chance to remix it for the CD. I'd never been happy with my original mix on "Molasses to Rum to Slaves," which is a fabulous number. While editing and mixing, because we were so pressed for time, I really didn't manage to capture all the variety in the orchestration. When I got the chance to remix it, years and years later, I felt satisfied with my work at last. On the CD it's wonderful. I finally did justice to Eddie Sauter.

Dames at Sea (1969)

A couple months after finishing *1776*, I was back in the studio with an entirely different show, smaller in scale, but nonetheless, a gem.

Dames at Sea took a long time to make its way to Broadway. In fact, it hadn't gotten there at the time I recorded it—it was an Off-Broadway hit at that point and wouldn't be produced on Broadway until 2015. But it was a wonderful show, regardless of where it was playing.

It had originated as a ten-minute revue sketch spoofing the giddy 1930s musicals churned out by Warner Bros. and MGM, with their plucky heroines, daffy plots, catchy songs, and why-the-heck-not tap dances. The sketch proved popular, though, and in 1966 George Haimsohn and Robin Miller (book and lyrics) and Jim Wise (music) expanded it into a fifty-minute club show, by now titled *Dames at Sea: Or, Golddiggers Afloat*, which was presented at the tiny Caffe Cino, a Greenwich Village coffeehouse where they'd pass the hat after each performance and divide the take among the actors, the piano player, and the director; that was all the pay they got. There were any number of shows like it going on in 1960s New York, and there was no reason to expect anything more to come of this particular one.

It had a lot going for it, though. The plot was funny and in its own right, more than simply a mockery of the movie plots. The catchy songs captured the spirit of the 1930s originals but were good enough to charm audiences thirty years later. And the tap dances were exhilarating. As for the plucky heroine, she was played by an up-and-coming actress named Bernadette Peters, who was a whole show in herself.

Dames at Sea ran for 148 performances at the Caffe Cino (about 140 more than that kind of show usually got), and two years later the creators managed to raise the money to launch a full-length version at the Bouwerie Lane Theatre on December 20, 1968 (by the time we recorded it, it had transferred to a larger house, the Theater de Lys).

The show was still a tiny affair, with a cast of only six, but it had an ace in the hole: Bernadette, who (in defiance of any career advice she may have gotten, I'd imagine) had left *George M!* to resume her role as Ruby, the plucky young actress in what was now simply called *Dames at Sea*. Besides a steep pay cut, leaving a Broadway hit for an Off-Broadway show meant a sharp drop in visibility, but she knew the material and the people who had created it, and I guess she had a good feeling about it. And rightly so because it ran for 575 performances and spawned a London version, a 1971 television production that starred Ann-Margret, several Off-Broadway revivals, and eventually that 2015 Broadway version—which ran for only 85 performances, maybe suggesting part of the original's charm was its small scale.

I didn't choose to record this show, as a matter of fact. A few other people at Columbia Records, including my friend and lyricist Charlie Burr, had gone down and seen it, and they came back and recommended it to Clive as something we should do.

They were right. In a certain sense the show was reminiscent of *O Say Can You See!*, which back in 1962 had been my first original-cast recording. They were both parodies of old-time Hollywood musicals.

The score of *Dames at Sea* is very clever, both musically and lyrically. Yes, it's a parody, rather than a true original, but it's done so well, and it was cast so well. The director, Neal Kenyon, had a great feel for this kind of thing. Doing a spoof can be tricky because it has to be done affectionately—you can't seem to be mocking the original source because your audience will be mostly people who loved the original—but it needs to have a satiric edge. And of course, the material has to work on its own because you can't assume everyone in your audience has seen the movies you're parodying. *Dames at Sea* did all that.

There were only two or three players in the orchestra—I remember a piano and a harp, I think; I'm not sure what else—and the show's producers obviously saved money in every way they could.

That tiny band was a problem, though. It worked in an Off-Broadway theater, but I didn't want to record the show with only a couple of instruments. I wanted it to have more substance. And this was to lead to my first encounter with a man who would become a friend and colleague.

It all goes back to David Rosen, my fellow pianist on that long-ago summer tour of *Lil' Abner*. I'd stayed in touch with him, and I recalled that he once urged me to check out the work of an orchestrator he knew. They'd been classmates at the high school now known as the Fiorello H. LaGuardia High School of Music & Art and Performing Arts.

David's classmate turned out to be none other than Jonathan Tunick. He had made his Broadway debut back in 1960, as co-orchestrator of a revue called *From A to Z*, which was a hotbed of up-and-coming talent: among the creators of its songs were Jerry Herman and Fred Ebb, and one of the three sketch writers was Woody Allen. The cast included Virginia Vestoff and Hermione Gingold, who was the show's "name." It was a twenty-one-performance flop, though, and Jonathan wouldn't be back on Broadway until *Promises, Promises* (1968).

That one was a hit, but Jonathan was still fairly new in this business when I called him and asked him to do all-new orchestrations for our upcoming recording of *Dames at Sea*. It would still be relatively small, a sixteen- or seventeen-piece orchestra, but a lot bigger than the tiny band in the theater.

Those new orchestrations were to be conducted for the recording by the show's music director, Richard Leonard. But on the day of the recording session, when it was time to start, Richard hadn't shown up. Nobody could get in touch with him, and we couldn't afford to wait, so Jonathan took his place. This may have been his first professional conducting job, and he had no time at all to prep for it, but he did a great job. Leonard came in about three hours later, still bleary, and took over from Jonathan. He's credited on the album as conductor, but Jonathan conducted several of the songs.

I could tell, even then, that Jonathan Tunick was something special. He's arguably the greatest Broadway orchestrator of the last third of the twentieth century, the way Robert Russell Bennett was for the middle third; there are other contenders for that title, but Jonathan is right up there. He became associated with the work of Stephen Sondheim, so we've worked together many, many times since then.

Dames at Sea was a lot of fun for me. The material itself didn't pose any particular problems, so I got to have fun with audible tap dancing and various stereo effects. The biggest challenge was several places in the show, particularly in the finale, where the band had to pretend to sound "Hollywood" huge, even though all we had were those sixteen players. So I had to employ a lot of electronic gadgetry and trickery to make the ending sound grandiose.

The cast was unfazed, new orchestrations notwithstanding. Steve Elmore, who would later appear in *Company*, was in that cast, and of course there was Bernadette. She and I have worked together through the years, with *George M!*, *Sunday in the Park with George*, and the Andrew Lloyd Webber show *Song and Dance*. I've had a lot of history with Bernadette.

It couldn't help but be a fretful day because when your music director doesn't show up, and when no one in the cast has ever heard the orchestrations before, everything takes extra time. But when all was said and done, it came out very well.

15

Annus Mirabilis

AFTER THE REORGANIZATION OF COLUMBIA RECORDS IN 1966, I went a couple of years doing almost no show recordings. But once Clive opened the gates with *George M!* in 1968, shows and other related projects seemed to come at me in waves. It was a very exciting time.

Every year brings its own highs and lows, but surely 1970 was among the most important ones in my career. I was in the studio constantly, and the projects I undertook were substantial ones with lasting consequences. When the 1970/1971 Tony Award nominations came out, I was surprised to learn I had recorded two of the three nominees for Best Musical; two of the three for Best Book of a Musical; two of the three for Best Original Score; and three of the four for Best Actor in a Musical, Best Actress in a Musical, and Best Director of a Musical. I'd recorded all three nominees for Best Choreographer, Best Featured Actor, and Best Featured Actress in a Musical. I've had some remarkable years since then, but none quite like 1970.

This single year launched the two collaborations that rank as the most substantial of my career, one with an icon of Broadway's past and the other with an icon of its future; it let me work with two of my lifelong heroes; it brought my most successful recording ever, as well as my first involvement with the movies, and my first (and only) involvement with radio; and it saw me at ground zero for the end of a legendary Broadway collaboration.

The Sesame Street Book and Record (1970)

When people walk into my home office, the two gold records on the wall always catch their eye. A gold record is a big deal in the music business because it signifies sales of more than half a million copies. That's not so unusual in the pop world, in which many artists have dozens, but in classical music and in Broadway it's very unusual because these parts of the industry serve niche markets—big niches, but still niches.

That's why people are curious when they see my gold records on my studio wall. Most assume one of the Sondheim shows, perhaps *Sweeney Todd* or *Sunday in the Park with George*, or maybe *42nd Street* or *La Cage aux Folles*; or if they're into classical, they may guess it was *Porgy and Bess*, my *Brahms German Requiem* with James Levine and the Chicago Symphony Orchestra, or my all-star *Beethoven's Ninth*. One of my two is predictable, *La Cage aux Folles*. Nobody ever guesses the other one, the best-selling record I've ever produced: *The Sesame Street Book and Record*.

The roots of this one go back to 1966, when Irene was cast in an Off-Broadway show called *The Mad Show*, which was playing only three blocks from where we lived—at the New Theater, on 54th Street and Lexington Avenue. She was brought in to cover for both Carol Morley and Jo Anne Worley, doing four shows a week, two in each of those parts.

The Mad Show was an offshoot of *Mad* magazine, a collection of skits and spoofs with music by Mary Rodgers and lyrics by at least three people, including Stephen Sondheim, who wrote the lyrics for a parody of "The Girl from Ipanema" under an assumed name. The show might not have been an all-time classic, but it was very funny—it ran for 871 performances, which was extremely good for an Off-Broadway show, and it had been recorded and released several years earlier on Columbia Records (not produced by me!).

The music director of *The Mad Show* was Joe Raposo. Joe was a very gifted man: a great arranger, accompanist, music director, and composer—twenty years later he would collaborate with Sheldon Harnick on a musical version of *It's a Wonderful Life*, the classic Frank Capra movie. Joe was a people collector, so when Irene introduced me to him, and he heard what I did for a living, I think he put me into his mental Rolodex as somebody worth remembering.

Flash forward three years to 1969, and Joe was conducting and writing songs for a new children's television show called *Sesame Street*. He wrote "Bein' Green," "C Is for Cookie," and "Sing," which was later recorded by the Carpenters and made it to No. 3 on the Billboard Top 40. Joe was indeed very creative.

One day he telephoned me and said, "Look, the Children's Television Workshop has made a deal with Time-Life for a record of songs from *Sesame Street* to be distributed through the mail. But they haven't yet made a deal for retail sales. Do you think Columbia would be interested?"

I thought we would be. I knew we would be! *Sesame Street* was brand new, still in its first season, but it had great reviews and good ratings, and I had a four-year-old daughter, so of course I'd seen it. It wasn't a perfect match for Columbia because the fact the mail rights had already gone to Time-Life meant we couldn't sell it through the Record Club, but it still was well worth pursuing.

As it turned out, Columbia's children's department was absolutely foaming at the mouth to get their hands on it. *Sesame Street* was hot, and so we sat down with fellow Columbia employee Arthur Shimkin, an unpleasant guy who had worked for Simon & Schuster and had once come up with the idea for the Little Golden Records label for kids. Arthur really wanted this and we agreed that he could pluck singles from our album for Columbia's Children's Department.

We issued two differently-packaged LPs: one was a deluxe version that sold at a higher price, a double-fold album that was an illustrated, annotated book—*The Sesame Street Book and Record*—and the other was released in regular packaging because CTW wanted a version that was affordable for anyone.

The recording sessions were fun because, although I was pretty familiar with *Sesame Street*, I knew only the Muppets I could see on the screen plus a few live people playing human characters on the show. In the recording studio, of course, nobody was in costume, and it was quite striking, hearing these familiar voices coming out of regular human beings.

The recording had only a small orchestra, which we recorded separately. All vocals were then overdubbed, added over the prerecorded orchestra tracks.

Everything went very smoothly, even though most of the people involved didn't know much about making records. I got to know Bob McGrath and Loretta Long, two of the original humans on the show, and also the puppeteers, including Frank Oz—later a successful film director, and of course, the voice and puppeteer of Yoda in the *Star Wars* movies—and Caroll Spinney, who played Big Bird for so long. Joe Raposo's contractor for the orchestra was Danny Epstein, who became a friend and colleague of mine: a few years later, when I wrote the score for the movie *Such Good Friends* and we needed to film a live band on a rooftop, I asked Danny to recruit the players.

I also got to know Jim Henson—creator of the Muppets and the voice of Kermit the Frog—and I actually lost my temper with him, which I don't often do on the job. Jim wanted one more take of one of his vocals, and because we were working with a limited number of tracks, this meant erasing the vocal track he had already made, which I thought was very good. But he insisted, and I had to go along with it—and in my opinion, perhaps we got a more perfect performance but lost some of the charm of the earlier take. Nowadays, of course, that sort of thing never happens because with digital recording you can do a million takes and still have room for one more.

(I'd often dreamed of engendering a new classical work for children in the tradition of "Peter and the Wolf." Columbia Masterworks had the great composer Aaron Copland under contract to conduct his own works. At this stage of his life, he wasn't composing any more. So I thought, "Why don't we introduce him to Jim Henson and see if that inspires him?" So Tom Frost and I took Copland up to Children's Television Workshop, and Jim Henson trotted out all his stuff, including his recently invented Snuffleupagus. Aaron was very attentive and smiling and all, and I was very excited, because I thought perhaps I had made a new team: Copland/Henson, but at the end, Aaron said to Jim, "Well, if you can think of anything for us, let me know." He just wasn't inspired. He lived another seventeen years, but I don't think he ever wrote any more music. It was a wonderful idea to bring these two giants together, but it didn't work.)

That *The Sesame Street Book and Record* was going to be successful was clear from early on. It had been announced in the papers before we'd even made the recording, and an executive from another, smaller record company called me and offered me personally a hundred thousand dollars if I would bring the recording to his label instead of to Columbia. Well, of course I said no, not only for ethical reasons—I would never have double-crossed Columbia—but also the thought of me taking a bribe was preposterous.

This recording also kindled my lifelong friendship with Christopher Cerf, a renaissance man of sorts—songwriter, composer, author, editor, voice actor, television producer, record producer, and more. Chris's work writing songs for *Sesame Street* was still in the future (his credits include the immortal "Put Down the Duckie" and "Dance Myself to Sleep"), but he was already there as a producer, and he and I clicked immediately. Many years later Chris invented *Between the Lions* (2000–2010), the PBS children's-literacy show, and he hired me and several others to write music for the show. So the link that runs from *The Mad Show* through *The Sesame Street Book and Record* extends through *Between the Lions* as well.

The Sesame Street Book and Record did extremely well. Now, this was 1970, when I worked for Columbia and was strictly a salaried employee; I had no royalty agreement. This record sold millions—it's the most successful recording I've ever made—and if I'd gotten just a few pennies on each record sold, I could have retired early!

It was so successful that someone in the pop department said, "Why don't we try issuing 'Rubber Duckie' as a single?" And wonder of wonders, the song (written by Jeff Moss and arranged by Joe Raposo) became a hit single, peaking at No. 16 on the pop chart. Some people credited what were perceived as double entendres in the lyrics, which may or may not be so, but, for whatever reason, it was a hit. Both the single and the album were nominated for the Grammy Award as Best Recording for Children; the album won, but I was OK with either one, since I had produced both.

But for me, there was one snag: The Grammy Awards for a song or an album are usually presented to the artist and to the record's producer. When the Grammy nominations for *The Sesame Street Book and Record* and "Rubber Duckie" came out, however, even though I was credited on the album as its producer, the nominations listed the producer as Joan Ganz Cooney, founder and president of Children's Television Workshop, and she was the one who collected the award, which made me very unhappy, obviously—yes, she did a wonderful thing by creating *Sesame Street*, but she had nothing to do with the making of the album. She wasn't at the session, and to this day I've never met her.

Many years later, though, I became friendly with Michael Greene, who was president of the organization that presents the Grammys (then the National Academy of Recording Arts and Sciences or NARAS, since then renamed the Recording Academy). I happened to mention my grievance, and he looked into it and said to me, "Yeah, you're right, that isn't fair." He was able to make it up to me, and that's how I got my twelfth Grammy, long after the record had been released.

The Year of Roosevelt Franklin (1971)

The success of *The Sesame Street Book and Record* led to a spinoff album. A year or so later, I got a call from Matt Robinson, who played Gordon on the show and voiced Roosevelt Franklin, a Black Muppet character who often spoke in verse. He wanted to do an album based on Roosevelt Franklin.

Well, the first recording had been so successful that we didn't have to be sold very hard, so the next year I produced the recording of *The Year of Roosevelt Franklin*, again in cooperation with CTW. Matt Robinson had worked out the whole album, and he and Joe Raposo had written all the songs. Roosevelt's mother, also a character on *Sesame Street*, was also on the album. Loretta Long, who played Susan on the show, also voiced Roosevelt's mother and his sister, Mary Frances, but Matt decided that on the album she should be replaced by Rosalind Cash.

For such a cute album, it sold very poorly. It was reissued in 1974 as *My Name Is Roosevelt Franklin*, but I don't think it did any better. However, it was the first of many records centered on specific characters from *Sesame Street*, so in that way at least it had an impact.

Bob and Ray: The Two and Only (1970)

The number two was big for me in 1970, with two recordings that featured that number in their titles. The first was *Bob and Ray: The Two and Only*. This was a very unusual record for me, but then it was a very unusual show for Broadway.

Bob Elliott and Ray Goulding were gleeful anachronisms, even in 1970. They had met in 1946 at the Boston radio station WHDH, where Elliott was a disc jockey and Goulding a newsreader. They had a lot in common—they were both Boston-area natives and newly returned veterans of World War II—so after Goulding had read the news on Elliott's show, he'd occasionally linger in the studio and goof around with Elliott on the air. Their senses of humor were similar, so they'd improvise brief skits satirizing radio commercials, soap operas, pompous newscasters, and other conventions of radio, which in those days was still the biggest media presence in American society.

It turned out listeners loved their byplay, and soon WHDH offered them their own radio show, *Matinee with Bob and Ray*, on weekday mornings. (Their professional name was "Bob and Ray" because "Ray" and "Matinee" rhymed; if their show had been on in the afternoon, Goulding used to joke, it would have been called *On the Job with Ray and Bob*, and he would have had top billing for the next forty-five years.)

They continued to play records and give the news, but it was their improvised comedy sketches the listeners loved best, sketches in which they'd do a myriad of characters, voicing all of them themselves. *Matinee with Bob and Ray*, originally fifteen minutes, soon turned into a half-hour show and then, after NBC bought out their contracts, went national. By this time there was no question Bob and Ray were a radio comedy team, in the tradition of Burns and Allen, Amos 'n' Andy, or Lum and Abner.

Radio was on its way out, however, superseded by television, and most radio stars were transitioning to the new medium. The two landed their own NBC show, *Bob & Ray* (1951–1953), which featured first Audrey Meadows and then Cloris Leachman playing the female roles (usually voiced on the radio by Goulding).

Television wasn't suited to the Bob & Ray vibe, though, because it discouraged improvisation and didn't allow the two to play several different roles in the same sketch, limiting their comic possibilities. While they would occasionally be seen on television after the cancellation of *Bob & Ray*, the two returned full-time to radio, where they built a fan base passionate enough to support them, even as the golden age of radio fizzled out, leaving them practically the only comedians left on a medium increasingly devoted to music, sports, and news (all of which, naturally, they spoofed relentlessly).

That fan base was passionate enough to justify a Broadway show called *Bob & Ray: The Two and Only*, in which Elliott and Goulding essentially performed their radio act for a live audience paying Broadway ticket prices for something they could listen to for free at home. Don't laugh—the show ran for two weeks of previews and then 138 performances, making it a solid hit and (given its cast and writers together totaled two people) made it almost certainly, in terms of return on investment, the most profitable Broadway show of the 1970–1971 season.

Among those passionate fans was Bruce Lundvall, who was vice president of marketing at Columbia Records. He went to see the show, and as soon as he saw it, decided we should record it. The responsibility of doing so fell to me.

Needless to say, this wasn't like any cast album I'd ever made, or ever would make again. I was used to dealing with a big room packed with actors, chorus members, and orchestra musicians, plus a legion of orchestrators, copyists, conductors, playwrights, music directors, directors, producers, and hangers-on of all descriptions. When the team from *Bob and Ray: The Two and Only* arrived at the session, they were, well, director Joe Hardy was there, so call them the three and only.

I was also used to dealing with people who were out of their element. Most people involved in musical theater spend their days in rehearsal halls and their nights either onstage or in an orchestra pit. They get to know those surroundings very well and develop routines with which they're very comfortable. When they suddenly find themselves in a studio they've never seen before, with rows of mikes, miles of cable, no sets, no costumes, no lights, and no audience, they're very much off their native turf. This makes most of them tentative and some of them insecure and difficult, as they try to figure out how to translate what they normally do into the new, sound-only language of the studio.

Bob and Ray, on the other hand, were sound-only veterans, two guys who had been sitting next to each other and talking into mikes practically every day since I was ten years old, and they didn't need a record producer to tell them how to do their job. To a considerable extent, all we had to do was to turn on a couple of mikes and let them talk. Nonetheless, I feel I did contribute something important to what turned out to be a fine recording.

Normally my preference is to have as few people as possible in the studio on a recording session. After all, every person in the room is a sneeze, a stumble, or a distraction waiting to happen. Unavoidably, a big show or a classical orchestra requires a lot of people in the room, but even then, I do my best to keep it to a minimum. Less, as they say, is more.

For *The Two and Only*, though, I decided more would be more. It's tough doing comedy in an empty room because, without people laughing, it's hard to tell if you're being funny. Bob and Ray had, of course, been doing comedy in empty radio studios for the past twenty-five years, but they'd been doing this material every night for a theater full of people, and I knew—professionals or not—they'd feel the absence of laughter in the studio, and it was bound to affect their performances.

So for the recording session, which, for Broadway, was usually held on a Sunday, I brought in an invited audience of roughly fifty, most of them Columbia Records staff. We set up chairs in rows and had a full buffet for a Sunday brunch. Joe Hardy re-created, as much as possible, the set used on the stage, and they'd brought the props and the recorded sound effects they used in the theater, so it was like a command performance of the show for a private audience. And it was a very receptive, friendly audience, so the laughs were where they needed to be—the laughter you hear on the recording is the studio audience, not a laugh track—and Bob and Ray were obviously immediately at ease.

The recording went very well. All I had to do was see to it that everything went as planned, and it did. There were probably a half dozen retakes of a few minor sections, but basically what you hear on the recording is the show in its original continuity. I've never had a recording session go so quickly and so smoothly, and I doubt I ever will again.

One nice touch about the LP, which unfortunately is lost on the CD, was the way we opened the second side. The first side ends with one of the classic Bob and Ray routines, "Slow Talkers of America," in which Ray is trying to interview a guy, played by Bob, who represents an organization of people who talk very slowly. The humor comes from Ray getting increasingly frustrated and trying to finish Bob's sentences for him, which Bob won't let him do. So we faded out on the slow talker—but when we began the second side, he was still droning on. What a great place for a side break.

(The placement of side breaks was a major consideration when producing an LP because it represents a pause and a break in the rhythm of the record, as the listener must flip the record over to continue listening. With show records, of course, the ideal moment for the side break was at the end of the first act. It was always frustrating when, because one act ran significantly longer than the other, or the first act ended on an unusually long number, the side break had to be placed before or after the act break. Fortunately, such instances were very rare.)

I had very little communication with Bob and Ray during the session because I didn't need to. They'd been doing some of these routines for twenty-five years, and they knew what they were doing. You have to know when not to interfere. They had their act, they had their timing, and all we had to do was leave them alone, so that's what I did. It's a good album. I think it delivers the show very nicely.

The Rothschilds (1970)

Oscar Hammerstein died in 1960, the same year Fritz Loewe retired from Broadway, so by 1970 Jerry Bock and Sheldon Harnick were the most celebrated Broadway songwriting team. Their only real rivals were John Kander and Fred Ebb, who hadn't yet written *Chicago*, whose 1996 revival is the second-longest-running musical in Broadway history. As of 1970 they hadn't yet produced a hit on the scale of Bock & Harnick's *Fiddler on the Roof* (1964). *Fiddler* was a generational work, one whose impact extends far beyond its original record-breaking run of nearly ten years, its hit film adaptation, and its frequent revivals across the ensuing decades.

Composer Jerry Bock and lyricist Sheldon Harnick first met in 1956. Their first musical, *The Body Beautiful* (1958), was a flop, but their second, *Fiorello!* (1959), was a runaway hit that earned them not only the Tony Award as Best Musical (shared with *The Sound of Music*) but also the Pulitzer Prize in Drama, an honor only nine other musicals have ever received. They went on to another hit, the charming *She Loves Me* (1963), which followed on the heels of the innovative-but-unappreciated musical *The Man in the Moon* (1963), which teamed them with puppeteer Bil Baird. *The Man in the Moon* had opened less than two weeks before *She Loves Me*—but nonetheless closed before *She Loves Me* opened.

Following the monumental success of *Fiddler on the Roof*, Bock & Harnick went in a different direction for *The Apple Tree* (1966), an anthology show featuring three one-acts based on stories by Mark Twain, Frank R. Stockton, and Jules Feiffer. It was much smaller in scale than *Fiddler* but was a substantial hit, running for 463 performances.

I had worked with Jerry and Sheldon's material when they contributed a few songs to the World's Fair revue *To Broadway with Love*, but hadn't gotten to know either of them—and of course, they had grown immensely in prestige in the intervening six years. They came into *The Rothschilds* as dual titans of Broadway, and I relished the chance to work on a new Bock & Harnick show. Little did I know it would be their last.

I almost didn't get to do the recording at all. When I first heard the score, I liked it, but I didn't jump up and down with joy, and the producer of the show, Hillard Elkins, became convinced I didn't like it—which was not true at all—and thus he didn't want me to produce the recording. I didn't know this at the time, but apparently he complained to Clive and Goddard, objecting to me being assigned the show. To their credit, they had my back: they calmed Hilly down, and I kept the assignment.

The Rothschilds is a complicated show, with a large cast and a book that spans forty-six years and most of Europe. It was a modest hit—it ran for 505 performances—but was no rival to *Fiddler on the Roof*. Nothing would be, of course: *Fiddler* was its own separate phenomenon, and it was unfair (though unavoidable) that it should be the yardstick used to judge everything else Jerry or Sheldon would do, together or separately, for the rest of their lives.

With a complicated show, generally the right approach to the recording is to keep things simple—you don't want to make the show any more difficult for listeners to follow. The only trick I can remember bringing to bear is that I asked the stage crew of the show to bring the prop rifles to the recording session: there's a distinctive sound when a rifle is cocked, and that's the sound I wanted for one scene. I also manipulated the sound quality for the town crier, making sure he sounded "outdoors" when he's announcing curfew, ringing the bell for the Jews to get back into the ghetto.

But mostly, as I say, I kept the approach simple, and the recording sessions were very smooth. It was a great cast. Hal Linden made a wonderful Mayer Rothschild. The rest of the cast was equally excellent, including all ten of the five sons (they were played by boys in the early scenes and by men later). One of the grown-up sons, Amshel Rothschild, was played by Tim Jerome, who became a good friend and with whom I've worked (and whom I've occasionally hired!) many times over the years.

The score was as good as anything Bock & Harnick had ever done. And of course it featured a Bock & Harnick hallmark: an extremely energetic, optimistic, and infectious song for a male principal. In *Fiddler on the Roof* it's "Wonder of Wonders, Miracle of Miracles," in *She Loves Me* it's the title song, and in *The Rothschilds* it was "I'm in Love! I'm in Love!," sung by Paul Hecht as Nathan. For me this song is one of the high points of *The Rothschilds*.

It's a heavily male show, with no chorus girls and—except for Leila Martin as Gutele Rothschild, and in the second act, Jill Clayburgh as Hannah Cohen—no other women. There's only one female solo in the show, and it's a reprise. But the men were great, and the show was exceptional. We already felt, when we were making the recording, that it was going to be a limited success: it had gotten mixed notices, and it wasn't filling the theater every night. But it was a show of such quality, with such wonderful songs, and it was satisfying for me to record it.

After the recording was done, I got a couple of very nice notes from people in the cast. I also got one from Jerry Bock, which particularly pleased me. They were extremely nice letters, and I sent the one from Jerry on to Clive and Goddard, with a little note from me saying, "I'm not used to blowing my own horn like this, but I thought you should see what these guys said." And Goddard sent a note to Clive saying, "Send this to Elkins." I don't know if Clive sent it or not.

If anyone had told me then I'd just worked on the last Bock & Harnick show, I'd have thought they were crazy, but that turned out to be the case. Jerry and Sheldon had made a very effective effort to keep people from sensing what was going on between them—but by the time we made this recording, I think they both knew that their partnership was over. They did get together one more time, to write a piece of special material, a new song, for a revival of *Fiddler on the Roof* some years later, but the partnership really ended with *The Rothschilds*.

The cause, apparently, was the firing of *The Rothschilds*'s original director, Derek Goldby, who was replaced by Michael Kidd while the show was previewing out of town. In production discussions the songwriters usually try to speak in one voice, but apparently Sheldon and Jerry disagreed on the change, and there were some meetings Jerry wasn't in on, and it drove a wedge between them that couldn't be overcome.

Writing and staging a show is a hugely stressful enterprise, and tempers flare daily. But most of the time, particularly if the show turns out to be a hit, people put those resentments behind them. In this case they couldn't, and a legendary partnership was ruined. Jerry lived another forty years and Sheldon another fifty-three, and we'll never know what they might have done together if it hadn't been for this quarrel.

It's rare for a session to be actively unpleasant. *The Decline and Fall of the Entire World as Seen Through the Eyes of Cole Porter* was one, *42nd Street* would be another, but by and large these people are professionals, and they maintain a professional tone. But there are occasional times—*Pacific Overtures* would be another one, a few years later—when everything just seems to flow, and whatever hitches may come up along the way, they're resolved with ease and a kind of good-natured optimism that nothing is really going to go wrong. *The Rothschilds* was one of those experiences. Whether *The Rothschilds* was a big hit, a semi-hit, or not a hit at all, a Bock & Harnick show was a prestigious project, and it meant a lot to me.

On a personal level, of course, the most important aspect of the recording may have been that it cemented my lifelong friendship with Sheldon Harnick. *To Broadway with Love* came and went, but we really started to bond during *The Rothschilds*. Sheldon was one of the closest people in my life, outside of my immediate family. Sheldon and Margie, Irene and me, we were good friends for more than half a century.

He would come to our apartment on 54th Street with his violin, and we would play chamber music together. Just for fun, I made (and still have) recordings of us playing Mozart and Brahms violin-and-piano sonatas. They're not stellar performances, but they're quite good, and we had a wonderful time. It's one of the ironies of theater that Sheldon, a lyricist, was a person who loved music passionately, who played music for the sheer pleasure of it and was, in fact, a very good composer himself.

And I was pleased to be able to help him in various ways. Back in 1961 he had written a show called *Smiling, the Boy Fell Dead*, with music by David Baker, and many years later he was doing something with it, and it turned out the sheet music for the show couldn't be found. He needed the whole thing recreated by ear, working from a recording of the show. I spent months listening and listening to the recording, transcribing every note, and then later he asked me to orchestrate it, which I did.

I would do this twice more for him, once on his adaptation of Norman Juster's book *The Phantom Tollbooth*, with music by Arnold Black, and again in 2012 for a one-man version of the adaptation of *A Christmas Carol* that Sheldon had done back in 1981 with composer Michel LeGrand.

All of that is in addition to two one-act operas we wrote together, his words and my music: *That Pig of a Molette* (1988) and *A Question of Faith* (1990). Those were great projects, and I was thrilled when they were presented in New York by Musical Theater Works in 1991.

So Sheldon and I were collaborators, in one form or another, ever since we finished the cast album of *The Rothschilds*.

Two by Two (1970)

The number two was back—twice—with this show, which brought me face to face with two of my lifelong heroes.

Clive Davis was in charge of Columbia Records in 1970, which meant he was in charge of Masterworks, but, surprisingly, he was not in charge of all the Broadway cast recordings. Goddard Lieberson may have been kicked upstairs, but there were still certain Broadway people with whom he had long-lasting relationships, and if those people were doing business with Columbia, Goddard was the person they wanted to work with. And one of those people was Richard Rodgers.

Other than Irving Berlin, there was no more legendary figure in the world of Broadway musicals in 1970 than Richard Rodgers. He and lyricist Lorenz Hart had written some of the most sparkling musicals of the years before World War II, and then—after Hart's alcoholism rendered him unable to continue and led to his death in 1943—Rodgers had teamed with a new lyricist, Oscar Hammerstein II, to redefine the Broadway musical and take it to heights of popularity it had never before experienced. All the great Broadway musical creators of the 1950s and 1960s—Lerner & Loewe, Frank Loesser, Jerry Herman, Bock & Harnick, Kander & Ebb—had been profoundly influenced by Rodgers & Hart, and especially by Rodgers & Hammerstein. Richard Rodgers was an icon.

The difference between him and Berlin was that, while Berlin had been retired for years by 1970, Rodgers was still very much a creative force on Broadway. Oscar Hammerstein had retired after *The Sound of Music* (1959) and died the following year, but Rodgers had no intention of retiring, and while he continued to oversee the legacy he'd created with Hart and Hammerstein, he also continued to create new shows.

That said, the 1960s hadn't been a productive decade for Rodgers. He had been unable to find a new collaborator on a par with Hart or Hammerstein—he'd been remarkably fortunate to find two such lyricists because most songwriters are lucky to find one great partner—and he'd done only three new shows in the 1960s, as opposed to six in the 1950s. He'd written his own lyrics for *No Strings* (1962) and the television musical *Androcles and the Lion* (1967), and had collaborated with Hammerstein protégé Stephen Sondheim on *Do I Hear a Waltz?* (1965). None of those shows was a hit, and in 1970 he returned to Broadway with a new lyricist, Martin Charnin, for an adaptation of the Noah's Ark story called *Two by Two*.

I had met Rodgers before, back in 1965. Goddard was doing the cast recording for the television remake of the Rodgers & Hammerstein TV musical *Cinderella*, and after they'd done the session, it turned out they needed to have a track overdubbed, with Stuart Damon, as the prince, singing "Loneliness of Evening." Goddard had other commitments, so he asked me to handle the session—which I was happy to do because it gave me a chance to meet Richard Rodgers. It was also a thrill to meet Johnny Green, the conductor, who was a jack of all musical trades—conductor, composer, arranger, music director—but was best known as the conductor of such iconic film musicals as *An American in Paris*, *West Side Story*, and *Oliver!*. But I really hadn't had anything to do on that session. I'd had no input at all—they just needed somebody to be there with the recording engineer.

That wouldn't be the case for whomever produced *Two by Two*, which was a new Broadway show and would be getting a full-fledged original-cast album. But I had no expectation it would fall to me, even after I heard Columbia was going to release the album. Goddard's history with Rodgers was well known, and I assumed he'd be producing the album.

However, one day Goddard, now on the 52nd floor with an office next to William Paley, called me in and explained that, because of his new responsibilities at Columbia, it wasn't practical for him to produce *Two by Two*.

"Look," he told me, "I've reached the point where, if I say yes to one composer and no to another, it's going to set up bad feelings."

So he wanted me to do it, which of course I was more than willing to do. And he'd called me in to say he wanted me to come with him to a meeting with Rodgers and Charnin, a couple of days later, where he'd tell Rodgers he couldn't do the show and would officially introduce me to him and Martin Charnin—thereby giving me his stamp of approval, so to speak.

Now, this was no ordinary meeting, and while I'd produced a good number of Broadway cast albums by then, this was the biggest show I'd ever been offered—it was a Richard Rodgers show, so by definition it was huge—and I very much wanted to make a good impression. I wanted to show Rodgers and Charnin, and Goddard too, their project would be in good hands with me. So I prepared scrupulously. Learning that *Two by Two* was based on a Clifford Odets play called *The Flowering Peach* (1954), I got my hands on a copy of the abbreviated script and read it, familiarizing myself with the story of the show.

Everybody knows the story of Noah's Ark, of course, but the real story of this play, and of the musical, is about the conflict between Noah and his rebellious son, Japheth (which, since I was only reading it, I thought was pronounced "JAH-feth," though I learned later it was actually "JAY-feth"). Odets had turned Noah and his family into an old-fashioned Jewish family with a rebellious teenage son—and in 1970 every family knew what it was like to have a rebellious teenager!

So two days later, Goddard invited me to ride with him in his limo to the meeting, which would be held at the office of the Rodgers & Hammerstein Organization. (The Rodgers & Hammerstein Organization was and still is a major force on Broadway, administering the copyrights of the Rodgers & Hart and Rodgers & Hammerstein canons, as well as *Show Boat* and many other musicals.)

The ride over gave me the chance to tell Goddard I had read *The Flowering Peach*, and I gave him a rundown on the story as we headed downtown. He didn't say whether he was familiar with it or not, but I suspect he wasn't because he never corrected my pronunciation of "Japheth." And I explained one of the key plot points, which is that Noah and Japheth argue over whether the ark needs a rudder, with Japheth (who is a very rebellious but practical young man) arguing that every ship needs a rudder, and Noah insisting that, even without a rudder, the ark will survive because it's under God's protection. They have a big fight over this, and Noah rips the rudder off the ark; but in the end, as they're about to go down in a storm, Noah says, "Japheth, put back the rudder." And the ark is saved because Noah, who's a stubborn old man, has come to understand that his son may have a point after all.

So we got to the meeting, and Goddard introduced me as the one who'd be producing the record. Rodgers and Charnin were probably surprised, but they accepted it, and we sat down to listen to them explain the plot. And when they were talking about removing the rudder from the ark, Goddard threw in, "Well, doesn't Japheth put it back?" And Rodgers looked at him and said, "Oh, Goddard, you're just showing off."

And that was amazing to me because Rodgers couldn't have realized it, but I knew it was actually true. Goddard hadn't known this at all, it was something he'd learned from me in the car on the way over. I kept myself from laughing, but it was a funny moment.

Rodgers was very businesslike, and in three recordings I did with him, he raised his voice only once. There are some creative people who want to be active participants in the recording, but Rodgers wasn't one of them. He chose people he trusted to make his recordings, and very seldom got involved. He was always in a three-piece suit, looking more like a banker than a composer, and he sat in the control room, listened to what was going on, and said very little. What he said, though, you listened to—he was a sophisticated, well-spoken, and highly educated man who had been at the center of America's cultural life for a half-century.

So of course I was very sensitive to his reactions on the *Two by Two* recording session, watching him out of the corner of my eye, and since he didn't say anything, I could only assume that he was pleased with the way the recording went.

Rodgers wasn't the only one of my heroes involved in this show, though. To play Noah, he and the producers had lured Danny Kaye back to Broadway for the first time since *Lady in the Dark* in 1941. I had been a huge Danny Kaye fan from the time I was a kid, knowing by heart his famous patter songs like "Anatole of Paris" and "Tchaikovsky," and it's a mark of honor to me if a man can recite Kaye's "pellet with the poison" routine from *The Court Jester* (1955). So I was very gratified by the idea of meeting and working with him.

I went up to New Haven, where *Two by Two* was in early rehearsals, weeks before the previews began, and they were still blocking some of it. One of the producers introduced me to the cast, including Kaye, and then I went out into the auditorium to watch. A routine in which Kaye didn't appear was being worked on, and he came out into the house and sat down next to me.

And he said, "Will you look at those fucking kalyakes?" That's a Yiddish word—a kalyake is a fool, a klutz, or a combination of both. He was criticizing the other people in the cast, but I didn't yet know him or them, so I didn't say anything.

Kaye was notoriously difficult to work with, prickly, sensitive, insecure, and demanding. He insisted on being treated like the star he was. That was certainly the case during the production of *Two by Two*: he got bored with doing the same show every night—he hadn't been onstage in almost thirty years—and started improvising a lot of his dialogue, lyrics, and music, frequently talking to the audience, and even criticizing the performances of his costars. This amused some people in the audience but offended others, not to mention his fellow actors, and of course, the author and composer of the show. In his autobiography, *Musical Stages*, Rodgers didn't hide his disdain for Kaye and his improvisation, noting, "He began improvising his own lines and singing in the wrong tempos. He even made a curtain speech after the performances in which he said, 'I'm glad you're here, but I'm glad the authors aren't.'"

A couple months after he made our recording, Kaye was doing an improvised dance when he fell and tore a tendon in his leg. For months afterward—supposedly long after the tendon had healed—he played the younger Noah on crutches and the older Noah in a wheelchair, integrating the crutches and the wheelchair into his improvisation, chasing other actors around the stage, and according to Rodgers, using a crutch to goose the girls. None of this went down well with his fellow actors.

I hasten to add that I saw no signs of this on the recording session. Kaye was on time; he was prepared, and he took care of business. I am told by other people who were present that day that Kaye often muttered under his breath, and after I would make a comment or suggestion, he'd mutter, "Kiss my ass." If that's true, he was quiet enough that I never heard him.

He did no improvising in the recording—in fact, when Kaye altered a line, he readily corrected it at my request. But I think I pissed him off. The song "Two by Two" includes the line, "It's catchy, no?" And on the session Kaye said, "It's funny, isn't it?" It wasn't necessarily a significant alteration, of course, but this was for posterity, so I wanted it exactly right. I went on the talkback and said to him, "Would you please put back the words that you did in the show?" Which he did, but I think he was surprised that anybody would even have noticed, let alone called attention to it.

But he didn't make a big deal out of it. Throughout the session, whether or not he was muttering behind my back, he was entirely cooperative when it counted. This isn't too surprising: I've worked with many performers who are famously difficult and found them to be fine to work with. The reason, I think, is I'm not meeting them on their turf, they're meeting me on mine. Danny Kaye had made some records, of course, but it wasn't something he knew well, so he went along with the people who knew what they were doing.

Although he wasn't adversarial on the session, Kaye was nevertheless self-contained, aloof. He didn't mingle with the rest of the company, he didn't mix. He kept to himself. Possibly he was just nervous about recording, because at the end of the session he loosened up a great deal. Rodgers's birthday happened to be around the time of the session, and Charnin had written a parody verse for one of the songs in the show. After we were through, Kaye sang it, and we recorded it as a birthday gift for Rodgers. It was the end of the day, and things can get looser at the end of the day.

Rodgers was essentially happy with the session and he said very little. Once he went out into the studio to talk to Madeline Kahn about the way she was singing a phrase in "The Golden Ram"; I'm not sure what he wanted her to change because it was a private conversation. But otherwise he stayed in the control room next to me and said very little.

He and Kaye came to my office right after I'd finished editing and mixing the recording, and I played it for them. They were completely happy with it and both in very good moods. They presented me with a picture of the two of them, which they'd both autographed to me.

I thought Madeline Kahn was terrific. So were Marilyn Cooper, Harry Goz, and most particularly, Joan Copeland, who played Esther, Noah's wife. It was a wonderful cast, and the songs had a lot of charm. There were also some chances for me to have fun when I was later doing the mixing on the recording: in the title song, for instance, the animals come marching onto the ark, which onstage was done with pictures of the animals, but when we were mixing the edited tapes, I laid my hands on some animal recordings—I don't even remember now where they came from—and I had so much fun putting in what sounded like elephants, tigers, lions, and God knows what else.

I really liked this show, although it was only a modest success. Peter Stone did the book, and there were some weaknesses there; but the music was wonderful, and Martin Charnin's lyrics were beautifully crafted.

Martin also played the thunder sheet on the recording. I don't know how it was done in the show, if it was done by a member of the orchestra or played offstage by a stagehand, but Martin decided he wanted to do this himself—which is very important because, in the first number of the show, the thunder represents the voice of God talking to Noah and therefore God's thunderous responses had to be carefully crafted.

If there was ever anybody I just gravitated toward, simply because I so much enjoyed his company, it was Martin. We went back a long way—years before, when Charlie Burr and I had written a revue called "Blaming It on You" based on group therapy, we went through a host of producers. Martin took a great interest in it and worked with us on it for a while. The last time we worked together was in 2013, on the cast album for the 2012 revival of *Annie*.

He died in 2019. I remember once sitting with Martin at an audition for a new revue that included a very mean-spirited parody of Stephen Sondheim. We both knew and liked Steve, of course, but we started laughing, the two of us, because the parody was in a way so accurate, but so mean, and I don't think I've ever laughed so hard or so long in my life.

Although I don't often go back to see the shows I've recorded, simply because I've spent so much time on them before the session that I'm sated, but I did return to see *Two by Two*. I wanted to take my daughter, who was about four years old at the time and was already coming with me to previews and recording sessions. Elizabeth really liked the recording of *Two by Two* and had memorized all the songs. We were sitting very close to the stage, in the second or third row center, and she was wonderfully well-behaved, but apparently she was mouthing all the words because I remember Joan Copeland looking down and catching her at it. I think she winked at us. Elizabeth really did know every word on the recording; she may have known Joan's songs as well as Joan did.

The capper for me, though, came some months later, when I was taking Elizabeth out to Central Park to ride her bicycle. We were crossing 59th Street, and we ran into Dick and Dorothy Rodgers, who were then living, I believe, at the Sherry-Netherland. And they said to me, "Hi, Tom!" And I said, "Hi, Dick! Hi, Dorothy!"

That was all there was to it, we went our separate ways. But I couldn't help thinking, "I ran into Richard and Dorothy Rodgers, and they both said hello to me. I've arrived! I now belong in the world of Broadway."

In recounting my remarkable 1970, though, I've intentionally left out what was undoubtedly the most consequential project I tackled that year. It didn't earn me a gold record, and it didn't mark the end of a legendary Broadway partnership, but it introduced me to the creative artist with whom I would do more show recordings than any other, launching a collaboration which, I'm fairly sure, will figure in the first sentence of my eventual obituary: the record was the original-cast album for a Broadway musical called *Company*, and the person was a songwriter named Stephen Sondheim.

16

"Mr. Shepard, Mr. Sondheim"

LONG BEFORE I'D STARTED RECORDING BROADWAY SHOWS, I knew who Stephen Sondheim was. Everybody who cared about Broadway knew who Sondheim was. Though only six years older than I was, he was already one of Broadway's most admired creators by the time I started at Columbia.

Born in New York City, Sondheim was the only child of a largely absent father and a difficult mother who divorced when he was ten. At that time he and his mother moved to Doylestown, Pennsylvania—not as far from Broadway as one might have thought: their neighbors included Oscar Hammerstein II, and Sondheim had become friends with Hammerstein's son, James. He soon developed a close relationship with the elder Hammerstein, who became a friend, mentor, and surrogate father to him.

This relationship fueled a fascination with both music and theater that had been kindled in Sondheim by frequent visits to the theater during his early years. Hammerstein's insightful critiques of Sondheim's early work helped shape him as an artist: after reading a musical the young man had written for his prep school, Hammerstein famously told him it was the worst thing he'd ever read—"but if you want to know why it's terrible, I'll tell you."

"In that afternoon," Sondheim later told a biographer, "I learned more about songwriting and the musical theater than most people learn in a lifetime."

Hammerstein's connections in New York theater also helped his protégé start his career with a bang: *West Side Story* would be one more brilliant feather in the cap of composer Leonard Bernstein and would make the Broadway careers of his three collaborators: playwright Arthur Laurents, choreographer Jerome Robbins, and lyricist Stephen Sondheim. Sondheim would have liked to write both music and lyrics; but when he was offered the job as lyricist alone, Hammerstein advised him to get a foot in the door however he could: once he had a hit or two under his belt, he could write his own music as well.

(Broadway composer/lyricists such as George M. Cohan, Irving Berlin, and Cole Porter had once been fairly common. By the late 1950s, however, they were an endangered species, with only Frank Loesser and Harold Rome still active. In the Broadway world of the 1970s and 1980s, Sondheim and Jerry Herman would be the only major composer/lyricists, though in the 1990s and 2000s Sondheim would mentor a later generation—notably *Rent* creator Jonathan Larson.)

His second show, *Gypsy* (1959), again teaming him with Laurents and Robbins, was another smash. Sondheim was originally asked to write the score for *Gypsy*, but he was still a novice on the Broadway scene—and Ethel Merman, a major star, was unwilling to put herself in the hands of an untried composer. Veteran composer Jule Styne would fill that role, and Merman accepted Sondheim as the lyricist on the strength of *West Side Story*.

As Hammerstein had predicted, Sondheim was able to leverage the success of those shows into a job writing both music and lyrics for *A Funny Thing Happened on the Way to the Forum* (1962), which wound up running longer than either *West Side Story* or *Gypsy*. In fact, its 964 performances would turn out to be the longest run of Sondheim's career.

Despite that success, however, Sondheim's talent and box-office appeal as a composer were still widely questioned. Conventional wisdom held that *Forum* was essentially a showcase for its cast of comedians, especially the great Zero Mostel as Pseudolus. Its success was not attributed to Sondheim the composer, though Sondheim the lyricist was generally conceded to have done a fine job.

Personally, I think *A Funny Thing Happened on the Way to the Forum* is a brilliant score, absolutely wonderful, and highly sophisticated. A few years ago I did a lecture on Sondheim at Yale University, and some people were surprised I spent as much time as I did talking about *Forum*, but I think this is a sadly underrated score, full of beautiful melodies and clever musical touches. "Pretty Little Picture," for example, is an utterly charming song, with clever lyrics, wonderful music, and some revealing character touches for Pseudolus, who sings it. I'm baffled that it's sometimes omitted in revivals—I love it, and from the moment I first heard it, I knew that independent of his talents as a lyricist, Steve Sondheim was a very skilled, very gifted composer.

That said, the remainder of the 1960s was not kind to Sondheim. His next show as composer and lyricist was *Anyone Can Whistle* (1964), a quirky show that—despite starring Angela Lansbury in her first Broadway role—proved to be a massive flop, running for only nine performances. *Do I Hear a Waltz?* (1965), which teamed him with composer Richard Rodgers, ran for 220 performances but still lost money, and given the pedigree of its songwriters, was considered a conspicuous flop.

Sondheim returned to writing both music and lyrics on his next project, a backstage musical about a showgirls' reunion called *The Girls Upstairs*. Although he and playwright James Goldman bogged down and gave up on the show, it would later be resurrected as *Follies* and would, a couple of decades later, be a major event in my life and career. In 1966 he and Goldman teamed for *Evening Primrose* (1966), a little-noticed musical episode of the anthology television series *ABC Stage 67*. An attempted reunion with Robbins and Bernstein (adding playwright John Guare) for an adaptation of Bertolt Brecht's *The Exception and the Rule* foundered due to problems among the collaborators and Sondheim's general dislike of the project.

Now there were good reasons why those particular projects didn't work out. *Anyone Can Whistle* has some wonderful songs, but Laurents's book is eccentric and complicated. The teaming of Rodgers and Sondheim for *Do I Hear a Waltz?* was a terrible idea from the beginning because the two men's goals were so different: Sondheim was interested in creating an entirely new approach to musical theater, whereas the sixty-three-year-old Rodgers, who had led one such revolution with Oscar Hammerstein and *Oklahoma!*, was in no mood to mount the barricades again more than twenty years later. The collaboration with Goldman was a problematic one that for its first fifteen years looked like a failure. As for *The Exception and the Rule*, Sondheim had agreed only reluctantly to work with Bernstein again—not because they didn't get along but because he was determined to set his own lyrics.

Nonetheless, Broadway was and is a commercial business, and in commercial terms Sondheim's career was on the skids by 1970. It had been eight years since his last hit, with nothing in the intervening years but two flops and a couple of projects that never even made it to opening night. It was easy for people to wonder if they'd already seen the best of Stephen Sondheim.

Company (1970)

When I was assigned to produce the original-cast album for *Company*, I quickly realized I'd never seen a show like this before. Nobody had.

For the past century or more, most Broadway musicals have fallen into one of two categories: the book musical and the revue. A revue was an old-style entertainment, like a vaudeville show that, instead of featuring a new show every few days or weeks, as a vaudeville theater did, might run for months in a legitimate theater. It featured an assortment of self-contained, usually comic sketches, many of which included a song or songs. There was no overall plot and there were no continuing characters. Often the contents of a particular revue would change during its run, which was almost unheard of with a book musical except for changes immediately after opening night. When you saw a revue, you knew it.

The revue's popularity persisted through the 1930s, but gradually it was supplanted by the book musical, which added the elements of singing and dancing to a straightforward story, often adapted from a novel or a nonmusical play. Book musicals began as light comedies such as Rodgers & Hart's *The Boys from Syracuse* or Cole Porter's *Anything Goes*, but gradually evolved into comedy-dramas such as *South Pacific* or *Fiddler on the Roof*. A tragic musical such as *West Side Story* was quite rare. Book musicals had become more ambitious after *Show Boat*, but they hadn't strayed far from that template. And again, when you saw a book musical, you knew it.

Company, directed by Harold Prince with a book by George Furth and a score by Sondheim, was a horse of a different color. Instead of a linear plot following its characters from conflict to resolution, it offered a series of vignettes, not necessarily in chronological order, and with only one unifying character: Bobby (Dean Jones), a thirty-five-year-old single man who dates one attractive woman after another, but resolutely refuses to open up to any of them. His friends are five married couples, all of whom are convinced he needs real love in his life—but he's basically rootless and unconnected, living for himself alone. Over the course of the show, which presents multiple views of marriage and married love, he comes to realize the emptiness of his apparently carefree bachelor existence. In the show's finale Bobby sings "Being Alive," a paean to the risks and the rewards of openness to other people, and especially, openness to love.

It was a complicated show, with grown-up themes and a biting wit that was a world away from the tradition of Rodgers & Hammerstein; but the songs were so great, the performances so good, and the book so sharp that it overcame mixed reviews (and the departure of its star after only a month) to run for 705 performances.

The question was, how could we shape this unique show to fit the unforgiving constraints of an original-cast album?

It was an important question to me because we all knew that this was no ordinary show. We couldn't have anticipated everything that lay ahead for Sondheim, nor predicted *Company*'s revolutionary effect on the Broadway musical, but I could certainly tell that this was the most important show I'd tackled to date, and that I had a lot to prove.

That was the case even before I heard, a week or so ahead of the recording date, that Columbia had agreed to allow the session to be filmed for a documentary by D. A. Pennebaker, which would originally be broadcast as *Original Cast Album: Company* (1970). So not only was I going to be running the most important session of my career to date, but there would be outsiders in the studio and the control booth, filming an hour-long movie that would air on Channel 5 in New York, with David Susskind as the host.

I felt ambivalent about the prospect—as indeed I do about the documentary itself, half a century later.

On the one hand, the chance to be seen on television was exciting. Not only would my friends and family be able to see me onscreen, but thousands of people would get a firsthand look at what I do. The work of a record producer, at least in the classical and Broadway fields, doesn't get a lot of attention. People in the industry understand and appreciate our work, but few record listeners have any idea what "Produced by Thomas Z. Shepard" (or by any of my many gifted colleagues) means. They think all there is to producing an original-cast album is assembling the cast and orchestra and turning on a tape recorder. The behind-the-scenes look provided by Pennebaker's cameras would be a unique opportunity for people to understand what it is we do, and perhaps, better appreciate the end product that ends up in their homes.

At the same time, I had qualms. I'd never been on camera before, and the prospect made me nervous. Not the ideal context in which to make my screen debut!

I've explained that a recording session for a cast album is a pressurized situation to begin with because it's imperative, if at all possible, to get the whole thing done in that one day. That's why I always keep outsiders out of the room as much as I can: I don't want distractions. Even if I have fifty or sixty people (singers, musicians, support personnel, and technical people) in the room, the sixty-first person could be the one who makes a noise or causes a distraction that ruins a take, maybe the best take of that song that we're going to get. Throw in the presence of a camera, and it takes distraction to a whole new level. In one of the first shots in Pennebaker's documentary, the camera zooms in on Elaine Stritch at a mike—and in the middle of the take, she looks over at the camera and winks. It's irrational to expect professional actors to ignore a camera, and they didn't. When Elaine ran into problems later in the session, I'm certain part of the problem was her awareness of the camera. How could it not have been?

But I had to make the best of it. So Pennebaker was there, roaming the room with his camera mounted on his shoulder—in the commentary on the Criterion edition, Steve says he was like a pirate with a parrot on his shoulder, and he was.

To give Pennebaker credit, one of the biggest worries I'd had—that the camera would make too much noise and ruin a take—didn't really come to pass. Partly this was because he and I had made a deal: by and large he and his crew shot only Take 1 of each number, so that camera noise wouldn't get in the way of succeeding takes, which were more likely to be the ones we'd end up using. In return, I gave him access to the raw takes from the session, before they got mixed down, so when the camera focused on the trumpets, the violins, or any other part of the orchestra, the sound could be those instruments, rather than the finished track in which they'd be in the background. So we were mutually helpful to that degree.

Even so, it was a distraction to everyone involved, and it made me nervous at a time when I needed to focus on what was going on around me. You can tell how self-conscious I was by how hard I was trying not to look self-conscious.

The film is what it is, and I've made my peace with it. My only regret is that many people's lasting sense of me and my work comes from a film made when I was still a smart-alecky young man. That said, I'm also happy to have it as a memento of a special recording of a special show—a show I watched take shape as I followed it out of town, to New Haven, and I think, to Boston as well. I watched a masterpiece being born. This wasn't the only time I'd have that experience, but you don't forget it when it happens.

I have some odd little memories of being with *Company* when it was out of town. You always do, during those weeks of rehearsals, because there's a lot of down time when a few company members are trying to fix a problem, and everybody else is at loose ends, except they can't leave the theater. Some people are reading, some napping, some knitting, and some are wandering around looking for somebody to talk to—somebody like me, for instance.

One day Elaine Stritch's understudy came over and sat with me while I was watching the rehearsal. A big believer in astrology, she wanted to know Irene's and my birthdays. And I guess Irene is Gemini and I'm Cancer, and so this woman said, "Oh, the marriage will never work." Well, Irene and I are still married, more than fifty years later, so maybe she wasn't reading the stars right.

Another time Elaine herself came out to sit with me, clearly in a bad mood over something that had just happened, I don't know what. She said, "You know the difference between Hal Prince and me?" I said, "What?" She said, "*I* believe *my* analyst." I nodded like I understood, but I had no idea what she meant; I've thought about it for fifty years, and I'm still not sure!

Charles Kimbrough, who played Harry, was one of my closest friends; he would later marry Beth Howland, who played Amy. I didn't get as close as that to everyone in the cast, but by the time I went into the studio with *Company*, I was no stranger to any of them. I wasn't just the guy in the control booth, talking to them through a glass wall. I was familiar to them; I'd been around during rehearsals and previews, they were used to my presence, and I'd also gotten to know all of them at least a little.

Even that early in my career, I usually had a pretty good idea, before I went into the studio, what the final recording was going to contain. I'd think extensively about how the songs would flow into one another—which orchestrations might need to be altered, which transitions or song endings we might have to change, that sort of thing. It's time-consuming and expensive to make those changes during the session, so I always planned ahead as thoroughly as I could. In the case of *Company*, Steve and I sat down well before the session and talked through the whole score and consulted with my old *Dames at Sea* friend Jonathan Tunick, *Company's* orchestrator, about any changes that needed to be made.

As the producer you're in charge of the session, so you want the cast and orchestra to feel confident you know what you're doing—if it seems like you're glancing at the score for the first time at the session, if you look like you're making it up as you go along, that makes everybody nervous. Sure, there's always room for a good idea that comes up on the session, but as much as possible you want to come into the room with those choices already made.

I was very, very stereo-conscious on this recording. Several points in the show, for example, feature a "battle of the sexes" with Bobby in the middle. For those moments I placed the men hard left and the women hard right, or vice versa.

Sixteen-track stereo was in use by this time, but we recorded *Company* in eight-track because I felt I could handle a small-cast show like this in eight. We also recorded it at double speed, at 30 rather than 15 inches per second. Some people think that makes for slightly better quality; it's debatable, but it made editing a great deal easier: when you're trying to find the exact moment at which a cut or a splice should be made, having twice as much space per second makes your target twice as big, and accordingly, twice as easy to hit.

For a lot of these songs, perspective is very important. Amy and Paul's wedding is a big musical number called "Getting Married Today," one of Steve's characteristic counterpoint songs, in this case comprising three distinct melodies. It opens with Jenny (Teri Ralston) singing a quasi-religious wedding song; then Paul (Steve Elmore) comes in with a warm, rhapsodizing solo, and then suddenly we have Amy (Beth Howland) singing this ratatat patter about her wedding-day cold feet. I had Terry step back from the mike because I wanted her to sound strong but distant, as though she was singing in a church. When Steve came in, he was closer to the mike, but still grand and public. When Beth starts singing, she's practically on top of the mike. That part of the song is an interior monologue, and it needed to be almost uncomfortably intimate.

Amy's line in "Getting Married Today" is a breakneck patter song. Beth Howland's performance was very impressive and has plagued generations of Amys who have struggled to sing it as fast and as crisply as Beth did, and to sing each verse in one breath, as she did on stage.

She didn't do so on our recording, though. There's a certain stunt aspect to singing patter fast and in a single breath, but I've done a lot of Gilbert & Sullivan in my time, and I know it doesn't generally produce the best results, in terms of either musical quality or audience comprehension. The tempo was a given with Steve's song, but I thought, "Let's take advantage of what a recording studio can do," and I asked Beth to sing up to a certain point and stop; then we backed up a bit, restarted the song, and she sang it the rest of the way. Then we edited the two takes so smoothly and seamlessly that it sounded as if it had been done in one breath—but because she didn't have to ration her breath to make it through, she was just as fresh at the end as she was at the beginning.

Now, that's not necessarily a good thing—some purists would argue it was inauthentic and a false representation of Beth's performance, and others might argue that her sounding absolutely winded by the end of the song is part of its author's intention. But its author was sitting right next to me at the time, and he didn't have any problem with it.

I imagine Steve saw it as I did, as the best of both worlds, in which Beth sings as fast and as crystal-clear as she always did, but without having to compromise her acting in order to make sure she didn't pass out in mid-song. The recorded version is one of the best performances of the song I've ever heard—not seen but heard.

In my earlier recordings, while I was still feeling my way, I'd stuck close to the way Goddard worked. By 1970, though, I'd begun to establish my own style—and one element of my style was that I like to incorporate dialogue, sound effects, transitional music, and the use of stereo to tell the story of the show.

That wasn't Goddard's style: other than in the 1951 *Porgy and Bess* recording that had made such an impression on me, he usually preferred to record the songs from a show without any effort to tell the story. For those who cared, a plot summary was included in the liner notes, but the actual recording was almost always only the songs. I went in a different direction. I'm sure he noticed it, but he never mentioned it to me, so I assume he was OK with it. His recordings were his recordings, mine were mine.

One of the most memorable songs in *Company* is "The Little Things You Do Together." Sung by Joanne (Elaine Stritch) and the ensemble, it's a sardonic take on marriage in the characteristic Sondheim style. By itself the song is funny, insightful, and lacerating—but on the stage there's an extra component, a karate match between Harry and Sarah (Charles Kimbrough and Barbara Barrie) that starts out playful but quickly gets serious. I don't know if the original idea for the karate match came from George Furth, Hal Prince, or Steve himself, but it adds a wonderful visual counterpoint to the song, and I wanted to have that on the record as well. Obviously, I wasn't going to have Charlie and Barbara throw each other around the recording studio, but without those noises the point would be lost. So I hired a sound-effects man (you can see him in the documentary) who simply drummed his hands and forearms on a special surface to produce a low-frequency thud that made the very convincing sound of a body falling.

My efforts didn't end there, though, because the thuds didn't mean anything without the dialogue, and the existing dialogue for that scene didn't paint the picture clearly because it didn't need to—the audience could see that it was a karate match just by looking at the stage. So I asked George to create a couple new lines of dialogue for Charles and Barbara to make it clear they were fighting one another.

Neither George nor Steve had any problem with this. This is one of the things I loved about working with Steve for so many years. He fully understood that a recording can be an independent work of art, separate and distinct from the stage version, and he was happy to do whatever it took to make that new work of art successful on its own terms.

It was to become a hallmark of Steve's style that he wrote scenes in which a song was being sung on one part of the stage while other characters were doing a dialogue scene on another part of the stage, or even singing a different song simultaneously. Sometimes he'd have three or four different things going on simultaneously. These songs were particularly challenging to record because the way the different components fit together was obvious to a theater audience but far from obvious to a listener with only her ears to make sense of what was happening.

Steve also appreciated the original-cast album as a chance to get some things right that hadn't been quite right onstage. If you watch the *Company* documentary, you'll see him coaching Beth Howland to fix a couple wrong notes that had slipped into "Getting Married Today," and helping Pamela Myers pronounce the Yiddish word "bubbe" correctly. These were details that, in the rush to opening night, he hadn't gotten the chance to fix, but he took the opportunity to do so in the studio.

He even agreed to have me make small changes. In "You Could Drive a Person Crazy," there's a line that goes, "Bobby is my hobby and I'm giving it up," which is a great payoff line—but Steve used it more than once in the song. And I asked him, "Could we leave it out when it comes in earlier, and just save it for the payoff?" He said, "Yes," and we did; to my mind, it made a great song even more effective.

Since I'd first started listening to *Company* in rehearsals, I'd been struck by the brilliance of Jonathan Tunick's orchestrations. I'd worked with him on *Dames at Sea*, of course, but that was a small orchestra. It was on *Company* that I became aware of just how extraordinary his gifts as an orchestrator were and really appreciated his theatrical instincts, the way he uses instrumentation to reflect and enhance what's going on with the story and characters.

Company was unusual in its contemporary setting, and Jonathan's orchestrations reflected that, going for a sound that reflected the present day. They included a Rocksichord, a keyboard instrument that was something like an electric harpsichord but with a sound very much of its time.

There's one little piece of the show that is not Sondheim. The credit goes to Tunick. It's the quote referencing Gustav Mahler in "The Ladies Who Lunch," after Elaine Stritch says, "And just a piece of Mahler," Jonathan gives the flute a quick line that is lifted from the first movement of the Mahler Fourth Symphony.

The thing everybody who has watched the documentary remembers the most is at the end, when Elaine starts in on "The Ladies Who Lunch" and everything goes wrong. It had been a long session—this was at 3:30 a.m., and we'd been there since 10 a.m.—but it had been going well until we got to this last number.

Elaine had specifically asked that it be the last number of the session. It was always going to be close to the end, of course, because in planning a session we always work from big-group numbers to small-group numbers and finally to solos, so most of the singers can get their work done while their voices are still fresh and go home (before we have to pay that extra week's salary!). Usually it doesn't matter too much in what order you do the solos. In this case, though, it would have been better if Elaine hadn't been last.

Elaine and the other twelve performers who play Bobby's various friends and girlfriends also serve as the chorus in the show; so by the time we got to "The Ladies Who Lunch," she'd been singing, off and on, for sixteen hours (allowing for meal breaks). This was a long, long day for any singing actress; she was exhausted, and so was her voice. That wasn't the only thing wrong with her performance, but it was a big contributing factor.

None of which changes the fact that Elaine also had a flask with her, from which she would sip occasionally before and after takes. Steve says on his commentary track for the DVD that it was brandy, and I'm sure he's right. By 3:30 she'd taken a lot of sips, and, although I wouldn't say she was drunk, she was certainly impaired. At this point in the documentary she can be seen playing with her dog, picking fights with other people, screaming in frustration, admitting to being scared, and having trouble following instructions from me and Steve, who at one point offers to take the whole song in a lower key to accommodate her.

I should emphasize that her performance wasn't bad—especially if you can see her performing it, as viewers of the documentary can. If you saw that performance onstage, you'd probably cheer. But Steve and I had seen her onstage, sober, rested, and in control of herself, and we knew what she was capable of—and this wasn't it.

We tried our best to coax, cajole, press, or drag a good take out of her, but it was quickly apparent we'd hit the point of diminishing returns. As take followed take, Elaine became more self-conscious, more embarrassed, and more frustrated.

And that's when I contributed to things going off the rails.

After yet another take we couldn't use, I said, "It's just flaccid."

This was not a constructive critique and that line has come back to haunt me more than once in the intervening half-century. And rightly so. because I shouldn't have said it; it was neither tactful nor kind, neither constructive nor helpful.

In the end Steve and I decided to lay down an orchestra track and have Elaine come back in the next day or two and record her vocal over it.

The difference in her performance is startling. She was like a different person. Rested, sober, and on top of her game. It became a great recording of a great song, a pivotal song in the show, and it's the single thing for which Elaine is best known today.

One of the things you get from watching the documentary is how long the *Company* session took.

Pennebaker's film cuts to the studio wall clock occasionally, so we can see just how much time is passing.

One reason *Company* took so long was the need for exceptional precision. Steve had written a very complicated score that asked a lot from the singers. I was just determined to get the best possible version of that score. That took time, and it was hard on all of us, but it was worth it because the recording shines, it glistens.

I wasn't the only one who thought so. Schuyler Chapin's son Ted was a friend of mine and a lifelong musical-theater enthusiast and expert, and he'd attended the recording session.. He must have liked what he heard because, within a week of the session, Schuyler phoned me and said, "Could Betty (Schuyler's wife), Ted, and I come over and listen to it?"

So the Chapins came over to our apartment and became the first people to ever hear the recording in its finished form, and they were delighted.

In one sense the original-cast album of *Company* was a relic almost as soon as it was released. Dean Jones was a movie star best known for his work in Disney family comedies such as *That Darn Cat!* (1965) and *The Love Bug* (1968). He'd done a couple of nonmusical Broadway plays in 1960, but for the next decade had lived in California.

At this time Dean was under a great deal of stress due to a difficult divorce proceeding. Apparently, he'd realized, even before opening night, that he was in no shape to endure a long Broadway run, and had told Hal Prince, *Company*'s director and producer, he wanted out. He wanted to go back to California and be with his children. Hal made a deal: if Dean would see the show through to opening and record the original-cast album, Hal would release him from his contract. That's what happened, and four weeks later Dean was on a plane for California.

Larry Kert, the original Tony in *West Side Story*, and Cliff for most of the original run of *Cabaret*, made an excellent replacement for Dean. Kert was so good, in fact, that—even though Dean had created the role of Bobby—the Tony Awards committee made a special dispensation allowing Larry to be nominated as Best Actor in a Musical. (The award ultimately went to Hal Linden for *The Rothschilds*.)

Some people who didn't know the real story may have assumed Dean was fired, but there's absolutely no truth to that. As anyone who's listened to my recording or watched Pennebaker's documentary knows, Dean Jones was just wonderful. He'd had a lot to deal with during the making of the show because it was a structurally problematic piece from the beginning and went through a great many changes during production, including three different finales at different times. Dean ended up closing the show with the third finale: "Being Alive."

In large part because of the documentary, this album and this session have kept coming back to me over the years. The first time I saw it in a theater was around 1978, when it was shown at a small theater for an invited audience that included some of the people who had been involved in the session. I was there with Irene and Elizabeth, who at the time was around eleven years old. And when it got to the part near the end when I was unkind to Elaine and said, "It's just flaccid," some of the audience actually hissed.

The next time I saw it in a theater was in 2019, at the premiere for a very odd project, a twenty-four-minute television parody version written by John Mulaney, Seth Meyers, and Fred Armisen. It was called *Original Cast Album: Co-Op*, and it apparently aired on the Independent Film Channel as part of a spoof series called

Documentary Now!. The cast included Renee Elise Goldberry and Richard Kind, Mulaney played the Sondheim character, Kind was the Dean Jones takeoff, Paula Pell spoofed Elaine, and Taran Killam played me, a character called "Benedict Juniper" who wore a bad wig. It was very funny but also a bit strange that it got made at all, so many years after the original documentary.

To promote the parody, they had an evening at the Greenwich Theater, where they screened first the original documentary and then the parody. Don Pennebaker was there. The writers had invited pretty much every surviving person from that session, including me. To my surprise, my daughter also happened to be there, sitting right in front of me. And when they got to the "it's just flaccid" point in the film, I said to Elizabeth, "I got booed for that." She said, "Yes, I remember."

One detail of the show I did get right—but it took me almost thirty years to do so! In the original opening of the show, which segues into the title song, there was what was intended to sound like a telephone busy signal but was an electric guitar doing a musical imitation. I decided to add a real busy signal on the recording, and when Steve first heard this, he was surprised and pleased. All the same, it turned out that putting an actual telephone busy signal into the middle of a song brings problems of its own.

We don't think of things like busy signals and dial tones as music, but a busy signal has a pitch and a rhythm—therefore it is music, albeit boring, repetitive music. The electric guitarist in the orchestra had imitated the rhythm of a busy signal, but on the pitch that works in the key of the song. When I stuck the real busy signal into the song, during the editing and mixing, I was pleased to find, entirely coincidentally, the tempo of the busy signal matched the tempo of the song perfectly—but its pitch was a tone lower than the guitar. I was sticking a measure or two of music into an existing song in an entirely different key, and it stuck out.

But I wanted to use the real busy signal because I thought it added a little dramatic pop to the recording.

All those years later, though, when Sony asked me to come back and remaster *Company* for compact disc, we were in the age of digital. I now had the power to keep the tempo of the busy signal exactly as it was, while also raising the pitch to match the guitar . . . something I couldn't do in the age of analog recording. So if you hear the album on the radio or online, and you wonder whether it's the original or the remastered version, the first way you can tell is by listening carefully to that busy signal. If it's in key with the guitar, then you're hearing the CD.

Company: The London Cast Recording (1970)

In some old bin of used records, enthusiasts may occasionally come across an album called *Company: The London Cast Recording* (1970). There was indeed a London production of *Company*, and several of the people on this recording were in that production. Nonetheless, this isn't the London-cast recording, title notwithstanding, if only because it was recorded more than a year before the London cast was even in rehearsal.

Larry Kert had been very successful replacing Dean Jones as Bobby. The following autumn, he was set to star in the upcoming London production of *Company*. Steve's publisher, Tommy Valando, talked Columbia into bringing in Larry and Susan Browning to overdub Bobby's major songs. This session took place on November 2, 1970. The resulting recording, with Larry's new tracks added to the rest of the recording, was never released in America; it wasn't released anywhere until after the original Broadway production had closed, on January 1, 1972.

At that point Larry and five members of the original cast—Steve Elmore (Paul), Beth Howland (Amy), Donna McKechnie (Kathy), Pamela Meyers (Martha), and Teri Ralston (Jenny)—flew to London, where on January 18 they opened in the London production of *Company*. At that point the so-called *London Cast Recording* was released in England.

Thus six of the singers on this album were in fact in the London cast in 1972, but five of them had recorded their tracks on May 3, 1970, and the sixth (Larry) on November 2, 1970; the other eight members of the London cast are not heard on this recording. The eight other singers who *are* heard were never in the London cast and recorded their tracks on May 2, 1970, except for Susan Browning, who recorded her overdubbed tracks six months later, with Larry. Not a note on either album was recorded in London or in 1972, the year the London production opened.

So it's hard to say what this album is, other than that it's neither the original-cast recording nor the London-cast recording of *Company*. It's its own unique thing, and I believe that it's quite rare and presumably valuable to Larry Kert fans and to Stephen Sondheim collectors.

It's not valuable to me because it's technically quite imperfect. I had never anticipated any Kert overdubs, so during the original recording session I didn't put any vocalists into isolation booths to entirely separate them from the orchestra tracks. As a consequence, on the "London" recording, there is audible leakage.

When Larry is singing, you can faintly hear a little of Dean Jones, who sounds as if he's standing some distance from the mike, singing along with Larry.

I have never been pleased with this concocted recording.

17

The Movies and Me

AS THE 1960S WANED, I'D BEEN WORKING AT COLUMBIA for nearly a decade. In many respects that decade had been a dream, but it had also been a demanding ten years, and I was tired and in need of a change. I said as much to Clive one day and offered a suggestion: I would step away from the bulk of my classical-music responsibilities in favor of new ones in an entirely different area: movie-soundtrack albums.

Clive had no problem with this, so that's what happened. Over the next several years I worked on the soundtrack albums for more than a dozen movies, a list that included *The Swimmer* (1968), *The Reivers* (1969), *The Royal Hunt of the Sun* (1969), *Tell Me that You Love Me, Junie Moon* (1969), *Scrooge* (1970), *M.A.S.H.* (1970), *A Man Called Horse* (1970), *The Owl and the Pussycat* (1971), *Little Big Man* (1971), *Who Is Harry Kellerman and Why Is He Saying Those Terrible Things About Me* (1971), *Le Mans* (1971), *The Last Picture Show* (1971), and *Sleuth* (1973).

Some of these movies were classics, some were bombs, but each posed the same basic problems for me as a producer.

Except in the case of a musical, a soundtrack album is overwhelmingly made up of instrumental music newly composed for the film. Songs sung within a scene or heard within the scene on a record player, radio, or jukebox aren't the work of the film's composer and therefore don't usually make it onto the soundtrack album. The composer's work is to compose instrumental music meant not to call too much attention to itself because it's intended to enhance dialogue scenes without distracting the audience from what the actors are saying.

In short, movie music is rarely if ever created to engage the listener's full attention, whereas record albums are made to be listened to. The challenge to the soundtrack-album producer is to assemble bits and pieces of music written for particular scenes into a coherent whole that people will want to listen to. After having no voice in the music's composition or at its recording session (I attended the actual session for only one of the thirteen movies listed above), you have to make some musical sense out of the pieces the studio sends you, assembling them into a different product that will fulfill a different purpose.

Whenever possible, I make it a point to get the dialogue tracks as well as the music tracks. As with a cast album, sometimes a snippet of dialogue can make a world of difference in setting the tone for a musical excerpt. (In the case of one of my soundtracks it was much more than a snippet, and it made the whole album possible.)

Most of these albums were straightforward editing jobs, but a handful stick in my mind, mostly because of their eventual impact on my future career.

The Reivers (1969)

The music for this Faulkner adaptation was by the jazz pianist formerly known as Johnny Williams, an experienced film composer who that year had changed his professional name to "John Williams." He would go on to write the music for *Jaws* (1975), *Star Wars* (1977), *Schindler's List* (1993), and other classic scores, winning a slew of Oscars along the way.

When I got the tapes for *The Reivers*, I was surprised and delighted that it contained very beautiful music. They were mostly very short cues, though, some of them less than a minute long, some of them a minute and a half, a few of them four or five minutes. I used whatever compositional skills I had to turn these scattered scraps into larger segments, sometimes putting things out of the movie sequence, sometimes repeating a section.

I was pleased with the results. I wasn't the only one, either: after the record came out, I got a letter from John Williams thanking me for the creative work I did on this album.

I didn't hear from John for another couple of decades—but in 1991, when he had become the conductor of the Boston Pops, and the Pops had newly signed with Sony (the successor to Columbia), he asked me to be the producer of their recordings, and one of them was a 1994 recording of the music from *The Reivers*.

M.A.S.H. (1970)

When Columbia was considering picking up the soundtrack for Robert Altman's irreverent comedy, I was asked to see the film and to determine whether or not we should pursue making a deal for the soundtrack recording. So one day in late 1969 or early 1970, the film studio did a special screening for me. I sat there, alone in the theater, and I couldn't stop laughing. Afterward I said to Irene, "This is the funniest damn film I've ever seen."

I was also struck by its use of music. There was incidental music by Johnny Mandel, but the film's most notable musical elements were the theme song, "Suicide Is Painless," written by Mandel and Mike Altman, and a series of ersatz Japanese renditions of such old-time American songs as "Chattanooga Choo-Choo," "My Blue Heaven," and "Happy Days Are Here Again," heard throughout the movie over the army base's public-address system. There's no other movie that sounds like *M.A.S.H.* I couldn't wait to get my hands on it.

So we made the deal, and in due course I received all the music and all the dialogue, the latter of which already had the sound effects incorporated into it. I decided that there was no point in trying to turn a movie that sounded like no other into a conventional soundtrack album.

So I started with the script instead of the music, going through it to decide which dialogue I wanted to keep—which turned out to be a lot more than I've ever heard on any other soundtrack album. I wound up with a kind of skeletal version of the screenplay and then I placed the music to fit that outline, bringing the dialogue in and out as necessary to trace some of the film's plot lines, running gags, and signature bits.

Listening to it today, I say to myself, "My God, that's good!"

Tell Me that You Love Me, Junie Moon (1970)

This bizarre mix of comedy and drama was a huge flop that didn't make any money, and its soundtrack album didn't sell at all, but I'm still very pleased and very fortunate that I made the soundtrack album.

The film was produced and directed by the famous Otto Preminger, who today is perhaps best known to some for playing the smugly evil Nazi commandant in Billy Wilder's *Stalag 17* (1953). He brought some of that same approach to directing. "Imperious" was a word often associated with him, as were "temperamental," "demanding," "impatient," and "controlling."

When Columbia picked up the picture, Otto insisted we send one of our people out to Hollywood to musically supervise the recording session. That person, of course, was me. This already was unusual, but Otto ensured it would get even more unusual.

For whatever reason, Otto had hired an erudite composer named Philip Springer. His atonal score for *Tell Me that You Love Me, Junie Moon* was very, very difficult, not only to listen to, but also to play. The orchestra musicians, who were seeing the music for the first time, had to read it, understand it, and then perform it under trying conditions, getting it right while synchronizing the music to the film. Unavoidably, this took time, and Otto wasn't happy at all.

I had never met him before, and frankly I thought he was a bully. He had no patience and no manners. Every five minutes, it seemed, he'd bellow, "Mr. Springer! Mr. Springer! Ve haff to get on with zis!" I could see Phil was trying his best to get the musicians to play his abstruse, difficult score, and Otto's intervention was only making things worse. I had no desire to antagonize him, but I'd been at a lot of recording sessions by then, and I could see that we wouldn't get anywhere until Otto calmed down and let Phil do what he had to do.

"You know, Mr. Preminger, I think we ought to have a little more patience with this guy," I said to him. "I mean, he really needs the time to get it going."

Otto turned to me and said, "Mr. Shepard! If you keep on defending incompetence, you vill die a poor man."

I replied, "I am a poor man, Mr. Preminger."

"Ah, perhaps so," Otto said, "but I didn't know you were so ready to die."

Then he added, "You're a musician, right? OK, you're going to write my next movie."

I didn't take him seriously.

Such Good Friends (1971)

Since I hadn't known Otto Preminger, and he didn't know my work, I took his remark to be nothing more than a sardonic aside to his ongoing quarrel with Phil Springer. I was to learn, however, that Otto was a man of impulse, a filmmaker who trusted his instincts, made decisions in a hurry, and generally stuck with them. He usually got what he wanted, and one of the things he wanted was for me to compose the score for *Such Good Friends*.

Not many people today have seen *Such Good Friends*, which got only a limited release and was a box-office flop, but it was and is an interesting movie with an excellent cast and strong direction. Characteristically for Otto in his later years, it was a quirky mix of comedy and drama, with a scathing attitude toward human character.

Dyan Cannon played Julie Messenger, an affluent New York housewife whose life is suddenly upended when her husband (Laurence Luckenbill) goes into a coma after what was supposed to be minor surgery. As he lies insensible, she stumbles across his "little black book" and discovers he's been cheating with various friends of hers. Thrown for a loop, she initially reacts by having affairs with several of his male friends, but by the end of the movie (after her husband's death) she emerges as a stronger, emotionally healthier woman ready for a life on her own.

Otto insisted the score's composer (me) be present for as much as possible of the filming, which was done in New York. He felt that it would help me get a heightened awareness for the emotional undercurrents of the characters and the story.

Well, what could be more delightful? I was there for at least two-thirds of the filming, and it was a pleasure getting to know Dyan, who is a charming woman. Our friend Virginia Vestoff, who had played Abigail Adams in *1776*, was also in the cast. They were all fascinating people—Ken Howard, Burgess Meredith, Jimmy Coco, Nina Foch. It was a great experience for me. Back in college I had dreamed of writing film scores. Otto wasn't an easy man to deal with, but I'll always be grateful to him for the chance to live out that dream, even briefly.

I had a lot of fun writing *Such Good Friends* because the contemporary setting and the mixture of drama and comedy let me write in a variety of styles. There are dramatic moments, there's a giddy waltz, there are moments of musical humor.

There's even a scene for which I decided that I wanted to use a kazoo. I brought in Anita Darian, the wonderful singer whom I'd worked with on several studio-cast albums in the early 1960s. I remembered that, back in 1960, she'd played the solo part in Mark Bucci's "Kazoo Concerto" on one of Leonard Bernstein's Young People's Concerts. It sounds silly because anyone can play the kazoo, but for this scene in the film I was writing a lengthy and bizarre solo, and I needed a pro. I needed Anita.

I wanted very much to have a song to run over the end credits of *Such Good Friends*, a song expressing Julie's joy at finally finding herself free and clear of her cheating husband and their hypocritical friends. I wrote the music for the song and gave it to my usual lyricist, Charlie Burr. Charlie couldn't latch on to it, somehow. So I turned to Robert Brittan. He was later to write the lyrics for the musical "Raisin," and I had known him from Lehman Engel's musical theater workshop. Bob wound up writing a terrific lyric.

Now, I hadn't discussed an end-credit song with Otto. When Bob and I finished the song, I played it for Otto with some trepidation. Otto wasn't diplomatic with his opinions, and he could be very hurtful. To our delight, he liked the song very much and he agreed to use it over the end credits. It was sung by O. C. Smith and was published later as sheet music. In 1974 Lena Horne sang it in *Tony and Lena Sing*, the Broadway show she did with Tony Bennett at the Minskoff Theatre.

Ironically, there was never a commercially released soundtrack album for *Such Good Friends*. But I assembled one for my own pleasure. I had a hundred LPs pressed, and I shared them with various family members and friends.

I would have loved the chance to score more films, but so far no other opportunity has come my way. It was in every way a memorable experience.

18

Nanette, Irene, and Friends

THE THREE YEARS BETWEEN 1971 AND 1974 WERE VERY FRUITFUL ones, for both Columbia Records and me. John McClure, the previous director of Masterworks, had left, and Tom Frost and I were named the new co-directors. Tom and I were good friends and colleagues and we got along very well. We never viewed each other as rivals. If the corporate powers that be had decided to pit us against each other to see who would win, it wasn't going to turn out that way.

That said, my new position as codirector entailed substantial administrative duties, which significantly reduced the time I could spend producing original-cast albums. I was obliged to turn over to other hands some shows that would have been fun to do. In those three years I recorded only as many shows as I had done in 1970 alone.

Several of them were very interesting projects, though.

No, No, Nanette (1971/1973)

The early 1970s saw a nostalgia movement of sorts on Broadway, and the musical that kicked it off was *No, No, Nanette*. The show had been a hit both on Broadway in 1924 and on London's West End in 1925, but it had remained a historical footnote for almost a half century during which it was best known not for itself, but for the myth that Red Sox owner Harry Frazee financed it by selling Babe Ruth's contract to the Yankees. Which isn't exactly true. Be that as it may, a revival came out of nowhere to become one of the biggest Broadway hits of 1971.

The inspiration for the revival came from producer Harry Rigby, but coproducer Cyma Rubin (who eventually squeezed Rigby out) was responsible for the lavishness of the production, which was a major part of the show's appeal. Production designer Raoul Péne Du Bois provided sets and costumes in the style of the famed 1920s Art Deco designer Erté, and the show had a glamorous flair that enhanced the lovely score (largely intact from the 1924 version) and the silly book (substantially revised by Burt Shevelove).

The production's other major influence was classic black-and-white Hollywood musicals of the late 1920s and early 1930s, especially those produced by Warner Bros. Former Hollywood director and choreographer Busby Berkeley was credited as "production supervisor," and Donald Saddler's choreography incorporated the Charleston and other period dances. The cast included several veterans of the era's movies, including Ruby Keeler and Patsy Kelly, as well as Bobby Van, Susan Walton, Helen Gallagher, and Jack Gilford.

The greatest delight of the show, for me, was the chance to work with Ruby Keeler. Ruby was a movie star from so long ago that I didn't remember her. She had once been married to Al Jolson (they had divorced in 1939, and I was advised never to mention his name within earshot of her), and they made a string of films with him singing and her tap dancing. People today are most likely to remember Ruby as the star of *42nd Street* (1933).

Ruby was in her sixties by this time, a totally unpretentious, soft-spoken matron. She did nothing to glamorize herself offstage or on, but she could still tap dance. Maybe not as flamboyantly as she could forty years earlier, but she was awfully good. I love the sound of tap dancing and I try to include it in the recording of any show I do that has tap in it.

Tap is tricky to do in recordings, though, especially in a show like *No, No, Nanette*, which has a lot of chorus tapping. You can't just have the chorus do their dance because it's a fact of life that twenty-five tap dancers are never entirely together. In the theater, a visual medium, you don't notice, but on a recording, no picture, only sound, it needs acoustic perfection. So what you do is take the four or five dancers selected by the choreographer, record their dancing, and then record them doing this a few more times so that five dancers can now sound like twenty-five dancers in perfect sync.

I will also rent what is called a tap floor, a large mat lined with slats of wood, not unlike a Venetian blind. There's an impact when the dancer's foot hits the wood, and then a second impact—so close together the ear can't discern the difference—when the wood hits the floor under the mat.

I pulled out all the stops for the Act I finale, a massive tap number for Ruby and the chorus that was based on "I Want to Be Happy," featuring a bunch of onstage banjos which I requested to be brought to our sessions. It was a delight. The machine-gun patter of the chorus taps, suddenly giving way to the solo taps of Ruby, was audible even if not visible. I love taps.

Another highlight of the show was Jack Gilford, who played the millionaire Bible publisher and philanthropist Jimmy Smith. This was the first time I had met him. The whole spirit of the room, the whole zeitgeist, everything changed when Jack was there. Later in my life, I got to know Jack and his wife, Madeline, socially. They were a great couple.

Bobby Van was also in that show, but I didn't much like him; he was a smartass. I don't usually have that kind of reaction to people, but there was just something about him that rubbed me the wrong way. I also finally got to work with Helen Gallagher, whom I had tried and failed to get for the role of Ado Annie on my *Oklahoma!* studio album some years earlier. I told her about my having spoken to her agent when I was hoping to hire her, and she said, "I never heard anything about that."

As often happened in those days, *No, No, Nanette* was too long for one LP and too short for two. This meant some material from the show—in this case, one song—didn't make it onto the original-cast album. That was "Peach on the Beach," sung by Susan Watson as Nanette, a fun little song that unfortunately happened to run exactly the length of time we needed to cut, and so was left out. When I remastered the recording for the CD almost thirty years later, I included it.

Also on the CD was "Only a Moment Ago," a song that had been cut during out-of-town tryouts. It had been written specially for the revival, as a duet between Jack and Ruby.

When I had a chance to remaster this recording for CD release, almost thirty years later, I decided to include the song. I still think don't think much of it, but in the intervening time, I'd come to appreciate the nostalgic value of a Jack Gilford/Ruby Keeler duet, so I made it a bonus track on the CD.

I actually did *No, No, Nanette* twice because I also went to England to record the British production. That was in 1973.

In the British production, in the same spirit of casting Ruby Keeler, they recruited Dame Anna Neagle to play Sue. She was sixty-nine at that time and had been maybe the biggest movie star in Britain during and immediately after World War II. As her movie career declined in the 1950s, she returned to the stage and became a star all over again. Between 1965 and 1971 she was the female lead in a musical called *Charlie Girl*, of which I know absolutely nothing except that it ran for 2,062 performances, and Anna Neagle never missed a single one—a feat that got her into the *Guinness Book of World Records*!

Her husband, British producer and director Herbert Wilcox, had discovered her—and married her—in a stage play in 1931. He was eighty-three when we recorded *No, No, Nanette*, and I remember that, as they walked in on the recording session, he didn't see a step down as you came into the control room. So my first introduction to Anna Neagle was picking her husband up off the floor.

Anne Rogers played Lucille, whose big song is "Too Many Rings Around Rosie." I remember working very hard with her, trying to get some pathos into it, instead of its just being a play on words. It was my Lieberson moment, like Goddard with Judy Holliday. Whether I succeeded or not, I can't judge.

The book of *No, No, Nanette* had been rewritten for the revival by Burt Shevelove, and it turned out he and I were distant cousins. He wasn't there for either of the sessions. I think I met him only once, years later. But although I really didn't know Burt, his mother happened to live right across the street from my parents in East Orange. So my family knew his family quite well.

70, Girls, 70 (1971)

It was a good year to be an old actor on Broadway in 1971, especially if you could sing and dance. Two musicals that year gave substantial roles to many actors and actresses in their sixties and seventies: Stephen Sondheim's *Follies* and Kander & Ebb's *70, Girls, 70*, which opened within two weeks of one another that April.

I very much wanted to produce the *Follies* recording and given the success I'd had working with Steve on *Company*, I had every reason to think I would. But it was not to be.

The problem, believe it or not, involved Cinema Center Films, Columbia's movie-production company. A year earlier Hal Prince had directed his first film, *Something for Everyone* (1970); it had been distributed by Cinema Center, and it had not been successful.

For this, Hal blamed Goddard Lieberson. Goddard had been named the head of Cinema Center Films, and Hal felt he'd failed to give the film the kind of publicity build-up it should have gotten. He took it personally and decided to punish Goddard by depriving Columbia of *Follies*, which he placed with Capitol Records. But when Capitol produced the recording, what they recorded had been drastically cut—mutilated, many of us thought—in order to squeeze it onto a single disk. The result satisfied nobody and it broke Steve's heart. It wasn't until a decade later that a proper recording was made . . . when I finally got a chance to do *Follies* and do it right. But that's a story for another chapter!

But we were happily involved with *70, Girls, 70*. It was the first of several times I would work with John Kander and Fred Ebb. John in particular became a good friend of mine. Among the things we have in common are Oberlin—John had graduated in 1951—and a wide-ranging interest in music and musical theater, and Gilbert & Sullivan. John's interests extended to many other things like taking a lot of photographs during the recording session.

One of the things about the show that particularly interested me was Lillian Roth's presence in the cast. She was an accomplished stage and screen actress and singer whose sixty-year career included Ernst Lubitsch's *The Love Parade* (1929) and the Marx Bros.'s *Animal Crackers* (1930). She particularly fascinated me because I'd seen the Susan Hayward movie *I'll Cry Tomorrow* (1955), in which Hayward delivered an Oscar-nominated performance as Lillian Roth. The movie was based on Roth's 1954 autobiography, a best-seller in which she wrote candidly about her struggle with alcoholism.

If I hadn't known her back story, I'd never have guessed how much it took for her to rebuild her career and wind up on Broadway in 1971. She seemed like a perfectly pleasant woman who performed very well in a decent-sized role—one of many good performers in the show.

And then there was Dorothea Freitag, who not only had to sing and dance, but also had to play the piano onstage. Mildred Natwick—John called her "Natty"—was the star, and I got a great kick out of Henrietta Jacobson, who had one of the show's best songs, "Go Visit Your Grandmother."

The show was based on Peter Coke's play *Breath of Spring* (1958), which had previously been adapted as the British movie *Make Mine Mink* (1960). It's a caper story in which a bunch of senior citizens stage a string of robberies to raise money to save the retirement hotel where they all live, confident nobody would ever suspect a bunch of elderly men and women.

The problem with a show whose cast is elderly is that unanticipated things can happen. I saw the show out of town, in Philadelphia, and was particularly taken with David Burns, who was uniquely amusing. I made a cassette recording of that performance—which is probably the only permanent record of Burns's funny and charming work in this show, because a few days later he had a heart attack onstage and died a half hour later. It was a shock to the entire company.

Burns was replaced by Hans Conreid, who completely changed the conception of the part, doing it essentially far less humorously. I thought the show had lost something special with David Burns. And I didn't enjoy working with Conreid. On one occasion on the session I pointed out what I thought had been a mistake, and he responded with hostility.

By the time we completed the cast album, it was clear the show wouldn't be around much longer. The reviews hadn't been kind, the box office was not doing well, and everybody knew the writing was on the wall. But maybe for that reason, making the record was a joyful experience. The score was terrific, and everything was so smooth and so happy. A weak show, perhaps, but a charming recording nevertheless.

Man of La Mancha (1972)

On the face of it, *Man of La Mancha* (1965) was an unlikely candidate for Broadway success. It was, after all, inspired by a classic novel (*Don Quixote*) and adapted from a television screenplay. In addition, the creative team was largely new to Broadway. Author Dale Wasserman adapted his own television screenplay, *I, Don Quixote* (1959), despite never having written a musical. Composer Mitch Leigh had never worked on Broadway, and lyricist Joe Darion had only one prior Broadway credit, the unsuccessful *Shinbone Alley* (1958).

Nonetheless the show became an immediate smash. Beginning Off-Broadway and moving to Broadway in mid-run, it ran for more than six years, won five Tony Awards (including Best Musical, and for star Richard Kiley, Best Actor in a Musical) and lasted for 2,328 performances. None of its creators would ever again have a Broadway hit, but it didn't matter—everything had come together for them in 1965, and they'd created a Broadway classic.

I didn't record that production, nor any of the four subsequent Broadway revivals. All the same, I've recorded *Man of La Mancha* not once, but twice.

The first one came about in early 1972, when I got a call from Jack Gold, who was the head of A&R at Columbia. Jim Nabors was a contract artist for the pop department, and Jack wanted Nabors to do a recording of highlights from *Man of La Mancha*. He asked me to produce it.

Nabors had gotten his big break on television, joining *The Andy Griffith Show* (1960–1968) in its third season as the bumbling Gomer Pyle. Gomer was a comic character, but an early episode of *Andy Griffith* revealed Nabors had a beautiful singing voice—a big, rich baritone. In 1965 Columbia signed Nabors to a record deal that eventually led to twenty albums and thirteen singles, including three gold records. Meanwhile he'd left Mayberry to star in *Gomer Pyle, U.S.M.C.* (1964–1969). By 1972, when I got that call from Jack, Nabors was a big, big star, both as a vocalist and as a comic actor.

Jack's idea for the *Man of La Mancha* album was inspired by a 1967 episode of *Gomer Pyle* that took the befuddled private to Washington to sing at a Navy relief show, backed by the United States Marine Band. Gomer delivered a rousing performance that brought tears to people's eyes. The song was "The Impossible Dream," the biggest hit from *Man of La Mancha*, which Columbia released as a Nabors single the following year to strong sales.

So the idea of Jim making a record of songs from *Man of La Mancha* for his twelfth Columbia album was a promising one. It sounded good to me, especially when it turned out Jim was a good friend of Marilyn Horne, whom he knew from her days in Hollywood. He wanted her to sing Aldonza/Dulcinea on the album, and she'd agreed. I was a great admirer of Marilyn Horne and way back when, my lawyer father and my real-estate-agent mother closed on the house that she and Henry Lewis were purchasing.

But I felt that instead of merely recording an album of some of the songs from the show, we should make a full studio-cast recording of *Man of La Mancha*, with a supporting cast of equivalent excellence.

So I headed for the West Coast to meet with Paul Weston, who was going to be the conductor. I went to Paul's house and we sat by his pool to talk through the whole project. He agreed with me that we should try to do the entire score. The plan that we evolved was that we would record Jim, Paul, and the orchestra—only sixteen musicians as in the original Broadway production—on the West Coast; then I'd record Marilyn in New York and recruit the rest of the cast there.

The only thing about that meeting that disappointed me slightly was I'd hoped to meet Paul's wife, singer Jo Stafford.

"I hope I can meet your wife," I said to Paul.

"I don't believe she's coming downstairs today," he said. He didn't explain why, but that was that, and I never met Jo Stafford.

I liked working with Paul. He recruited the sixteen players we needed, and the sessions went smoothly.

Jim Nabors also turned out to be a particularly friendly person. He had bought a big house that he told me had cost him $1 million, which he'd paid for in cash.

The funny thing to me was he was that in the recording studio, he was like two different people—one of them a hick from the sticks, the other a gifted legitimate baritone. He was from Sylacauga, Alabama. I have no idea where that is, but I'm sure it's a small place, and when he talked, he sounded like Gomer Pyle, high-pitched and with a strong Southern accent. I remember, in the studio, he'd listen to a playback and drawl, "Tahm, ya wan' me t'do it again?" I'd say, "Yes, Jim, I think we can do it better." And he'd say, "OK!" and then suddenly boom out in an entirely different voice, "To dream the impossible dream!"

And then I got on a plane and headed back to New York with a lot of work to do because I had the orchestra parts and Jim's songs, but other than Marilyn I didn't have a cast.

Marilyn, obviously, was no problem. She possessed an incredible and far-ranging mezzosoprano voice; in my opinion it may have been possibly the greatest of the twentieth century. This was the first time I'd worked with her, but it wouldn't be the last.

As for the rest of the singers, I went with the choices that made sense to me.

Ever since I'd done *No, No, Nanette*, the year before, I'd been wishing I could work with Jack Gilford again, so I asked him to play Sancho Panza. And again, he was warm, funny, creative, and great fun to work with.

The role of the Padre is a small but important one, calling for a strong tenor with a lyrical side. I had an ace in my pocket: Richard Tucker, with whom I had by this time worked for many years.

For the two smaller male roles—the innkeeper and the barber—I went with singers whose work onstage had impressed me. Ron Husmann had made his Broadway debut in Bock & Harnick's *Fiorello!* (1959) and had just finished a run in the Broadway revival of *On the Town* (1971); and Charlie Burr and I had hired him to sing in the backers' auditions for our show *Blaming It on You*. He had the big-but-flexible voice I wanted for "Knight of the Woeful Countenance."

David Bender, whom I hadn't worked with previously, had a light tenor voice that was just right for the Barber, whose material is comic.

For the role of Antonia, Don Quixote's hard-headed niece, I asked Madeline Kahn, with whom I'd worked on *Two by Two*. There was nobody funnier than Madeline onstage or on camera, but it was strange working with her because she hardly volunteered a word. She came in, sort of smiled, said hello, did one or two takes, said "Thank you," and went home. We didn't develop any actual rapport. Maybe that's not surprising, since her part in *Two by Two* was basically one big number, and my interaction with her on those sessions was minimal. And her part in *La Mancha* was so easy for her that she could have phoned it in. Regardless, she did the job and she sounds great on the recording.

Madeline's big number, "I'm Only Thinking of Him," is part of a trio, with the Padre and Quixote's housekeeper, a nice little role that I only had to look across the breakfast table to fill: I offered the part to my wife, Irene Clark, who at the time was still performing onstage.

Now, when I say Irene "sang opposite Richard Tucker and Madeline Kahn," I don't mean she was in the same room with them, or with the orchestra. This was a layered recording—Jim Nabors was the only singer who worked live with the orchestra; all the other singers were overdubs.

Overdubbing has its advantages . It might never have been possible to put together a single session involving Jim Nabors, Marilyn Horne, Paul Weston, Jack Gilford, Richard Tucker, and Madeline Kahn. These were very busy people, and some of them lived three thousand miles apart. But the proof of the pudding is in the eating, and it turned out to be a fine album, one which couldn't have been made any other way than on all those separate sessions.

Of Thee I Sing (1972)

Over the course of my career I've had only occasional brushes with television. That's natural because television has rarely been much interested in either musical theater or classical music, which have been my specialties as a producer.

Nevertheless, there have been a few. One was *The Sesame Street Book and Record*, and another one was the television production of *Of Thee I Sing*, which aired on October 24, 1972.

Of Thee I Sing is a political satire written by George S. Kaufman and Morrie Ryskind, with a score by George and Ira Gershwin. When it opened in 1931, it was an unexpected smash—political satire almost never seems to work on the Broadway stage—and ran for more than a year. Even more surprising, it was embraced by the critics and became the first musical ever to win the Pulitzer Prize for Drama.

By its nature political satire dates very quickly, and revivals of *Of Thee I Sing* in 1933 and in 1952 (both directed by Kaufman) failed to achieve anything like the same success: while the original production had run 441 performances, the revivals ran for only 32 and 72, respectively. A 1933 sequel by the same authors. *Let 'Em Eat Cake*, featured much of the *Of Thee I Sing* cast returning to their roles, but closed after only 89 performances.

After that the show pretty much dropped off the radar, and I wasn't even aware that CBS was going to air a television version until I got a phone call from Peter Matz, the music director whom I had first met and worked with on *Harold Sings Arlen*.

He told me he was serving as music director for a new *Of Thee I Sing*, a ninety-minute TV special starring Carroll O'Connor, whose *All in the Family* was CBS's biggest show, along with Cloris Leachman (a 1971 Oscar winner for *The Last Picture Show*), my new favorite Jack Gilford, and Michele Lee.

Peter thought it would make a good recording, and the more he told me about it, the more I was inclined to agree. We couldn't use the television tracks—at that time stereo television broadcasting was still a decade in the future—but Peter thought we could have a separate recording session and do all the material fresh. That sounded good to me. It also sounded good to the people at Columbia, who appreciated the names of the Gershwins and the production's stars. So I went out to California to make the recording.

I wouldn't say I was intimidated by Carroll O'Connor, but I had trouble separating him from Archie Bunker, the belligerent, argumentative character he played on *All in the Family*. Carroll was actually a fairly soft-spoken man in real life and was very nice to me. At the end of the session, I remember, he took me back to my hotel in his Rolls-Royce; his wife was driving.

After I finished editing the album, it felt to me like it was missing something—not surprisingly, since the TV version was an edited version of the Broadway show, and the remaining songs didn't necessarily tell the story by themselves. The original *Of Thee I Sing* had never had a cast album, and this was my chance to fill the gap. So I went back to the TV soundtrack, which I'd been given, and extracted a lot of the dialogue and inserted it into the recording.

From a technical standpoint that was less than ideal because there was no way I could make that sound match the rest. The sound quality from the TV recording was significantly worse than our studio work. I felt the end justified the means, though. The recording made more sense, and there were moments of dialogue—particularly with Jack Gilford—that were so funny, they cried out to be included on the recording.

Otherwise I don't think I had to do very much. Peter had the cast well prepared for the show, so I simply recorded it.

It was a good experience, though, because I generally don't get to work with Hollywood people. It was something of an adventure.

Dr. Selavy's Magic Theatre (1972)/ *Elephant Steps* (1974)

I've spent most of my career working in the theatrical mainstream, but there's a whole other world of New York theater, and occasionally, I've found myself briefly off the beaten track. *Dr. Selavy's Magic Theatre* (the doctor's name is pronounced like "c'est la vie") was one of those times.

The director Richard Foreman has been a mainstay of the Off-Broadway experimental-theater scene for half a century now, with his Ontological-Hysteric Theatre staging plays that defy the customary theatrical rules of characterization, narrative, and even cause-and-effect. His kind of theater isn't really to my taste, but Foreman is a big deal: among the honors he's received are a MacArthur Fellowship, seven Obie Awards (the Off-Broadway equivalent of the Tony Awards), and a lifetime-achievement award from the National Endowment for the Arts.

He was still in the early stages of his career when he staged *Dr. Selavy's Magic Theatre*, with music by Stanley Silverman and lyrics by Tom Hendry. As far as I can recall, I never saw the show, which was apparently crazy in the Foreman style, with no dialogue and no plot, just a man going through a series of bizarre medical treatments, expressed through dance and twenty-eight songs. The songs weren't especially experimental, though, and I had no trouble understanding them at the session.

I was brought into the project and could not be credited on the album because I was moonlighting to do a favor for a friend.

I just came in and got the best out of the performers that I could, and then I went home.

I knew Stanley Silverman, who had once been a classmate of Irene's at the Performing Arts High School in New York, which is how he knew me and thought of me for the recording. Stanley is an adept composer, guitarist, and conductor, and his music for *Dr. Selavy* was really good.

I started working on another Stanley Silverman/Richard Foreman original-cast album, *Elephant Steps*, in late 1973. Shortly after we made the deal, I left Columbia to go to RCA. The only thing I really remember about it is the cast included Larry Marshall, with whom I would cross paths five years later, when I recorded *Porgy and Bess* with him as Sportin' Life.

A Little Night Music (1973)

Today, my career spans more than sixty years, and I've accomplished a lot in that time—including making some memorable misjudgments along the way. I'm the guy who told Hal Prince a Webber & Rice musical about Eva Perón was a terrible idea that would never make it on Broadway. Fortunately, Hal ignored my opinion.

But the biggest one came in 1973, when Clive Davis called me into his office and told me he wanted me to go to Boston to see the new Stephen Sondheim musical that was in previews up there.

So I went to see *A Little Night Music* in Boston, and I loved it.

But I felt it was really an operetta, something the New York City Opera might do as part of a repertory season, but I didn't believe that it was the kind of show that could play eight times a week and make money. So when I got back and reported to Clive, I gave him both sides of the story: loved the show, but I don't think it's commercial. And so Clive turned it down.

Fortunately for Columbia, and perhaps for all the rest of us, Goddard Lieberson was still there, up on the 52nd floor in his office next to William Paley's, and he still had a lot to say about Columbia's Broadway recordings. When Goddard also saw the show, he decided it was just intrinsically too good to pass up, so he overruled Clive (and me). He decided that Columbia had to make this recording.

Goddard produced it himself, and I was there for the session because Steve liked what I had done with *Company* and wanted me there in some capacity, as did Hal Prince (who had calmed down in the two or three years since his fight with Goddard over *Something for Everyone*). It was Goddard's session, though, and my job basically was to set up extra microphones for a quadraphonic recording. Quad was supposed to be the next big thing, and Columbia decided it wanted to release a quad version of the show. That required a whole fresh setup of microphones, and my job was to oversee this.

It was getting late, close to midnight, and the only remaining thing to be recorded was the solo violin cadenza that ends the show. Goddard was tired, he put on his coat and he said, "Tom, you take care of it," and he went home. So I sat down in his chair, the concertmaster played the cadenza, and I said, "OK, that's it." And then we all went home.

The show turned out to be one of Steve's most successful musicals, and the recording made plenty of money for Columbia. The whole episode lingers in my mind because of what it says about Goddard and his way of doing business. I don't think he had an instinct that I was wrong and that, in fact, the show would actually be a hit—it's that he simply felt its quality was such as to override any other considerations. That wasn't the way Clive looked at things, and I was reporting to Clive, so I'd given him the advice I thought was congruent with his point of view.

I'm both grateful and relieved that Goddard overruled me, and it was a lesson I've tried never to forget. Eight years later I'd be in a similar situation with Steve's *Merrily We Roll Along*, and I might not have had the guts to say, "I don't think this recording will make a nickel, but it's a brilliant show and we should record it anyway," if I hadn't had Goddard's example to draw on.

Irene (1973)

After Cyma Rubin removed Harry Rigby from *No, No, Nanette*, it wouldn't have surprised me if he'd sworn off 1920s revivals for good. Instead he doubled down, took the same recipe that had made *No, No, Nanette* a hit, and did it all over again—and again scored a hit.

I had never heard of *Irene* until the revival was announced, but it turned out to be a show with a long and successful history. Based on James Montgomery's play *Irene O'Dare*, it opened in 1919, made a star out of Edith Day (who played the title role and sang the show's biggest hit, "Alice Blue Gown") and ran for 675 performances. This was the longest a Broadway musical had ever run—in fact, *Irene* held that crown until the 1940s, when *Oklahoma!* hit 676 performances—and kept right on going, to an eventual total of 2,212.

Unlike *No, No, Nanette*, which had retained many of the songs from the original, the 1973 *Irene* discarded all but four of the original songs. Instead there were other songs written by the original lyricist, Joseph McCarthy, notably his biggest hit, "You Made Me Love You"; original songs by Charles Gaynor and Otis Clements; and a few more by Wally Harper (whom I knew best as Barbara Cook's preferred accompanist and music director), who contributed the music for Irene's first song, "The World Must Be Bigger Than an Avenue." The book was rewritten by Hugh Wheeler, then re-rewritten by Joseph Stein during an extended out-of-town tryout that also saw director John Gielgud—an odd choice for a musical!—fired and replaced by Gower Champion.

Nonetheless, Rigby's recipe proved to be reliable. Instead of former movie star Ruby Keeler, he signed former movie star Debbie Reynolds. Patsy Kelly, who had won a Tony for her work in *No, No, Nanette*, returned for *Irene*, and another Hollywood veteran, Ruth Warrick (best remembered today for *Citizen Kane*), was also in the cast. Raoul Péne Du Bois was back to design over-the-top 1920s sets and costumes, and Ralph Burns provided the same pitch-perfect 1920s-pastiche orchestrations he had for *No, No, Nanette*. The show ran for 595 performances, with Joan Powell eventually replacing Debbie Reynolds, and spawned a 1976 London production that ran for more than two and a half years.

To me, of course, *Irene* is most memorable as the recording on which I worked with Debbie Reynolds. Of course, she was a very talented woman, and she'd starred in *Singin' in the Rain*, one of the all-time-great film musicals. But if you wonder what she was like, I can't really tell you. I've generally liked the people I've worked with in the studio, or sometimes I've disliked them very much—but either way, that always presupposes some interaction, something on a visceral, emotional level that prompts my response. This didn't happen with Debbie; I couldn't make any emotional connection with her, and therefore I guess she couldn't with me either. There was never a moment when we had the same thought or laughed at the same thing. There was some kind of invisible shield between us, and it didn't go away.

She was very professional, of course. She knew what she wanted to do and how to do it, and she was a very seasoned performer. She didn't need a lot of takes on anything; in fact, this was one of my shorter Broadway sessions. But I came away from it without any sense of what she was like as a person. There was a toughness about her, and there were invisible boundaries I couldn't cross.

This may be because she had a lot on her mind. That morning her fifteen-year-old son, Todd Fisher, had shot himself in the finger, so she was on the telephone with him a lot of the time during the course of that day. But when she needed to be at the microphone, she was all business.

Debbie had sung a wonderful song onstage, "I'm Always Chasing Rainbows" (1917), until for some reason it was cut from the show. Naturally I wanted it back, and we restored it for the album.

The only other contribution I remember making had to do with the actor George S. Irving, who would later win a Tony Award for his performance in *Irene*. He had a fun song called "They Go Wild, Simply Wild Over Me." I suggested he do it with a French accent, and he said, "Oh, what a wonderful idea," and he did.

Patsy Kelly was as funny in *Irene* as she had been in *No, No, Nanette*. She was a tough woman; she should have been a boxer. She was in her sixties by this time, and she had done everything there was to do in show business—vaudeville, theater, radio, movies, slapstick comedy, drama, even horror movies (she was in *Rosemary's Baby* in 1968), and she knew exactly what she was doing. She had been an out lesbian for her entire career, which was almost unique for an actress at that time, and there were various rumors about which women in the cast she was sleeping with.

This was very much like *No, No, Nanette* to me because it was an homage to the same bygone era. The story was so lightweight that I didn't need to think about it, and even the new songs were old-fashioned, self-contained numbers. All I really had to do was see to it that the stuff sounded good—there wasn't much opportunity for me to be creative. (I wish I could blow my own horn here, but I don't think I did anything particularly noteworthy.)

Shelter (1973)

Shelter was an interesting little musical, written and performed by talented people, which closed after thirty-one performances. This isn't to say it wasn't good—it was simply an odd little show, deliberately small in scale, a chamber musical in an age when big productions were the norm.

The story was a crazy one, involving a writer of television commercials who lives on the set of a television show he's constructed in his studio; there is Maud, an actress who seems attracted to him; Wednesday, his cleaning lady, who is crazy about him; and Gloria, his wife and the mother of his seven (offstage) children. The songs by lyricist Gretchen Cryer (who also wrote the book) and composer Nancy Ford were the best thing about the show. Gretchen and Nancy were, and are, delightful, gifted women whose biggest success would be with the Off-Broadway hit *I'm Getting My Act Together and Taking It on the Road* (1978).

Columbia had contracted to make the original-cast album, but the reviews were mixed, the box office was so-so, and it was clear the show wasn't going to make it. Although there was a contract in place, Clive really didn't want to spend the money it would take to record it, so he made a deal with them: he would pay them almost the same amount they'd have been due for the cast album, but instead we would release only a single. It was called *Songs from Shelter*, one side of which was "Run, Little Girl" and the other "Woke Up Today." "Woke Up Today" was sung by Marcia Rodd and Tony Wells, and "Run, Little Girl" was only Tony Wells. They're really good songs. The recording came out very well. Because it was only a single, and we had virtually a whole day to record it, we spent a lot of time on it, more than I normally would on a 45 single. The show closed shortly thereafter, and the single probably sold nothing.

I crossed paths with Gretchen and Nancy again in the mid-1990s, when they were hired to write a musical based on the American Girl dolls, to be performed in small theaters in their stores. Gretchen and Nancy recommended to the company that I be hired to come out to Chicago and produce a recording of the show. They were the only other real professionals involved in the project, and all kinds of snags came up. I oversaw some of the sessions but didn't do the editing or mixing. If the recording ever was issued, I've never seen or heard it.

Many years later, cleaning out my attic in 2020, I came across something I didn't know I had—a cassette I'd made (illicitly) of a performance of *Shelter* before Clive decided to pull the plug on the cast album. So my little homemade cassette, surreptitiously taped in the theater, is the closest *Shelter* came to having an original-cast recording.

Raisin (1973)

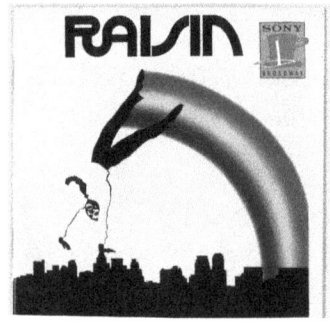

In a genre that leans heavily toward escapism, *Raisin* was an outlier. Based on Lorraine Hansberry's acclaimed play *A Raisin in the Sun* (1959), with a book cowritten by Hansberry's ex-husband, Robert Nemiroff, it had some humorous moments, but was basically an earnest, realistic look at an African American family living in 1950s Chicago. Its domestic focus, its attention to economic issues, its willingness to address racism, and of course, its putting a Black family front and center were all unusual on Broadway in the 1970s.

However, if a show is good enough, it doesn't have to be typical, and *Raisin*, the musical, was very good indeed. Its book—always the essential element to a musical—hewed closely to Hansberry's play but broadened its scope to show more of the neighborhood than the play's tight focus had allowed. The score was full of heart and gave everybody in a fine cast opportunities to shine. The show won the Tony Award as Best Musical and certainly deserved it. It was nominated in all the major categories, with Virginia Capers winning as Best Actress in a Musical for her performance as the family matriarch, Mama Lena Younger. But everybody was good: Joe Morton was terrific as Walter, as was Debbie Allen, who played Beneatha.

This show was close to my heart because the score was written by friends of mine: lyricist Robert Brittan, who also had written the words for my song "Suddenly It's All Tomorrow," from *Such Good Friends*, and composer Judd Woldin. We were all in Lehman Engel's BMI Theater Workshop, and I'd known their work for years. Seeing two people who'd been in Lehman's class with me and Charlie Burr score a hit on Broadway was inspiring.

Raisin had been workshopped to some degree, so I'd heard quite a bit of the material as it was being created. Judd Woldin was already in his forties, and Bob Brittan was in his thirties when *Raisin* got put on, and it's unusual for Broadway songwriters to begin that late—particularly Judd, obviously.

The show was recorded with very little adaptation from the way the songs were performed onstage. Virginia Capers had one spectacular number, "A Whole Lotta Sunlight," which was a combination of a lot of dialogue and a lot of singing. Usually I love that sort of thing, but this time I took out all the dialogue in the editing—it didn't seem that it was needed. It stuck out from all the rest. But many years later, I had second thoughts and, when I was asked by Sony to remaster the recording for CD, I put it all back in again.

I hadn't known Robert Nemiroff, and he quickly became a thorn in my side. Hansberry had died in 1965, and although they had been divorced the year before she died, Nemiroff was the keeper of the flame. He was the driving force who got *Raisin* created and produced, and there wasn't any aspect of the show he didn't feel personally invested in.

Normally the book writer doesn't say much on the recording session, but Nemiroff, he had plenty to say. I felt undermined. I no longer remember whether the things he was saying had much merit, but I do clearly recall the frustration of being unable to get out from under him. Even though I loved the show, and the songwriters were friends of mine, Nemiroff's interference made it one of my very rare unpleasant sessions because he had so many opinions about so many things. And I had no choice but to put up with him.

It was also a stressful day for me because Irene and I had just gotten a dog for our daughter, Elizabeth, who was just six at the time, and the little puppy refused to eat anything and was apparently dying. Irene often came to recording sessions, but she wasn't at this one because of the dog, and during the day I had several distressing phone calls from her. It had a happy ending. When Irene gave Sammy some steak instead of dog food, she ate like a trouper. We had her for ten more years. But in the studio, at the time I thought my daughter's dog was dying, and there I was, stuck in the studio with Nemiroff, a difficult, humorless, tactless man who had something to say about everything. I was so happy when that session, maybe the most difficult and unpleasant of my career, ended. Thank God, Nemiroff wasn't there for the editing and mixing. And thank God I never saw him again.

As is usually the case, all the trouble at the session didn't come through on the album. It won the Grammy as Best Original Cast Album, and it was a wonderful moment for me accepting the Grammy with my two friends who had written it.

Candide (1974)

Back when I was a grad student at Yale, I became friends with a fellow student named Mitch, an architecture major who was a native of New Haven. We shared a taste for Broadway musicals, and one day he said to me, "Have you ever heard Bernstein's *Candide*?"

I hadn't, as it happened. I had been at Oberlin when the show—with a libretto by Lillian Hellman (based on the classic novella by Voltaire) and lyrics by a half-dozen different writers, including James Agee, Dorothy Parker, Richard Wilbur, Lenny, his wife Felicia, and Hellman herself—had opened in 1956, and it closed only two months later, before I could see it. I hadn't heard the original-cast recording, so all I knew about it in 1959 was that Leonard Bernstein had written the music for four Broadway hits and one flop, *Candide*.

But Mitch was a big fan, and when I told him I had never heard the recording, he insisted on lending me his copy. And when I listened to the recording, I understood his enthusiasm. Whatever problems there might have been with the show, they certainly weren't with the music.

My next encounter with the show came in 1963, when Schuyler Chapin gave me an unusual assignment. Goddard had produced the original-cast album back in 1956, and he'd done it in mono, as all Broadway cast albums were done at that point. However, even then, everyone knew stereo was on the horizon, so Goddard and his crew also made an experiment in stereo recording, setting up extra mikes at the session. Nothing had ever been done with those stereo tapes. By 1963, however, a stereo release of *Candide* was commercially viable. I was able to locate those tapes, which I then edited and mixed into the long-awaited stereo version of the album—which, I must say, turned out to be worth the wait.

And for another decade that seemed to be the end of the story. *Candide* had been a monumental flop, and even those who admired the music (which was practically everyone who'd heard it) didn't see much chance it would ever be revived.

The man who changed all that was Harold Prince, who saw something in it that had escaped most others. In the 1970s he became the show's greatest champion.

Hal knew that the problems with the show were entirely with the book. Broadway fans may often think of shows mostly in terms of the songs and the production, but in American musical theater, from *Show Boat* onward, if the book doesn't work, the show fails. Oscar Hammerstein once said, "Audiences do not respond with their head, they respond with their heart." He was right. If you can't grab them with the characters and story, the songs can be as wonderful as you want, but the show still won't work.

Dealing with this problem, Hal commissioned Hugh Wheeler, the librettist of *A Little Night Music*, to write an entirely new book, adapting Voltaire's work directly rather than attempting to revise Hellman's adaptation.

I first heard about Hal's project from my good friend, the great arranger/orchestrator Hershy Kay. Hershy had done the original orchestrations for *Candide*, and he informed me he had been asked to scale down those arrangements for a new production with a thirteen-piece orchestra. The new version would play at the Chelsea Theater Company Center at the Brooklyn Academy of Music (and the next year it would move to the Broadway Theater, where its 740 performances were more than ten times the run of the original production). Naturally Hershy thought Columbia might be interested in making a new cast album.

I was immediately intrigued. I loved the score, of course, and Bernstein, along with Stephen Sondheim, who was writing some new lyrics, and Prince were a magic combination. But the thing that fascinated me most was that Hal was staging it, to use the then-emerging term, environmentally: instead of a conventional placement, with the audience seated facing a single, stationary stage, Hal and set designer Eugene Lee put the action on a series of platforms throughout the theater, in front of, behind, and even within the audience. Even the orchestra was scattered around the hall.

Now, at this point Columbia and many other record labels were experimenting with quadraphonic recording, which instead of the two perspectives of stereo recording (left and right) used four speakers (left front, right front, left rear, and right rear) to produce a richer, more realistic surround-sound environment. I was extremely enthusiastic about quadraphonic sound, especially surround sound. (Most four-channel recordings put the main sound sources in the front and used the rear mostly for reverberation. But when used to its fullest, with important sound sources on all four channels, quad could surround the listener, creating the sense he or she was in the center of things, with the action or the music coming from all over the place.)

I had already done a few quad recordings at Columbia, with Pierre Boulez and the New York Philharmonic, but *Candide* would be the first show I'd done with quad. So I committed Columbia to this show, which would cost us around a hundred thousand dollars to make the recording.

I began by meeting with Hal and Hugh, to explain the capabilities of quadraphonic recording and explore how we could best use it to record *Candide*. I also asked Hal—who had been to countless recording sessions but always as an observer—to take a more active role this time, directing the actors in the dialogue we needed for the recording. He agreed, and even said to me on the session, "Hey, this is fun."

I needed Hal in that capacity because the unusual aspects of this production didn't end with the environmental staging. The double role of Dr. Pangloss/Voltaire was played by Lewis J. Stadlen, with June Gable as the Old Lady, and they were fantastic. The other cast members, though, were much less experienced. Hugh had written his new version with the idea of casting young actors as the teenage characters.

It was a wonderful idea, with actual young people playing idealistic youths and actual older people playing the older generation who are constantly screwing up the young people's lives.

I had great fun doing this recording and playing with the possibilities of quad recording. Hugh, Hal, and I worked hard to translate any strong visual reference onstage into sound on the recording. We added small changes to the dialogue and we added sounds that weren't heard in the show—for example, the boar hounds that can be heard barking during the hunt, which aren't mentioned in the show; the sound of a storm at sea; and the sound of Candide pushing a statue and killing Maximilian. All these things were conveyed through sound and were further enriched by the availability of quadraphonic techniques.

Unbeknownst to all but a very few, I had begun *Candide* in full knowledge I wouldn't be able to be there for the post-production work. I already knew I would be leaving Columbia for RCA only a few weeks after the recording session, and that the editing and mixing would be left to other hands.

Fortunately they were the capable hands of Jay David Saks, whom Tom Frost and I had brought on as an assistant producer and who had quickly demonstrated formidable talent in this area. Jay joined me at RCA not long afterward and has gone on to a wonderful career of his own, producing such original-cast recordings as *Into the Woods, Jerome Robbins' Broadway, Once on This Island, Assassins, My Favorite Year, Chicago, Cabaret, Ragtime, Fosse, Urinetown,* and *Avenue Q,* among others. He's very gifted and has an awful lot of technical expertise, far more than I've ever had—he can run a console himself, which isn't something I can do.

I left for RCA and Jay did all the heavy lifting on *Candide,* and he did a fabulous job, proving himself a master of detail—editing and mixing the music and then all the added effects: everything from Candide hurling the statue to the ground, to the rustle of a sheet of paper—and doing it with great expertise and taste.

Candide was released in a four-channel version as well as in a conventional two-channel stereo version. (I no longer have the equipment on which to play quadraphonic recordings, which is a pity because there's a magic to the quad version that's not quite there on the stereo version.)

Even in that version—and that's the version I most often listen to now because I can play it in my car—I love the recording. Yes, the orchestra is small, but it's still a beautiful recording.

Hal's revival was a big success, and it marked the resurrection of *Candide* as a viable property. Hal kept coming back to it, with new revisions and expansions each time: in 1982 he directed an "operatic" version at the New York City Opera, which was very well received—the original orchestrations were back to their original glory—and was broadcast on the PBS series *Live from Lincoln Center.* That version was recorded by City Opera in 1986 and won a Grammy Award as Best Opera Recording. Hal brought the show back to Broadway in 1997, where it ran for another 104 performances, and revived it for City Opera in 2017. That was his last show, an appropriate finale for the man who, more than anyone else, established *Candide's* place in the musical-theater canon.

I liked Hal very, very much. He was a Broadway powerhouse, but he was also a kind, generous man who treated superstars, working professionals and "civilians" with equal courtesy.

One little story that crosses my mind makes that point: if you look at the back cover of the *Candide* recording, you'll find a bunch of little circles with the names of each person who was part of the show, whether it's Hal Prince, Hershy Kay, or whomever. I had left the company before the recording came out, and I worried that the back cover of this recording—a recording I was very proud of—wouldn't have my name on it, because the cover art was in the hands of the art director, John Berg, and he and I didn't really like each other. With me no longer at Columbia, I had no control over my billing.

So I asked Hal, "Just in case my usual billing isn't there, can you get Columbia to add me as one of the many names on the back cover, an additional circled credit balloon along with all the others?" He said, "Sure," and he saw that it was done.

I've worked with a lot of very talented people, but there were few that I liked as much as Hal.

19

All Good Things Must End

COLUMBIA RECORDS WAS CAMELOT TO ME. I had some very good years at RCA and MCA, but Columbia still holds a special place in my heart.

I suppose everybody feels that way about their first major venture and Columbia was definitely a great adventure for me. I came to the company in 1960, fresh from dropping out of Yale, without a clue what the record business was all about.

But I learned fast. I'd never really thought about a phonograph record as a manufactured product—it always seemed to me it was something unique and magical—but I learned how records are made. I'd barely realized there was such a thing as editing or mixing a record, but I learned how to do both, and how to do them well. I'd seen the words "Produced by" on records, without knowing what that meant at all, but I learned to be a producer myself. I learned to work with artists, I learned how to cast a studio-cast album, I learned how to work within a big corporation.

And I learned them from the best people in the business—Goddard Lieberson, the king of our Camelot, above all, and so many others as well. I learned how to run a recording session from Howard Scott, and I learned about editing and mixing from him and Jim Foglesong. Schuyler Chapin taught me invaluable lessons about how to decide which recordings to make in the first place. Then there were the other producers, especially Tom Frost and John McClure; the best engineers in the business, men like Buddy Graham and Fred Plaut, and so many others.

Working at Columbia led to my rubbing elbows with some of the greatest creative artists and performers of our time—Leonard Bernstein, Barbara Cook, Fred Ebb, Sheldon Harnick, Marilyn Horne, John Kander, Danny Kaye, Carroll O'Connor, Anthony Quinn, Florence Henderson, Richard Rodgers, Stephen Sondheim, Richard Tucker, and the rest. It was a magic place to me, and it always will be.

By the early 1970s, however, the magic was wearing off. My foray into movie soundtracks had been a symptom of larger problems, and while I'd enjoyed my tenure as codirector of Masterworks, the problems at Columbia began well above the level that Tom Frost and I occupied.

My years in the corporate world have taught me I am not and have never been a natural as a corporate executive, either by instinct or inclination. I never aspired to climb the corporate ladder any higher than necessary to make the kind of recordings I wanted to make. Perhaps Goddard was wrong—you can't make a businessman into a musician, but sometimes you can't make a musician into a businessman, either!

The happiest times in my professional life have been when I was working under the aegis of persons who shared my approach to the record business but were adept at the kind of in-house politics with which I've never felt comfortable. Left to run my end of the company while my boss fended off the slings and arrows of corporate politics, I was perfectly happy.

In the case of Columbia, Goddard Lieberson was that man. It was under his watchful-but-benevolent eye that Masterworks became a Camelot. His bond with William Paley was such that for many years no one was looking over his shoulder; he was free to run Columbia Records as he saw fit. Given his artistry as a producer and as a musician, and the sophistication of his taste, he was the perfect monarch for a kingdom run by musicians.

As I've mentioned, the chink in Goddard's armor was he neither liked nor understood rock 'n' roll. He was surprisingly knowledgeable not only about his own favorite category, classical music, but also about jazz, pop, Broadway—really, everything except rock. He understood folk music, and under his leadership in the 1960s Columbia had signed Bob Dylan and Simon & Garfunkel, but we'd missed on (or I think, hadn't really tried for) Elvis Presley, the Beatles, the Rolling Stones, the Beach Boys, and the other 1960s bands that ruled the teen market, and hence, the record market.

With so much money to be made from rock 'n' roll, it was perhaps in hindsight, inevitable CBS would take the company away from Goddard and turn it over to somebody who cared more about the current musical scene. As I've already recounted, Clive Davis turned out to have a perfect ear for rock, signed many important artists and bands, and made Columbia a major player on the rock scene in only a few years. But in 1973 Clive was forced out under a cloud of suspicion, supposedly for using Columbia's money to pay for his son's bar mitzvah.

Given Clive's enormous contributions to the company, his lavish expense account, and the fact that, in the entertainment world, people do a lot of legitimate business at the parties they host, I find it hard to believe that his downfall was only about a bar mitzvah. I assume it was the result of his losing some corporate power struggle far above my level of knowledge.

It was amazing how completely Clive was expunged after his departure. By the time of that year's big summer convention, a gathering of Columbia's nationwide sales force, he wasn't just a guy, a president, who'd left the company, he was a nonperson. Columbia's creative-services department spent a huge amount of money redoing any promotional materials that referred to Clive. Anything that had to do with him was erased completely. It was as if he'd never existed.

With Clive's downfall, Goddard returned as head of CBS Records, but things were not the same. For one thing, Goddard was almost sixty-five, which meant he'd have to leave Columbia very soon due to an iron-clad retirement policy (to which Bill Paley was the only exception).

When Goddard turned sixty-five, Irwin Siegelstein took over from Goddard as president of CBS Records; he was a very decent man, but he had absolutely zero experience in the record business. Shortly before I left Columbia—and after I'd already agreed to move to RCA, though I hadn't yet told anybody at Columbia—Irwin called me in to reprimand me for having committed a hundred thousand dollars of Masterworks money to record *Candide* without consulting him.

I had certainly done that, but it hadn't occurred to me to consult him. In 1974 I was the co-director of Masterworks, and Tom Frost and I were entitled to make that kind of decision, the same way our predecessors had. Although I liked Irwin, the episode reminded me that things at Columbia had been changing for some time and it confirmed that my decision to leave was the right one.

More important, though, I had somewhere else I very much wanted to go.

In my later years at Columbia, I had gotten to know Kenneth Glancy, a big, jovial, good-looking, intelligent, cultured, suave executive with an outgoing demeanor and a canny business sense. He seemed to have been created very much in Lieberson's image. (He was also a serious alcoholic, but that became clear to me only in later years.)

Where Ken was different from me was that he was a happy corporate warrior, a man who always had his ear to the ground within the industry and who had a chess player's knack for seeing the board several moves ahead. He was climbing up the Columbia corporate ladder.

Goddard's impending retirement had touched off a scrum between two very important Columbia executives, each of whom wanted to be chosen to run the company at one level below the president, and thus, to be the heir apparent when Goddard retired. One of those men was Bill Gallagher and the other was Ken Glancy.

They were different in almost every way. Bill was intelligent, but he was a street guy—not particularly well educated, aggressive and very political. He was a big, fat man who could be ruthless if you stood between him and something he wanted. He had begun at Columbia in 1950 and by the mid-1960s had worked his way up to vice president for sales and marketing, a good job from which to pursue the top spot.

He was the antithesis of Ken Glancy, a man of culture who had a certain ease Bill could never quite match. After fighting in Europe during World War II, Ken had begun at Columbia with a part-time job as a salesman, while he was working on a doctorate in education at the University of Michigan. He ended up giving up his plans to be a teacher, instead becoming the Midwestern sales manager for Columbia. The throughline of Ken's career is that, at whatever level he found himself, he was a brilliant salesman. By the early 1960s he was in the main office in New York as vice president for production—which, because it covered every category of Columbia records, was also a good place for a prospective heir to Goddard.

One of them had to go, and initially Bill came out on top. He was put in charge of running both pop and classical at Columbia, while Ken was sent off into exile in London, as head of Columbia's British division, which was called CBS Records.

In the end, though, Ken was the big winner. Under his leadership CBS Records became a very aggressive, very successful label. They came up with hit after hit, doing so well that eventually RCA lured Ken away to run its own British division. The people he hired adored him, he had a beautiful apartment on Park Lane, and he and his wife, Peg, lived an extraordinarily gracious life. Ken's success in London was so remarkable that in 1973 Robert Sarnoff, chairman of the RCA Corporation, brought him back to New York to take over as president of RCA Records worldwide..

Ken and I had great rapport. He was an important part of Columbia Records. I think Goddard felt Ken was the man most formed in Goddard's own image: when Ken left CBS Records to head RCA England, Goddard said to Ken, "I wish you had discussed this with me first."

I was happy for Ken when he was made president of RCA, but it was nonetheless a surprise when, six months or so after he'd assumed that position, Ken reached out to me to talk about becoming head of RCA's renowned classical-music division, Red Seal. This was RCA's analog to Masterworks, of which I was then cohead, so in a certain sense this would be a lateral move, but there were many things about the offer that enticed me.

It would be a new beginning, which was appealing after fourteen years at Columbia, and I'd be head of my own department, with the title of vice president. At a time when I was feeling under-appreciated at Columbia, this was a very flattering offer. The money would be substantially better, including something I'd never had at Columbia: royalty participation in the records I produced. The per-record amount was tiny, but it added up.

And Ken, as I mentioned, was an extremely good salesman. He offered me some nice perks such as: benefits, stock options, and a company car (RCA owned Hertz Rent-a-Car). And there was even a company plane, on which a few years later, Ken, his wife Maida, Irene and I would fly to Washington to watch President Ford present Arthur Rubinstein with the Presidential Medal of Freedom. (On the way home, just for the hell of it, our pilot took a loop around the Statue of Liberty—one of my most vivid memories.)

Most of all, though, the appeal of a jump to RCA involved Ken himself. At a time when I was being nickel-and-dimed at Columbia and had no real idea who would be in charge when Goddard left, the chance to work for Ken was one I couldn't turn down. His vision for Red Seal was much like my own—he immediately agreed, for example, to transfer RCA's Broadway recordings from the pop department to Red Seal, the way Goddard had with Masterworks, and he promised me the resources I'd need to hit the ground running.

If I was going to leave the only professional home I'd ever known, I wanted to go to the best classical company in America, and that was exactly what Ken wanted Red Seal to be. We sent that message when, within a year of my arrival, we signed the legendary pianist Vladimir Horowitz, who for more than a decade had recorded with Columbia.

One aspect of my move to RCA has been widely misunderstood: I've read in numerous places that I brought Stephen Sondheim with me from Columbia to RCA. I wasn't as powerful as all that, but it is is an understandable error because, from 1964 to 1973, the cast albums of all Steve's shows except *Follies* were recorded at Columbia, and from 1974 to 1990 they were recorded at RCA. It looks very much like we signed Steve away from Columbia.

This wasn't in fact the case, however. Sondheim was never signed to either Columbia or RCA because record companies don't sign songwriters; they sign performers—singers and instrumentalists. The contract for a cast recording is between the record company and the show's producer, and it covers only that show.

Ken and I certainly discussed Sondheim, because we were about to make a bid for his next show, *Pacific Overtures*. We both saw Steve in the same light: not necessarily as a guaranteed money maker, a la Rodgers & Hammerstein, but as a unique artist whose work was the sort of thing we wanted the public to associate with the words "Red Seal."

We had some competitive advantages. Steve and Hal Prince had both thought well of my work on *Company* and had specifically asked Goddard to involve me in the original-cast album for *A Little Night Music*, which Goddard produced.

And both Ken and I were friendly with the publisher Tommy Valando, who represented Steve, Bock & Harnick, Kander & Ebb, and many other Broadway songwriters. We did a lot of business together, and we often saw each other socially. At that time Tommy had quite a bit of influence over Sondheim, and the fact Tommy vouched for us, as it were, helped Steve get comfortable with the idea of working with a new record company—or rather, with people he knew and trusted who were now working at a new record company. And why not? Even if Hal and Steve had stayed with Columbia, they'd have had to get used to working with new people because, by the time *Pacific Overtures* opened, Goddard had retired, and I'd moved to RCA.

As Hal Prince was the producer of *Pacific Overtures*, the final decision on the cast album was his, not Steve's. In the end they chose our offer. The same process would be repeated with every Sondheim show for the rest of his career.

Ken wanted us to make Red Seal the kind of place where artists like Sondheim, Horowitz, and any number of other classical and Broadway stars would feel at home. I certainly felt at home there myself. In fact, with a packed slate of interesting projects, full support from the company, and Ken there to shield me from frustrating, time-consuming office politics, I looked forward to coming to work every day for the next several years.

My wife Irene and our daughter Elizabeth have stood by me through a long and varied career. *Courtesy Shepard Family*

My father and myself, in the early 1940s. Though not himself musical, he loved music and supported my musical interests from the beginning. *Courtesy Shepard Family*

Left: My mother, Dorothy Kahn Shepard, about 1950. She was a very intelligent woman, a teacher from whom I inherited my lifelong love of reading. *Courtesy Shepard Family*

My brother, Lewis Shepard, is one of the best people I know. I can honestly say that we've never fought, as boys or since then. *Courtesy Shepard Family*

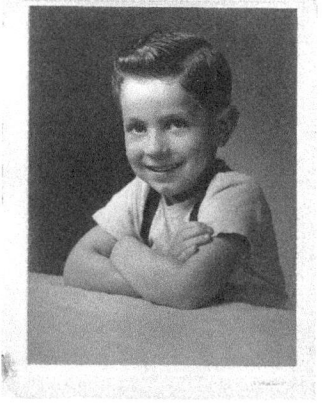

I'm not sure what amused me while this photo was being taken, but it clearly was entertaining. *Courtesy Shepard Family*

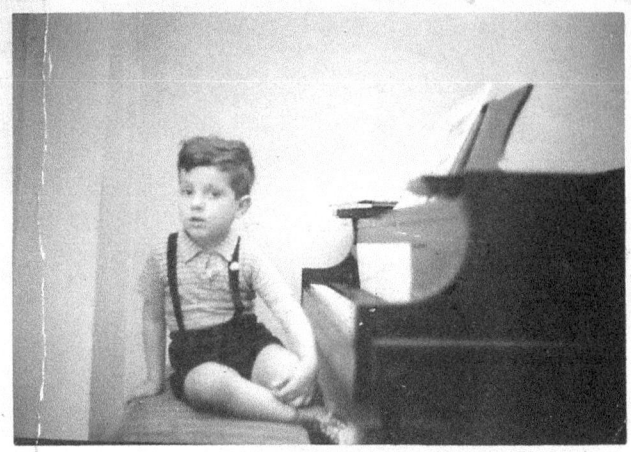

I've loved playing the piano since the beginning. I haven't loved practicing nearly as much. *Courtesy Shepard Family*

It was sheer happenstance that I ended up at Oberlin College in 1954, and I've always been grateful. *Oberlin College Archives/Courtesy Oberlin College*

I met Irene Clark in 1959, when she was playing Moonbeam McSwine in a touring production of *Lil' Abner*, for which I was one of two pianists. We've been married for more than 60 years, and it's hard now to imagine what my life might have been like if we hadn't met. *Courtesy Shepard Family*

I was the proverbial fly on the wall at the recording session for Irving Berlin's final show, *Mr. President*. Berlin is at right, talking with producer Goddard Lieberson and singer Anita Gillette. The sharp-eyed will spot me in the background, eyes and ears open, mouth shut. ©*1962 Columbia Records*

From left, me, bass/baritone Walter Berry, Leonard Bernstein, and mezzosoprano Christa Ludwig, during a 1969 recording session. After first winning Lenny's favor as an editor, I went on to produce 25 recordings with him over the course of 13 years. ©*1969 Columbia Records*

Bajour, starring Gus Trikonis and Chita Rivera, was my first Broadway original-cast recording. Working with Chita was a great first step! ©*1964 Columbia Records*

Legendary songwriter Harold Arlen (left rear) and arranger Peter Matz (right) listen to a playback with me and a very young Barbra Streisand—only 23 at the time, but already very sharp in musical matters. ©1966 Columbia Records

Angela Lansbury played a madwoman in *Dear World*, a show that flopped despite a fine Jerry Herman score. It would be the first of many times that Angela and I would work together. *Photofest*

Songwriter Sherman Edwards (second from left) came up with the idea of a musical based on America's founding fathers, and *1776* turned out to be a Broadway hit. Listening to a playback are, from left, me, Edwards, director Peter Hunt and book author Peter Stone. ©1989 Columbia Records

That's me and Bernadette Peters listening to a replay at the *Dames at Sea* session. Engineer Fred Plaut stands behind us, and barely visible at left is Charles Burr, my friend, lyricist and Columbia colleague. ©1969 Columbia Records

Two very different people, each in his way a genius: Danny Kaye and Richard Rodgers during the recording session for *Two by Two*. ©*1970 Columbia Records*

From left, me, conductor Milton Greene and star Hal Linden during the session for *The Rothschilds*. ©*1970 Columbia Records*

Company was a groundbreaking musical, with Dean Jones (left) starring as the commitment-shy Bobby and Stephen Sondheim (right) producing music and lyrics like nothing Broadway had heard before. ©*1970 Columbia Records*

The recording studio as it looked during the *Company* recording session. Conductor Hal Hastings is on the podium. Note the cameraman at right rear, shooting footage for D.A. Pennebaker's documentary. ©*1970 Columbia Records*

A song is born: Me and singer O.C. Smith (right center) talk over "Suddenly It's All Tomorrow" with director Otto Preminger at the recording session as lyricist Robert Brittan looks on. Bob and I wrote the song for *Such Good Friends* without clearing the idea with Otto, and were relieved when he liked it. ©1971 Otto Preminger Films

70, Girls, 70 was the first show on which I ever worked with John Kander (left, with conductor Oscar Kosarin). We've worked on several other shows since, and have become friends. ©1971 Columbia Records

My lack of faith in *A Little Night Music* cost me a chance to produce the original-cast album. Instead I acted as an assistant to Goddard (center, with Sondheim at left), because Steve and director Hal Prince, pleased with my work on *Company*, wanted me to be involved. ©1973 Columbia Records

Ruby Keeler lays down some taps during the recording of *No, No, Nanette*. The tap floor laid beneath her feet makes her steps crisper and clearer. ©1971 Columbia Records / Photofest

The combative Robert Nemiroff (left) caused headaches for everybody else involved with the recording of *Raisin*, including (from left center) conductor Howard Roberts, me, actor Joe Morton, and lyricist Robert Brittan. (I have no idea who the man between me and Morton is, but he doesn't seem happy with Nemiroff either.) ©1973 Columbia Records

Ralph Carter lets it fly in a song from *Raisin*. ©1973 Columbia Records

Book author Hugh Wheeler (center), director Harold Prince (right) and I seem to be having a good time during the recording session for *Candide*. Conductor John Mauceri is ignoring us, but also seems pretty relaxed. © 1974 Columbia Records

The Brain Trust: At the *Pacific Overtures* recording session, from left: Conductor Paul Gemignani, me, RCA Records president Ken Glancy (rear), songwriter Stephen Sondheim and director Harold Prince. ©1976 RCA Records

Working with Constance Towers on *The King and I*. Yul Brynner was the headliner of that revival, but the show is as much about Anna as it is about the King. ©1977 RCA Records

In real life, Angela Lansbury and Len Cariou couldn't have been further from the deranged characters they played in *Sweeney Todd*. ©1979 RCA Records. Courtesy Yale University.

Angela Lansbury and Len Cariou relax during the recording session for *Sweeney Todd*. ©1979 RCA Records / Courtesy Yale University

Clockwise from top center, that's me, director and book co-author Richard Maltby, Nell Carter, Armelia McQueen and Charlayne Woodard posing during the *Ain't Misbehavin'* session. ©1978 RCA Records

Gregory Hines and I face off on the session for *Sophisticated Ladies*. Judith Jamison is at center; she wasn't speaking to Greg, and he wasn't listening to me. ©1980 RCA Records

Lee Roy Reams (left), Jerry Orbach and Karen Prunczik belt one out on the recording session for *42nd Street*. The show was a joy, the recording session much less so. ©1979 RCA Records / *Courtesy Yale University.*

That there was ever an original-cast album for *Merrily We Roll Along*, which was a dismal flop in its initial run, is attributable to three people: Me, who produced it; Steve Sondheim, who wrote the songs; and RCA president Robert Summer (right), who backed my decision to make the album even though it would almost certainly lose us a lot of money. The picture is from the National Academy of Recording Arts & Sciences' annual Governors Award presentation in 1984, when I was given the award. *Photo by John A. Bright / © 1984 NARAS*

I'm not sure what Steve was saying at the *Merrily We Roll Along* session, but he seems to have felt strongly about it. ©*1981 RCA Records / Photofest*

Steve and I share a quiet moment during the *Merrily We Roll Along* session. The sweatshirt I'm wearing is a copy of the name-labeled sweatshirts the cast of the show wore onstage. ©*1983 RCA Records*

Sharing a laugh with Anthony Quinn on the recording session for *Zorba*. I'd gotten to California only the previous day, and gone straight into the session the next morning—but everything worked out well. ©*1983 RCA Records / Photofest*

The recording session for *La Cage aux Folles* was actually conducted before the show even opened—it was obvious to everybody that the show was going to be a hit. That includes (clockwise from left) songwriter Jerry Herman, director Arthur Laurents, stars George Hearn and Gene Barry, me and Fritz Holt, co-producer of the show. ©*1983 RCA Records / Photofest*

Sometime during the recording session for *Sunday in the Park with George*, Jim Lapine had an idea that moved him greatly. I seem interested, but Steve Sondheim has his doubts. ©1984 RCA Records

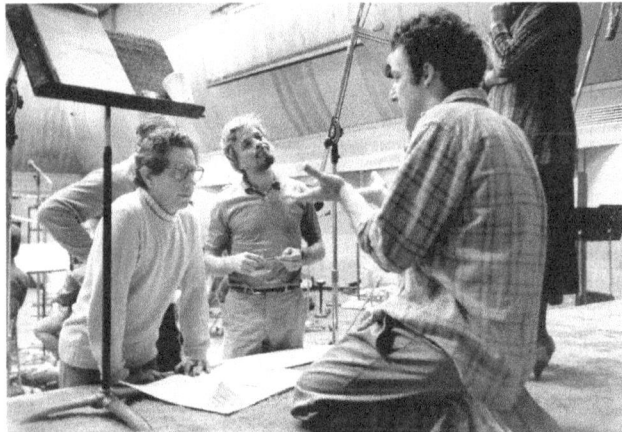

Mandy Patinkin, star of *Sunday in the Park with George*, is giving Steve and me his take on whatever we're recording at the moment. I don't remember what the issue was, but everybody seems a bit nonplussed. ©1984 RCA Records

Jay David Saks and I celebrate the Grammies we won in 1985. Jay first worked for me at Columbia Records, and for more than a decade we were a team at RCA, where he succeeded me after I left for MCA. ©1985 RCA Records

Stephen Sondheim and I, hard at work during the *Merrily We Roll Along* recording session. ©1981 RCA Records

Bottom left: Bernadette Peters was the entire cast of *Song and Dance: The Songs*, singing a fine score by Andrew Lloyd Webber. It's the only one of his shows I've ever gotten to record. *Photofest*

Bottom right: Maryann Plunkett and Robert Lindsay starred in *Me and My Girl*, the first major show that I recorded for MCA. Capturing Lindsay's infectious energy on tape was a formidable challenge. *Photofest*

All Smiles: Taking a break from the *Kismet* recording session for a publicity photo are, from left, Jerry Hadley, conductor Paul Gemignani, Ruth Ann Swenson and me. ©*1991 Sony Rec-ords / Photofest*

Mandy Patinkin and Daisy Eagan share a dramatic moment in a scene from *The Secret Garden* on Broadway. *Photo by Bob Marshak / Photofest*

I've always loved tap dancing, and Savion Glover (left) and Gregory Hines were among the world's greatest tap dancers when they shared the role of Jelly Roll Morton in *Jelly's Last Jam*. On the recording, however, all the taps are by Savion—Greg had come to the session without his tap shoes. *Photofest*

Vanessa Williams headed the replacement cast in *Kiss of the Spider Woman*, but the producers deemed her performance (and those of fellow replacement stars Howard McGillin and Brian Stokes Mitchell) worthy of a second-cast album—and rightly so. It's one of the recordings I'm proudest to have made. *Photofest*

PART III
RCA (1974–1986)

20

Sondheim Times Three

RCA WAS FAR MORE POLITICAL THAN COLUMBIA HAD BEEN, but in some ways they were similar. At Columbia I had been working for a record company that was a minor division of a television network. William S. Paley, founder of CBS, was still the chairman of the network. He knew he owned a record company, of course, but he didn't spend a lot of time thinking about it. No matter how well or how poorly Columbia Records did, it would never produce more than a fraction of CBS's revenue. Paley had bigger things to worry about.

At RCA I was working for a record company that was a minor division of a corporate empire. Founder David Sarnoff had retired in 1970 and died in 1971, after heading the company since 1919. As the founder of NBC, he had been Paley's chief rival for decades. He built RCA—originally the Radio Corporation of America—into a conglomerate whose holdings included NBC, RKO Pictures, Random House books, Hertz car rentals, and Gibson greeting cards, as well as manufacturing radios, television sets, record players, and other electronics. Amid all that, RCA Records was very small although very prestigious.

In one respect this was good for me and for Red Seal, as it had been for Goddard and Columbia Records: because the health of the parent company didn't depend on record sales, we could count on a certain amount of benign neglect, as long as we didn't run up significant losses—which we didn't.

On the other hand, in both companies, I wound up often reporting to people who disdained what I did. There simply wasn't enough money in Broadway or classical for them to respect Masterworks, Red Seal, or the people who ran them.

Paley was hands-off, though. If he had wanted something from me, he would have communicated it to Goddard, who would have communicated it to me. But RCA corporate—you just couldn't get rid of them. No matter how well things might be going, there was always somebody there who knew better what we should be doing.

For example, when I first arrived at RCA, Robert Sarnoff—who had succeeded his father at the helm of RCA—was about to marry Anna Moffo, one of RCA's classical artists. She had once been a beautiful operatic soprano, but her voice was beginning to fail her, and her career was on a downswing. Nevertheless, before I came to the label, Anna had been slated to star in a new recording of the opera *Thais*. It wasn't bad, but it was disdained by the music critics because they all knew that this recording would never have taken place if Anna hadn't become Mrs. Robert Sarnoff.

In my twelve years at RCA, I had some excellent, simpatico bosses, notably Ken Glancy and Robert Summer, and also, at the corporate level, the chairman of the board Thornton Bradshaw and the executive vice president Herb Schlosser. But on a day-to-day basis I had to answer to people who didn't know or care much about classical or Broadway. . . . but they knew how to cut costs.

Now, for most of my tenure at RCA, I had some pretty substantial hits, Broadway and classical alike. Shows like *Sweeney Todd* and *La Cage aux Folles* sold a lot of records. But perhaps I lasted as long as I did at Red Seal because of our inventiveness in repackaging and remarketing RCA's huge catalog of existing classical and Broadway recordings, which of course cost us next to nothing.

In 1975 though, all that was still in the future. When I arrived at RCA, Ken Glancy was riding high, I was his latest acquisition and he put the muscle of the whole company behind what we were doing. For the first time in my career, I was running my own shop, and it was exhilarating.

A Little Night Music (1975)

As I mentioned a couple of chapters back, I had only a small role in the Columbia original-cast album of this Sondheim classic. Even though I had been present for Goddard's session, I had little to do.

Columbia was run by very intelligent people, and I have no idea why, having made the original-cast recording, they apparently made no effort to lock up any future recordings of future productions. For some reason they hadn't acquired the recording rights for the London staging of the show. Ken Glancy grabbed it.

The London production starred the glamorous Jean Simmons as Desirée. She had a layer of toughness that was quite unlike the ladylike fragility of Glynis Johns in the American production. Simmons really turned it into her own role, tougher and more hard-edged; it was an interesting and effective performance, but her singing was no more than adequate.

Joss Ackland was Fredrik, replacing Len Cariou. He didn't have the commanding presence Cariou had, but he was fine. Hermione Gingold was the only one of the Broadway cast who came to England for the show, repeating her performance as Madame Armfeldt. David Kernan played Karl-Magnus and was very good—but he was not as good, in my opinion, as Laurence Guittard was in New York.

Diane Langton, who sang "The Miller's Son," was an interesting choice as Petra because she was somewhat Cockney, which made her sound more like a housemaid. But I loved D'Jamin Bartlett, who had sung the song wonderfully on Broadway. Judy Prince, Hal's wife, took an active role in a lot of his musical decisions, and I believe that it was Judy who first heard Bartlett and recommended her to Hal for Petra. So by and large, I would say the American cast was stronger than the English one.

I always pay a lot of attention on my recording sessions to the overtures or, if there isn't an overture, to how my recordings begin, probably for the simple reason that I often feel they are capable of improvement.

A Little Night Music has that fascinating vocal overture, which begins not with an actual tune but with the "liebeslieder singers" warming up.

But since they were only "warming up" I thought it might make a nice point if they cleared their throats before they sang.

The opening song, "Now/Later/Soon," is actually three solos, which are introduced individually and then combined into a complex trio. In the opening solo, Fredrik sings over an obbligato of his wife, Anne, who's chattering in the background, talking under the music. Goddard didn't like the chatter and chose to have it almost immediately fade so far into the background that Anne's words are unintelligible. It was an interesting creative choice, but I didn't see that it made the album any better, and I kept her chatter up and audible throughout. I tend to gravitate toward preserving what happened onstage unless there's something specific to be gained by making a change. Besides, to me there's a charm in hearing Anne prattle on that is lost if she fades out.

The session went very smoothly, one long day in London, and I stayed on for several days and did the editing and mixing of the show there. The only real snag was with Hermione, who had been taken ill and wasn't able to be at the session. So on the session we recorded the orchestra doing "Liaisons" and then, about a week later, after I had left London, Charles Gerhardt recorded Hermione singing "Liaisons" to the prerecorded orchestra track.

That was fine with me because Chuck Gerhardt was a brilliant conductor and producer. Ken Glancy had told me Chuck was a major talent, and he really was. Chuck attended the session and hung around while I was doing the mixing, watching me, and seeing how I went about it.

"In a way you're kind of layering it," he said. "You put something on, and then you layer something else onto it, and then something else."

Well, I never thought of it that way, but it's certainly one way of looking at it. Then and now, my approach is to get certain basic balances locked in, and then I keep on adding, subtracting, and experimenting.

I'm very mix-conscious. You've got to figure out the kind of sound you want every step of the way. Is it hard, is it soft, is it dry, is it wet? Is it aggressive, is it nostalgic? Is it dreamlike? Does it hit you over the head? Sound is all you've got on a recording.

Naturally, I choose to think that my English cast recording of *A Little Night Music* is very good. That said, there's a tenderness and a kind of lyricism in the American cast recording that I greatly admire.

Goodtime Charley (1975)

The British *A Little Night Music* had been Ken Glancy's doing, a quick-witted jump to take advantage of an unexpected opportunity. The first show I signed myself, using my new clout at RCA, was *Goodtime Charley*—and after that I had nowhere to go but up! I liked *Goodtime Charley* very much, and it looked like a winner to me, but it turned out to be a flop.

With music by Larry Grossman and words by Hal Hackady, *Goodtime Charley* had a great score and two outstanding leads: Joel Grey, at the peak of his fame, as the Dauphin (the future Charles VII of France), and Ann Reinking as Joan of Arc. Louis Zorich, Susan Browning, and Richard B. Schull were also in the cast. Joel and Ann were both nominated for Tony Awards, as were Susan and Richard.

In retrospect the real problem wasn't the cast or the score, but the book, which was by Sidney Michaels. That's often the case. When people talk about musicals, they usually identify them by the songwriters ("a Cole Porter show," "a Stephen Sondheim show"), but the book is what really makes the difference. I don't know if I've ever seen a show in which a great book was dragged down by a second-rate score, but *Goodtime Charley* is one of many in which a fine score has been sabotaged by a weak book.

The biggest problem, I suppose, was inconsistency of tone. The story of Joan of Arc ends tragically, of course, but when they knew they had Joel Grey—who was back on Broadway for the first time since the one-two punch of *Cabaret* (1966) and *George M!* (1968) and was fresh from an Oscar as Best Supporting Actor for *Cabaret* (1973)—they built up the role of Charley, who's not really the natural center of the story (the show was originally called *Charley and Joan*) and wrote in a lot of comic shtick for Joel.

The result was a show that was neither fish nor fowl—a drama with too many laughs, or maybe a comedy with too many long, unfunny sequences. Whatever the reason, the show went through a lot of rewriting out of town and was panned by most New York critics. Joel and Ann got great notices, though, and it might have run longer than 104 performances on their star power alone, except Joel had a movie commitment in Hollywood and had to leave. They couldn't find another star of that caliber to replace him, so they closed the show.

But the writing was already on the wall by the end of the first week, when we got into the studio to make the recording. *Goodtime Charley* was a failure and living on borrowed time, and that cast a bit of a pall over the session. Things took longer than they ought to have and, given that the show was clearly not going to succeed, there were limits on how much time and money we could put into the recording. When we got to the final number we needed to record, we had only about twenty minutes left before serious overtime would kick in.

That number happened to be my favorite song in the show, "Merci Bon Dieu," a beautiful duet for Susan (whom I'd known since she played April in *Company*) and Richard. It was sad and meditative, and it made a big impression on me. Unfortunately, under the circumstances, I had to do it in one take—but they hit it the first time, and it was lovely, but with more time, it would have been better.

This record didn't make any money, but it's a good recording. Book problems or not, it's a wonderful score, and I believe it deserved to be preserved.

So my first Broadway venture at RCA was a swing and a miss. But it would be the last one for a while because we were about to go on a winning streak.

Pacific Overtures (1976)

One of the most enjoyable things about the fifteen years I spent working with Steve Sondheim was the sheer diversity of his projects. Except for his first outing as a composer/lyricist, *A Funny Thing Happened on the Way to the Forum*, and perhaps *A Little Night Music*, each of his shows seemed to go further from any conventional idea of what a Broadway musical should be like or should be about.

Anyone Can Whistle was a peculiar, allegorical fable. *Company* was a psychological study of a contemporary New Yorker that didn't like what it found. *Follies* brought the aging process—and the disillusionment that so often comes with it—to center stage.

But none of these was as unlikely as *Pacific Overtures*, an avant-garde, Kabuki-style retelling of the nineteenth-century forcible opening of Japan to the West. It has a large cast made up almost exclusively of Asian American men, most of them playing several different parts, including female roles. It has no love story, no conventional leading man or leading lady. It's not merely a musical set in a historical time and place, but a musical about history itself. There had never been a Broadway show like it, and—almost a half-century later—there never has been another.

It was a happy recording session. There are certain times this happens, when things just flow, and even though there may be difficulties along the way, there's a buoyancy and an optimism that informs the room in some way or other. That was true of *The Rothschilds*, and it was true of *Pacific Overtures*. It was such an unusual show, and I think the actors had a sense of mission. They knew this was something different, something important, and they wanted to make a lasting record of their work. And it was basically an all-boys club, full of funny, clever actors who were having a good time.

A little digression: back at Columbia, probably in 1972, Tom Frost and I were running Masterworks, and we needed some extra hands, kind of the way Schuyler Chapin did when I got hired, back in 1960. So we brought in two younger guys as Masterworks assistants. One of them was Steven Epstein, who went on to a wonderful career producing classical recordings and such cast albums as *Into the Woods* (2002), *The Light in the Piazza* (2005), and *Once* (2013).

The other was Jay David Saks, who had a flair for both classical and Broadway, and soon was assisting me in the studio. Soon after getting to RCA and taking over Red Seal, I brought in Jay. He joined me at RCA, and *Pacific Overtures* was the first show we did together there.

This time he did the heavy lifting on the editing and mixing himself, and he did a fantastic job. The recording sounds larger than life. That was absolutely by design: I wanted it to sound spectacular. I wanted the sound of those cannons coming off the boats to be hugely frightening. Jay took what I believe was an eight-track master and mixed it down to what eventually became a two-track, making hundreds of important decisions about whether this particular moment needed a little more treble, a little less bass, a little more reverberation, or whatever.

From the very beginning, when the Reciter (Mako) says "Nippon!" and there's this big, percussive crash, Jay saw to it that there was real scope and tremendous drama in the sound. He took great care with everything he did, irrespective of whether he or I produced it. We were a team for a long time, and I've always been grateful to have worked with Jay for so long.

Jonathan Tunick's orchestrations were beautiful, of course—fresh and imaginative, weaving in Japanese elements without turning the show into pastiche. He also managed to give the show a nice sense of balance, even though the ensemble consisted almost entirely of men: there was only one woman in the cast in a credited role—Freda Foh Shen, who played the non-singing role of the Shogun's wife. On the recording, you hear women's voices only twice. At the very beginning of the show, you hear three musicians who vocalize and play traditional instruments. One of these was Fusako Yoshida, who played the shamisen, a kind of Japanese guitar. The second time is in the show's final song, "Next," which presents contemporary Japan. This number shows the full company, male and female, in Western dress. Apart from "Next," however, all the female roles in the show were sung by men.

Mako, the leading man who played the Reciter, had great difficulty pronouncing the letter R—his mouth just didn't want to form that particular sound. So naturally Steve gave him the hardest line in the world, right at the start of the show:

> In the middle of the world we float,
> in the middle of the sea.
> The __realities remain remote__
> in the middle of the sea.

It wasn't an easy show to record. A lot of the musical numbers were unusually long and complicated, demanding a lot of attention to detail to get things right. I don't recall being particularly helpful or creative in any sense on the recording session. The show was already so original, so imaginative, that it didn't need much from me.

One thing I do remember is a revision I suggested on the song "Pretty Lady," a trio for three sailors. There's a refrain line, "I sailed the world for you," which is a beautiful melodic line—so beautiful I thought it was a mistake for Steve to put it in the song twice, once in the middle and again at the end. So as I'd also done with "Bobby is my hobby and I'm giving it up," back in *Company*, I asked Steve if he would be willing not to have it sung in the earlier section but to save it for the end. And he agreed.

But I can't think of many similar suggestions on my part. Nevertheless, I had a really good time, because it's such an unusual show and posed such interesting challenges. And it's one wonderful song after another: "There Is No Other Way," "Welcome to Kanagawa," "Please Hello," and "Someone in a Tree," which at least to that point was Steve's favorite of all his own songs.

One of the most unique things about Steve is that no two of his shows are alike. He had not only the courage, but also the intellectual curiosity to see to it that whatever he was doing now was not like what he had done before. I don't suppose anything he wrote was more courageous than *Pacific Overtures*.

A lot of that has to do with John Weidman, of course, who wrote the book for *Pacific Overtures* and for *Assassins* (1990). Weidman is a very gifted writer. He and

Steve produced a different kind of show than when Steve worked with James Goldman, Hugh Wheeler, or James Lapine. Maybe it's coincidental, but neither *Pacific Overtures* nor *Assassins* has either a lot of women or a chorus line in it. And they're tougher shows. *Pacific Overtures*, as charming as it is, is rigorous: you have to pay attention to these numbers, and if you've only seen the show once, as is the case with most audience members, I imagine you walk out of there a little perplexed. It didn't surprise me that it ran for only six months.

Because I had the advantage of having seen it perhaps half a dozen times before I went into the studio, I was not perplexed. I paid attention every time, and I saw how the pieces fit together. I just admired it enormously. So did my wife, Irene, who saw all the same shows I did and loved *Pacific Overtures* more than anything else Sondheim ever wrote.

Side by Side by Sondheim (1976)

This was another one I owed to Ken Glancy because it was playing in London, and Ken, even though he was no longer based in England, remained very aware of what was going on in London. I didn't even know it existed until Ken told me he had picked it up.

Side by Side by Sondheim was a revue of songs from Steve's earlier musicals, plus some rarities, and it was one of those things that start small and organically grows. There's a theater called The Stables in a small English town called Wavendon, and the people running the theater wanted to put on a benefit performance. They asked David Kernan, a Sondheim devotee who had been in the London cast of *A Little Night Music*, to put together a revue that focused on Sondheim. Kernan got in touch with the director Ned Sherrin, and they lined up two actresses, Millicent Martin and Julia McKenzie. Sherrin directed and narrated, and Kernan, Martin, and McKenzie were the cast.

That would have been it, but British producer Cameron Mackintosh heard about the show and decided to bring it to London. It became a hit, running at three different theaters for a total of 806 performances.

Hal Prince bought the American rights. I don't know how he managed it, but somehow he convinced Actors' Equity (the theatrical union, which generally requires imported British shows to be recast with American actors) to allow the entire British cast to come over, so the show that opened at the Music Box and then transferred to the Morosco Theater had the same director and the same cast that had played in Wavendon.

Now, the Music Box and the Morosco (which since then has been torn down) were Broadway theaters, but this wasn't the usual Broadway show. The cast was unique, but there were only three of them, plus Sherrin who was still the narrator, and they were all British. There was no orchestra, just two pianos. The whole thing was kind of Noel Coward-ish, like a great night's entertainment at some posh house party.

It ran for 384 performances, and all four cast members were nominated for Tony Awards as Best Featured Actor or Actress. None of them won. After it closed there was a national tour, with Millicent Martin joined by Barbara Heuman and Larry Kert, with Hermione Gingold as the narrator.

Sondheim aficionados embraced the show because, while it contained some Sondheim classics, it also contained plenty of rarities, some of which had never been publicly performed. *Side by Side* included not only "Comedy Tonight," the opening number from *A Funny Thing Happened on the Way to the Forum*, but also "Love Is in the Air," one of two earlier opening numbers for *Forum* that got scrapped along the way. "I Remember Sky" is a gorgeous song from the television musical *Evening Primrose* (1966), which had never been released as a recording. Then there was "Can That Boy Foxtrot," a rather suggestive song cut from *Follies*, and "I Never Do Anything Twice," written for Nicholas Meyer's film *The Seven-Per-Cent Solution* (1976)—which I happen not to like (I do like the film, but the song is one of those clever numbers that I find very tiresome!).

And there was "We're Gonna Be All Right," from *Do I Hear a Waltz?* and the *Mad Show* song "The Boy from Tacaremba," originally sung by Linda Lavin, her successor Carol Morley or Morley's understudy, my wife Irene Clark. So for the obsessive Sondheim fan, of whom there were and are a good many, this revue offered a lot to like.

We recorded the show over a three-day period, which was a pretty relaxed schedule, but made it easier on the three people who had to do all the singing. These were easy sessions for me because, with a revue, you don't need a lot of the detailed preparation and execution that you do for a book musical. It was not a difficult show to do, given that it was extremely well rehearsed, had been running in London for some time, and had only three people in the cast. Steve was there for the sessions, and he was in a good mood the whole time—I think very happy to have some of his little-known and even unknown songs getting new attention. All I had to do was try to get the best performances possible.

I very much enjoyed working with these people. They were all in their thirties or forties, and all of them appreciated how unlikely and delightful it was that this little show had taken them from Wavendon to the West End and on to Broadway. My favorite was Millicent Martin, who would put down stakes in America and later earn a second Tony nomination for her performance in *Kings of Hearts* (1979) before becoming a television favorite with a recurring role on *Frasier* (2000–2003) as the loud-mouthed mother of Jane Leaves's character.

It also turned out she and I had friends in common. She was a good friend of Sheldon Harnick's wife, Margie, who was an actress under her maiden name, Margery Gray. Margie and Millicent had been together in the national tour of *The Boy Friend* in 1955.

I have a reputation as something of a Sondheim expert, and it dates from these years. I'd done *Company* for Columbia, but these three Sondheim shows I did in 1975/1976 were really a meaningful extension of my education in Steve's work. Over the course of the next decade, I'd learn a lot more about him and his music.

21

Richard Rodgers and Me

IN 1976 I USHERED MY LONGTIME HERO RICHARD RODGERS back into my professional life. Rodgers had continued to write shows, and of course his past hits continued to receive major revivals. I was lucky enough to produce cast albums for one new show, *Rex*, and for a revival of one of my old favorites, *The King and I*.

Rex (1976)

In 1976 Goddard Lieberson was no longer at Columbia Records; if he had been, most likely RCA (and I) would never have gotten a crack at *Rex*, a new musical by Richard Rodgers and Sheldon Harnick. Rodgers and Lieberson went back a long way, and that relationship would almost certainly have brought the show to Columbia. Goddard had left Columbia, though, which meant RCA had a good shot at *Rex*. If we wanted it.

Given the pace at which Rodgers had worked for most of his career, it spoke volumes that *Rex* was his first show since *Two by Two* (1970). Since he and Lorenz Hart had debuted with *One Minute, Please* in 1917, Rodgers had never gone more than three years between shows.

He was seventy-two, and a recent laryngectomy had left him with only a hoarse rasp of a voice. Revivals of his shows played regularly on Broadway, but he hadn't had a blockbuster since *The Sound of Music* (1959). When he published his memoirs in 1975, many assumed they'd heard the last from Rodgers.

They hadn't. *Rex* teamed him with another new lyricist—Sheldon Harnick, by now clearly out of his longtime partnership with Jerry Bock—for an exploration of the life and loves of Henry VIII (Nicol Williamson). The show spans more than a decade and all six wives (although Nos. 4 and 5 come and go between acts).

The shows Rodgers wrote during the 1960s were considered disappointments only because he had had so many huge hits before that. *No Strings* had notched 580 performances, followed by 220 for *Do I Hear a Waltz?* and 351 for *Two by Two*. For many composers, these would have been encouraging numbers.

Not so with *Rex*. The influential *New York Times* critic Clive Barnes called it "one of the most interminable musicals in years," and it closed after only forty-eight performances. In retrospect the handwriting had been on the wall since the show's out-of-town run, during which Hal Prince had been brought in as director (unofficially) in a vain attempt to rescue it.

In short, despite the golden pedigrees of its composer and lyricist, *Rex* had "failure" written all over it. Ken Glancy and I both had heard the buzz, and we hesitated to put in a bid on the show. In the end, though, Ken felt we couldn't turn it down. He knew this might very likely be the last show of Rodgers's storied career, and the unique combination of Rodgers & Harnick might never be seen again.

I agreed. We didn't kid ourselves that *Rex* was likely to be a surprise blockbuster, but we felt something almost like a sense of duty, driven by our respect for Rodgers. We were also on something of a winning streak, so Ken didn't think twice before agreeing to take a chance on something that was clearly risky. It was ultimately his call, but of course it made me very happy because of my past working relationship with Rodgers and my personal friendship with Sheldon.

The book for *Rex* was a paradox, a story that on the one hand was overly familiar in its broad outlines, but unfamiliar to most Americans in its details.

This was one show that didn't need book problems to be in trouble, though. Something always seemed to be happening, and it was never anything good. At the end of a late rehearsal, perhaps it was even the final dress rehearsal, one of the chorus boys, when they were finally told they could go home, breathed a sigh of relief and said, "Well, that's a wrap." And Nicol Williamson lunged at him and punched him in the face. As matters subsequently developed, Nicol had heard it as, "Well, that's crap."

This was nothing unusual for Williamson, who was generally agreed to be hard to work with, mostly because he drank constantly, and it made him highly unpredictable. During an out-of-town tryout for *Inadmissible Evidence* (1965), he famously punched producer David Merrick in the face (had Merrick said, "That's a wrap?"). In *I Hate Hamlet* (1981), he apparently felt costar Evan Handler was upstaging him and responded by hitting Handler with a sword onstage. (Based on my own experience, I could understand the urge to punch Merrick, but I'll save that for another chapter!)

Because of Nicol's reputation, I approached the *Rex* session with some caution. I was relieved and pleased that, on the session, he turned out to be prepared, quiet, well-behaved, and entirely professional—much as the difficult-onstage Danny Kaye had been in *Two By Two*.

Hal Prince's role, as the unofficial would-be savior of the show, was to look at things, to suggest changes, and to redirect anything that seemed to need it. (Edwin Sherin remained the director of record.) One of the things Hal did was to take out a song I particularly liked, "The Pears of Anjou." But the show resisted nips and tucks; its complicated plot was grounded in history, and it seemed there was very little anyone could do that would make much difference. Even Hal ended up saying, ruefully, "You know, I don't know if I've made it better or if I've just messed it up worse."

I do think, though, that a Broadway musical about a guy who kills a few of his wives had better be awfully amusing—a black comedy or something of that nature. What Sheldon, Dick Rodgers, and librettist Sherman Yellen tried to do was to make Henry's relationships real from an emotional point of view, to depict Henry as a man who just kept on falling in love, who may have killed or divorced most of them later, but who meant it at the time. It's a bold idea, granted, but I'm not sure it was ever going to work.

By the time we got in the studio, everybody knew the closing notices were only a matter of time. The reviews were too bad, and the box office was too feeble. It had the effect of rendering the sessions quiet and subdued. Everything seemed very, very calm, no sense of urgency or pressure.

Rodgers was there for the session, but as always, he said little, sitting in the control room and watching imperturbably.

He may have been playing out the string, but Rodgers still had some great tunes in him. "Away from You," a duet between Henry and Anne Boleyn, is absolutely gorgeous. Years later, when I was putting together an album of Broadway songs for Sarah Brightman, I remembered that song and suggested it to her, and she did it on her album.

Sheldon admitted to me that he'd had a hard time working with Rodgers. Following the same process he'd used with Hammerstein (but not with Hart), Rodgers wanted all the lyrics first, but there were certain rhyme schemes he would dismiss out of hand, saying, "I can't do this, I don't understand it, I can't do it." Now, Sheldon was a lyricist respected around the world, but Rodgers was Rodgers, and he was getting old, so there was no discussion—Sheldon simply had to start over and write something else.

Rodgers really was on a different plane from us mere mortals. For the longest while, Sheldon said, he kept calling his new partner "Mr. Rodgers"—he just couldn't bring himself to call him "Dick." But one day Rodgers played a song for him, I believe that it was "Away from You," and Sheldon just loved it. Without thinking, he exclaimed, "Oh, God, Dick, that's beautiful!"

"And I saw Rodgers relax," he recalled. "Even Richard Rodgers wanted to know that the person he was working with really loved the material."

As it turned out, *Rex* was not Rodgers's final show. He wrote one more, *I Remember Mama* (1979), for which Martin Charnin was the lyricist. It ran for a little over three months.

It was another show that was in deep trouble, even out of town, and changed directors during tryouts. The book was actually written after the songs were, and it never quite gelled. People talk about the lyricists Rodgers went through trying to find a new Hammerstein, and it's an impressive list—Sondheim, Charnin, Harnick—but I can't help thinking what Rodgers lost most when Hammerstein retired was a lyricist who was also a brilliant book writer.

I don't recall even discussing it. Recording *Rex* had been a nice gesture, but not the kind you make twice. There was no original-cast album for *I Remember Mama*, from RCA, Columbia, or anyone else.

What's harder for me to make sense of is that *Rex* was also the last show Sheldon Harnick ever brought to Broadway, except for "additional lyrics" for *Cyrano: The Musical* (1993). Sheldon was only fifty-two when he did *Rex*, and he had written lyrics for three Broadway classics. Nonetheless, none of his post-*Rex* Broadway-bound musicals ever made it. Just as Rodgers never quite recovered from Hammerstein's retirement and death, Sheldon never quite recovered from his split with Jerry Bock.

The King and I (1977)

Rex wasn't the last time I worked with Rodgers, though. As it turned out, we had one more, and almost another.

I had always loved *The King and I*.

And back in 1964 I had done a studio album of the show, with Barbara Cook and Theodore Bikel. But, when I next crossed paths with *The King and I*, it was on a whole different level—because this was the first revival to star the original King, Yul Brynner himself, returning to his most famous role for the first time since the 1956 film.

I had never met or worked with either Brynner or Constance Towers, who was playing Anna. She was a lovely woman, married to the actor John Gavin, who would soon be named ambassador to Mexico under the Reagan administration. She had an unshakable dignity; she sang reasonably well, and she really looked like Anna Leonowens. I mean, she was just perfect. She and Brynner were well-matched.

Brynner had been second-billed in the original production, which had been written as a star vehicle for Gertrude Lawrence as Anna, and the Tony Award he won that year was as Best Featured Actor, not Best Actor. However, after playing the part on Broadway, starring in the movie, and winning an Oscar as Best Actor, he had become strongly identified with the role and was very much the star of this production. The press duly reported that he had refused to go on at the Uris Theater (now the Gershwin) until its then-shabby dressing rooms were remodeled to his standards.

There was one significant difference between Brynner's 1953 King and his 1977 one: if you compare the original-cast *King and I* with my recording of the revival, you'll notice he's singing in lower keys. On average, he's probably about a fourth lower than the original keys. He'd been thirty-three when the show first opened on Broadway; he was now fifty-seven, and while he was still in excellent physical condition, his voice wasn't quite what it had been.

Brynner was eager to make a new recording because much of the King's music had been omitted from the original-cast album, including one verse of "A Puzzlement" and the entire "Song of the King." He might have been prepared to make a big issue of it, but had no need to do so, since I love nothing more than restoring previously omitted material. If Brynner thought he would have to badger me into recording everything he did, he must have been disappointed. I like completeness. I like not having to decide what there is and isn't room for. This recording is a very complete *King and I*.

Rodgers was at the session, and for most of the time, he was his usual august but silent presence in the control room. There was a brief period, though, when he got very upset—the only time I ever saw him get angry. He was not only upset, but frustrated as well because, since his laryngectomy, he couldn't raise his voice—and he clearly wanted to shout. He got up suddenly and tried to use the talkback, the control-room microphone that lets the producer talk through a loudspeaker into the room. He hit the button, but he could barely be heard, which upset him even more.

It was no big deal, actually. It was during the instrumental polka that follows "Shall We Dance?" the big song in which Anna and the King finally dance together. The conductor, Milton Rosenstock, was taking it at a very fast pace. It's a big moment in the show, and I thought the tempo was a bit fast myself, but Rodgers was really seeing red. Of course, it was easy to fix—Rosenstock just took it slower, Rodgers sat back down, and the crisis was over.

His voice was hardly there at all by that time. (Rodgers had a sense of humor about it—someone once asked him if his nephew, Adam Guettel, had a good singing voice, and Rodgers replied, "Better than mine.")

There are several classic musicals that share a notable aspect in common: they don't end with a big final song. *My Fair Lady* ends with an almost-silent parlor interaction between Eliza and Higgins. *West Side Story* ends on a funeral procession, with no songs or dialogue in its final moments. And *1776* ends with the cast forming a tableau in imitation of a famous painting. In all these cases, the stage business is very powerful, and the audience doesn't feel the lack of a big final number. On a recording, though, in which the audience can't see the stage business, this sort of ending risks wrapping up the show on an anticlimactic note.

The King and I is one of those shows. The musical climax of the show is "Shall We Dance?"—a big, crowd-pleasing dance number—but the show has a lot more left to do, culminating in the death of the King and the succession of his young son. Rodgers chose to add musical underscoring to this final scene, which adds considerably to its emotional impact, but until now this scene had never been included on a recording of the show. I thought it had to be. I thought it was essential if we were going to, using sound alone, create a finale that would have the same kind of impact as what the audience in the theater saw.

My finale begins with Rodgers's underscoring of "Something Wonderful," Lady Thiang's song about the King, over which we hear Anna reading a letter from the King, written on his deathbed. As she is speaking, I do a radio cross-fade, bringing her reading down while bringing up his speaking voice. Now we are in the final dialogue between Anna and the King, underscored by a slow, melancholy version of "Shall We Dance."

That dialogue segues into the young Prince Chulalongkorn announcing a list of proclamations, underscored once again by "Something Wonderful" as the son begins to assume his father's role. He starts with childish decrees of fireworks and boat races but sounds increasingly older and more mature as he continues to a decree against groveling before the King. After that decree, he anxiously asks, "You are angry with me, my father?" And Brynner responds, "Why do you ask question? If you are King, you are King."

For the very ending, I borrowed an idea from my recording of *1776*: the King orders all his retainers to rise, in obedience to the new King, and says there will be "no more bowing for showing respect of King." To this Chulalongkorn responds by proclaiming a new form of respect: that instead of "bowing like toad," "You will stand with shoulders square back, and chin high." As he finishes, the orchestra gets louder and louder with a big, sweeping version of "Something Wonderful," until finally the orchestra overwhelms everything, and that's the ending.

It's an absolutely thrilling finale, and a lot of its success was due to conductor Milton Rosenstock, who had to space the music we'd chosen for the underscoring to match the duration of the edited dialogue and peak at the right moment. And it's perfect, just perfect.

Rodgers sat there and watched us putting all the pieces together, and he didn't say a thing.

That day in the studio was the last time I ever saw Richard Rodgers. Two years later, when I produced the recording for the 1979 revival of *Oklahoma!*, I had looked forward to seeing him again, but he died a week before the session.

A week or two after the *King and I* session, I got a telephone call from Yul Brynner: "Tom, is it finished?"

I said, "Yeah."

"It's all done, it's mixed and everything?"

"Yeah," I said, "it's all done. I've sent it to the plant."

"Oh," he said. And then, after a moment: "Listen, Tom, there's one thing. I'd like to . . ."

"Yul," I said, "it's on the way to the plant. There's no *one thing*. Not now."

"Oh," he said. "Oh, OK."

I never did find out what he wanted to have changed, but it can't have been anything important. It's an awfully good recording.

22

The High-Water Mark

AT THE RISK OF APPEARING ARROGANT, I THINK OF MYSELF AS AN ARTIST—as a composer, an arranger, and a pianist, of course, but also as a producer. I choose to believe that the records I produce can be themselves works of art, not simply a reproduction of somebody else's art, whether that person is Ludwig van Beethoven, Richard Rodgers, or Joel Grey.

Obviously, I'm not the primary creative force at work on my recordings. If Dick Rodgers and Oscar Hammerstein hadn't written *The King and I*, my 1977 recording of that show wouldn't exist.

Richard Rodgers, like Beethoven and like Jerry Herman, Steve Sondheim, and any other songwriter or composer whose work I've produced on record, was a creative artist. He took a blank sheet of paper and turned it into something wonderful and distinctively, unmistakably his. Hearing two minutes of my recording, most people will recognize it as Rodgers & Hammerstein; even my wife probably won't recognize it as Thomas Z. Shepard.

But I think of myself as an interpretive artist, not unlike Harold Prince, Barbara Cook, or Mandy Patinkin. An interpretive artist applies his or her particular talents in the service of a creative artist, helping that artist's work to reach an audience. The *performing* arts are called that for a reason: unlike a novelist, a painter, or a sculptor, the work of a songwriter, composer, playwright, choreographer, or screenwriter is incomplete, arguably nonexistent, until it's bolstered by the work of an interpretive artist—usually many interpretive artists. The original creative spark is essential to the process, but so is the interpretation on a stage, on film or, yes, on a recording.

Our society tends to value creative artists more than interpretive ones, though the money often flows in the other direction—rare is the screenwriter or playwright who earns as much as the actor starring in his work. But creative artists get the prestige: movie stars notoriously long to direct, but you'll seldom hear a filmmaker say, "What I really want to do is to act."

I share that perspective. If I could relive my life with the songwriting talents of Dick Rodgers or Steve Sondheim, but only at the cost of all the recordings I've ever produced, I'd probably take that deal. I think any producer would. Would anyone rather play, conduct, or record Mozart than be Mozart?

I bring this up at this point because, when I talk to audiences or to interviewers, I am often asked—like any artist who's reached a certain age—which of my recordings is my favorite? which makes me proudest? which is my masterpiece?

I always end up pointing to the same recording.

Porgy and Bess (1977)

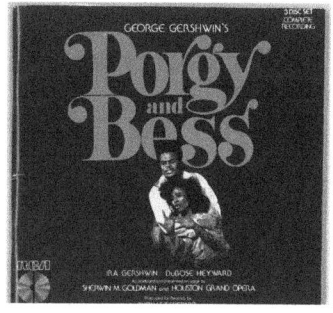

As I've written earlier in this book, Gershwin's *Porgy and Bess* has always been a special work for me. Goddard's 1951 recording of the opera changed my way of thinking about what a recording could be. I'd never really thought about the question before (I was probably fifteen at the time), but if I'd been asked, I'd have said that a recording of a show was a recording of the songs from that show. It had never crossed my mind that so much could be conveyed with sound alone—that a recording of a show could, in a real sense, be a show unto itself. (And of course that name stuck out, "Goddard Lieberson"—I mean, how many people are there whose nickname could be "God"?)

It would be nine more years before I was myself involved in making recordings, and in that time, I never heard another show recording that was so complete, that made such brilliant use of dialogue, sound effects, and so on. Even Goddard's other show recordings—and there were many—didn't do what he'd done on *Porgy and Bess*. He'd invented this way of recording a show and just left it there. Frankly, I'm not sure if there was another recording that even tried to do what he'd done in that album until I started producing my own recordings. But I never forgot that recording, and when I found myself in a position to apply those lessons, I tried to do so.

And then, in 1977, a Houston Grand Opera *Porgy and Bess* came to New York. Irene and I went to see it, and I was completely blown away. It was complete—and I mean complete! I hadn't realized until then that, even though the Lieberson recording was billed as complete, it had made a lot of small cuts (none of which, as far as I was concerned, had made the piece any better).

I badly wanted to record this production. But it wasn't going to be easy.

To begin with, for decades *Porgy and Bess* had been widely considered a brilliant but problematic work. It had debuted in 1935, with music by George Gershwin and lyrics by DuBose Heyward (mostly) and Ira Gershwin, based on Heyward's 1925 novel *Porgy*. The opera opened in 1933 and was a *succès d'estime*, with the caliber of its music recognized at once, but in a commercial sense it fared only moderately well on Broadway.

Part of the problem was that, while it opened at the Alvin Theatre, a popular Broadway house, it clearly wasn't a Broadway show. Gershwin called it a "folk opera" (meaning an opera written in a popular idiom), and when it was previewed for invited audiences at Carnegie Hall in September 1935, it ran more than four hours long. Gershwin then made substantial cuts during the show's trial run in Boston, but it opened on Broadway at roughly three hours and twenty minutes long. Moreover, it was definitely an opera in terms of style and substance.

There had been a time, certainly in Gilbert & Sullivan's heyday in the 1870s and 1980s, when operas did big business on Broadway. Even as late as the years after

World War I, Victor Herbert, Rudolph Friml and assorted imported Viennese operettas were notching impressive runs. There was certainly a large crossover audience between opera and operetta, as they have in common a similar style of singing and a similar symphonic orchestral accompaniment. There are even the last gasps of a distinctly American take on operetta in *Show Boat* and in the big chorus numbers of *Carousel*. But by the 1930s opera and operetta fans didn't look to Broadway, and Broadway fans didn't look to opera.

Throw in the fact that the show required a large cast (twenty-two lead roles) and an onstage choir, nearly all of them African Americans, and a substantial orchestra, and it was a hard show to keep open on Broadway. Everybody recognized the show was something special, and there were four revivals between 1942 and 1953, the last and most successful of which ran nearly a year, but all of them lost money. As with most operas, *Porgy and Bess* was too expensive to make money unless it sold out big theaters, but it remained too much of a rarefied taste to sell out big theaters.

And then, after 1953, there wasn't another revival for twenty-three years. *Porgy and Bess* suffered the fate that had befallen many Black-themed musicals that had opened in the 1930s, 1940s, and 1950s: in the changing racial climate of the late 1950s and 1960s, shows that earlier had seemed progressive for their embrace of Black characters and Black themes, now became problematic for their treatment of those characters and themes.

Porgy and Bess was set in an impoverished community, treated themes of violence, crime, gambling, prostitution, drugs and domestic abuse, and featured lyrics and spoken dialogue (only for white characters) all performed in dialect.

Some of the opera's songs—"Summertime," "I Got Plenty o' Nuttin," "There's a Boat dat's Leavin' Soon for New York," "It Ain't Necessarily So"—became standards and were widely recorded in both instrumental and vocal versions, by both Black and white musicians, but the opera itself was infrequently commercially produced. A 1958 film adaptation, directed by (my future employer) Otto Preminger and featuring Sidney Poitier and Dorothy Dandridge lip-syncing, bombed and lost half of its $7 million budget.

And so matters stood until a producer named Sherwin M. Goldman somehow saw or became aware of a new *Porgy and Bess* by the Houston Grand Opera, directed by a then-unknown named Jack O'Brien. I never asked Goldman, who worked out of New York, how he came across the Houston production, but he was captivated by it and resolved to bring it to Broadway. He managed to convince the Gershwin and Heyward estates that it was time for a new look at this iconic masterpiece.

There were some advantages to this approach: because he would be bringing an existing production to New York, he'd save the costs of an out-of-town run, and the sets and costumes would be in hand from the start. The cast members were almost all newcomers, so far as Broadway was concerned, but that meant they'd be relatively inexpensive. All these savings would be useful in mounting a show that, because of the size of its cast and orchestra, came with some intimidating built-in costs.

It was a huge gamble on a show that remained controversial and—since O'Brien and music director John DeMain had restored all of Gershwin's 1935 cuts—was still a very long show and a hard sell in a world in which opera was rarely seen in commercial theaters.

It was a successful gamble, though. The critics were unanimously favorable, and the show—originally scheduled for a two-month run at the Uris Theatre—wound up being held over for another month at the Mark Hellinger Theatre.

When I got in touch with Goldman, I found he was interested in having a recording but seemed to feel no sense of urgency about making up his mind. I also found that my offer wasn't the only one on the table: no less than Goddard Lieberson himself, now a freelance producer, wanted to produce it. I imagine he would have taken it to Columbia, but at this stage it was Goddard bidding for himself.

Goddard's credibility, both as a producer and as a producer of *Porgy and Bess*, was obviously unassailable. However, we did have some advantages. Red Seal was on a roll, for one thing, and Goddard was asking a lot: he wanted a producer's fee of a hundred thousand dollars on top of the costs of production, which was a hundred thousand dollars more than I'd cost, being a staff producer for RCA.

In addition, it turned out I had an in with Goldman. Back when he was an undergraduate at Yale, he'd roomed with Robert Kimball, who went on to write several books about musical theater. Kimball and I had known each other for a long time and had done several projects together, so he was pitching me to his old roommate. (Bob eventually wound up writing the liner notes for our recording.)

Goldman was a canny producer, though, and a very, very tough negotiator. On behalf of RCA, I wound up agreeing to pay half of the $150,000 the recording would cost.

Selling opera recordings was a tricky business, as it still is, and one obvious marketing tool was potentially a Grammy for Best Opera Recording of the Year. I normally would have felt sure we had a good shot at the award. As it happened, though, in 1976 the Grammy had gone to Lorin Maazel and the Cleveland Orchestra for—the first-ever complete recording of *Porgy and Bess*.

This Grammy-winning recording had, obviously, been a very high-profile affair, and our recording couldn't help but be confused with theirs in the minds of record-buyers and Grammy nominators. And the fact it had been a complete recording stole a great deal of our thunder, making it seem as if Red Seal had arrived a year late for the party. Furthermore, I didn't like it very much.

But I wanted this one desperately. I loved the production, and I was bursting with ideas for the recording. I threw everything I could think of at the corporate guys: not only would we be paying only half the costs, for example, but we'd benefit from the fact that, since *Porgy and Bess* is an opera, the orchestra would fall under the musicians' union's classical rates and regulations, not pop rates. A classical recording could have sessions as long as four hours, as opposed to three hours for a musical, and you could book two four-hour sessions in a day, as long as you allowed adequate time between them. And there were a lot of singers, but because none of them were stars, they were all working for scale, so the chances of the costs getting out of hand were very small.

I told them all sorts of things, and eventually it worked. Maybe it wouldn't have, because Goldman was maddeningly slow to make up his mind, but for some reason he had to go to Europe, and while he was gone, his lawyer concluded the deal with us. By the time he got back, everything was set. It would be, unfortunately, the second-ever complete recording, yes, but we were going to do this *Porgy and Bess*.

The obvious difference between recording an opera and recording a musical—and I hadn't recorded a lot of operas previously, since Columbia didn't record many—was it involved an orchestra of around sixty-five. Unlike many producers of Broadway recordings, though, whose work is done through the pop departments of their labels, I had worked with plenty of orchestras this large or larger, notably the New York Philharmonic. I knew how to set up a big orchestra, where the mikes needed to be, how to schedule it—all skills that would come in handy on *Porgy and Bess*.

A little detail from my past turned out to be useful, as well: The Houston Grand Opera, knowing a Broadway run involved eight shows a week and that so demanding a schedule was rare for operatic singers, had come to New York with three different casts. Obviously, all the singers wanted to be on the recording, and there was the risk of fights breaking out among three Porgys and three Besses, all wanting to do the session. It was an awkward issue for us and for Goldman, who was getting it from all sides.

I'd faced this issue once before, though, on *To Broadway with Love*, of all things, and had thought it through then. The answer was to simply declare that, as with any Broadway musical, RCA was making an original-cast recording, meaning the Broadway cast on opening night was ours as well. That still left two unhappy Porgys and two disappointed Besses, but at least we (and Sherwin Goldman) could say it wasn't personal. It wasn't a case of us preferring one singer over another, it was just the customary protocol.

We got some very touching letters from some of the other cast members, who understandably were deeply disappointed at not being given a shot at this. But the truth is, as good as those other two Besses were, Clamma Dale was extraordinary in her voice, her acting, her vocal coloring. We weren't playing favorites, but if we had been, she'd have been the easy choice. She was really the star of that production. Donnie Rae Albert was very, very good as Porgy, but Clamma was fantastic.

Larry Marshall was Sportin' Life. I had worked with Larry back in 1973, working fairly briefly on the original-cast recording of *Elephant Steps* prior to my leaving Columbia, so we already had a rapport. That came in handy because I had been particularly struck by the way, in the movie, Sammy Davis Jr. had sung the words "Come with me" in "There's a Boat dat's Leavin' Soon for New York." It was so seductive, the way he sang those three syllables, and I wanted to get that out of Larry. I sang it and Larry went with it.

Usually I work closely with the singers, but less so this time. This was an opera, not a musical, and these performances were engraved in these people's minds. I made little effort to make any adjustments because it wasn't necessary.

Now and then I did, of course. There's a photograph of me standing with Porgy and Crown, played by Albert Smith, talking to them about how they should audibly stage their fight scene. It's a cute picture—this little Jewish guy standing between these two big Black guys, looking like a referee as we talk about how they're going to fight each other—where the grunts come, the groans, and the body falls. We recorded it both ways, with them grunting and groaning over the music, and then again in a clear background, so we could put these sounds in wherever we chose.

Carol Brice played Maria. I knew her from one of those old Columbia 78s I had listened to when I was a kid, Fritz Reiner conducting de Falla's *El Amor Brujo*, with Carol singing the solo in "Ritual Fire Dance." Carol was almost sixty in 1977, but she still had a fantastic voice and did a superb job on the recording.

Conductor John DeMain was a very soft-spoken guy who was only thirty-three, but already had been the music director of the Houston Grand Opera for many years. He's had a good career since then, although I haven't run into him again in all these years, since he's based in Madison, Wisconsin. John is a highly gifted conductor. He really understood and absorbed the music to its core.

Jack O'Brien was not nearly as famous then as he has become in the intervening years, but was a very good director. I say that, though he frustrated me by getting more involved in the recording session than directors usually do.

There's a moment in the opera after Robbins is killed and Crown has to flee, that Bess is left alone and friendless. Then Porgy opens his door, silently beckons to Bess, and she walks across the stage to his house and goes inside. Of course, on a recording you can't see Porgy beckoning, so for his 1951 recording Goddard added a line for Porgy (Lawrence Winters): "Bess, Bess, Porgy will take you." I thought it was a good solution, but Jack objected. He said, "I don't want that line. I've directed Porgy to be much more passive than that, and the Porgy I've directed wouldn't speak."

Now, he had no actual right to interfere with me on this, but for once in my life I thought twice and stepped back from a challenge. I had wanted the line, and Donnie Rae was willing to do it, but I realized this wasn't worth a fight. The tone of the session was very good, and the last thing I needed was to kindle an air of conflict.

Instead, in post-production I created the sound of Bess's footsteps going from center to stage right. Then you hear a door (Porgy's) creak open, and then you hear it shut. It doesn't take too much imagination to realize Bess has gone to one side and been let in a door, which is then closed behind her. In the fullness of time, I've come to think it's perhaps a better solution than Goddard's line of dialogue.

During the protracted negotiations for the recording rights, I'd had plenty of time to think about how I wanted this recording to sound and to plot out which character would be on which microphone, and whether they would be placed in the foreground, middle ground, or background. Knowing most of these singers had never recorded before, and trying to be as efficient as possible, I made a point of getting hold of the principals' piano/vocal scores before the recording session and I wrote into each singer's score which mike they needed to be at for each of their lines.

The RCA studio had an actual stage—an unusual amenity for a recording studio. So we set up seven mikes across the apron of the stage, spacing them far enough apart that we could acoustically divide the stage into far left, left, left center, center, right center, right, and far right, creating a smooth horizontal progression across the imaginary stage in the listener's mind. Because the singers knew their material by heart, they needed their scores only to cue their movement from one microphone to the next. As long as they could do that without shuffling their feet—which is always a hazard—it was easy.

Porgy and Bess is a long opera! We broke it up into exactly a hundred pieces—big takes, little takes, and inserts—and we were able to record them all in three days of two four-hour sessions apiece. That was possible only because the orchestra members were being paid opera rates. If we'd had to follow the union rules for musicals, we'd probably have had to do it all in substantially less time for financial reasons, and the results never would have been so good.

As for me, three eight-hour days, instead of one of up to twenty hours, afforded me ample recording time to realize all the extra things, the special effects that I wanted to insert into this recording. For several weeks before the recording session, I gave a lot of thought to how I would proceed.

For example, the first thing the audience hears after the overture in *Porgy and Bess* is an onstage piano being played by Jazzbo Brown. As he's playing it, the chorus is singing "doo-wah-wah, doo-wah." It goes on for a long time, and—probably because it's outside of the story—Goddard had omitted it entirely in his 1951 recording. I wanted to include it, and I had asked myself, "What should that piano sound like?" Most recording studios have an excellent piano, but if I'd used that, it would have sounded too good. Jazzbo shouldn't be playing a Steinway. But if I chose a honky-tonk instrument, a sort of barroom piano, it would have sounded hokey or cartoonish. I needed a piano that just sounded ordinary, unglamorous.

As it happened, my perfect piano was close at hand, in the office of one of my fellow producers at RCA. It was a humble spinet that had probably been tuned within the past two or three years and on which, thank God, all the keys worked. So one of the first decisions I made was to use this ordinary-but-believable piano for the Jazzbo Brown sequence. We also weren't going to mike it closely because Jazzbo is way upstage somewhere and should sound far-off.

Next question: Who did I want to play that piano? The *Porgy and Bess* pit pianist was Ross Reimuller, who happened to be a former classmate of mine at Oberlin, but I wanted a more idiomatic sound for Jazzbo. So I got in touch with Dick Hyman, the great jazz pianist, and he agreed to do it. (He wound up being double-credited on the album: as an orchestra member because he was an instrumentalist, and as an actor because Jazzbo is an onstage character.)

Now, this opening number is very long, about five minutes, and cutting it in half would not have been a bad thing. I wanted to leave it intact, though, because it has a gradual accretion of voices, which is very powerful, more and more people singing as it goes along, and the longer this process continues, the more powerful it is. So I decided to keep the complete musical sequence and use it to create, in sound, the entire breadth of the stage. All the "wah-doo-wahs" would start out in one corner but gradually get more and more downstage and closer to the center and would start to move more and more horizontally until we reached the final "wah-doo-wahs," when our imaginary stage of the recording would be filled with people, the entire community of Catfish Row.

Sometimes, I didn't know in advance what "inspiration" might come to me as I went later into post-production. For example, while mixing the completely edited recording, we added the sound of wind at the end of the hurricane. It would be normal and reasonable to have the wind stop just as the music ends, but for some reason, I suddenly felt that to make the scene end more effectively, I would let the hurricane wind trail off for a few more seconds after the music stopped. I still don't know why that's such a perfect touch, but as I listen to it now . . . it is.

There are so many strange little details I remember. I remember, weeks after the sessions, my executive assistant, Susan Krauss, who was the most wonderful assistant I've ever worked with, trying on different pairs of shoes because she's on the recording—when Bess is walking quickly to Porgy's house, the feet you hear walking, belong to Susan.

We had our whole chorus of kids, and early in the opera, when Robbins (Glover Parham) asks, "Who wants a cotton hook?" he then slides the cotton hook across the stage. I don't remember what we used to sound like that we thought a cotton hook might sound like, but I know we panned it from one side to the other. We did this in post-production—on the session, there was no cotton hook, so I said to the children, "I want you to laugh and run like the cotton hook is coming to you."

I even got into the act myself, which I almost never do. In the finale, when Porgy is giving out gifts to the various people on Catfish Row, one of the gifts he gives to Scipio is a harmonica. And on the recording, you can hear him playing a lick of "Oh, I Can't Sit Down" as he walks off. But that was me playing the harmonica.

Sherwin Goldman was not there for the sessions—he was still in Europe—and it's probably just as well. He came back after the recording was finished, and we got into a nasty argument. He wanted to be listed as executive producer of the recording, as if he'd supervised my work. That made me very angry because he wasn't even present on the session. So I dug in my heels and refused to give him that credit, and he bore me a grudge for many years afterward.

He was so angry at me that when he learned Jack O'Brien had vetoed my putting in the line, "Bess, Bess, Porgy'll take you," that filled him with delight. Years later, when we happened to run into each other, he brought it up again and said, "See, you couldn't do everything you wanted, you know? You didn't do that the way you wanted." And he's right, I didn't.

That story has a nice ending, though. Sometime in the mid-2010s, I was at one of the Metropolitan Opera Guild luncheons, and there was Sherwin Goldman, thirty-five years older but looking exactly the same. We said hello, we smiled at each other, and I said to him and to the people we were with, "You know, the greatest recording experience of my life was doing *Porgy and Bess*."

I could just sort of feel him relax, and me too—like, after all those years of tension, he thought he'd finally gotten the acknowledgment from me he deserved.

And he did deserve it, because the Houston Grand Opera production would never have come to New York—and played a major role in "rehabilitating" *Porgy and Bess* for generations to come—if Goldman hadn't seen the potential and made it happen. He's remained a passionate advocate of the opera: he held the professional-production rights for many years thereafter, and he brought it back to New York in 1983 for a forty-five-performance run at Radio City Music Hall, again directed by Jack O'Brien, and to City Opera in 2000, this time directed by Tazewell Thompson.

We had the first playbacks of the discs in my office at RCA, months later. It could have been sooner, but Goldman was giving us a hard time, not coming up with the money that had been promised, so we didn't want to complete the post-production until he'd lived up to his deal, which eventually he did.

Besides, because this was a limited run and the recording would be released well after the show had closed, we had the luxury of time, with no deadline to meet. I'd asked Jay David Saks to do most of the editing and mixing, and Jay always appreciates the time to really get into it. So he edited and mixed it over the space of three or four months. That gave us the time to think about everything—timing each roll of the dice, each throwing-down of coins, and each rustle of paper. When Bess sniffs happy dust and then runs off with Sportin' Life, what's that going to sound like—how loud will the sniff be, and what exactly will we hear as they run off, receding further and further into the distance, very high and laughing? A police car is arriving, do we hear it? When the sheriff comes in and starts pacing, do we hear him pace, hear his voice moving, or is it too gimmicky?

We had time to think about all of that. And sometimes, yes, maybe it is too gimmicky. I like to bring a lot of detail to these things, but you have to be careful not to interfere with the music, not to let the gadgetry distract the listener from a magnificent score.

So, months after the sessions, John DeMain came to my office, along with Clamma Dale, Donnie Rae Albert, and I think, Carol Brice as well. We went through three hours of listening, and I don't think anybody said a word. We came to the end, and Clamma was crying. I didn't know why she was crying, and my first thought was, "Oh, my God, what did I do wrong? What do I have to fix?"

No, she was crying because her father had recently died, and she said, "I was crying because I wish he had been alive to hear me do this."

And then, like the cherry on the sundae, the next year at the Grammy Awards, we won Best Opera Recording—just one year after another recording of the same opera. It had never happened before, and it's never happened again. I suppose I was surprised—I'd been very pleased just to be nominated, and I certainly didn't think the odds favored us—I was gratified. These awards can be very political, and they don't always go the way they should. But on this occasion, they did. I say this, believe me, as dispassionately as I possibly can: it is one of the greatest recordings ever made.

Everything I knew or imagined about making a recording went into this one. It's the best work I've ever done. If there's a claim for my work as art, it's this recording.

23

A Man Named Sweeney Todd

Sweeney Todd: The Demon Barber of Fleet Street (1979)

Early in 1978, Steve Sondheim invited Irene and me to an afternoon gathering at Mary Lea Johnson's house, where he sang through the songs he'd finished for a new show he was working on, an offbeat musical called *Sweeney Todd*. The songs were impressive, but it was far from the whole score, and there was enough missing that it was hard to get a feeling for the show itself.

A few months later he invited us to another gathering at Hal Prince's house, where he and Hal ran through the songs together for about fifty of Hal's closest friends. This time Steve had more of the finished score, and he and Hal did their best to convey the story and characters as well. In fact, one of my favorite memories of my years with Steve and Hal is that evening, as they made up for their limitations as actors or singers with their sheer enthusiasm for a show that clearly excited both of them very much.

I can't say, however, that at this early date I recognized that I was hearing what arguably stands as Steve's masterpiece, the most ambitious, most completely successful work in his long and storied career. I think the score wasn't finished even then, and while I did get more of the story, neither of these early presentations really captured the show's unique tone. It was not until I saw it onstage that I fully realized what this show really was.

Sweeney Todd is as close as Steve ever came to writing an opera, and it surges with dark, twisted passion. The show is a perfect rebuttal to anyone who ever charged Steve with writing cerebral, clever-but-detached shows. Whatever else one might say about *Sweeney Todd*, it's a cauldron of emotion from beginning to end. And yet, except for *A Funny Thing Happened on the Way to the Forum*, it's also his funniest show, a riotous black comedy that never fails to evoke tears of laughter. The tension between these two aspects, and the ease with which Steve and Hugh Wheeler (author of the book) balance them, makes for a tone unlike any other show that Steve—or anybody else—ever wrote.

Sweeney Todd: The Demon Barber of Fleet Street is a musical adaptation of Christopher Bond's 1970 play *Sweeney Todd*, which had a brief run in London in 1973. It was almost happenstance that Steve went to see it one night. That put the idea in his head and inspired him to secure the musical rights.

The story went back much further than Bond's play, all the way back to Elizabethan times, when the grisly tale of a barber who dispatches his customers, usually to steal their money, was used to caution country folk against venturing into the big city. James Malcolm Ryder's 1846 serial novel, *The String of Pearls: A Romance*, is the first work known to have given the barber a name, and to have introduced Mrs. Lovett, her gruesome meat pies, and Mr. Todd's trick barber chair that whisks the corpses to the cellar.

In 1847 George Dibdin Pitt adapted Ryder's novel into a hit stage melodrama, *The String of Pearls: or The Fiend of Fleet Street*. Over the next century or so, the story was retold on stage and screen numerous times. There was an American knockoff novel, Harry Hazel's *Sweeney Todd: or the Ruffian Barber: A Tale of Terror of the Seas and the Mysteries of the City* (1852), and the film *The Demon Barber of Fleet Street* (1936), which seems to have contributed the subtitle to the musical and starred Tod Slaughter, a melodrama actor who specialized in villains and apparently actually was named "Slaughter."

None of these previous versions, however, has the operatic scope or the sardonic humor that defines the Sondheim/Wheeler musical. Those are very definitely its own.

It wasn't automatic that we'd record *Sweeney Todd*. Steve and Hal had been happy with my work on *Company* and *Pacific Overtures* and would be happy to have us record their new show, but not everyone thought *Sweeney Todd* would be worth recording. The word on the street was negative. People were going to previews and not liking it very much. There was no strong feeling that the show was going to be a hit. Among the people who heard the bad buzz was Robert Summer, then in his first year as president of RCA Records.

"OK," he said to me, "you've got to tell me, are we going ahead with this or not?" Which I read as my new boss telling me, "If we do this, it's your neck if it doesn't work out."

But I had confidence in the show, so I said, "Yes, we're going ahead with it. This is a masterpiece we've got on our hands, and we're going to record it."

That was enough for Bob, who would turn out to be the longest-serving president of RCA Records during my twelve years there and one of the best bosses I ever had. I'd have a long and rewarding relationship with him, in which he backed me up whenever he could, but it started off with a gamble. He let me make the call, and thank God, I was right.

It was never a question of quality, as far as I was concerned, but just a question of whether *Sweeney Todd* would find its audience. Because you never know. I remember seeing a show called *Drat! The Cat!* out of town in 1965. It was a musical about a Victorian-era cat burglar with book and lyrics by Ira Levin and music by Milton Schafer, and I adored it. I saw it in either Boston or New Haven, and it was just the most delightful show, and the audience ate it up. It came to New York, and it laid an egg right away, ran for only eight performances. There are no guarantees.

Whatever the problem was with *Sweeney Todd* in previews (I'd bet on its tone, because tone is always a delicate thing to calibrate), it was fixed by opening night. The reviews were some of the best Steve ever got, and the word of mouth was terrific. *Sweeney Todd* became a show you had to see, and it went on to win the Tony Award for Best Musical. By the time the cast assembled for our recording session, we all knew the show was going to be around for a good long time.

The recording of *Sweeney Todd* began, as the recording of any cast album does (or should), with a planning meeting scheduled several weeks before the sessions. In late February Jay Saks and I met with Steve, Hal, conductor Paul Gemignani, copyists Mathilde Pincus and Al Miller, orchestrator Jonathan Tunick, and librettist Hugh Wheeler. Our purpose was twofold: to agree on the broad parameters for the recording—what would be in it and what wouldn't—and to identify and if possible, resolve potential problems before we were on the clock at the session itself.

The broad outline was easy enough: we all agreed the recorded version of *Sweeney Todd* should be constructed like a radio play, guiding the listener through the story with the judicious use of dialogue, sound effects, and technological resources such as stereo. We spent several hours going over the material, song by song and scene by scene, to create a master plan and determine what to include and what to excise. Most notably, we decided to sacrifice two onstage murders (those of Pirelli and the Beadle) because they did not take place during musical scenes and therefore would interrupt the flow of the recording.

Once this master plan had been devised, Steve and Hugh were tasked with reshaping the material to fit the plan, trimming the dialogue to an absolute minimum, and if necessary, writing new, shorter transitions to replace longer, more complicated scenes. (In the liner notes for the album, Steve would explain whatever action took place onstage but wasn't depicted on the recording.)

The plan we devised also called for small changes in the orchestrations, for altering the sequence of some selections and for adjustments, during the recording sessions, of actors' performances to ensure that the intentions and motivations of the characters would come across, even without the listener seeing them and hearing the full dialogue.

By the end of the planning meeting, we all had our work cut out for us, but we were pleased with the plan and convinced it would serve the show well.

During the next couple weeks, I studied the music, pored over Hugh's recording script, and returned to see the show several more times. Having done so, I devised a recording schedule that encompassed six three-hour recording sessions spread over two days (unavoidable, given union rules and the amount of music in what would be a two-disk LP), utilizing the full company at first and whittling down to major soloists on later sessions.

The finished recording would have twenty-nine tracks, ranging in length from 31 seconds to 13 minutes. I structured the three-hour sessions to be able to extract 15 minutes of usable material from each one. In all, I expected to get about 90 minutes of music recorded in those 18 hours.

On the morning of the first session, March 12, 1979, I got there at 9 a.m., an hour before the session was to start, in order to see that the orchestra chairs and music stands had been set up on the studio floor and to help engineer Tony Salvatore position eight mikes on the stage and sixteen or so on the floor.

There were three unexpected early arrivals in the form of Hal's wife, Judy Prince, and their two kids, Charlie and Daisy. Judy asked me to walk them through and to tell them why things were set up as they were, and—as I had some spare time, since Tony had everything well in hand—I took them around the studio.

The prepared floor was strewn with cables and several small isolation booths for vocal soloists, plus a large table and three chairs for the music copyists, who attend every session to enter any small changes we might need into the orchestra parts. Tony was in the control room, preparing the recording console, the tape machines, the work space, the talkback from the control room to the studio, and additional chairs for the privileged few who had been invited to watch the recording in progress.

Charlie Prince, who today is an orchestral conductor, was particularly interested in the seating arrangement of the orchestra, which was different from the customary arrangement for the pit orchestra. I explained to him that the differences were due to the capabilities of stereo and reflected my personal preferences.

As in the standard orchestral setup, the high strings—the first and second violins—were to the conductor's left, the violas in the center, and the cellos on the right. The double-basses are normally placed behind the cellos at the conductor's right, but I prefer to put them in the center because I want their deep sound to be reproduced from both loudspeakers when the recording is played in stereo.

In my orchestra setup, the percussion instruments are spread out in a straight line behind the rest of the orchestra. The woodwinds are behind the violas, with the high brass—the trumpets—on the right, behind the low strings, sitting on risers so their bells will be above the heads of the string players, sending their sound directly into the air. The French horns are on the left, along with the harp. Normally the trombones would also be on the left, but I prefer them to be in the center, again to be sure their deeper sound will emanate from both loudspeakers.

All three Princes seemed interested, and it was fun for me to walk them through it. It put me in a good mood for what would prove to be a very enjoyable series of recording sessions.

This was an unusually complicated show, with many opportunities for things to get out of whack and throw us behind schedule. What saved us was the extraordinary professionalism of the cast. They were just so good and so ready—nobody was hoarse, nobody was sick, nobody had to dub anything in later. It was just a very good bunch of people, eager and celebratory because, of course, the show had looked like a looming failure and now suddenly looked like a great success. That sense of gratification, that all their hard work was finally paying off, energized the whole session.

In particular, the two leads were superb. Steve's post-1970 musicals are usually ensemble shows, with either many stars or no stars at all, depending on how you look at it. One glance at the poster for this one, though, and you knew it was a show that would live or die by the performances of Len Cariou as Sweeney and Angela Lansbury as Mrs. Lovett. There's hardly a minute of the show when at least one of them isn't onstage.

Len was wonderful, with a dark performance that was almost painfully intense, except every now and then he'd have a sardonic line that was hilarious for being so unexpected. Steve told me he'd heard that Len had a daughter whom he hadn't seen in a long time, somewhere in Canada, and Steve took that as having been a key to his performance as a tormented father seeking his lost daughter.

When you're talking about calibrating the tone of *Sweeney Todd*, you're really talking about Angela Lansbury. Mrs. Lovett is a very difficult role. Sweeney is much easier, a relentless, driven avenger from start to finish. He's almost a one-note character. Mrs. Lovett starts out as the comic relief in a very dark show, but before "The Worst Pies in London" is over, we already know she's as callous as she is hilarious. It's her idea to dispose of the murdered Pirelli (and Sweeney's future customers) in her pies, and despite her soft spot for Sweeney, she feels no sympathy or understanding for his obsession with revenge. On the other hand, she keeps us laughing through much of the first half of the show. This mix of the hilarious and the horrifying makes it a role that challenges everyone who plays it, but nobody has ever done it better than Angela did.

And of course, as a personality type, Angela couldn't have been further from Mrs. Lovett. She was such a nice person to be around—I don't know anybody who didn't love her.

I remember, when we were recording "The Worst Pies in London," she finished a wonderful take, her second one, and I was completely satisfied. I said, "That's great," and I was prepared to move on, but Angela said, "Tom, would you mind if I did just one more?" I didn't see any need for another take, but naturally I said, "Of course not"—and she sang it even better. I hadn't expected it.

Another Angela memory I've mentioned before: once we started the editing and mixing, I realized I needed her to come back in to redo one line. She hadn't made a mistake; I just needed a different reading of that particular line. (The line was "So it is you, Benjamin Barker," leading into "These Are My Friends.") She didn't make a fuss about it but came in, did the one line, and went home—and never sent us a bill. As she put it, "What are friends for?" That was very generous of her. She was a very gracious lady.

There was never any question that *Sweeney Todd* would have to be a two-disc set. Even to try to shoehorn it onto a single disc would be to repeat the mistake Capitol had made with *Follies*. There was too much music, and it was too good.

Everything about the way we presented and packaged this recording was top of the line. We included the full lyrics of the show, and I have no idea how much time Nancy Swift, who was our literary editor at Red Seal, put into sitting with Steve and making sure that the lyrics and text were going to be printed flawlessly.

As usual for the recording, Steve was eager to restore one or two things that had been cut from the stage production. For example, large sections of the shaving contest between Pirelli and Todd had been deleted, and Steve made sure that they were put back for the recording, making the song almost twice as long.

There are two songs sung onstage called "Johanna," but three on the recording. The extra one, known as "the Judge's Johanna," is a solo sung by Judge Turpin while masturbating and whipping himself as he watches Johanna through a keyhole. It was just too much for the Broadway audience, and Hal and Steve agreed it had to go—but Steve wanted to have it restored for the recording.

He also agreed to a two-word, who-sings-what change that I suggested: Late in Act Two there's a scene and song ("The Letter") in which the wily Sweeney writes a letter to lure Judge Turpin back to his shop. But Sweeney himself doesn't sing in "The Letter," it's all sung by a vocal quintet, one of whom sings the two final words, "Sweeney Todd."

I suggested it might be highly effective if Len sang those last two words. Steve liked the idea, and it plays very well on the recording.

The orchestrations for *Sweeney Todd* are magnificent. Jonathan Tunick did a phenomenal job. He said to me, years later, "This was when I first felt that I knew exactly what I was doing, that I was in total command of my own resources."

To achieve the symphonic sound Jonathan and I thought the show required, we agreed to expand the size of the orchestra. The orchestra in the pit of any theater is limited by budgets and the size of the orchestra pit and with Broadway producers generally hiring the minimum they think they can get away with, and of course nowadays there are synthesizers, and everything is heavily miked.

But romantic musicals, period dramas, and shows of extraordinary scope lean heavily on the strings, unlike most of today's musicals, which tend to emphasize winds and brass. A show like *Sweeney Todd* really needs more strings than you'll find in any modern Broadway orchestra. The difference is not volume because ten violins aren't significantly louder than five: mathematically speaking, doubling the number of strings on a part, whether you're turning five into ten or fifty into a hundred, adds only three decibels.

The difference is the richness of sound. Where two violins can clash audibly because of tiny differences in pitch, vibrato, and so on, six violins will mask or blend those differences and you've got the beginnings of a rich ensemble. That's why we generally double the strings for a recording; if the pit had five violins, we'll bring it up to ten in the studio. The *Sweeney Todd* pit was unusually large already, with twenty-six players, but we added another twelve strings, plus an extra French horn and one more percussionist.

There's a song near the beginning of *Sweeney Todd* called "Poor Thing," in which Mrs. Lovett narrates what happened to Sweeney's wife after he was sentenced to exile. The orchestration for this scene is big, until suddenly it switches to a minuet that's played onstage by a trio in Judge Turpin's house. I took those three players out of the orchestra and put them somewhere else in the studio, just for that minuet, so they were no longer sounding as though they were part of the orchestra but had the effect, for the listener, of an onstage ensemble.

Sweeney Todd has no overture. Instead there's a long, ominous organ solo, which ends with the shriek of the factory whistle that heralds the beginning of the action. Now, I may have a reputation as a completist, someone who likes to keep every note of the score and then some, but that can't always be true.

In this case the long organ solo is there only to set a mood. In the theater it helps the audience settle in, but on a recording its length is unnecessary and perhaps distracting. This organ music is not particularly noteworthy, mostly a lot of block chords, so I cut it to 30 seconds or so before I slammed in the sound of that harsh, ear-splitting whistle.

On the recording, the purpose of the organ solo is simply to establish a churchlike tone to be shockingly disrupted by the whistle, and the only purpose of the whistle is to get your attention for the prologue—and that the prologue is one of the best things Steve ever wrote.

Just look at that first word, which couldn't have been more perfectly chosen. There's that whistle, a sudden quiet, and then we hear a solo voice: "Attend the tale of Sweeney Todd." "Attend" is such an antiquated word, one that puts you right there into Victorian England. No one today uses the word "attend." And then there's the alliteration, all those T's: aTTend, Tale, Todd. Six words into the show, you can already tell you're listening to something unique, archaic.

From there the score only gets more impressive. Instead of following the old-fashioned musical template of dialogue that explicates a minimal plot and builds to a mood that motivates the song, *Sweeney Todd* does almost the opposite. In a style similar to that of opera, the plot explication is often done as recitative or within a song, and the emotional pivots take place within the music as often as within the dialogue. The dialogue/music interplay is much more unpredictable, and the audience has to pay close attention to both.

Steve's score is wildly diverse. There are concerted numbers more than ten minutes long and dialogue scenes almost that long. He employs counterpoint, musical clues to the story, leitmotifs, a recurring use of the medieval chant "Dies Irae" (first heard as "Swing your razor wide, Sweeney"), a reference to Bernard Herrmann's music for *Psycho* (1960), and so much more.

One of the joys of recording something like *Sweeney Todd* is the opportunity to turn it into a full-blown radio play. Some of the plots of Steve's shows—*Pacific Overtures*, for example, or *Assassins*—are so complex as to defy being reproduced in a recording, but *Sweeney Todd* has a clear, linear narrative that can be told through sound.

When I do lectures and want to explain what I mean by the art of telling the story of a show with sound alone, I always take as my example a track from *Sweeney Todd*. It comes early in Act II, a quartet called "Johanna"—the recording's third song with that name. It's a classic example of Steve's penchant for complex songs that are easily understood on the stage and seemingly impossible to capture on a recording, and just the kind of challenge that turns on my creative juices.

To the audience, what's going on is busy but not confusing: they can see Sweeney's barbershop (a raised area at the audience's right) and watch as he sings about Johanna while shaving two customers, slashing their throats, and dropping their bodies down to the basement to be baked into pies. When Anthony enters at left, singing about his quest for his abducted love Johanna, the audience can see that he's on the other side of the stage at ground level, obviously somewhere else in London because he's lit differently and walking between lampposts. When Johanna joins in, they can see that she's very far upstage, singing through the barred window of the madhouse (Bedlam) to which Judge Turpin has committed her, out of earshot of Anthony or Sweeney. As for the Beggar Woman wandering in and out, they can tell she's also on the street, but never crossing paths with Anthony.

So there's a lot going on, but it's easy for audience members to sort out because they can see it.

This need to establish that four different things are happening in four different parts of the stage is made for stereo. When Anthony (Victor Garber) opens the song, he's at far left; when Sweeney (Len Cariou) joins in, he's at far right. Johanna (Sarah Rice) is singing further from the microphone, making her sound remote from both of them. Finally, while the others stay in their specific locations, the crazed beggar woman (Merle Louise) is constantly moving from microphone to microphone left of center, conveying to the listener the sense that she's wandering. (Anthony and the Beggar Woman are both in the streets, but I fade him out before she appears, and fade her out before he returns—they're in the same place, but not at the same time.)

This is all very effective, but it takes us only so far. To anyone watching the show, the visual anchor of this scene is Sweeney's shop, where in the course of this single song he kills two customers. How can we depict the shop so a listener can understand what's going on? The answer is a bell that tinkles whenever the door is opened, and footsteps (shoes on wood) as each customer comes up the stairs and into the shop.

But what happens to them? Onstage Sweeney pulls a lever, and the special barber's chair catapults them down the chute into the basement. We sent two RCA recording engineers to the Uris Theater, before a Wednesday matinee, to record the sound of the chair as well as the shrieking factory whistle that was the production's acoustic signature.

In the theater, it was easy enough to see a newly killed victim being ousted from the barber chair and then falling through a trap door, crashing a moment later into the basement. For the recording, it wasn't difficult for us to create the sound of a body fall and its unceremonious landing, but I had to deal with an immutable reality: that a stereo recording may contain sounds that flow from one side to another, left to right, right to left, and all permutations in between, but a stereo recording does not have an up and down! No vertical component. So our recorded victims would need to travel right to left or left to right because there was no way they could travel top to bottom.

I was fortunate to have the remarkably talented Jay David Saks, who was young, healthy, and particularly athletic—which qualified him to play Sweeney's sonic victims. With microphones hovering above him, he didn't seem to mind shoving himself around the floor many times over, until we got the thuds and swishes that seemed to work best. He was also very willing to throw himself to the ground to replicate what it might sound like when a fresh corpse lands. After a (literally) bruising hour, we had the effect we would need to add when we did our final editing.

For the final mix, we positioned the sound of the chair hard right. We then took the sliding-on-the-floor effect and electronically moved it from hard right to hard left, as fast as if it were in a vertical free fall. As the "corpse" got to the left side, we added the dull thud as the body of the victim (Jay's) lands hard in the left loudspeaker. We nicknamed the entire venture "The Horizontal Laundry Chute."

Jay and I both worked very hard on the editing and post-production. I occasionally also had my eleven-year-old daughter, Elizabeth, sitting with me when I was editing *Sweeney Todd*. She was a smart kid who attended many recording sessions, and in the editing cubicle, she listened closely. Her ability to point out what might be worth my attention was very, very perceptive. (She had a great ear—she still does.)

In the final sequence, more than thirteen minutes long, "The Ballad of Sweeney Todd," we are clearly in the presence of Sondheim the theater composer, not the "songwriter." There is stage business here that is germane to the show, but not appropriate to advance the narrative of the recording. As Tobias is sampling pies down below, he finds a hair and a fingernail: the body of the Beadle has descended. Mrs. Lovett tells Todd that Tobias has guessed what's going on, but Todd is fixed on killing Judge Turpin.

There is a lot of tension here, screaming, hysteria, the factory whistle, and then the lunatics from Bedlam singing "City on Fire." The general hysteria leads into Johanna, released from Bedlam, joining Anthony to reprise "Kiss Me" with "We Will Be Married on Sunday," and then the recording goes into the bakehouse as Mrs. Lovett and Sweeney try to coax out a traumatized Tobias. It's a dramatic riot with the lunatics and the Beggar Woman who is looking for the Beadle. And then comes a great melodic-dramatic clue: as the Beggar Woman turns the word "Beadle" into "Deedle," she starts to rock an imaginary infant with a lullaby that is the same tune that was played by the string trio in the home of Judge Turpin when he raped Lucy. So the Beggar Woman is Lucy! The astute listener may well latch on to this clue.

Sweeney, now back in his tonsorial parlor, encounters her. He doesn't recognize who she is, but clearly she is in his way. He slits her throat and sends her down the chute. The judge enters, he settles into Sweeney's chair, and then he and Todd reprise "Pretty Women," ending when Sweeney reveals that he is Benjamin Barker. As the judge screams, we bring in the factory whistle as Sweeney's razor slices, the chair squeals, and the Judge's body slides, drops, and lands with its inevitable thud in the bakehouse. Sweeney goes back down to the bakehouse, he recognizes the Beggar Woman as his wife, Lucy. He realizes that Mrs. Lovett never told him that Lucy still lived, that she was, in fact, the Beggar Woman.

There are now two potential victims left: Mrs. Lovett and Tobias. Todd flings Mrs. Lovett into the oven as Toby wanders in. He grapples with Todd, picks up a razor from the floor, and while Todd grieves for Lucy, Toby kills him. In an abbreviated form, this is what we present on the recording. At the end of the show, there are only three survivors: Tobias, Johanna, and Anthony. They will be the first who sing the Epilogue.

If it weren't for Jay, *Sweeney Todd*, *Porgy and Bess*, and any number of other albums would not be nearly as good as they are. I don't think I would ever have had the patience to milk the material to the last drop the way Jay did. *Porgy and Bess* and *Sweeney Todd* were Grammy winners, and Jay was credited as associate producer on both. He may have started out as my assistant, but by this time, he was really my partner and not anonymous by any means.

* * *

It took at least three weeks to finish the editing and mixing of *Sweeney Todd*. During that time something happened that nobody saw coming: Steve had a heart attack.

Nobody was aware of this at the time—including me, because at one point Steve (who could tell a tale very convincingly) called me at home about something relating to the recording, and he didn't say, "I'm in the hospital." Instead he said, "You can't get back to me, I'm in a phone booth."

After a few days we found out, of course, and we were shocked. Steve was only forty-nine at the time, and while he'd lived an unhealthy lifestyle for some time, he didn't look that bad. As it turned out, it was a minor attack that, fortunately, did very little damage. He started taking care of himself better after that and lived for another forty-two years.

A couple weeks later, when Steve was back home recovering, I went over to his house, carrying the master discs (the acetates that had been cut but not pressed) so he could hear the recording for the first time. We put them on, and the three of us—he, Judy Prince (who was visiting when I got there), and I—sat and listened listened straight through, without a word. The recording finished, and Steve had started to cry, which was not at all typical of him in my experience. I was very moved.

Then I began to tear up. "I really did this for you," I said. "It was really important to me that you should be happy."

And he was. The closest Steve usually got to a smile in those days was a wry twist of the mouth, but that day he was beaming. He was very pleased with the recording; he didn't neglect to give Jay his due credit: he phoned him shortly thereafter and thanked him as well for the great work he'd done on the recording.

The rest is history. After the Tony Award for the show in 1979 came the Grammy Award for the recording in 1980. In 2013 the Library of Congress added the album to its National Recording Registry, which "highlights the richness of the nation's audio legacy and underscores the importance of assuring the long-term preservation of that legacy for future generations." Only twenty-five recordings a year are added to the registry; it's considered the highest honor an American recording can receive.

It's a great comfort to know that, for as long as there is a Library of Congress, there will also be our recording of *Sweeney Todd*.

The Ballad of Sweeney Todd (1979)

Now and then I've done a record unlike any other. *The Ballad of Sweeney Todd* is one of them. The idea was inspired by an RCA colleague of mine named Mitch Farber. He had done some work for the pop department and was something of a disco maven. It was 1979, and the disco craze was in full swing.

For some reason, maybe because I'd spent too many hours editing and mixing, I wanted to do something flat-out wild. I decided we should come up with a disco version of "The Ballad of Sweeney Todd," taking the song from the musical and giving it a driving disco beat and an abundance of spooky sound effects.

Mitch and I worked together, and in the process, he gave me a crash course in the rules of disco, which apparently involved maintaining the beat relentlessly and coming back to it again and again because the dance had to be something like eight minutes long. And given the subject matter, we decided to pepper the record with sound effects of people being stabbed—daggers into watermelons, that sort of thing—to create something bloody and disgusting. It was fun.

It was a single, and instead of Red Seal I released it on a "new" RCA label called Red Seals. The art director at RCA, whose name was Joseph Stelmach, turned out to have the same kind of peculiar streak I have. He loved the whole idea of doing something irreverent on Red Seal and designed a clever label for Red Seals, which had two seals looking at each other.

Steve enjoyed it. He did feel "The Ballad of Sweeney Todd" should have had some kind of contrasting musical section, that it was too much of the same thing over and over. According to Mitch, though, that's what disco is all about. Anyway, Steve got a kick out of it.

I have no idea how it sold. Probably very badly. I have two copies, and maybe they're the only ones left in the world.

24

Everything Old Is New Again

ONE INTERESTING ASPECT OF THE DEVELOPMENT of the Broadway musical over the past century is its evolution into a vehicle for nostalgia. In the 1920s and 1930s, Broadway musicals were typically set in the present day and made extensive reference to contemporary events. The Gershwins, Rodgers & Hart, and their peers presented lighthearted looks at the world in which their audience lived. (The same was true of the great movie musicals of the 1930s, many of which were backstage stories about putting on a Broadway musical.) There certainly were spectacular period pieces—*Show Boat* most prominent among them—but most Broadway shows took place squarely in the present.

That changed after World War II. Clearly the tastes of the audience had shifted from contemporary stories to nostalgic looks backward. We can see this in the career of Rodgers & Hammerstein. Of their nine musicals, the contemporary stories (*Allegro, Me and Juliet, Pipe Dream, Flower Drum Song*) were usually either outright flops or had only a modest success and are rarely seen today. The only big hit they had with a contemporary story was *South Pacific*, probably because it addressed the recent, universally shared, and deeply emotional experience of World War II; everyone in the audience could identify with the characters and situations. For the most part, though, audiences responded much more strongly to the period stories: *Oklahoma!, Carousel, The King and I*, and *The Sound of Music* were all smash hits.

Learning from this, Broadway creators from Lerner & Loewe to Andrew Lloyd Webber leaned overwhelmingly on period pieces. The occasional shows with a contemporary setting, such as *West Side Story* (1957), *Company* (1970), *The Life* (1990), or *In the Heights* (2008), were striking in part for that very fact. Even when they scored hits, however, they did nothing to change the new order on Broadway. If Hollywood billed itself as "the dream factory," Broadway was "the nostalgia factory."

This was particularly noticeable for me in the years between 1978 and 1981, when all five of the major Broadway cast albums I produced were for shows that had period settings. That they included two revues, a revival, and a movie adaptation also spoke volumes about where Broadway was heading, but that's another story.

Ain't Misbehavin' (1978)

Ain't Misbehavin' has the distinction of being the first songwriter-revue "jukebox musical" to make the transfer to Broadway. The show began as a Manhattan Theatre Club presentation on February 8, 1978. It was the brainchild of a wonderful guy named Murray Horwitz, who was a cousin of my wife, Irene.

Murray co-conceived the show with Richard Maltby as a tribute to the music of Fats Waller (1904–1943), a jazz-piano master who—with frequent collaborators Andy Razaf and Harry Brooks—wrote hundreds of popular songs during a brief, troubled life. A big, heavy-set man (hence his nickname), he performed with an infectious brio that still comes through on his recordings, almost a century later.

Murray and Maltby teamed with director Arthur Faria and arranger/orchestrator/onstage pianist Luther Henderson to use a series of musical sketches, employing Waller's songs and minimal dialogue, to depict a series of scenes in Black nightclubs of the 1920s, Waller's own stamping-grounds. This concept was brought to life Off-Broadway by a gifted cast that included Irene Cara, Nell Carter, Andre DeShields, Armelia McQueen, and Ken Page; when *Ain't Misbehavin'* opened on Broadway on May 9, 1978, the cast was the same except for Cara, who had been replaced by Charlayne Woodard. The show earned rave reviews and ran for 1,604 performances.

My biggest problem with the show came right at the beginning: Richard Maltby didn't want me producing the recording. Knowing my recordings of *Porgy and Bess* and *Company*, on which I'd taken a very elaborate approach, he may have worried I'd make an overblown mess of his simple, straightforward show. He may also have been concerned that as a classical-music and more traditional Broadway specialist, I wouldn't have a feel for this kind of show.

Neither concern was valid, I'm happy to say. My father had a reasonably eclectic record collection that included several Fats Waller recordings, so I already know a lot of the music. And of course, as a pianist I certainly appreciated what Waller did at the keyboard. Besides, I had such an affection and such a friendship with Luther Henderson that I just knew the project was going to work out.

Despite his earlier misgivings, Maltby and I got along wonderfully well. He was very pleased with my work and with the resulting album, and while we haven't worked together since then, we're always happy to see each other when we meet.

The sessions generally went very smoothly. Nell Carter had a reputation for being difficult, and indeed she did start out by complaining about something. I can't even recall now what it was; it must have been a minor matter, though, because I acceded to her request immediately, and from that point on she was good as gold. I think she felt she had to assert herself early on, but as soon as she saw that she'd be treated with respect, she relaxed and did a great job.

Ain't Misbehavin' was really easy to produce, being a revue and having such an accomplished cast. In a way, doing this sort of show is like recording classical music: the songs are classics, and I'm not going to try to change an orchestration or to persuade the composer to make any changes. The singers are masters in their field, and I have no reason to want to ask them to reinterpret their performances. My job is simply to make sure these performances are crisp and clear, and that the brilliance of the music comes through. I do that for Beethoven and Brahms, and I did it for Fats Waller, the same way I would a couple of years later for Duke Ellington.

I'm very pleased with the original-cast recording of *Ain't Misbehavin'*. It captures the joyous good humor of much of Waller's music and the energy and excitement of the show. It won a Grammy Award as Best Cast Show Album.

Oklahoma! (1979)

The first Broadway show I ever saw, *Oklahoma!* remains a personal favorite. However, even if I hadn't seen the original production, and even if I hadn't had a thoroughly enjoyable experience making a studio recording of the show, it would still be near to my heart for the recording I made of the 1979 Broadway revival.

This wasn't one I had to pursue. This revival was produced by the Rodgers & Hammerstein Organization itself and directed by Oscar Hammerstein's son William. Richard Rodgers' daughter, Mary Rodgers Guettel was also very much involved. They wanted the recording to be done by RCA and for me to produce it.

This was my second time around on *Oklahoma!*, and I came into it, I think, with both a deeper understanding of the show (from seeing this revival, which was brilliantly done) and a stronger sense of what could be done with a show recording.

One of the things I'd learned in the interim was the value of completeness. Our 1964 recording had restored "Lonely Room" and "The Farmer and the Cowhand," but this time I also restored the Act I song for Ali Hakim and the chorus, "It's a Scandal, It's an Outrage," which had never been recorded, as well as two or three important reprises.

I had put some thought into how to convey the relationship between Curly and Laurey, because there's a combative aspect to it which doesn't show up in their only duet, "People Will Say We're in Love."

"Surrey with the Fringe on Top," for example, is a beautiful song, and it does give you a sense of who Curly is and what he wants from Laurey. But you don't truly understand why he's singing it unless you realize it's a reaction to the dialogue preceding the song, a back-and-forth in which Laurey greets him with a dismissive "Oh, I thought you was somebody." Including that one line, as I did on the recording, gives the song a different shape, a bantering, teasing tone that is missing from the song alone.

And although "People Will Say We're in Love" is one of the most beautiful melodies in the show, there's almost nothing in its lyrics that bears any relationship to the characters. In a rare misfire from Hammerstein, in my opinion, the lyrics are generic.

Without belaboring the point, the opening lyric of "People Will Say We're in Love" is "Don't throw bouquets at me"—but Curly never threw Laurey a bouquet. The next line is "Don't please my folks too much"—but we don't know if Curly has any folks, and Laurey lives with her aunt. The next line, "Don't laugh at my jokes too much" falls on deaf ears because up to now, Laurey hasn't laughed at any of Curly's jokes. Later on comes the line "Give me my rose and my glove" but there has never been a rose nor a glove in sight! And yet it's a great song which no one has ever complained about.

Hearing the song by itself, you have no idea who Curly and Laurey are. Onstage Larry Guittard and Christine Andreas had a wonderful, scrappy, sexy, playful relationship as Curly and Laurey. I loved that when I saw them in the show, and I was determined to make sure it came across on the album. I was totally captivated by their performances. Christine's rendition of "Out of My Dreams" was a high point. I often think that "Out of My Dreams" is one of the most beautiful waltzes in the whole world.

On many albums reprises are omitted as a matter of course, but sometimes the reprise isn't just a repetition; sometimes it conveys something important about the story in altered lyrics because it builds on an earlier lyric. That's certainly the case at the end of *Oklahoma!*, when Curly proposes to Laurey, and despite her pretend hesitance, thinks he's talking her into it, which leads into a reprise of "People Will Say We're in Love," which now ends with an exuberant "Let people say we're in love!" Their love just explodes, and it's wonderful.

One thing that's different in recording a revival, as opposed to an original-cast album, is you don't have to be a slave to pacing. When I'm recording a revival, I'm recording a known quantity, and I'm no longer so concerned about the forward energy. This lets me focus more on realizing (or re-realizing) the arc of the show to its fullest extent. There are things that maybe needed to be cut from the original-cast recording, or even the original production itself, but may merit being restored for the recording of a revival. That reprise is a great example.

The cast was good from top to bottom. When I went to see *Oklahoma!* during previews, I thought it was sensational. Mary Wickes, the Hollywood character actress who thirteen years later would have a late-career renaissance as a hardnosed nun in *Sister Act*, was a terrific Aunt Eller. Martin Vidnovic took the role of Jud in a very dark direction and was excellent. Harry Groener was a wonderful Will Parker, and Bruce Adler was charming and eccentric as the peddler, Ali Hakeem. Christine Ebersole was Ado Annie, and I think did it better than Celeste Holm in the original production. And of course Larry and Christine were a perfect pair of leads.

The conductor knew the score to *Oklahoma!* probably better than anyone else alive at that point: Jay Blackton had not only conducted the original production, but also had done the original orchestrations and shared an Oscar for Best Musical Score in the 1956 film adaptation of *Oklahoma!* Jay—whose last name was a translation of his original name, Schwartzberg—always conducted from a sitting position because he had a bum leg and walked with a limp. He was a sweet-natured, very talented man.

There was an empty chair in the control room, though, metaphorically speaking: Richard Rodgers had died, barely a week before we gathered to make the recording.

I missed him because I admired him tremendously and I liked working with him.

But we weren't recording under a cloud—it was a fun, joyful occasion—and I think we all took some inspiration from the fact that this production was Dick's legacy, the final Richard Rodgers show to open on Broadway in his lifetime. Dick had had a sixty-two-year Broadway career, premiering *I Remember Mama* only seven months before his death, but that career ended with this show.

Oklahoma! has been recorded many times, and many of those recordings are excellent. How could they not be, given such delightful material? I haven't heard them all, and I can't pretend to be objective about this recording, but in my heart of hearts, I think it's the best *Oklahoma!* recording ever made.

42nd Street (1980)

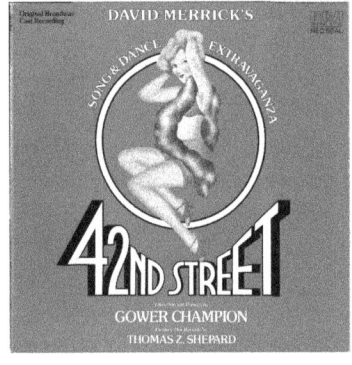

Today, when two of every three new Broadway musicals seem to be based on hit Hollywood movies of the past, it's hard to realize how much of a risk *42nd Street* was in 1980. At that time there had been only a handful of Broadway musicals based on Hollywood movies, and nearly all of them had been flops. (An exception was *On the Twentieth Century*, from 1978.) Every once in a while, Broadway musicals were made into movies, but movies weren't made into Broadway musicals. Since book musicals became popular in the 1920s, the formula had been straightforward: musicals were based on plays, or they were based on books.

Nonetheless, veteran producer David Merrick had a hunch that a musical based on a forty-six-year-old, black-and-white movie called *42nd Street* would catch audience's eyes and ears. He reasoned that the success of revivals of *No, No, Nanette* (1971), *Irene* (1973), and *Very Good, Eddie* (1975), the last of which he himself had produced, had demonstrated Broadway audiences' appetite for old-school song and dance, and big production numbers. And he was ready to put his money where his mouth was: in an era when choruses of twelve men and twelve women were considered extravagant, *42nd Street* opened with the clattering of forty pairs of tap shoes. Merrick may have been taking a gamble, but he wasn't afraid to push all his chips into the center of the table. In the age of Stephen Sondheim and Kander & Ebb, purveyors of dark, complex adult musicals, Broadway was starved for old-time glamour, pretty chorus girls in scanty costumes, simple, relatable stories.

And he had a lot to lose. Merrick was sixty-nine in 1980, and health problems, financial difficulties, and a failed venture in Hollywood had kept him from mounting a Broadway production in the five years since *Very Good, Eddie* and *Travesties* in 1975. *42nd Street* would be either his big comeback or his last hurrah. As it turned out, it was both: he would live another twenty years, but he suffered a debilitating stroke in 1983, and *42nd Street*, arguably his biggest hit, was his last.

By 1980 most Broadway shows were mounted by teams of producers, but Merrick was a fiercely proud lone wolf, staking his own money on plays and musicals based on nothing but his personal instincts. For decades, it had been enough: in 1966 *Time* profiled him in a cover story and estimated 20 percent of all Broadway actors, musicians, and crew members were working for Merrick.

His gamble on *42nd Street* was his most expensive ever, and it turned out to be a spectacular success. The opening-night reviews were golden, the show earned Tony Awards for Best Musical and Best Choreography (going posthumously to director/choreographer Gower Champion, who had died the morning of opening night), and it went on to run for more than eight years.

Though he had many admirers, Merrick was also known as a cruel, domineering man, especially to the people who worked for him. He had a long-running feud with Richard Rodgers, for example, and—even though Dick was dead by this time—when Merrick gave Dorothy Rodgers complimentary seats for *42nd Street*, they were in the upper balcony. Asked once by an interviewer why people said that he was mean, Merrick replied, "Because I am mean—what else?"

I would come to understand, firsthand, that his reputation was well deserved. For many years Merrick had released his original-cast albums through RCA, where he had strong personal connections, but those connections were long gone by the time I arrived.

So I was surprised when Jon Maas, a most pleasant and very smart person who worked for Merrick, somehow latched onto me—I'm not even sure when or where we met—and told me he was determined that I should produce the original-cast album of *42nd Street*.

Maas told me candidly that, at the time, Merrick wasn't even interested in having a recording, but he told me he'd bring Merrick around, and he did. I met Merrick for the first time at our recording sessions.

Shortly before we were scheduled to record the show, I phoned Harry Warren, who had written the songs for the movie with lyricist Al Dubin. Warren was then eighty-six years old, retired, and living in California (Dubin had died in 1945), and I asked him if he was interested in coming to New York to attend the recording sessions.

"No," he said. "That son of a bitch Merrick, you go to the show, and you look at the front of the theater, and what does it say? It says, 'David Merrick's Song & Dance Extravaganza, 42nd Street.' Underneath it says, 'Directed by Gower Champion.' There's no mention of me, and I wrote the damn thing."

So he didn't come, and I took a look at the poster for the show, and it was true. Merrick's name was there in big letters over the title, Champion's name was listed in big letters under the title. But Harry Warren and Al Dubin were nowhere to be seen.

The album cover is the same way, except under Champion's name it says, "Produced for Records by Thomas Z. Shepard." (In obscenely large type, I think, looking at it now!) Still no mention of Dubin or Warren, but that must have been contractual, and I had no control over it. But they are both mentioned prominently on the back cover.

So maybe it shouldn't have surprised me when things went crazy practically as soon as the session began.

It was a big session, with a large orchestra and that forty-member company. The opening number of the show is set in a rehearsal hall, where the entire company is running through a big dance number. We were in the control room and we'd done only a few takes of a scene in which stage director Julian Marsh (Jerry Orbach) is rehearsing his dancers, when Merrick suddenly said out of nowhere, "Kill all the orchestra mikes."

I'm sure by now I've conveyed how much it gets my back up when somebody tries to tell me how to manage a recording session. Over the past few decades, particularly since I began freelancing in 1989, I've become more amenable to discussing things and reasoning with people. In 1980, though, I had a visceral, angry reaction when anyone interfered and tried to dictate to me how to run a recording session. Especially if, like Merrick, he didn't take me aside or ask it as a question but issued an order.

So I said, "No."

I wasn't being merely stubborn or arbitrary. I knew that without an energetic musical accompaniment, the taps would sound awful.

Merrick wasn't a guy that people said "No" to. His response was, "OK, then, the recording session is over." With that he went out into the studio and announced to the cast that the recording was off and they should all go home.

Now, today my first instinct would be to avoid confrontation and try to de-escalate the situation. OK, no, that would be my second instinct, but I'd know better than to follow my first instinct, which would be to do exactly what I did: I got on the talkback in the control room, so the whole cast could hear me, and I said, "You're not working for Mr. Merrick today, you're being paid by RCA. You can't go."

That was perfectly true, of course, but it put the cast in a very difficult position. Most of them would never see me again after that day, but they'd have to work for Merrick for months, if not years, to come. It was such an awful fix that we had to take time out for the company's Equity rep to call the union office and ask what they ought to do. In the meantime the actors milled around nervously. They were scared and uncomfortable, and neither Merrick nor I gave them any help at all.

In the end we didn't have to get a ruling from Equity. RCA Records president Bob Summer happened to be in the building that day, and he came down and brokered a sort of peace between Merrick and me. And that led to something very good.

Seeing he wasn't going to get what he wanted—which would have sounded terrible—Merrick said, "OK, since it's supposed to be a rehearsal, what if we did it with only piano, instead of with orchestra?" I said, "That's a great idea." So that's what we did, and it was the perfect compromise.

But it should never have gotten that far. If the more mature Tom Shepard could have taken over from the younger one, at the point that Merrick said, "Kill the mikes," the older me would have said, "Why?" Then we're talking between ourselves, instead of fighting in front of the whole company. He would have made his objection, whatever it was, and—neither of us having drawn a line in the sand—I would then have explained how coarse and unpleasant it would sound if the tap dancers had no music behind them.

As it turned out, of course, word of this got into the papers. The cast members were asked about it later, but they didn't really know what the issue was. But Jon

Maas later said, "Tom Shepard was right, and David Merrick was wrong." And there was one unfortunate consequence because there were certain key lines of dialogue I wanted to get into the recording, but at that point Merrick only wanted to win his battle, so he refused to let me record them. It didn't spoil the recording, which is rather good, despite everything. But it could have been better.

Worst of all for me personally, Elizabeth, my twelve-year-old daughter, was there, and she started to cry because her father was being raked over the coals.

I was so aggravated by Merrick, so aggravated by the whole experience that I said to Bob Summer, "I think you should leave my name off the album cover." He said no. By that time, perhaps, I was well-known enough that my name on the cover of a recording was a modest sales asset. And maybe he thought it was going to be a good recording, and that perhaps, as time went by, I'd be happy to have my name on it.

He was right.

Sophisticated Ladies (1981)

Sophisticated Ladies was surely inspired by the success of *Ain't Misbehavin'*, three years before, because it followed the template of the earlier show closely: it cherrypicked the greatest hits of an iconic African American composer, this time Duke Ellington, and assembled them into a loose-knit revue that featured a small number of gifted Black singer/dancers.

The two shows opened on Broadway three years apart, and both were hits. They overlapped on Broadway for almost a year.

Sophisticated Ladies was, as its name suggested, a more elaborate production with an elegance in its style and presentation that *Ain't Misbehavin'* hadn't aspired to. This is appropriate, perhaps, in that Ellington was a trained musician who thought of himself as a serious composer, while Waller was an unabashed songwriter whose songs are characterized more by sass and strut than by class and refinement.

(There was some controversy, during the run of the show, as to whether it gave appropriate credit to Billy Strayhorn, who was the writer or cowriter of many of the songs associated with Ellington, such as "Take the A Train.")

Strangely, though my longtime friend and colleague Luther Henderson was an authority on the music of Duke Ellington, had orchestrated many songs for Ellington (including Ellington's only Broadway musical, the 1946 *Beggar's Holiday*), had known the composer well, and had even spent part of his childhood living next door to the Ellingtons, yet, he wasn't involved in *Sophisticated Ladies*.

Duke's son, Mercer Ellington, was the conductor, and despite his lack of Broadway experience, proved to be very capable, a low-key presence who kept the music well in hand.

I recorded the orchestra first and tracked in the singers subsequently on at least half the numbers, the first time I'd ever done that so extensively. A lot of Ellington's songs establish a rhythm and then keep going steadily, with very little rubato, and that rhythmic precision makes it relatively easy to overdub the vocals later.

I've said that revues are usually the easiest type of show for a producer to record, but in this case the human element came into play and made things tense. Gregory Hines and Judith Jamison, who were the leads in *Sophisticated Ladies*, were not on speaking terms.

The fault must have been with Greg, who was a difficult man to work with. He was wonderfully talented, a brilliant tap dancer who could also sing and act and could have achieved much more than he did if he hadn't had the misfortune to be born a few decades too late, coming of age in an era in which tap dancing was usually a second thought, if that. Greg had the skills to have been a Fred Astaire or a Gene Kelly, but he wound up making his mark mainly as a dramatic actor starring in such movies as *White Nights* (in which, admittedly, he dances up a storm) and *Running Scared*.

That Judith found it impossible to deal with Greg wasn't surprising, because many people felt that way. It was common knowledge that even Greg's brother and former dance partner, Maurice Hines, didn't get along with him. (Maurice replaced Greg late in the run of *Sophisticated Ladies*.)

Two stars who aren't speaking to each other makes for an uncomfortable atmosphere, but even setting that aside, I found Greg exasperating because his talent wasn't matched by his professionalism. He didn't like being told much of anything. When I'd say, "It's time for a take," he might suddenly decide to walk out of the studio to make a phone call. He came back in when he felt like coming back. No one was going to tell Gregory Hines when to stay and when to leave.

But he was a great performer, and he did a very good job on the recording, despite being cold and confrontational. Some years later, when I found myself working with him again on the recording of *Jelly's Last Jam*, things were perhaps just a little easier.

Otherwise the cast was very cooperative, including Judith, Gregg Burge, Hinton Battle (who later won a Tony as Best Featured Actor for his performance), and Terri Klausner. It was also a pleasure to get to know the music of Ellington and Strayhorn better—the score includes such enduring hits as "Don't Get Around Much Anymore," "In a Sentimental Mood," "It Don't Mean a Thing (If It Ain't Got That Swing)," "Mood Indigo," "Sophisticated Lady," and "Take the A Train." So the music was wonderful, and Mercer was very easy to work with.

The producers of the show were very kind to me, exceedingly happy with the way the recording sessions went and how the recording itself turned out. After my experience with David Merrick, it was gratifying—and a huge relief—to work on a very professional basis with the producers of *Sophisticated Ladies*.

25

Sondheim Times Three, Again

I SOMETIMES THINK OF MY TENURE AT RCA as "the Sondheim years" and find it hard to remember that my work with Steve was only a part of what I did at RCA. Most of my time during those twelve years was spent on classical music, not Broadway, and fewer than half of the twenty-one cast albums I produced there were by Steve.

Nonetheless, there were certain periods when it felt like I spent at least some of every day working on Sondheim shows. In 1975–1976 alone I did three Sondheim projects, and in 1981–1983 I did another three: one revue, one live concert, and one Broadway show.

Marry Me a Little (1981)

Marry Me a Little is, if nothing else, a unique entry in the Stephen Sondheim canon. It's a revue made up entirely of material that had been removed from Steve's early shows, and then stitched together in the service of an entirely different plot.

It was a very gentle Off-Broadway show, conceived by Craig Lucas and Norman René. Directed by René, it was about an unnamed man (Lucas) and an unnamed woman (Suzanne Henry), who have seen each other but have never actually spoken, sitting in their lonely New York apartments and imagining what sort of relationship they might have, if either ever got up the nerve to speak.

The nineteen songs consisted of three from Steve's then-unproduced first musical *Saturday Night* (1955), one from the unproduced musical *The Last Resorts*, one from Steve's incidental music for S. Richard Nash's 1956 play *The Girls of Summer*, and the rest had been cut from five of his Broadway musicals before they opened. It was a lovely show, very small scale, with a tiny orchestra and a cast of only those two, neither of whom was well-known in show business (Craig would only later establish himself as a playwright).

At this time I was getting flak from some of the middle-management people at RCA—not from Bob Summer, with whom I generally agreed, but from people one level down. Through the years, there were always various RCA corporate people to whom I had to report. I'm not even sure who the person was at this time because they all seem to blur together. They were very hard on me, probably because they didn't like the idea that I had an independent production contract, and so they were always a little suspicious that, whenever I wanted to produce a show or a classical project, it was in order to put extra money in my own pocket.

That wasn't the case, of course. I thought *Marry Me a Little* was a charming little show, Off-Broadway but still of interest, particularly to Steve's many fans, and I knew it would be so inexpensive to make—certainly no more than fifty thousand dollars, and perhaps less—that there was no significant reason not to go forward. But my immediate superior wouldn't approve the project. I was stymied. Probably I could have gone over his head and gotten Bob Summer to approve the project, since it was important to him that we nurture our relationship with Steve, but instead I resorted to subterfuge.

We never booked an official recording session for *Marry Me a Little*. I listed it as an audition, which meant there were no talent costs, and I did it without having contracts drawn up with the producers, singers, or musicians. They just came in and went through their material, officially to help us decide if it was worth recording, and as they did so, we recorded it. It went very smoothly. Nothing needed more than two or three takes, and it was probably done in eight or nine hours, long for an audition but short for a recording session. Then I took the tapes and edited and mixed them into an album that, officially, still didn't exist at all.

Only then, with the whole thing recorded, edited, mixed, and ready to go, and when I knew exactly how little it would cost, did I bring it back to the arrogant mid-level executive to whom I officially reported and say, "You know, this is only forty or fifty thousand dollars, you'd be crazy not to release it." He agreed!!! So the contracts were drawn up, and signed. It's a modest little album, and it didn't sell a lot, but it still made a profit because it cost so little to make (I even waived my contractually guaranteed producer's fee).

My motivation was simple loyalty to Steve. I wanted to produce his work, and I really liked this piece, so I did what I needed to do to get it recorded.

The project turned out to have one additional benefit I couldn't have predicted. Four years later I assembled a four-LP set called *A Collector's Sondheim*, which consisted of both well-known Sondheim material as well as Sondheim rarities. Ten of the songs on that album were from *Marry Me a Little*. The only reason I could have had access to these songs was because we'd recorded this little show.

Although this battle ended well for me and for Sondheim fans, it showed how much I had to learn about walking between the raindrops at RCA. It wasn't just the marketing guys; there was also a lot of resentment toward Red Seal from the pop department because they couldn't understand why a department with our modest sales occasionally posted such high costs (particularly for orchestral recordings and Broadway cast albums). They neither understood nor liked classical music, and they resented the fact that the cast albums, some of which were very strong sellers, were making money for my department rather than theirs, as had been the case until I joined RCA.

I didn't spend a lot of time thinking about *Marry Me a Little*, though, because throughout the time we'd been working on it I'd been engrossed in a far more complex and demanding project, the original-cast album for Steve Sondheim's latest Broadway show, which was released a month to the day after *Marry Me a Little*.

Merrily We Roll Along (1981)

With *Merrily We Roll Along*, for once, Steve took up a thoroughly familiar, Broadway-friendly subject matter: friendship and conflict between songwriting partners, fresh out of school and longing for their big break on Broadway. The show opened in 1981, but it could easily have opened in 1941 or even 1921 and had no trouble finding investors.

And it turned out to be his biggest flop.

Partly this was due to the treatment of the theme: instead of charting the rise of two underdogs to Broadway stardom, Steve, George Furth (book), and Hal Prince (director) wove a story of betrayed idealism. The protagonist, Franklin Shepard, is a talented composer who, over the course of the play, does indeed achieve fame and success—but only at the price of selling out his talent, his partner, and his loving wife. Additionally, many in the cast were unknown teenagers.

Mostly, though, the show's box-office failure was due to its narrative structure. Having settled on relatively conventional subject matter, Steve and Hal chose to treat it in an extravagantly unconventional way: like the play on which it's based, Kaufman & Hart's *Merrily We Roll Along* (1934), the musical unfolds in reverse. The play runs from 1934 to 1916, while the musical starts in 1980 and presents eleven subsequent scenes, each earlier than the previous one, that take the story back to 1955.

The combination of the dark turn of the plot and the reverse chronology means that by the time we reach the final scene and see Frank and Charley as idealistic would-be world-beaters, seeing them that way is crushingly ironic and cynical because we know what's to come, even if they don't.

Taken together, the form and the tone constituted a challenge that even Steve, George, and Hal, the same trio who had made an unlikely hit out of *Company* eleven years before, couldn't overcome. Audiences and critics alike found the rewinding plot hard to follow, as conventional cause and effect were turned on their heads, and the corrosive cynicism embodied in the final vision of doomed idealism struck many as making it the most depressing show Steve had ever written.

The curtain came down on *Merrily We Roll Along* after only sixteen performances. Two weeks after it opened, the show was history. But history can take strange turns: subsequent revivals since 1981 (with a revised book and more adults in the cast) have been successful.

There's almost always an escape clause in the recording contract for any Broadway show, a provision that allows the record company to pull out if the show doesn't make it to twenty-one performances. Since the show closed the night before it was scheduled to be recorded, RCA had no obligation to go forward with a *Merrily We Roll Along* cast album.

Bob Summer called me into his office and we discussed whether or not we should let loyalty and prestige override our better business sense. When I'd advised Clive Davis at Columbia not to commit to *A Little Night Music*, I did so because I was obliged to go by Clive's yardstick, which was the bottom line. At RCA when it came to a Broadway cast album, the only yardsticks I needed to consult was my own and Bob's.

Bob felt that we should go forward, that we should keep up our very close relationship with Hal and Steve, and that we should buck the tide to such a degree that we would issue the recording in a very lavish package. More about this later.

Two or three years earlier, Judy Prince, who was a major influence on Hal, had suggested he do a show with and about teenagers. Intrigued by the Kaufman/Hart play and interested in making it into a musical, Hal thought this might be the perfect vehicle for Judy's idea and made it part of his initial pitch of the show to Steve and George. They wound up casting twenty-seven actors in their teens and twenties, twenty of whom were making their Broadway debuts and only one of whom had previously been heard on a Broadway cast album. (Frank is the only character played by two actors: Geoffrey Horne, at age forty-three, in the show's opening scene, and young Jim Walton thereafter.)

So when we gathered to record the cast album on November 29, 1981, it looked almost like a Dalton School production—complete with Daisy Prince, who played Meg and who attended Dalton with my daughter, Elizabeth.

Those actors may have been green, but they were wonderfully enthusiastic and so grateful to be there. The show had closed only the day before. It's hard even for veteran actors to handle working for months on a show, only to have it get bad reviews and close ignominiously; for a cast who were little more than children, it was particularly harsh. But the recording session was one last time for them to all be together, and the cast album meant the show would have a continued life, and they were thrilled. They'd all grown up with Steve's shows, and they were overflowing with gratitude to have been cast in a Sondheim show in the first place.

About a month before the show opened, Lonny Price, who played Charley, had hosted a party for the cast and crew at his parents' house somewhere in Greenwich Village, where he was still living.

It was a very young crowd, but Steve and I were both there, and I remember Steve saying to me then, "You know, what Goddard Lieberson was to you, you are to them. That's the generational thing." I knew they felt that way about him, but it hadn't occurred to me they might see me that way as well. I was only forty-five at the time, I didn't feel like an old master. But I think he was right, to those kids we were both heroes.

People always talk about Steve writing adult musicals, and certainly he was always attracted to complex, adult characters. The ingenues are there, sure, but they are rarely the center of our attention: the main protagonists are likely to be mature adults, such as Fredrik and Desirée in *A Little Night Music*, the Reciter in *Pacific Overtures*, or Sweeney and Mrs. Lovett in *Sweeney Todd*.

In *Merrily We Roll Along*, the major characters are over forty when we first meet them. By the time we see them as ingenues, at the end, we know what's going to happen to them, and there's nothing simple or romantic about it. If anything, we feel sorry for them because they're so young and starry-eyed, and they can't see what's coming.

Steve himself said in an interview that the characters of Frank, Charley, and Mary were modeled—very loosely—on himself, Hal, and Mary Rodgers, so this is Steve's most autobiographical show, and in its cynicism about the business to which he'd chosen to devote his life, one of his darker ones. His shows featured a lot of cynical, jaded characters, but this is the one in which he shows us how they got that way. There's a lot of pain in *Merrily We Roll Along*.

The reviews had not been the first clue to me, or to anybody else, that this show wasn't going to make it on Broadway. The show had not been taken out of town; that tried-and-true Broadway practice was beginning to go out of fashion. Instead it had six weeks of previews right in the heart of Broadway, at the Alvin Theater (since renamed the Neil Simon). The word of mouth was terrible, the opening was delayed twice, and halfway through this preview period, the choreographer and leading man were both replaced. If you've heard the phrase that a show is "in trouble out of town," *Merrily We Roll Along* defines the concept, except its out-of-town troubles took place in the full glare of the spotlight.

It was a lot of pressure for a young and largely inexperienced cast to withstand. Steve and Hal kept tinkering with the show during previews, and in my opinion, they didn't make it much better—and sometimes, I thought, they made it worse. They certainly made it confusing for a young cast that had never been through anything like this before.

For all of that, though, there was a lot to like about *Merrily We Roll Along*. It's a beautiful score, a fact recognized by many of the critics, even as they dismissed the show as bitter and confusing. I thought it was Steve at his best, and I was determined to create an original-cast album that would do it full justice.

I had the advantage of having seen the show many times before opening night, an advantage denied to the audiences and critics. There were certainly things that escaped me the first time I saw it, but the more I saw and heard it, the more I understood it and the better I liked it.

Merrily We Roll Along is organically composed, with themes, sequences, and leitmotifs that are reused throughout the show, changing and evolving as they go along. The song at the very beginning, "Beyond the Hills of Tomorrow," was originally written by Frank (music) and Charley (lyrics) as a high-school graduation anthem, and that melody is used over and over, in various guises, for the rest of the show. Even the hit song the team writes, "It Started Out Like a Song," is built on thematic material from that opening number.

This was a particularly hard show to record in terms of helping the audience follow the story. We didn't consider the possibility of putting the songs in chronological order for the album—like it or not, the backward chronology was the show's signature aspect and remains so to this day.

The stage version of the show is full of in-front-of-the-curtain bits, brief signpost scenes in which the chorus tells the audience in which year the next scene will be set, singing "1968!" or whatever. We were in a huge crunch for album space, but I put as many of those bits on the recording as we could. We didn't have room for them all, but Steve and I went over the scenes and decided which ones were most important, and they're on the album—we don't even list them as separate tracks. Without them, I think the listener would be even more lost than some of the people in the audience were.

That said, we simply had too much to fit onto one record—and much as I appreciated Bob Summer's support in making the recording, I knew better than to go back to him to ask for a two-disc recording of a show that had run for only two weeks. Something had to go, so Steve and I decided we could live without the song "It's a Hit." It gave me a pang, but it wasn't crucial, so on the LP of the original-cast album, you don't hear that song. We did record it, though, and when we issued *Merrily We Roll Along* on compact disc, with all that additional real estate at our disposal, I went back, edited and mixed "It's a Hit," and added it to the recording where it belonged.

Some of my favorite Sondheim lyrics are from this show. I could point to many examples, but a single word in the song "Not a Day Goes By"—which is a beautiful song, sung by Beth (Sally Klein) in Act I and then, in a rare Sondheim reprise, by Beth, Frank (Jim Walton), and Mary (Ann Morrison) in Act II—always catches me when I hear it. (During all the tinkering during previews, Steve, Hal, and George reassigned the song to Frank. However, they ultimately restored the song to Beth.)

There's a line in there, "not a blessed day," and I've never heard "blessed" used as an adjective in any other lyric. It's just such a perfect choice. It could have been "not a lovely day," "not a goddam day," "not a funny day," but it's "not a blessed day." There's something about the word that sets the whole tone of the song apart. It makes it serious and very mature, because a kid doesn't talk like that. I don't know what went through Steve's mind when he wrote it, but to me that has everything to do with placing the number contextually in the show. Sung by Beth in 1966, it's a song of disillusionment, a woman saying goodbye forever to the husband she still loves. And of course, it makes the second-act reprise, which is sung in 1960 at their wedding, all the more heart-rending.

I had a lot of fun with "Opening Doors," the number in which the young Frank, Charley, and Mary are scrambling for their first break. "Opening Doors" is all about people in your face or people on the telephone. Well, give me a number where somebody's talking on the phone, and you might as well call it a tap dance. I made sure, as we mixed that number, that every time somebody was phoning somebody else, the other person would sound like he was at the other end of the telephone. That was important to me because it has a lot to do with the audible energy of the song: there are people in the same room, but there are lots of people who are being contacted elsewhere, and it gives the song the same machine-gun energy it had onstage.

A little detail on "It's a Hit" pleased me disproportionately in the mixing: when the stage door opens and shuts, you hear the audience applauding, but then, as the door shuts, you can hear the applause being shut out as well. It's a tiny detail that probably hardly anybody notices, but it was fun for me.

Because audience members apparently were having trouble telling the characters apart, Hal made a late decision to redo all the costumes. Instead of wearing clothing that reflected the styles of the story's twenty-five-year time span, for the first couple of scenes the actors all wore T-shirts or sweatshirts with their character's names or their relationship to Frank printed in big letters across the chest.

I didn't think it was much of an idea, because it made the whole thing look even more like a Dalton School show, but when I got to the recording session, they had a shirt for me that said "Mr. Shepard." I put it on, of course, and you can see it in the pictures from the session. That was probably the only time I was ever sloppily dressed for a recording session—otherwise I always came in either jacket and tie or turtlenecks.

I never knew quite what to make of the fact that Steve, George, and Hal gave my name to Franklin Shepard (complete with its unusual spelling, not "Shepherd" but "Shepard"), the composer who sells out and becomes a one-man mega-corporation. The character is named Richard Niles in the Kaufman/Hart play, so the character name in the musical was their choice.

Was it some kind of dig at me? I find it hard to believe that it was—I had been producing recordings for them for eleven years by this point, but I don't think I was important enough in any of their lives for it to be a crack. And anyway, all three of them were very clever with words, and if they'd meant it as a dig, I assume I'd have gotten the joke. But it piqued my interest then, and still does. Maybe it was meant as a compliment. I'll never know.

Another thing I remember from the session is being introduced, at the end of the day, to the playwrights Ruth Gordon and Garson Kanin, who had just shown up. They were friends of Steve and Hal.

Steve very seldom got involved in the editing and mixing. He was interested in the creative work at the session. However, Lonny Price's big song, "Franklin Shepard Inc.," was an exception—in fact, it's one of the very few times I remember him coming into the editing facility.

On the stage there were a certain number of orchestra vamps—repeated bars of music—between sections of the song, to allow Lonny to catch his breath for the next section. Steve had just come back from Hollywood, where he had written the music for *Reds*, directed by and starring Warren Beatty. He was with Beatty for some of the editing, to match his music to what was going on onscreen, and Steve was fascinated by the way Beatty tightened things up, taking out tiny moments of dead air to juice up the pacing.

So to my surprise, when we got around to that number, Steve actually showed up for the editing because he wanted all those little instrumental bridges made as short as possible, so the number would move more quickly. He said that he'd learned this from Beatty. So if you listen to that number on the recording, Warren Beatty had a lot to do with the way it turned out.

The CD of *Merrily We Roll Along* is the better option for those wishing to listen to the recording today, preferable to the LP for its better sound quality and the inclusion of "It's a Hit," and preferable to online and streaming versions for a CD player's superior sound performance. In one respect, though, the LP has never been surpassed.

I was grateful to Bob Summer for agreeing to make the recording at all, even though the show had closed, and we both knew we'd lose money on the album. But he and I were both very pleased with the recording, and Bob insisted it be packaged as elegantly as if it were a guaranteed money-maker.

"Look," he said, "we're not going to apologize for this recording. We're going to treat this as first-class as anything else we've done."

And indeed, if you have the LP, you'll notice the front cover features Al Hirschfeld sketches of the original cast, surrounding a center cutout of a photo of Stephen Sondheim. When you pull the record out of the sleeve, you discover it's a slip cover, and the inner sleeve is decorated not only with the photo of Steve, but also lavish color photographs from the show itself. The LP album also included a complete booklet of lyrics. The CD has the same booklet and the same photos, but of course they're much smaller.

The LP outer jacket is really a beautiful piece of work, and the concept for it came from Bob himself. He had studied fine arts at Carnegie Mellon University and graduated with a degree in printing management, so he was highly visually oriented and aware of packaging. This was his brainchild, and besides showcasing his visual sense, it also demonstrated how smart a marketer he was: given a cast of unknowns in a show that had been an epic flop, our best selling point was Steve himself, so Bob put him front and center.

It really was a pleasure working with Bob, who had great appreciation for the theater and for classical music. Red Seal was a well-run operation, but it was never going to be a big money-maker for RCA, and some company presidents basically ignored us until it was time for a round of cost-cutting. Bob took the time to understand what we were doing, and to support us in it. Even at the time I appreciated this, and with passing years I've appreciated it more and more. Professionally speaking, Bob was the best thing to happen to me since Ken Glancy.

One thing about working with a cast of young, up-and-coming unknowns is that, in the ensuing years, you have the pleasure of watching them make their own marks in the world. Not everybody associated with that production has gone on to stardom, but they keep turning up, more than forty years later.

Jason Alexander made his Broadway debut as producer Joe Josephson in *Merrily We Roll Along* and since then has gone on to fame and fortune playing George Costanza on *Seinfeld* (1989–1998). Jason was at this time very young, still had hair, and was already extremely talented. His biggest moment in the show was "It's a Hit." I'm sure he was disappointed not to hear it on the LP, but after all these years, I am sure he has the CD.

He also had one of my favorite moments in the show, a throwaway line in "Opening Doors," in which Joe admonishes Frank that his tunes aren't hummable enough: "There's not a tune you can hum,/there's not a tune you go bum-bum-bum-di-dum./ You need a tune to go bum-bum-bum-di-dum—/Give me a melodee-dee-dee-dee-dee-dee," and hums the first two lines of the *South Pacific* classic "Some Enchanted Evening." Everybody picks up on the humor of Sondheim, who has often been accused of writing unhummable tunes, jabbing at the clueless producer, but not everybody notices that, when Joe (Jason) hums the song, he actually gets the tune wrong. It's a subtle little extra dig.

Liz Callaway (Nightclub Waitress) was another debutante, kicking off a career onstage and in cabaret in which she has been something of a Sondheim specialist (we would be reunited a few years later for *Follies in Concert).* She also played Ellen in the original Broadway cast of *Miss Saigon* (1991) and has voiced several animated roles, notably singing for the title character in *Anastasia* (1997) and voicing a dancing napkin ring in *Beauty and the Beast* (1991).

Giancarlo Esposito (Valedictorian) has gone on to almost two hundred film and television roles. He's a favorite of director Spike Lee, and I was pleased to spot him playing Gus Fring on *Breaking Bad* (2009–2011), one of my favorite television shows.

Tonya Pinkins (Gwen) and I would cross paths again a decade later, when she earned a Tony Award for her performance as Sweet Anita in *Jelly's Last Jam* (1992). She also created the title role in *Caroline, or Change* (2004).

Not everybody chose a performance route. Lonny Price, the original Charley, continues to act on occasion, but is best known today as a director and producer. He's particularly noted for a string of concert and semi-staged musicals with the New York Philharmonic, in which capacity I worked with him again (me as producer, Lonny as director) on Lerner & Loewe's *Camelot* in 2008.

A few years ago I got a call from an instructor at Barnard College in Manhattan, who wondered if I'd be willing to come and speak to her musical-theater class. To my pleasure, Adjunct Professor Mana Allen turned out to be Marianna Allen, who played the Auditioning Girl in *Merrily We Roll Along.* I spoke to the class, of course, and enjoyed catching up with Mana.

The recording is still in the catalog, more than four decades later. The show itself has returned to New York in three major Off-Broadway productions since then, in 1994, 2019 and 2022, the last of which moved to Broadway in 2023—not to mention any number of revivals at major regional theaters—and has always been far better received than it was originally. The creators made changes to it along the way (the sweatshirt experiment was never repeated), and perhaps some of the changes account for the change in audience response. Today *Merrily We Roll Along* is widely accepted as a Sondheim classic and as one of Steve's greatest scores.

I can't prove the existence of an excellent cast album made any of these subsequent developments possible. I will say, though, that precious few saw the show in its brief original run, and fewer liked it. If it's grown on thousands of people in the intervening years, our recording certainly hasn't hurt.

A Stephen Sondheim Evening (1983)

Late in 1982 a producer/director I knew named Paul Lazarus called me and said that he was producing a concert of Sondheim music at the Whitney Museum of American Art in Manhattan. He read me a list of the talent involved—Liz Callaway, Chris Groenendaal, Bob Gunton, George Hearn, Steven Jacob, Judy Kaye, Angela Lansbury, and Victoria Mallory, with Paul Gemignani as music director—and then he asked me, "Would you like to record it?"

I said, "Yes." I liked the cast, we were always looking to build on our relationship with Steve, and live recordings are typically easy to do. They're also relatively inexpensive because a concert is always much shorter than a day of recording.

So I brought an engineer and crew to the concert, and we recorded it. That was all there was to it—sometimes, after live events, if somebody has messed up a song, we'll stick around afterward and rerecord it, but I don't believe that we did any retakes on this one. We just took it as it was. The recording as you hear it is basically a documentary of the concert.

My favorite moment was at the end when Steve came out and took over the piano to accompany Angela on "Send in the Clowns" and then joined her to sing "Old Friends," from *Merrily We Roll Along*, leading into the finale. Steve didn't have a great voice like Angela did, but he had a serviceable voice, and it was a charming moment.

And like *Marry Me a Little*, *A Stephen Sondheim Evening* provided me with material for *A Collector's Sondheim*, eleven songs in all. One thing I've learned in the record business: hang onto everything you record! You never know when it may come in handy down the line.

26

Trips to Greece and France

Zorba (1983)

It is rare for a revival to get a cast album. It's rarer yet for a revival that wasn't particularly successful in its original production, and it's especially rare for a revival that features no big-name Broadway stars. But the 1983 revival of *Zorba* was no ordinary revival.

The genesis of this production began with a 1946 novel by Nikos Kazantzakis, published in English as *Zorba the Greek*. It's the story of a young Greek intellectual (also named Nikos) whose bookish existence is overturned when he meets a charming, earthy Cretan peasant named Alexis Zorba. The novel's seize-the-day, live-for-life message caught on in America and made it a best seller.

In 1964 *Zorba the Greek* was adapted into a movie, directed by Michael Cacoyannis, with Alan Bates as Nikos and Anthony Quinn as the mercurial Zorba. The movie was a hit and was nominated for four Oscars, including Best Picture, Best Director, and for Quinn, Best Actor. Lila Kedrova won as Best Supporting Actress for her performance as Madame Hortense, an aging former courtesan who is smitten with Zorba.

In its turn the movie was adapted into the 1968 Broadway musical, *Zorba*, with a book by Joseph Stein and songs by John Kander and Fred Ebb. Directed by Hal Prince, the show starred Herschel Bernardi as Zorba, John Cunningham as Nikos, and Maria Karnilova as Madame Hortense. It enjoyed a run of nearly a year and received Tony nominations for Prince, Bernardi, and Karnilova, though its only win was for Boris Aronson's set designs. In a crowded year for musicals—others included *Dear World*, *George M!*, *Promises, Promises*, and *1776*—it didn't attract a lot of attention, and after it closed it wasn't heard from again for more than a decade.

In May 1983, however, Bob Summer called me into his office and told me, "We've just agreed to record the revival of *Zorba*. It's in Los Angeles. I want you to go out there and make the recording."

I'm not sure I was even aware there was a revival of *Zorba*. It had been touring the country since January, I subsequently learned, and arrangements had just been made for a Broadway run that would begin on October 16. The idea was for me to fly to Los Angeles and make a cast album that would be released on June 1, so it could be sold at the various tour stops as the show worked its way to Broadway.)

The hook to this revival was in the timing and the casting. The runaway success of *42nd Street* had kicked off a spate of movie-based musicals, including three in 1982: *Nine*, *Seven Brides for Seven Brothers*, and the long-running Off-Broadway hit *Little Shop of Horrors*, which would make it to Broadway in 2003.

The revived *Zorba* fit into this trend, but with a crucial difference. Unlike all previous film-based Broadway shows, this *Zorba* featured two of the movie's stars, with the Oscar-nominated Anthony Quinn and the Oscar-winning Lila Kedrova recreating their screen roles, this time onstage and singing. That was enough to give an old musical new life and to get it back to Broadway, where it would run for nearly a year before spending a further year touring the United States.

In later years, working as a freelance producer, I would get used to the occasional short-notice job, but this was by far the shortest notice I'd ever had for a Broadway recording. Barely a week after receiving the assignment, I'd be walking into a recording studio in Burbank, California.

So it was a very steep learning curve. I'd seen the movie, of course, but I hadn't seen the musical in 1968. I learned what I could by listening to the original-cast album. To see what might have been in the show but not on the album, I studied the published libretto and the piano/vocal score. I was still going over this material on the plane out west with RCA's Paul Goodman, who would be my engineer for the project.

I was glad to have Paul—with whom I'd worked on various previous projects, including a recording of Mahler's Seventh Symphony the year before—because almost everything else about this recording would be a leap into the unknown. I had never worked with any of the cast members before, so I'd be meeting them all for the first time at the session; I knew Kander and Ebb, of course, but they wouldn't be there for this out-of-town recording, and neither would the orchestrator, given it was a revival. I'd be recording in Evergreen Studios, a place I'd never worked before, and so far as I knew I'd be working with the touring orchestra as it stood, without the extra musicians I'd almost certainly have wanted for the recording. I didn't have an advance recording of the production, and as far as I can recall, there wasn't even time for me to see the show on stage once I arrived.

Quinn was very imposing because he was so tall and burly. There's a photo of the two of us on the recording session, and it looks like I'm going over the score with Paul Bunyan. He was also a very charismatic man, one of those people your eyes go to in a room, which made him seem even bigger. He was three-fourths Mexican and one-fourth Irish, which gave him a sort of generally ethnic look—in Hollywood he was cast as Italians, Greeks, Arabs, Frenchmen, and Atilla the Hun, and occasionally even as a Mexican.

Quinn had actually recorded before. He made some pop records for Capitol in the 1960s, but basically he'd murmured seductively over a chorus and orchestra; in *Zorba* he actually had to sing. By 1983 he was sixty-eight years old, and his voice was rather hoarse, though still tuneful. He kind of half-sang, half-acted his songs in *Zorba*, and it was very effective—like a bigger, more emotional Rex Harrison. He was a senior citizen, but still very sexy, with a lot of animal magnetism.

I didn't really get to know Kedrova, but I got a big kick out of her. She was a Russian expatriate who at this point was sixty-five and had been acting since the 1930s, and she knew exactly how to play this part. Madame Hortense is a cute, eccentric little old lady, and Kedrova played it perfectly. Her song "No Boom Boom" was just delightful.

Robert Westenberg played Nikos. I would later work with him again on *Sunday in the Park with George*, in which he played the Soldiers. He's a very good actor, but what I remember from *Zorba* is a silly detail: for some reason we had to do take after take of a scene in which he knocks on a door and then comes in; after we'd done several takes, he joked that he was going to change his character's name from Niko to Knocko.

Also in the cast was Debbie Shapiro (later Debbie Shapiro Gravitte), who was very young and just beginning her career. She was a wonderful singer and very easy to work with. It doesn't surprise me at all that she has gone on to a very successful career as an actress and concert singer, most notably winning a Tony as Best Featured Actress for *Jerome Robbins' Broadway* in 1989.

One other member of the cast also went on to bigger things, though I can't say I remember him. Rob Marshall was in the chorus and played a monk. At the time he was a dancer, but later on an injury derailed that career, so he transitioned to choreographing and directing—and it couldn't have worked out better for him because he's won four Emmy Awards, been nominated for five Tonys, and won one Oscar (for directing the musical *Chicago*).

I don't have a lot more memories of the experience of recording *Zorba*, simply because things moved so quickly. I'm proud of it, though, because it came out well despite the many difficulties posed by the accelerated schedule.

La Cage aux Folles (1983)

One of my regrets about my recording career is that I got to do only two shows with Jerry Herman. He was such a nice person and so very talented a songwriter that I'd have liked to have produced the recording of all his shows. Instead, after *Dear World* in 1969, I got to do only one more.

I do take comfort in the fact that in *La Cage aux Folles*, I got to do the best of his shows. There's an argument to be made for *Hello, Dolly!* (1964) or *Mame* (1966), and certainly those are wonderful scores, but I'm comfortable saying that as an overall show, *La Cage* is the best thing he ever did.

Many people think *La Cage aux Folles* was based on the 1978 French film of the same name, but technically that wasn't the case. Producer Allan Carr wanted to adapt the film but found the rights were unavailable. Undeterred, he acquired the rights to the 1973 play on which the movie had been based.

(The most obvious effect of basing the musical on the play, instead of the film, is the absence of Jean-Michel's mother. Because that character had been created for the film, she couldn't be included in the musical, though she's in *The Birdcage*, the 1996 American movie adapted from the French film.)

It took five years for Carr to get the musical to Broadway, and it's a miracle it didn't take longer. He'd signed some top talent for the project, including Jay Presson Allen to write the book, Maury Yeston to write the songs, Mike Nichols to direct, and Tommy Tune to choreograph. The show was to be set in New Orleans and be titled *The Queen of Basin Street*. Carr had trouble coming up with the financing, however, until he brought in two executive producers, Fritz Holt and Barry Brown, who proceeded to bring in their own creative team and start over.

Predictably, a blizzard of lawsuits resulted (Yeston won his and received a percentage of the show's profits), but slowly the show moved forward, now once again set in France and called *La Cage aux Folles*. The new team included Harvey Fierstein as book writer, Arthur Laurents as director, and Scott Salmon as choreographer. Jerry Herman replaced Yeston as songwriter.

Half a century later, when gay-themed shows—including such hit musicals as *Rent*, *The Boy from Oz*, and *Fun Home*—are so routine on Broadway that the fact is rarely even discussed, it's hard to realize how ground-breaking *La Cage aux Folles* was or how nervous everyone involved in the show was about its prospects.

The history of the Broadway musical can't be told without the work of gay or bisexual creators from Cole Porter and Lorenz Hart to Stephen Sondheim and Elton John, but they weren't able to live their lives so openly, and until *La Cage* they hadn't written overtly about issues of sexuality. Their main characters were always overtly heterosexual—Broadway was famous for "boy meets girl" stories, not "boy meets boy" or "girl meets girl."

La Cage aux Folles was very consciously something different. The success of the movie with mainstream audiences had led Carr to think a musical could have the same success, and everyone involved in it realized that, while this was a show that needed to entertain audiences and make money at the box office, there was much more riding on it. Set in and around a drag club and built around the love between two gay men and their son, it was a test case, an experiment into whether American audiences of the 1980s—an era in which the AIDS epidemic had spurred a surge of homophobia—was ready for an unambiguously gay-centered show. It aimed for nothing less than to legitimize gay love, to make an audience feel for Georges and Albin the way they felt for Laurey and Curly or Tony and Maria.

The story and its lead characters were carefully shaped to avoid hurtful stereotypes of gay men, but also to avoid stripping them of their gay identities. This same concern was reflected in the costumes, the set designs, and the choreography. Nothing in the show was explicitly sexual, but every kiss, hug, and hand-hold was weighed in the balance. The lead roles of Georges and Albin were given to Gene Barry and George Hearn, both known to be straight—and they played their parts very conscious of the fact they were embodying the first onstage gay romance that many audience members would ever have seen. They made sure Georges and Albin were never caricatures but always two very simpatico human beings.

All of this was important, but of course it wouldn't matter if the show didn't also deliver the clever lyrics, catchy tunes, and general razzle-dazzle Broadway audiences have always loved. That's where Jerry came in.

As I've said previously, Jerry was razzle-dazzle personified, a writer of big, flashy show tunes that embodied an older Broadway, not only before the darker, more nuanced shows of Steve Sondheim, Andrew Lloyd Webber, and Kander & Ebb, but also before the more integrated, emotionally realistic shows of Rodgers & Hammerstein. Jerry was the artistic heir of Irving Berlin, Jerome Kern, Cole Porter, and the Gershwins.

And Jerry was also a man who needed a hit badly. I'd met him on *Dear World*, which had been a flop in 1969, and the 1970s had brought him nothing but two more failures, *Mack and Mabel* and *The Grand Tour*. Both contained good material, and *Mack and Mabel* was nominated for eight Tonys, but both shows flopped with audiences and closed in a matter of weeks. Jerry was fifty-two years old by 1983, and if he wasn't wondering if Broadway had finally passed him by, certainly other people were. He very much wanted *La Cage aux Folles* to succeed because of its subject matter and social significance, but he desperately wanted it to be a hit for his own legacy as well.

It was. *La Cage aux Folles* played its previews in Boston, where audiences were considered to be especially conservative, and was warmly received. Its New York previews went well, and its opening night earned rave reviews. The show was nominated for nine Tony Awards and won six, including Best Musical, Best Book, Best Score, and Best Direction; George Hearn and Gene Barry were both nominated as Best Actor in a Musical, with George winning. The show went on to run for more than four years and had two successful revivals, in 2004 and 2010, each of which won the Tony for Best Revival of a Musical—making *La Cage* the only show to accomplish that feat.

In certain respects this was one of the easiest recordings I've ever made. I first heard the songs played on the piano by Jerry during a kind of backer's audition at his apartment, and I felt this was a show that couldn't miss. There were representatives of other labels there, but the show-business lawyer Allen Grubman, who was representing Carr and the other producers (and would later represent me), took me aside and said, "You know, we're going through this as a pro-forma thing, but you guys have it." I assumed (correctly, as it turned out) that he and Bob Summer had already agreed on a deal. So I didn't need to worry about getting the rights, I could just sit back and listen to the wonderful songs.

We actually recorded the show before it opened, even before its New York previews began. It had been frozen in Boston, before it even came to New York—meaning the script and score were essentially finished, with only minor changes still to come.

This was very unusual. Producers and directors typically want to see how New York audiences respond to a show, so they can use the preview period to make any necessary changes. If you study the original-cast album of a show you've seen, you'll sometimes find the list of songs has them in a different order or even includes a song or two that wasn't in the show when you saw it. That's because the person doing the liner notes got the list of songs during tryouts, wrote up the notes on that basis, and then further cuts and changes were made when it was too late to change the notes.

That wasn't going to be the case with *La Cage aux Folles*. The creative team liked what they'd seen and heard in Boston so much they were willing to guarantee the material was substantively final. That let us make the recording on August 4, before the first preview on August 9, and well before the opening on August 21. The cast album was actually for sale at the theater on opening night.

Maybe because we were recording the show early, well before the frenzy around opening night, and because everybody was feeling good about the show—which isn't always the case—the cast was very easy to deal with.

This was my first time working with George Hearn, who previously had made his name mainly as a replacement actor, stepping in as John Dickinson in *1776*, and notably, as Sweeney in *Sweeney Todd*. He'd participated in *A Stephen Sondheim Evening*, the Whitney Museum concert I'd recorded, but that was a live event, and I'd had no occasion to interact with him then. He was a very impressive performer. Albin is a big, flamboyant character whose emotions are all over the place, but George's performance was meticulous, every detail exactly right—Albin might be wildly impulsive, but George knew exactly what he was doing.

Gene Barry arguably had a tougher role than George did. Albin is a big, showy character who delights audiences, while Georges is the stable center of their house, a gay man who isn't showy, can function in straight society, and serves as the family's—and the audience's—liaison between the two worlds. He played the part brilliantly.

I didn't really get to know Harvey Fierstein because he was the book writer, and we didn't interact that much. But I got very good at imitating his Brooklyn accent and I can do it perfectly. I mean, poifictly.

Conductor Don Pippin was always a pleasure to work with, though he did take a little dig at me when it came to the overture. He'd also been the conductor for *Dear World*, during which he'd been frustrated by my repeated stops to tweak the overture. This was fourteen years later, but they started playing the overture, and almost immediately, I stopped him and asked for a change—and Don, whom everybody knew to be an even-tempered guy, threw up his hands theatrically and said, "For God's sakes, Tom, can't we at least go through the whole thing once?" What could I say, except "Of course."

The stone in my shoe for this show, as he always was whenever we crossed paths, was Arthur Laurents, the director. Arthur was a brilliant writer and a very smart man—he wrote the movies *Rope* (1948), *The Way We Were* (1973), and *The Turning Point* (1977); he wrote the books for *Gypsy*, *West Side Story*, and *Anyone Can Whistle*; and he did a great job directing *La Cage aux Folles*—but he was also very nasty. A lot of what he had to say on this session was right on the money, but if he had a suggestion to offer, he always said it in the rudest, most offensive way.

Even when he agreed with me, Arthur found a way to make it unpleasant. I remember him telling me we needed more dialogue to make a particular scene understandable. This was exactly the sort of thing I'd been saying to directors for years—it was funny hearing it from somebody else! And he was absolutely right, we added the dialogue, and it was better. But the way he expressed his opinion was so critical that it left a sour taste in my mouth.

The biggest fight I had with him wasn't face to face. Anyone who's looked at my more recent albums knows my name is always last in the credits on the front cover, the way the director's name is last in movie credits. It's something I've done for a long time, and at RCA and MCA I believe that it was in my contract.

But Arthur Laurents didn't like that. He wanted to be listed last. And I was ready to make an issue of it. In the end, though, Bob Summer came up with a compromise that, in the end, kind of stuck it to Arthur.

If you look at the album cover, you'll see that Arthur Laurents is indeed listed last in the credits, just as he insisted he should be. But my name isn't above his—it's off to one side, in a place all its own, and while the credits are against a black background, my name is against a red background. It's very eye-catching, and I'm sure if Arthur had been given the choice, he'd have wanted a red spotlight shining on his name.

Putting my credit alone and to one side was Bob Summer's idea, which was very characteristic of Bob. He was cleverer than I was at finding an elegant way around a problem. I was more prone to dig in for a fight.

Jerry Herman was the antithesis of Arthur—invariably respectful, friendly, and utterly unpretentious. Jerry wrote in his memoirs that, during the previews in Boston—which began very badly, with the first preview canceled due to technical problems with the set—he had a panic attack before the second night, convinced they were in the wrong city, that the Boston audience wouldn't be open to a gay-themed show. The applause that night had washed away his worries, and by the time of our recording session he'd realized the hit he'd been waiting for was finally here.

In some respects this was a typical Jerry Herman show. Jerry loved shows that were built around a very strong woman, a star role in the Ethel Merman tradition. *Hello, Dolly!*, *Mame*, and *Dear World* had all been showcases for their female stars. On the face of it, *La Cage aux Folles* doesn't look like that because its starring roles are for men. But Albin is a gay-male version of that same Jerry Herman heroine, and his big solo "I Am What I Am" is a classic Dolly-or-Mame kind of song, bringing down the first-act curtain on a defiant note of confidence.

Albin also leads "The Best of Times," another classic Herman kind of song. That song was an outlier in *La Cage*, in that it was an "extractable" song, one that played just as well if taken out of the context of the show and put into some completely different context. Jerry said to me he'd written it "to be sung at every wedding and bar mitzvah there is"; he may have been joking, but it was that kind of song, and Jerry had spent his whole career writing extractable songs, even as Broadway trended more and more toward integrated scores in which the songs were closely tied to character and situation.

La Cage was a different kind of show, though, and Jerry wrote a different kind of score for it. His past shows had been old-school, daffy comedies in which the audience didn't really take the plot or the characters too seriously, but just waited for the next extractable song, and Jerry had felt the same way. In *La Cage*, though, he cared deeply about the story and the characters, and he wanted the audience to care too. "The Best of Times" is one of only a couple of songs in *La Cage*—the other would be "Song on the Sand"—that aren't tightly woven into the characters and the situation. "(A Little More) Mascara," "We Are What We Are," "Masculinity," "La Cage aux Folles," "I Am What I Am"—these songs couldn't be in any show but this one. It's a much more integrated show, and Jerry proved he could be just as good at that kind of show.

I've always said that sometimes a cast album needs to tell the story of the show, and sometimes it simply needs to be a great recording of the songs—and Steve Sondheim is my example of the first kind, and Jerry Herman is my example of the second kind. And it's true, with most of his shows (including my recording of *Dear World*), the songs are usually divorced from the action of the story, and I don't need to tailor the dialogue, to integrate sound effects and so forth. A Jerry Herman show is like a Cole Porter show, with songs that come easily out of the context of the show; you don't need to know what's happening to understand them.

But *La Cage aux Folles* was a more sophisticated show, and at certain points I had to look at it, maybe not like a Sondheim show, but certainly like a Rodgers & Hammerstein or Kander & Ebb show. "Cocktail Counterpoint" isn't just a song, for example: it's a scene in which each of the characters has his or her own separate song, and they go back and forth until, at the end, they're woven together in a big climax that ends with a crowning single word of dialogue—"Mother!"—as Albin enters, disguised as Jean-Michel's mother. In the show the various songs are separated by dialogue until the end, but I knew it would work best on the recording if I took out the dialogue and wove the songs together from the beginning of the scene. This took a lot of help from Jerry, Don, and orchestrator Jim Tyler, not to mention a lot of editing and mixing by Jay Saks and me.

I think *La Cage* is Jerry's best show, and I think maybe he felt the same way. He lived another thirty-five years, and he didn't stop writing, but he never wrote another Broadway musical. He wrote his memoirs, did a couple of revues of his previous stuff, and wrote the songs for a television movie called *Mrs. Santa Claus* (1996), starring Angela Lansbury; but the only subsequent musical he worked on, *Miss Spectacular*, was never staged.

Maybe he felt it would be impossible to top *La Cage aux Folles*, or maybe he thought he didn't have to top it, that he'd written a show—not some great songs, but a show—that would live long after him. I don't know, of course, but if he thought that, I think he was right.

27

Sunday in the Park with Steve

AS MY YEARS WITH RCA DREW TO A CLOSE, I found myself increasingly involved with Stephen Sondheim's past, as well as his present. In 1984 I recorded my final one of his original-cast albums, but also delved deeply into his past catalogue and began planning an ambitious effort to redeem what stood, to that point, as the one lingering sour note in his twenty-two-year career on recordings as a lyricist/composer.

All three were fascinating projects and each, in its own way, is among my proudest moments in my own long career.

Sunday in the Park with George (1984)

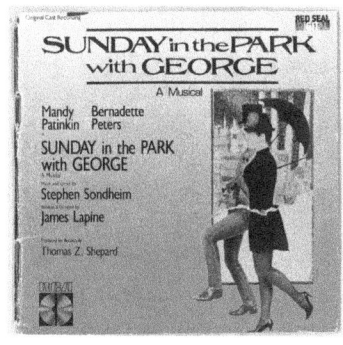

After finishing with *1776*, back in 1969, I thought I'd finished recording musicals in which a classic oil painting played a significant role. As it turned out, I was only getting warmed up. If anything, *Sunday in the Park with George* was even more challenging as a translation into a nonvisual medium: in *1776* only the final moments of the final song evoked a classic painting, but in *Sunday* the entire first act was built around a great painting, as were the opening number of the second act and the show's finale. Even the title of the show was an homage to Georges Seurat's 1886 masterpiece, *A Sunday Afternoon on the Island of La Grande Jatte*.

There has rarely, if ever, been a show as visually oriented as *Sunday in the Park with George*. The lead characters (one in each act) are visual artists—one a painter, the other what we'd call today a mixed-media artist, working with light, laser technology, and sound. Steve and author/director James Lapine were deeply concerned with the painter's art and, indeed, with art itself. Though it was nominated for ten Tony Awards, the show won only two (both visual!), for Tony Straiges's scenic design and Richard Nelson's lighting design. The show's visual look was widely applauded: as

Frank Rich wrote in *The New York Times*, "What Mr. Lapine, his designers, and the special-effects wizard Bran Ferren have arranged is simply gorgeous."

To make a viable recording of a show so dependent on its visuals (the special effects to which Rich referred included state-of-the-art projection mapping and laser lighting) was no small task. While *Sunday* was more audience-friendly than *Merrily We Roll Along*, it was arguably the most challenging show for a record producer that Steve had ever written, or ever would.

As usual with a new show, I had a preliminary meeting with Jim and Steve, sitting down in one of the large meeting rooms at RCA to discuss plans for the recording (also present were associate producer Jay Saks and Nancy Swift, who would be in charge of the liner notes and a full printed libretto to be included in the album, and also the *New York Times* writer Bernard Holland, who was profiling me for the paper's Sunday magazine). I borrowed a term from Gilbert & Sullivan to describe what I wanted to do with the show: their one-act operetta *Trial by Jury*, a favorite of mine, is subtitled "A Dramatic Cantata," so one of the first things I said to Jim and Steve was, "I would like this to be a dramatic cantata, in that it should feel continuous, and even if we physically have band breaks on the CD or the LP, I want the thing to keep flowing."

They may not have picked up the Gilbert & Sullivan reference, but Jim and Steve had no problem with my idea. I think, in fact, that they were relieved to hear it, because *Sunday* is a very integrated show, and trying to chop it up for the recording would have been very difficult.

So the two of them went back to work on the show, revising it to make sure it would be comprehensible to a listener deprived of the stage production's stunning visuals. I think they did a great job.

Steve was excited by the chance to revisit the creative process. I remember him saying to Jim, "Oh, now we can put the girls and the soldiers back where we wanted." Apparently, they'd had to move that sequence (involving the two Celestes and two soldiers, one of them a cardboard cutout and the other Robert Westenberg) from one part of the show to another for staging reasons, but now they could restore it to its original place.

So right from the start, we committed to the idea that this wasn't going to be a collection of songs from a show at the Booth Theatre, but rather an effort to tell a complicated, visually oriented story through sound alone. We were trying to put the listener not in the theater with Mandy Patinkin and Bernadette Peters, but on the Island of La Grande Jatte with George and Dot.

Sunday was different in kind from previous Sondheim shows, not only in its content, but also in the process by which it was created.

After the failure of *Merrily We Roll Along*, Steve and director Hal Prince parted professional ways, although they remained good friends. Steve formed a new partnership with writer/director James Lapine, one which sent him off in a new direction.

Jim was the antithesis of Hal, who was a Broadway director to his fingertips. Hal's specialty was big, glorious, romantic shows that at least aimed to have mainstream appeal, working largely the same way Broadway shows had been done for the past half-century or more. Jim's natural habitat was not Broadway, but among repertory companies like the Roundabout Theatre Company or Playwrights Horizons, where he could try things out, experiment, and gradually build a show in a continuously evolving process. *Sunday* initially opened at Playwrights Horizons, while *Into the Woods*, which again teamed Steve with Jim, opened at the Old Globe Theatre in San Diego. *Assassins* (directed initially by Jerry Zaks and with a book by John Weidman, who had written *Pacific Overtures*) returned Steve to Playwrights Horizons.

Working with Lapine was a whole new way of doing a show for Steve, and he liked it. A lot of the process was hands-on collaborative, really sitting in a room together, and if you take a hard look at *Sunday*, you'll see the result. Many of the numbers are not quite complete in the usual Broadway sense—the show is to a considerable extent through-composed, with songs yielding to other songs or to dialogue without the clear beginnings and payoff endings of most of Steve's previous work. It was a comprehensive change, and there's a clear dividing line in Steve's career after *Merrily We Roll Along*. *Sunday* would be a modest success on Broadway and *Into the Woods* a hit, but in a certain sense Steve had stopped being a Broadway songwriter.

I came into the recording session with certain expectations, but I was caught off guard by how extraordinarily moved I would be by the score. This was by no means a new show to me. I'd first heard it back in the summer of 1983, when it ran Off-Broadway at Playwrights Horizons. At that time it was only the first act because the show had not reached its final form, and the second act was unfinished. In fact, the finishing touches wouldn't be applied until only a few days before *Sunday* opened on Broadway, nine months later.

It was a difficult second act, jumping forward to the present day and with Mandy playing another George, the great-grandson of Georges Seurat, struggling to be a trendy artist in the present day. There were thirty-five Broadway previews, and for most of that time the second act really didn't hang together. Then Steve wrote "Children and Art." I don't know what it is about that song, but somehow or other it solidified the entire second act.

There were people who said that the second act didn't measure up to the first act, but I disagreed and still do. The second act also contains "Move On," which is a powerful song. Perhaps I find the show so moving because, like Steve and Jim, I identify with the struggles of both Georges and George to create meaningful art in a world that often offers nothing but obstacles. Listening to the recording today, I have the same reaction I did in the studio in 1984.

It was a very good cast, of course, headed by Mandy and Bernadette Peters. I've worked with Bernadette repeatedly through the years, going all the way back to *George M*. It's always a pleasure to do a project with her.

This was the first of many occasions on which I'd work with Mandy, who needs to be handled somewhat carefully. He's a bit neurotic as a performer and usually has to get rid of a flawed take or two before he can relax and say, "OK, I'm glad you're with me on that, let's do it again."

My good buddy Charles Kimbrough was in the cast. I'd known Charlie since my earliest days at Columbia Records, where he was with the Columbia Record Club as one of its classical-music advisors. We became close friends, and Irene and his then-wife Jane got to be close friends. Early on in our friendship, Charlie and Jane, who were both graduates of the Drama School at Yale, wanted to go back into show business. They were auditioning for one of Julius Monk's revues at the Plaza Hotel, and they wanted to perform "Carried Away" from *On the Town*. Charlie asked if I would rehearse the song with them and accompany them at the audition, which I did. (It turned out that going back into show business was a smart move for Charlie, who—besides playing Jules and the museum director in *Sunday in the Park*—wound up scoring a huge success as Jim Dial on *Murphy Brown*.)

So the recording studio was full of people I had a lot of history with—Charlie, Steve, Bernadette, and cast member Robert Westenberg, who had played Nikos in *Zorba*. Besides Mandy, Jim Lapine was the only major unknown quantity—I think it was the first time I'd met him. He was easy to be with, and it was a comfortable experience making this recording because we all knew and trusted one another.

I always put a lot of thought into how a recording should begin. The very first thing that happens onstage in *Sunday* is that George (Mandy Patinkin) proclaims, "White, a blank page or canvas! The challenge: bring order to the whole." As he continues speaking, delicate arpeggios punctuate the elements of art that he names: design, composition, balance, and so on, and the music resolves on his last line, "And harmony."

I thought the music should begin earlier—in fact, I wanted it to be the first thing we heard, so George's line "White. A blank page or canvas!" follows the music, rather than referring to the drawing pad he's holding or to the all-white stage, neither of which the listener can see. The extra arpeggio represented perhaps an audio representation for the color white, the color of the surface on which George will ultimately create the painting. It was a small change, and I'm not precisely sure how to explain it or defend it, but it felt right to me, and Steve said, "OK, fine." So the recording is, literally from the first note, a departure from the way the show was done onstage because you "hear" the color instead of seeing it.

In those days Steve and I were very much on the same page. I remember, after Bernadette finished singing "Everybody Loves Louis," I thought to myself, what if we took it much faster? And just as I was about to ask Steve, he said to me, "I think we should try it at breakneck speed." I said, "That's exactly what I was going to say to you." So we did one more take, with the tempo very, very fast—much faster than they do it onstage—and Bernadette was great.

That's a good example of something you can do in the studio that probably wouldn't work onstage. In the show the singer will always be a little out of breath, even before she starts the song, but in the studio, everybody is fresh, or will be if you've scheduled the session properly. And of course, on the stage you've got one shot—you either make it with that shot, or you don't. Bernadette got the faster tempo right the first time, but it was risky, and onstage she might not have wanted to take the chance, and the lyrics might not be so intelligible.

Steve and I didn't always agree, of course. In one scene Dot slams down her hairbrush on her dressing table and storms off the stage, so in the final mix, I added the sound of her slamming down the brush and then the sound of her footsteps walking out. And Steve liked the hairbrush slam, but he didn't like the footsteps—I have no idea why. He just said, "I don't like it. Take it out." I said, "OK."

We did the whole recording in the course of one long day, but the sessions were broken up in terms of the size of the orchestra, rather than the number of singers.

The orchestrations were by Michael Starobin, and as usual we augmented the stage orchestra with a number of extra strings. But the extra strings were not necessary for the entire piece. I divided *Sunday* into three different-sized instrumentations, not changing the orchestration at all, but simply making decisions on how many orchestra players to a part there should be on a given song or sequence. There may have been only four first violins in one third of the numbers, six in another third of the recording, and eight in another third. I don't recall the exact numbers at this point, but the purpose was to make sure the biggest numbers, like the chorus singing "Sunday," had the maximum forces.

One of the marvelous visual effects of the stage production was when at the end of Act I, as they began singing "Sunday," the actors walked to their positions onstage and formed a life-size tableau of Seurat's painting. The curtain rises on Act II with them in the same tableau—singing a song called "It's Hot Up Here," which comically presents their point of view about being trapped in a great work of art for all eternity. There's one moment in the number in which each character sings one line in turn, beginning with the Boatman (William Parry) on the audience's left. The characters sing their lines in the order of their position in the painting, ending with Dot (Bernadette), who sings the line "And I hate these people!" from her position on the audience's right. Thanks to stereo, I was able to place the singers at the appropriate mikes and recreate that stage picture in sound. When you listen to the recording, you can actually hear the sound travel from left to right in that number. It's a nice effect for the listening audience who can't see the painting.

I remember, as we were about to record that beautiful chorale "Sunday," I said, "This is what I've been waiting for, this is my favorite." And Steve said, "Be careful. You know, Mandy can hear you." He was afraid, I think, Mandy would be offended by my saying that a chorus song, rather than one of his solos, was my favorite. It never occurred to me that my offhand remark might be tactless (and in fact I don't think it was), but I understood Steve's caution. Actors can be very sensitive, and it's important to watch what you say to them to avoid being misinterpreted.

There was, for me, an odd postscript to *Sunday in the Park with George*, long afterward. More than thirty years later, I came across a Union Prayer Book and decided to set some of the prayers to music. I was extremely proud of one of them, which I modestly thought was gorgeous, until I suddenly thought, "Oh, my God, isn't this melismatic chorus line lifted from *Sunday in the Park with George*?" It wasn't an obvious steal, and of course it hadn't been done consciously; but once it occurred to me, I couldn't stop hearing it.

Steve and I hadn't been on good terms for a long time, but I emailed the setting to him anyway, apologizing for a little unintentional plagiarism and saying at least my subconscious was cribbing from the best. He sent me a very nice email in response, saying that to him it didn't sound like plagiarism—"I just hear some lovely music."

Given the ugly turn things had taken between us, I was amazed, in fact absolutely flabbergasted, to receive such kind words from him. It made me very happy.

A Collector's Sondheim (1985)

This entry in my Sondheim catalogue is unique in several ways: it's the longest, at four LPs or three CDs, and the most wide-ranging. It's also my only release of his work in which I never stepped into a recording studio.

I don't recall exactly when the idea for this project first occurred to me, but it was probably in 1983 or early 1984. It arose from two related recognitions.

First, I realized Steve had written a great deal more music than was to be found on the original-cast albums of the twelve musicals for which he'd written either the lyrics or the complete score. There were songs for movies or television, songs from projects that never reached the stage, and songs cut from the shows that did make it to Broadway. It added up to a lot of material. Second, I realized that at RCA I had access to a lot of that material—five RCA cast albums, plus the two revues and one live concert I'd produced.

Although I had so much material already in hand, there was still more I wanted. I knew there was a song written specially for the film version of *A Little Night Music*, another version of "The Glamorous Life" sung by Desiree's daughter (Elaine Tomkinson, the uncredited singing voice of Chloe Franks in the movie), a child's-eye view of the glamorous life as seen by the daughter of a star, a mother who is always on the road.

To get that number I needed to make a deal with Columbia, my old label, but fortunately I had a pretty good relationship with Joe Dash, my successor at Masterworks, and they gave it to us on reasonable terms. They got a piece of the royalty for the album, which amounted to almost nothing—when you're talking about only one or two of more than fifty selections, it's not going to be a lot. It was a courtesy on Joe's part, and I appreciated it.

Columbia also gave me another rarity, Lee Remick singing "There Won't Be Trumpets," from *Anyone Can Whistle*. Goddard had recorded the song for the original-cast album but not included it on the album. *A Collector's Sondheim* would be the first time this recording had ever been released. In all, there would be five tracks in the set that I had not originally produced: the two Columbia loaned me and three tracks from the French film *Stavisky*, for which Steve had composed the score.

This album didn't involve any new recording sessions and needed only a little editing and mixing, but it was nonetheless a lot of work, requiring a great deal of planning. I chose the selections myself. I was in touch with Steve, of course, but he never contradicted me about my choices, never told me there was anything he'd like to see on the album that I hadn't included. I think he was pleased I was digging so deeply into his catalogue, giving a new life to some wonderful songs that, because they weren't on cast albums, weren't available until *A Collector's Sondheim* came out.

I made a couple decisions early on: first, we wouldn't include anything from *West Side Story*, *Gypsy*, or *Do I Hear a Waltz* because we had a wealth of material already and would have needed a whole additional disc to do justice to these three shows for which Steve had written only the lyrics, not the music. And I preferred to have every word and every note of music be by Steve—after all, the title was *A Collector's Sondheim*. There was a purity to the way we did it that appealed to me.

Then I decided that, while the music would be presented in broadly chronological order of composition, I wouldn't be obsessive about it. If the natural flow of the material was better served by doing certain songs out of their order of composition, I was OK with that.

Ultimately, we wound up with an overview of Steve's entire career, starting with two tracks from his first show, *Saturday Night* (which had not then been produced onstage), and ending with two from *Sunday in the Park with George*. All of Steve's Broadway shows, from his hits to his ambitious failures, were represented—by both fan favorites and rarities. I also included a generous sampling of songs and/or instrumental music from his film and television work. A great deal of this material had never been heard by the general public and certainly never had been presented or collected in one place before.

Even the familiar songs were rarities in these particular recordings: only eight of the fifty-three songs were from Broadway cast albums. It was a collector's dream—and I knew because I was the collector. I included "Comedy Tonight," the iconic opening of *A Funny Thing Happened on the Way to the Forum*, but also "Love Is in the Air," originally intended to open the show. All three finales written for *Company* are on the collection, one after another. Jason Alexander's recording of "It's a Hit," which I'd had to excise from *Merrily We Roll Along* for time reasons, finally saw the light of day. (And when the CD of *Merrily We Roll Along* was released, it was returned to its rightful place in the show.)

This project really gave me a fresh sense of who Steve was as an artist, and it left me with an admiration that has only grown. Today I look at *A Collector's Sondheim* and think "My God, what a fantastic repertoire of material the man wrote!"

A Collector's Sondheim included thirteen songs from *Follies* because I (along with the entire Broadway community) felt the original-cast album recorded by Capitol lacked both quality and completeness. I'd been thinking about ways to fill that gap since one day in 1983, when Ted Chapin dropped by my office at RCA.

28

Two Nights at Avery Fisher Hall

Follies in Concert (1985)

As I've said before, the most important aspect of an original-cast album (or a revival-cast album, for that matter) is that it constitutes that production's enduring legacy.

Every show closes eventually, and even in this age when an occasional Broadway show may be filmed in the theater and shown on television or even in a movie house, the cast album is still the primary means by which that show will be known to posterity. Very few people are alive today who saw the original production of *Oklahoma!* (I'm one of them), but people are still listening to the original-cast album.

This is, of course, one of the most rewarding aspects of making cast albums. It's gratifying that shows like *Dear World* and *Goodtime Charley*, which never found an audience during their brief runs on Broadway, can still be known to future generations through my efforts. And I flatter myself that my original-cast album of *Merrily We Roll Along*, another ignominious Broadway flop, has had something to do with the show's subsequent rich, widely appreciated afterlife as a Broadway and regional success.

The flip side of the coin is that if a cast album is done poorly or not at all, it can permanently damage the legacy of the show. A show that doesn't get recorded seems as if it never existed, and a show that is represented by a badly done cast album can be unfairly pigeonholed as a badly done show. I don't believe that I've ever made a cast album that fell into that category—but I think all producers of cast albums view the risk of unfairly harming a show's legacy as a constant goad to put our all into every album we make.

Stephen Sondheim's legacy has, in general, been well served by the people who have made his original-cast albums. Every one of his shows has been recorded, and in all but one case recorded well. That one exception, however, was a bitter disappointment to Sondheim fans (myself definitely included) for more than a decade after 1971, when the original-cast album for *Follies* was made.

I knew all about *Follies*. Back in 1969 Goddard Lieberson had, as he often did, forwarded to me the script for an upcoming Broadway musical. He wanted to know whether I thought the show had promise, and specifically, whether Columbia ought to pursue the original-cast album.

This particular script was called *The Girls Upstairs* and was about a bunch of long-retired actors and actresses meeting to relive their past glories. The basic plot involved two mismatched couples who were still reliving the fights of thirty years before. The characters were complex and interesting, but the plot was contrived, and I had trouble imagining it winning over a Broadway audience. At this point I had yet to hear any of the songs, which were being written by Stephen Sondheim (who, with *Company* still a year in the future, hadn't had a hit since 1962), so I recommended to Goddard that we pass on the project.

That script was later reworked into *Follies*, but it took a lot of reworking. Based on what I had to look at, I think I made the right recommendation.

As it turned out, of course, we never had a chance to make that recording because of the quarrel between Hal Prince and Goddard that I described earlier. Hal had taken the show to Capitol Records. Capitol had produced some excellent original-cast albums, and producer Dick Jones was a veteran whose credits included *The Music Man* (1957), *Funny Girl* (1964), and even Steve's *A Funny Thing Happened on the Way to the Forum* (1962).

But Hal made the wrong choice. Despite Dick's excellent reputation, the *Follies* original-cast album was a disaster. For a host of reasons—a poorly chosen venue for the recording session, some problematic performances, and most of all, the misbegotten decision to excise so much of Steve's brilliant score in order to squeeze the show onto a single LP—it was recognized by many as a travesty from the moment it was released.

Many of us wondered whether the absence of a decent original-cast album was the reason *Follies* had languished in obscurity through the fourteen years following the original opening night. With no easy way for a Sondheim aficionado (or a Broadway aficionado) to hear the show in anything like its real glory, was it destined to be a "lost" show?

I certainly wondered, so I was immediately intrigued when, one day in 1983, Ted Chapin stopped by my office at RCA to tell me about an idea he'd had.

Ted, of course, was no stranger to me; he was Schuyler Chapin's son, and he'd been present at the recording session for *Company* back in 1970. Fourteen years younger than I was, Ted was a smart, talented young man with theater in his blood, and only two years before (when he was barely over thirty) had been named president of the Rodgers & Hammerstein Organization. This made him a major player on the Broadway scene, as the chief administrator controlling the rights to all the Rodgers & Hammerstein and Rodgers & Hart shows, as well as several other classics. But Ted didn't want to talk about Rodgers & Hammerstein that day. He wanted to talk about *Follies*.

We were both big fans of the show, but even I, after my long association with Steve and after recording numerous *Follies* songs in *Side by Side by Sondheim*, *Marry Me a Little*, and *A Stephen Sondheim Evening*, didn't know the show the way Ted did. As a college student, he'd worked on *Follies* as a production assistant, paying close attention to the backstage drama involved in the creation of the show and taking detailed notes, which later became the basis of his 2005 book, *Everything Was Possible: The Birth of the Musical* Follies. Like so many of us who loved the show, he'd never gotten over how bad the original-cast album was.

Ted wanted to do something about it. He was in my office that day to convince me that RCA should make a studio-cast album of *Follies*.

I was intrigued by Ted's pitch for a studio album that would finally do justice to *Follies*. The only problem was, I didn't think it would work.

Most of the very successful studio albums I'd done with Jim Foglesong at Columbia in the early 1960s had been based on great hits, iconic shows that were familiar to anybody who cared about musical theater. They had found a ready market among record-buyers who had already seen and loved those shows in one form or another. In addition, they were structurally simple, with easily recognizable character types and songs that were popular, in part, because they were so readily detached from the stories.

None of that could be said of *Follies*. It was a 1970s show that had scored only a modest success on Broadway, and unlike the subjects of our earlier studio albums, hadn't been filmed, revived on Broadway, or widely performed in regional or community theater. Moreover, its characters were complicated, and Steve's songs were complex and embedded in the scenes for which they had been written. I didn't think it would be possible to do justice to a show of such artistry and sophistication without a cast that had worked together in a staged production.

The last thing *Follies* needed was another failed recording, so I told Ted a studio album wasn't the answer to the problem.

But *Follies* had taken hold of me the same way it had taken hold of Ted, long before we ever sat down to talk about it. Once Ted got me thinking about it, I couldn't get the show out of my head.

Yes, its book was complicated, and its characters were more psychologically nuanced than Broadway musicals usually offered, but I found those characters enormously sympathetic. I loved what they had to say and the way they expressed themselves. As for Steve's songs, they were a constant revelation, each more beautiful, funnier, and more compelling than the last. From the moment I saw *Follies*, I was captivated by the beauty and power of the score, and I was heartbroken that, despite my success with *Company* only the year before, I had missed out on my chance to make the original-cast album. To this day, that's the single recording I didn't get to make but most wish I had.

So while I didn't think Ted's idea of a studio album was viable, it got me thinking about *Follies*—and of all things, the New York Philharmonic.

In 1980 the classical-music world had been rocked when Columbia Masterworks dropped the New York Philharmonic from its roster of exclusively contracted artists. Orchestral recordings had been getting more and more expensive, while sales revenues held steady or even declined, and there was no longer a Goddard Lieberson at Columbia to insist this decades-long relationship was too integral to Masterworks to simply be discarded. The decision may have made sense financially, but it was bad news for the Philharmonic, for classical music as a whole, and for the millions of people who loved it.

I toyed with the idea of signing the Philharmonic to Red Seal, but I ran the numbers, and they came out the same way they had for Columbia. Exclusive deals between orchestras and record labels were becoming less prevalent.

I still had faith in the Philharmonic, though, and their break with Columbia meant I could think about special projects that might make sense for both the orchestra and RCA. I was convinced the right project could work—and if it let me score a point off Joe Dash at Masterworks, well, so much the better. Joe was a friend, but we were still competitors.

The project I came up with was to team with the Philharmonic to produce a gala concert that would also be preserved as a live recording. Such a plan would require one-of-a-kind programming that would appeal both to the Philharmonic's concert-going public and to record buyers around the world. I hit upon the idea of an all-star performance of Beethoven's Ninth Symphony, featuring the talents of conductor Zubin Mehta, soprano Margaret Price, mezzo-soprano Marilyn Horne, tenor Jon Vickers, and bass Matti Salminen. To round out the program, Red Seal's hottest young pianist, Emanuel Ax, would join the orchestra and chorus for Beethoven's "Choral Fantasy."

The Philharmonic didn't plan this Beethoven concert and recruit RCA to record it. It was my idea, and I pitched it to the Philharmonic. This was a total departure from their usual way of working and a first for me in my recording history with them. Essentially it was an experiment.

We were all thrilled when the gamble paid off. It took a lot of work from everybody involved, but the Beethoven project wound up a huge success, both as a concert and as a recording. Among those particularly impressed were Albert Knickerbocker "Nick" Webster, general manager of the Philharmonic, who was delighted to be able to prove the orchestra could still sell records; and Thornton Bradshaw, CEO of the RCA Corporation, who appreciated the prestige that came with a high-profile pairing of RCA and one of the world's most famous orchestras.

So when I said to Ted that I thought the best way to bring *Follies* back to life would be to stage a concert performance of the show and record it live, I wasn't making up the notion out of whole cloth. I felt there was a good chance I could sell both the New York Philharmonic and RCA (along with Steve himself, of course) on the idea.

Which didn't mean it would be at all easy to do.

The easiest person to persuade was, of course, Steve. Nobody had been more disappointed with the original-cast album, and the prospect of a new recording done under optimal conditions by people he trusted was welcome news. Creative people always have a soft spot for their underappreciated pieces, and when Ted and I pitched him our idea, Steve was more than happy to give it his blessing.

The Philharmonic was going to be a tougher nut to crack. I'd certainly gained some credibility with our Beethoven project, but *Follies* was a Broadway show, not an opera or a symphonic work. We were asking the Philharmonic to step well outside its comfort zone, and it was by no means guaranteed that Nick Webster would sign on.

Nowadays it's not unusual for a major orchestra to accompany a concert performance of a Broadway musical. The New York Philharmonic has done other such concerts since 1985, some of them under my aegis, and even has accompanied screenings of movies such as *West Side Story*. This is true of the other major American orchestras as well. "Operatic" recordings of Broadway musicals featuring major orchestras and a mix of operatic and Broadway voices also had their moment in the late 1980s. The lines between classical and Broadway have in many areas blurred.

That wasn't the case in 1985. I can't say for certain that ours was the first such venture ever attempted—some orchestra, somewhere, may have done something similar previously—but for an orchestra with the stature and the history of the New York Philharmonic, it was unprecedented. The Philharmonic had done pops concerts for decades, but it had never been asked to function essentially as the pit orchestra for a cast of nonclassical singers. Due to the different style of music involved, we even felt that the conductor would need to be someone from the Broadway world, rather than Zubin or another classical conductor. We were asking a lot. It would take a leap of faith on Nick Webster's part for the orchestra to get involved.

To my relief, Ted and I got a very cordial reception from Nick, who was intrigued—but reluctant to make a firm commitment at that time. I understood his hesitation. The general manager has a lot of clout at the Philharmonic, but there are plenty of other stakeholders involved. How would this proposal sit with the musicians, the orchestra's board of directors, and even its patrons, who were faithful supporters of the orchestra but also, on the whole, devotees of tradition?

But almost immediately, Nick decided we would go forward. Ultimately it was decided the concert would be presented twice in September 1985 at Avery Fisher Hall. It would be the gala opening of the Philharmonic's 1985–1986 season, a high-ticket charity evening benefiting the orchestra's pension fund.

What we came up with was a tripartite plan that had an elegant symmetry to it. The New York Philharmonic would pay to produce its own concert, and RCA Red Seal would pay to produce the live recording. We also envisioned a video that would be made at the concert and released both for cable television (Showtime, as it turned out) and for consumer home video, all those expenses to be covered by the producer of the video.

With the Philharmonic in place, I took the project to Bob Summer and—as I had expected—found him both supportive and enthusiastic. RCA was on board. For the moment, at least.

Initially, Ted and I were to share responsibility, but that wasn't to be. Not long after our visit to Nick's office, Ted called me to report that his wife was expecting another child. Between his responsibilities as head of the Rodgers & Hammerstein Organization and as coproducer of what was now officially known as *Follies in Concert*, he was being spread too thin. Something had to go, and that something was *Follies in Concert*.

I was on my own and not too upset at the prospect of a chance to spread my wings. After fifteen years of having to explain to people I was a producer of Broadway cast albums, not of Broadway shows, I was finally the producer—the sole producer—of something that looked very much like a Broadway show.

The first step was to assemble a creative team with the talent, skill, and commitment that *Follies in Concert* would demand. Organizing the recording was a job for which I felt amply prepared, but organizing the concert was another thing altogether.

To get the recording we wanted, which was the primary goal of the whole project, we'd need to perform the complete score; we'd need dialogue, which meant hiring a writer, and a director; we'd need at least minimal dancing, which meant hiring a choreographer; we'd need a stage design. We'd need an extensive rehearsal schedule, a production budget, and more.

I'd expected I could talk Steve, the Philharmonic, and RCA into participating, and I'd been right. The next sales job was more complicated, though, because this time it was personal.

When I said that we'd need dialogue, I didn't mean the script of the stage musical, word for word. A musical, even a music-heavy one like *Follies*, typically includes at least an hour of dialogue. That's not feasible in a concert version. What we needed was a stripped-down version of the original text, one that hit the key narrative points but did it in much less time, getting the audience quickly from one song to the next. Most of the dialogue would need to be converted into narration. But the original text couldn't be revised or adapted except with the permission—ideally, the participation—of the original book author, James Goldman. The plot and characters of *Follies* had been cocreated by Goldman, so his consent for their use was necessary.

The problem was that Jim Goldman and Steve hadn't been on speaking terms for some years. Goldman's wife, Bobbie, was a decorator who had done some work on Steve's house, and there had been some kind of conflict between them, I don't know what. As a result, Steve made it very clear it would be me, not him, who reached out to Jim.

So I telephoned Jim and found him cordial and willing to get together to talk about it. He invited me to join him and Bobbie for a drink at their Fifth Avenue apartment.

The Goldmans lived in a bright, spacious penthouse overlooking Central Park. At that time, however, it was undergoing massive renovations and was strewn with construction debris. Jim and Bobbie greeted me graciously, got me a drink, and then led me through the rubble to a room that was something like a conservatory. We sat down, and over our drinks, I explained what we were trying to do with *Follies in Concert* and how Jim might fit into those plans.

I finished my spiel, there was a pause, and then Bobbie said, "Mr. Shepard, we don't give a shit about *Follies*."

That wasn't what I'd hoped to hear, but at least the conversation couldn't go anywhere but up! Bobbie then went into a monologue recounting the reasons she and Jim despised Steve and never wanted to see him again, let alone work with him on *Follies*. In fact, she told me, they were about to hire a composer to write a new score for *Evening Primrose*, jettisoning all of Steve's songs preparatory to bringing this new version to Broadway. (As it turned out, this never happened.)

I resisted the temptation to comment on any of this, keeping a smile on my face and resolutely directing the conversation back to *Follies* as smoothly as I could. I got the sense that, while Jim wasn't going to contradict his wife, he was open to the possibility. And indeed, after an hour or so, he agreed to take a new look at the *Follies* libretto and see if he saw a way to adapt it along the lines I had suggested.

Realizing this was as good as I was likely to get, I quickly made my farewells and headed back to the office, feeling I'd made progress. And indeed, before long Jim was working—with Steve—on the revised libretto. I believe that it was Jim who had the key idea of turning Weissman, a theatrical producer modeled on the famed impresario Flo Ziegfeld, into the narrator of the concert version.

With composer and author in line, I now turned my attention to our director. Given this would be a large cast tackling a difficult show in a severely truncated, two-week rehearsal period, this was a key hire. Nobody had ever done a project like this before. If our director couldn't handle it, everything would fall apart.

The right of first refusal obviously went to Hal Prince, who had directed the original Broadway production. Here again (and despite his long personal and professional history with Hal), Steve asked me to reach out to Hal instead of doing it himself.

Hal gracefully declined, saying he wasn't interested in staging a concert, but wishing us luck.

It worked out for the best, though, because Steve had another candidate ready to put forward, and I don't think anybody could have done the job better.

Herbert Ross was a true jack of all trades, an actor, dancer, and choreographer of theater and ballet who was best known as a producer and director of film, television, and theater. He had history with Steve, having choreographed *Anyone Can Whistle* and *Do I Hear a Waltz?* in the 1960s, and directed the 1973 film *The Last of Sheila*, for which Steve had cowritten the screenplay with Anthony Perkins.

Steve called Herb, and he readily agreed to do the job, asking only for his travel costs, and living expenses at the hotel of his choice. He lived in San Diego and would arrive in New York only a few weeks before opening night.

Herb was a dynamo, tall, highly energetic, and wildly creative. He took the full responsibility for getting *Follies in Concert* up and running. He brought in Danny Daniels as choreographer, and Steve and I asked a friend of ours, the talented director Paul Lazarus, to assist Herb.

The musical end of things was more easily handled. Apart from the New York Philharmonic, which was a new element in the *Follies* team, I was rounding up the old gang, music director Paul Gemignani and orchestrator Jonathan Tunick.

The Philharmonic OKed Paul, who jumped at the chance to work with one of America's most prestigious orchestras. He was uniquely qualified for *Follies in Concert*, having taken over as music director during the original run of the show and subsequently conducted its national tour. He'd gone on to be Steve's go-to music director.

He wouldn't be conducting the *Follies* score he'd led in 1971, however. Orchestrations written for a Broadway pit of twenty-five or so wouldn't work for a symphonic ensemble of seventy or more. We contacted Jonathan Tunick, the original orchestrator, to adapt his original orchestrations for this concert staging. He happily agreed.

Whatever might happen on the stage at Avery Fisher Hall, with a Sondheim score in the hands of Gemignani, Tunick, and myself as producer of the recording, we were on very solid ground so far as the music was concerned. I was sure the new recording would be exceptional.

With the creative team in place, we moved to the most enjoyable aspect of what was in some respects a glorified studio album.

Follies is an ensemble show. It has eighteen roles, including most notably Phyllis, Sally, Heidi, Buddy, and Ben, each of which is a double role, with a present-day, middle-aged version of the character and a flashback, young version. This was a show with many, many plum roles, and Steve, Paul, and I had great fun kicking them around and throwing out ideas.

Some of the choices were easy, or at least seemed that way, because Steve was also getting a team back together, lining up many of his favorite performers from previous shows. Mandy Patinkin (the erstwhile Georges Seurat) would play Buddy and George Hearn (a memorable replacement as Sweeney Todd) would play Ben, with Jim Walton (the original Franklin Shepard in *Merrily We Roll Along*) as the young Buddy and Howard McGillin (a replacement in *Sunday*) as the younger Ben.

Elaine Stritch (of *Company* fame) played Hattie, with Liz Callaway (a tremendous singer who'd made her Broadway debut in *Merrily We Roll Along*) as Young Sally. In the end our cast and crew included at least one veteran of every previous Sondheim show except *A Funny Thing Happened on the Way to the Forum*.

There were still plenty more roles to cast, and Steve suggested Barbara Cook, somebody I was always eager to work with, to play Sally.

Some of my own ideas were offbeat, none more so than my suggestion of Arthur Rubin to play Roscoe, the Ziegfeldian tenor who kicks off the show with "Beautiful Girls." Arthur was a top executive at the Nederlander Organization, which then and now seemed to own all the Broadway theaters that weren't owned by the Shubert Organization. Everyone on Broadway knew him, but few people remembered he could sing.

I was one who did. My memory of him stretched back to his performance in Frank Loesser's *The Most Happy Fella* (1956), in which he soloed on "Abbondanza." Back then he looked like what Roscoe would have looked like in the 1920s, and now—portly and bald—he looked like what Roscoe would look like in the 1980s. Hammy and just ungraceful enough for the part, he was the very model of a retired vaudevillian tenor.

Steve was delighted at the suggestion, and Arthur was more than happy to shake the rust off his pipes for one more show. (Steve even ventured to say I had a flair for casting, which considering future events would turn out to be ironic.)

Another one of my ideas was casting Licia Albanese as the older version of Heidi Schiller, with the young soprano Erie Mills as the young Heidi. Steve was less sure about this one. He deferred to my knowledge of classical music, of course, but he asked Paul to go with me to check out Albanese, who had been out of the spotlight for many years.

I didn't really know Albanese. I'd met her only once, at an RCA reception to launch a huge LP boxed set called *100 Years of the Metropolitan Opera and RCA Records*. She had left the Met in 1966 and had been largely unheard from since then, but of all the big opera names gathered for that reception—people like Anna Moffo, Roberta Peters, and Risë Stevens—Albanese fascinated me the most. I remembered her early *La Bohème* and *La Traviata* from 1946, and I had trouble reconciling the sweet, emotion-packed voice on those recordings with the little, round Italian lady sipping wine and eating hors d'oeuvres in RCA's executive dining room.

But that contrast was exactly what we were looking for in "One More Kiss," the *Follies* song in which the aged Heidi sings her signature song from long ago, which segues into the younger version of herself. When the old and young Heidi sing together at the end, it's an embodiment of what time does to us all, even great artists, and I could feel what it would look and sound like if it were sung by the seventy-six-year-old Albanese and the thirty-two-year-old Erie Mills. All I needed to do was to get Paul, and through him Steve, to feel it too.

So I telephoned her and asked if I could come up and discuss a project with her. After I briefly outlined what I had in mind, she invited me to her apartment to talk further and to go over the music together. A few days later Paul and I went to see her. Her apartment was very much what you'd expect from a retired diva, ornately furnished and decorated with a grand piano laden with photographs and other memorabilia of her career, most of them personal tributes from famous colleagues and conductors. Taking pride of place was a framed, signed photo of Arturo Toscanini, the legendary maestro who had been one of her greatest champions and the conductor on many of those recordings I remembered so well.

I sat down at that piano, Paul gave her the music to "One More Kiss," and Albanese sang. It was everything I had hoped it would be—aged, surely, and missing the sheen she'd once had, but still Licia Albanese.

The song was a waltz that she clearly understood, even if she didn't yet entirely understand the concept of the show, but she liked the song and was eager to participate in the project.

Paul had heard exactly what I'd heard. As we got to the street, after spending about an hour with her, he said, "She's perfect. I'm going to phone Steve."

He headed off to look for a phone booth, and I took a moment to bask in my relief and pleasure. I couldn't quite believe that we had coaxed the great Albanese out of retirement and into our project. It was a great coup. (As things developed, Albanese enjoyed the show, and a couple of years later played the same role in a Houston production of *Follies*. She was to live almost another thirty years, dying in 2014 at the age of 105.)

Not many people declined the chance to be in what was rapidly becoming one of the most talked-about productions of the new season, but I struck out twice in trying to fill the role of Weissman, the Florenz Ziegfeld figure who brings the rest of the cast together for a reunion at his soon-to-be-leveled old theater. Weissman doesn't have to sing or dance, but since he would serve as the narrator of Jim Goldman's new libretto, it would be an important role.

I asked a friend of mine, the Broadway producer Alexander Cohen, to play the role. He would have been perfect for the part, being a Florenz Ziegfeld figure in real life, but he didn't want to. The best he would do is to tell me that, since we were old friends, he'd do the role if I was really stuck at the eleventh hour. It was nice of Alex, but I could tell he didn't want to do it. Besides, I had another candidate in mind.

Alfred Drake had been Broadway's leading matinee idol of the 1940s and '50s, creating the lead roles in such classics as *Oklahoma!* (1943), *Kiss Me, Kate* (1948), and *Kismet* (1953). In 1985 he was all but retired and he walked with a cane, but he still had a magnificent speaking voice and had stage presence to burn. He was happy to hear from me and said that he was interested but wanted to see the script. To my great regret, he decided it was too small a role and he turned it down.

Steve then offered the part to a friend of his, the avant-garde director André Gregory. André, then best known as the writer and costar of Louis Malle's hit indie film *My Dinner with André* (1981), did a fine job in the part, assuming a nice, light Viennese accent and performing his narrations with great urbanity.

So gradually our cast took shape, emerging without a weak link. Betty Comden and Adolph Green filled the roles of Emily and Theodore Whitman, and Phyllis Newman, my old Ado Annie from *Oklahoma!*, played Stella and covered all the older women's roles. Television star Carol Burnett, known to Broadway fans since 1959 as the original Princess Winnifred in *Once Upon a Mattress*, returned to the stage to play Carlotta. Lee Remick was cast to play Phyllis, and that's a story I will tell later. Liliane Montevecchi, who had won a Tony for her work in *Nine* (1982), played Solange. And Daisy Prince took on the role of Young Phyllis.

The term "all-star cast" gets thrown around a lot, often loosely, but I honestly think that's what we had for *Follies in Concert*.

We could have put together quite a good cast from people we turned away, in fact. I still remember the day when my office phone rang and it was Lisa Kirk, who had been the original Lois/Bianca in *Kiss Me, Kate* alongside Alfred Drake. She wanted to know if there was a part for her in *Follies in Concert*—and I had to tell her there wasn't, we were already fully cast.

Everybody wanted to be in *Follies in Concert*. Most of the people we cast, whom we were asking to devote weeks of preparation for a two-night run and paying only scale, didn't push back or play hard to get. They thanked us for thinking of them and offering them such a unique opportunity.

So as *Follies in Concert* entered its stretch run in the summer of 1985, everything seemed to be falling into place. We had a terrific musical team, a gifted director heading our way, and a cast that couldn't be beat. Steve and Jim Goldman were working harmoniously in revising their show for our innovative production, the Philharmonic's leadership was squarely behind us, and the early buzz in the theatrical community was unanimously positive. All my concerns seemed to have been ironed out, and the show was looking like a sure thing.

As it turned out, though, I had been worrying about the wrong things. I ought to have been looking over my shoulder—and specifically, at the RCA executive to whom I directly reported, José Menéndez.

Four years later José would become a household name after he and his wife were murdered in a hail of gunfire. Seven months later his sons, Lyle and Erik, would be arrested, charged with the murder, and ultimately convicted.

In the early days after the killing, however, a grim joke made the rounds at RCA: we were all the usual suspects. Knock on any door at RCA headquarters, and you'd find somebody who hated José. He was a monster, devious, and abusive to his coworkers. (Fortunately the murders took place in Los Angeles, so we all had alibis.)

I wouldn't say I hated José enough to kill him, but I did dislike him intensely. It wasn't because he was clueless about classical music and spent his days crunching numbers and looking for an excuse to make my life miserable. . . . I'd reported to a lot of people at RCA who didn't understand what I did, and I'd endured a lot of budget cuts.

José was different. There was a meanness to the way he went about his business and an underhandedness I despised.

He had no particular interest in music or, as far as I could tell, the record business. The only thing that mattered to him was José Menéndez, and RCA and all the people who worked there were simply rungs on his personal climb to the top.

José had come to RCA Records via Hertz Rent-a-Car, which at the time was owned by the RCA Corporation. He had an MBA and considerable skill at trimming staff and slashing costs. At the time RCA Records wasn't doing very well, so one of the major corporate honchos, Frank Olsen, installed José as a watchdog with a mandate to make RCA Records more profitable.

The lines of authority were complex, I think intentionally so. In theory Bob Summer was my overall boss, which would imply that José reported to Bob, but José and Bob both reported to Frank, who was RCA's own George Patton—quiet, tough, and totally intimidating to one and all. In practice this meant Bob couldn't protect me from José's machinations. If José had it in for me, there wasn't much Bob could do about it.

And José did have it in for me. It seemed to bother him that I had managed to achieve a modest profit doing what I did. Unable to crack down on me as a money loser, he hassled me in all sorts of ways. For example, as the compact-disc revolution hit in the early 1980s, I requested CD players for my staff of five producers—and José turned me down, even though they wouldn't be able to check our own products without them.

That level of pettiness was an everyday reality of working under José Menéndez. Not long afterward, people asked me why I left a high-profile position at RCA to start a department from scratch at MCA. The answer was José Menéndez and the corporate system that kept elevating people like him—people who neither knew nor cared about the business of making records—to positions of authority.

To be fair, I wasn't without blame in our steadily deteriorating relationship. Corporate politics has never been my strong suit, and without meaning to do so I had stepped on the toes of José and several other RCA executives the year before *Follies in Concert*.

I've mentioned previously that in 1984 I cooperated with a *New York Times Magazine* feature about me that was written by the *Times* critic Bernard Holland. He and I got along very well and had a great deal of respect for each other's work. Perhaps that was why I let my guard down more than I should have and, in passing, admitted to Bernard that from my perspective the only one in the RCA Records leadership who gave me encouragement and support was Bob Summer.

This was perfectly true, but in retrospect it was foolish to say it to anybody, let alone to a *New York Times* writer with a notebook and a tape recorder. Bernard put it in the article, and when it came out, there was an awkward staff meeting at RCA (presided over by José) in which the interview came up. I answered truthfully: What I had said was simply the way I felt at that moment and wasn't intended to embarrass José or anybody else. I was simply trying to tell it like it was.

Clearly angered by my lack of repentance or subservience, José then said that he felt it was inappropriate for any of us to air our dirty laundry in public—with which of course I couldn't disagree. The meeting then went on to other matters, and I foolishly assumed the matter was over and done with. It clearly wasn't either over or done with for José, and the fact that I'd inadvertently embarrassed several other RCA executives probably lost me some support when the conflict between José and me came to a head the next year.

Bob did everything he could to get me to recognize I was treading on dangerous ground. He was very enthusiastic about my *Follies* project. But he was much more adept at corporate politics than I was, and he several times strongly suggested I needed to get José behind *Follies in Concert*. I ought to have listened, but I didn't.

The fact is, I didn't think I needed to. I was living in a bubble. My projects were going well, my department was making money, and the top men at RCA, CEO Thornton Bradshaw and Executive Vice President Herb Schlosser, were pleased with the direction in which I'd taken Red Seal. I knew José was dangerous, but I felt protected. I didn't think he'd dare to come after me.

Cannily, he bided his time. Instead of making his move when I was riding high, he waited. I wrote him a memo on *Follies in Concert* on February 7, 1984, and he let it go unanswered for fifteen months. Not until July 2, 1985, with the concert plans locked in and everything in full swing, did he respond with a brief memo, which I quote here in full:

> I have decided not to go ahead with the Follies project. After reviewing the information received from a variety of sources, I feel this appears to be a risky project with an uncertain payoff.
> While I share your enthusiasm for the overall idea, I am afraid that at this time I have to decline to proceed with the project.
> —J. E. Menéndez

This was a declaration of war, and it quickly became clear José had not been sitting idly by for the past fifteen months.

When I ran down to the office of Bob Summer, putatively José's boss, I was met—to my amazement and horror—with nothing but vague assurances that he'd see what he could do, but that I should lie low for a while. In this crisis, Bob couldn't help me.

I turned to Jim Alic, a very civilized executive who had recently been assigned to a high-level advisory position, something of a liaison between RCA Records and the company's corporate headquarters at Rockefeller Center. I laid it all out for him, and he was understanding and supportive—but also unwilling to intercede directly. He hinted obliquely that he might take up the issue with RCA's corporate chiefs, but like Bob, implied I should do nothing.

Time was, of course, the one thing I didn't have. Tickets would be on sale in less than four weeks, and opening night was scheduled for September 6. If I didn't immediately share the horrible news with Steve and with the Philharmonic, they inevitably would learn about it from some other source, and my lack of candor might blow up the whole project.

I had expected Steve would be supportive and sympathetic, given how much I'd already put into the project, but he was not. He had not a word of sympathy, empathy, or concern. His own reaction was paramount: he was deeply invested in the resurrection of *Follies*, and this was a body blow.

"Well, then," he barked, "what are we doing this concert for, if not for the recording? Now what are you going to do?"

I wondered that myself. With two months and counting, there was no time to lick my wounds or, as Bob and Jim Alic had suggested, to keep my head down and hope the storm would blow itself out. As far as I could see, my only remaining option was to get another record label to sweep in at the last minute and record *Follies in Concert*.

This was, of course, an extremely risky move. It would amount to going behind my bosses' backs and might well have spelled the end of my career at RCA.

But I was hugely invested in *Follies in Concert*, so I approached my old label, Columbia, about taking over the project. I put out feelers to Warner Bros., EMI, and Sony. I even tried to raise enough money to pay for the recording through such funding sources as Francis Goelet, a major patron of the Philharmonic; Richard Baskin, the ice-cream company heir and himself a composer; and Steve's publisher, Tommy Valando.

Again and again I heard the same response: it was a terrific project, and my predicament was appalling and undeserved. They might well want to rescue me, but they needed time to think about it, time I simply didn't have.

I didn't blame them. Record companies are rivals, of course, but their executives are professional colleagues. We move easily and often from one label to another, as I had done from Columbia to RCA, and we do our best to maintain cordial relationships with one another. (An obvious example was the help Joe Dash had given me on *A Collector's Sondheim*.) Anyone who stepped in to bail me out would have incurred José's eternal enmity and probably that of the top people at RCA, and *Follies in Concert* simply wasn't worth it.

A few weeks passed, and I didn't hear from anybody—not even from Columbia, where I still had friends and which seemed like my best alternative. I kept going to rehearsals, where (since of course everyone was now aware of the situation) I had to keep assuring people that, yes, we would have a recording, which privately seemed less likely with each passing day.

Then Bob Summer called me down to his office. I was hoping against hope he might have good news for me, but this was anything but good news. Bob asked me point-blank if it was true that I was shopping *Follies in Concert*, seeking support from other labels. Obviously, he'd heard I was, so I admitted it and said that since RCA had made clear it wouldn't be making the recording, I felt obliged to do so.

Bob understood my point but warned me that, as head of Red Seal, I couldn't hope to take the project elsewhere and keep my job.

I'd had time to think about this possibility, and while I'm not intrinsically brave, I'd decided, if it came to it, I'd have to draw a line in the sand. I told Bob I'd put too much into *Follies in Concert*, that I'd made too many promises to Steve, to the Philharmonic, to Paul Gemignani, and to the cast, to abandon the project now. If that meant I got fired, then so be it. (I didn't add, though he probably understood anyway, that the prospect of not working for RCA, and for José in particular, wasn't looking like such a bad thing.)

I left his office confused and very sad, and resolved not to convey this latest information to Steve, Paul, or the other people involved. Whether I was being heroic, stupid, or both, I kept it to myself. For the next few weeks I avoided Bob as much as I could, and he made no effort to engage me on the subject.

It's a matter of record that *Follies in Concert* was indeed released by RCA and went on to win the Grammy Award as Best Musical Theater Album. I would love to describe how I marshalled my resources, and in a masterly feat of corporate infighting, outmaneuvered José and talked the powers that be at RCA into backing the album. But I can't.

As it happened, I was rescued by someone more powerful than José Menéndez, Bob Summer, Thornton Bradshaw, or RCA itself: the New York theatergoer. The public can make a hit of the most unlikely show, or a flop of the most touted blockbuster, and in this case, it was on my side.

On August 11 the tickets for *Follies in Concert* went on sale at Lincoln Center, and both performances sold out in three hours. The advance buzz had not been misleading. People really, really wanted to see this. The Philharmonic's publicist made sure this information reached the city's newspapers, which duly reported it, and got extra juice into their stories by adding another tidbit that had reached their ears: "*FOLLIES IN CONCERT* SELLS OUT AS RCA CANCELS RECORDING." It was all the funnier when they mentioned that the project had itself been initiated by RCA's Red Seal label, only to have RCA bail out at the last moment.

Suddenly the press was having a field day at RCA's expense, and the people up the ladder at RCA didn't like that at all. Once again Bob Summer called me down to his office, but this time with better news. He had decided RCA would record *Follies in Concert* after all. I was, obviously, as delighted and relieved as I'd ever been.

I was less delighted when he told me that, to allow José to save face, I'd have to take a hit in a different area. He asked me to settle for a reduction in my contractually mandated producer's fee and royalties for both *Follies in Concert* and Andrew Lloyd Webber's *Song and Dance*, which we were about to record. This didn't sit well with me—why should I have to pay for having come up with an idea that RCA had finally realized was a good one?—but Bob strongly suggested I accept the terms gracefully, so I did.

If I had chosen to fight that battle, I might have won it. After all, RCA was in a very awkward position and at this point couldn't drop the project or take me off it without triggering another wave of mockery. But frankly, I was exhausted. Weeks of stress and anxiety were catching up with me, and I didn't have another fight in me right then.

Today, though, I very much regret having gone along with it. It simply wasn't fair.

Suddenly RCA was 100 percent behind *Follies in Concert*. The company's publicists made up for lost time, beating the drums far and wide. It was the greatest idea in the history of recording, a massive, incredibly prestigious project that stood squarely in the RCA tradition, the kind that only a storied label like RCA could hope to bring to fruition.

That change was immediately apparent in my daily life. RCA executives who had been giving me a wide berth for weeks were suddenly coming up to congratulate me and perhaps to try to associate themselves with the project in some way. After all, they'd been on my side all along, even if they hadn't said so to me, let alone to José.

With the dark cloud removed from over our heads, everything seemed to click into high gear. Everyone in the cast seemed to be working out. RCA was pumping out publicity, and Mary Rodgers Guettel (composer, author, old friend of Steve's, and an officer of the Dramatists' Guild) was getting out the word to all her theater contacts. The Philharmonic's entire staff was working only on the concert, and we'd recruited RCA art director Joe Stelmach to design our stage backdrop (the iconic *Follies* logo that also became our poster, program cover, and album cover). Paul Marantz, an old Oberlin friend of mine who is a partner in the architectural-lighting company Fisher Marantz Stone, handled our stage lighting.

The last phase of our three-part plan fell into place when I received a call from Ellen M. Krass, a video executive who was willing to front the costs of a home video, utilizing technical equipment and expertise from the BBC. Ellen was hyper-energetic and moved with the assurance of Ethel Merman, and she was sure she could place the video for both cable-television broadcast and VHS home video.

This seemed to me to be exactly what we'd been looking for, but when I told them about it, Jim and Steve were less excited. Apparently, there had been feelers from Hollywood about a film musical of *Follies*, and they were worried that having the whole show available on home video would put the kibosh on a possible movie deal.

So we compromised: the video would be a documentary about the production, mixing rehearsal footage with selected excerpts from the performances, but a few significant songs would be omitted entirely. The result is a very effective video, but I regret the absence of several of the show's best songs—and notice that, almost forty years later, the feature film has yet to materialize.

That said, it was particularly gratifying to see Steve and Jim working closely together on the revised script and clearly enjoying each other's company. What they came up with was very effective, a tightly constructed combination of narrations for Weissman and abbreviated dialogue for the actors that essentially functioned as lead-ins to each song.

Herb Ross arrived from California and quickly proved to be everything we'd hoped. His rehearsals were models of efficiency, making good use of every moment.

He ran the production with an iron grip on every detail and didn't hesitate to kick somebody—even an important member of our team—out of the room because he or she happened to talk while Herb was talking. Herb was very impressive—he kind of knocked me out. He was so smart and understood what needed to be done so well that I would never have interfered or even made a suggestion. He had everything under control and had *Follies in Concert* almost on its feet in a week.

A couple of our cast members were returning to the stage after years away and were a little more nervous than they needed to be. Carol Burnett hadn't had to memorize lyrics for the previous twenty years, which she'd spent on television. She requested a Teleprompter to help her get through "I'm Still Here." Barbara Cook, who hadn't performed in an ensemble for nearly as long, felt she needed a monitor, a small loudspeaker at her feet to let her hear the orchestra more clearly.

I went along with Carol's request gladly because the last thing I needed was for her to "go up" on her lines. I don't think she ended up using it, but she felt more secure because it was there. On the other hand, I didn't want to give Barbara a floor monitor for fear its additional sound would leak into her vocal mike. To my relief, as the rehearsals went on, she became secure enough to decide that she wouldn't need it. I was pleased.

Perhaps Herb's best idea was to split the New York Philharmonic in two. They were sitting upstage on risers, fully visible to the audience, and Herb came up with the idea of a center aisle or walkway between the two halves of the orchestra. On stage right would be all the strings and on stage left the winds, brass, and percussion. (There was also a trio of piano, drums, and bass to the left and in front of the main orchestra, and André Gregory was downstage with a microphone and podium all his own.)

This runway gave Herb the opportunity to introduce the women onstage, to the background of Arthur Rubin singing "Beautiful Girls," by having each of them enter upstage, one by one, cross to center stage and then turn and come downstage dramatically between the two halves of the orchestra, each getting her round of applause before taking her place in a line across the apron of the stage. The theatrical power of this staging was immense, but it was particularly welcome to me because the bifurcated orchestra gave the recording crew a very clean acoustic shot at the Philharmonic's strings, which in a normal setup were less acoustically isolated from the winds and brass among and behind them.

Miking the actors was more difficult than it would be today, when each would simply wear his or her own wireless mike. In 1985, however, wireless mikes were still works in progress, with mediocre sound quality and a bad habit of either making unexpected noises or failing just when they were needed most. Instead I chose to use traditional high-quality recording mikes arrayed on seven stands across the apron, despite the potential hazards of their inevitable masses of black wire.

Understanding the needs of the recording, Herb staged all the major solos and ensembles to take place in this downstage, miked area that included not only my recording mikes, but also those deployed by house-sound engineer Otts Munderloh to reach the audience. Getting those powerful loudspeakers placed in such a way as to avoid audio feedback into our stage mikes was a tricky business.

As the ten days of rehearsal went along, Paul Gemignani and the New York Philharmonic got to know each other, and they both seemed to enjoy the experience. Paul is a man of relatively few words but conveys an innate sense of authority—a combination that pleased most of the orchestra musicians. A few of them had expressed qualms about playing a Broadway show with a Broadway conductor, but Paul's professionalism and musicianship won them over. Nearly all the cast had worked with Paul before, so he, they, and the orchestra were literally and figuratively on the same page. As for those pages, Jonathan Tunick's reworked orchestrations sounded fantastic when played by the Philharmonic.

Our first staged run-through, a few days before the show, was done without an audience, except for a few people working on the show who happened to be in the house. I was one of them and will never forget the first time I saw "Beautiful Girls." I knew how it was being staged and had been at many of the rehearsals, but seeing it on the stage at Avery Fisher Hall was electrifying. Following a gorgeous overture, Arthur Rubin sang "Beautiful Girls" and each of the leading ladies in turn came down that aisle splitting the New York Philharmonic. Montevecchi, Cook, Burnett, Remick, Stritch, Comden—all the power of their beauty, their poise, and the aura of their legendary careers was packed into one moment, and it was explosive.

Suddenly I could see, I could feel what this concert was going to be, and it was better than I had ever imagined.

One of us wasn't going to see the show, though, because fate still had one more curveball to throw us. The day before our premiere, Herb Ross got word that his wife, the former ballerina Nora Kaye, had had a seizure and been hospitalized in Santa Monica with a diagnosis of cancer.

There was never any question of what he'd do. Herb turned over the last twenty-four hours of polishing to Paul Lazarus and caught the first plane to Los Angeles. Paul did a fine job, and Nora soon improved markedly, but it was a cruel irony that Herb, who had done so much to make *Follies in Concert* what it was, wouldn't be there in the flesh to see his great work come to life.

Our dress rehearsal took place on the afternoon of September 6, 1985, hours before our first performance. The audience was made up of friends, family members, and colleagues of the cast members, the production team, RCA, and the Philharmonic itself, many of them famous people. Strongly disposed to like the show, they were arguably the best audience we'd ever have, ready to applaud and cheer everything that happened onstage, except that I wouldn't let them.

This was one of only three opportunities we would have to record the event, and the only one where I could control one of the biggest hazards of any live performance: outbreaks of applause that interrupt the progress of the show. I desperately wanted one "clean" recording, so I spoke to the audience before the show, thanked them for coming, and then asked them not to applaud at all, at any time, for any reason, no matter how good a time they were having, until the final curtain.

The result was a very unusual experience, one that was particularly difficult for the audience themselves because their enthusiasm was at a fever pitch, and yet they were asked to maintain absolute silence, great song after great song, for more than two hours. When the dress rehearsal finally ended, the result was a surge of applause that was deafening, as if a dam had broken, as a frustrated and highly charged audience released all their pent-up emotions at once.

When the opening night finally arrived, I could hardly believe it. It seemed like I'd been working on *Follies in Concert* for years, riding waves of euphoria and despair for so long that to finally actually see opening night seemed almost unreal. It was magical beyond my ability to describe—I can only direct my readers to the CD and to the video, which are more eloquent than anything I can add.

From the moment Paul picked up his baton and the Philharmonic began the overture, and even more from the moment Arthur Rubin started "Beautiful Girls" and that line of fabulous women began parading down the stage, the audience became part of the drama, electrified by the moment and by the power of Steve's score.

I would have given a lot to be able to simply sit in the audience and watch the show, but I could spare only a few moments of self-indulgence. I stayed at the back of the auditorium through the overture and "Beautiful Girls"—I knew that it would be a magical moment, and I couldn't bear to miss it. And when it finally happened, and those beautifully dressed women came down the stage one by one, the audience exploded with a ferocity of cheering and applause such as I had never witnessed in my life. I simply let the sound wash over me and for a minute or two let myself savor the pride, the relief, and the exhilaration of seeing this dream come vividly to life.

And then I turned my back and walked out of the hall, bound for a van parked outside on West 65th Street that was packed with digital tape recorders and all the attendant equipment. There, in the nerve center of our live-recording operation, Jay David Saks was waiting for me, along with engineer Paul Goodman and an RCA crew. For the audience, *Follies in Concert* was a chance to kick back and enjoy a historic evening of musical theater. For us, it was a work night.

I did get to the party afterward, where I was joined by Irene and Elizabeth, who had been in the audience. I also talked to many, many other people. Among them was Hal Prince, who told me he'd enjoyed it very much. He added, "I guess maybe I should have directed this, huh?"

Most of RCA's top brass attended the opening night, with one conspicuous exception: José Menéndez was nowhere to be seen. He didn't attend the show, and I feel sure he never listened to the recording. Bob Summer, of course, was there on opening night and gave me his heartfelt congratulations.

Bob was a judicious man who watched his words and never let emotion cloud his judgment, so I know he spoke from the heart when, a few weeks later, I happened to mention José having skipped the opening night, and Bob responded feelingly, "Fuck Menéndez!"

Follies in Concert continues to have an impact today, almost four decades later. That impact began at the party on opening night, when a man came up to me and introduced himself as Cameron Mackintosh.

I knew who he was, of course. *The Phantom of the Opera* (1988) and *Miss Saigon* (1991) were still in his future, but he was arguably the top theatrical producer in London, where the soon-to-be-blockbuster *Les Misérables* was already in previews. And of course *Cats* had been playing on Broadway since 1982, on its way to a staggering eighteen-year run. The future Sir Cameron had another Broadway show in previews at the Royale: *Song and Dance*, about which I'll have more to say later.

So when Mackintosh shook my hand on opening night and told me that based on what he'd just seen, he had decided to produce a revival of *Follies* in London, I knew he was serious. And in 1987 *Follies* opened on the West End, newly revised by Steve and Jim in a less neurotic, more accessible production that Steve later called "the Jerry Herman version."

It ran for two years, and since then *Follies* has assumed its rightful place in the Sondheim canon, with Broadway revivals in 2001 and 2011, along with London revivals in 2002 and 2017, and professional productions around the world. And it all stems from the meeting Ted and I had in my office, back in 1983.

The idea of symphony orchestras accompanying concert versions of Broadway musicals (and later, movie screenings) caught on and continues to the present day. The New York Philharmonic has done many more (including *Camelot* and *My Fair Lady* with me as producer), and orchestras around the world have joined the fun. Increasingly, it seems the greatest Broadway musicals are being accepted as classics in their own right—and as someone who's devoted his life to Broadway and to classical music, I couldn't be happier about that.

Most surprising, perhaps, *Follies in Concert* itself has turned out to be a property with staying power. In the ensuing thirty-eight years (as I write this), it has been seen and heard in high-profile productions in cities as far apart as Los Angeles, Dublin, and Sydney, with great performers such as Patty Duke, Carol Lawrence, Lorna Luft, Millicent Martin, Donna McKechnie, Bob Gunton, and Ron Moody. A very special 2003 production in Detroit featured Broadway's original Young Sally, Phyllis, Buddy, and Ben—Marti Rolfe, Virginia Sandifur, Harvey Evans, and Kurt Peterson—this time playing the older versions of the characters they'd created.

The idea of semi-staged productions of under-appreciated Broadway musicals has also been institutionalized in the Encores! series of revivals at City Center in New York, a gem of the city's theater scene since 1994. A number of its productions have transferred to Broadway, including *Wonderful Town* (2000), *The Apple Tree* (2005), *Finian's Rainbow* (2009), and most notably, *Chicago* (1996), which has run more than seven times as long as its original 1975 production did, and now is the second-longest-running show Broadway has ever seen. I don't know whether they got the idea from us—but either way, it's a good one!

The recording is terrific. It filled three sides. We rounded out the LP release by reissuing Steve's music from the film *Stavisky*, which fit nicely on the fourth side and which originated around the same time as *Follies*.

Everything considered, *Follies in Concert* may have been the finest of my many collaborations with Steve Sondheim. As it turned out, it would also be the last.

29

Sondheim and Me

IN MANY RESPECTS THE HUGE SUCCESS of *Follies in Concert* marked the high point of my fifteen-year collaboration with Stephen Sondheim. That relationship had been built on my recording the original productions of shows he'd created for Broadway, but *Follies in Concert* was something different. It had come about largely as the result of my efforts and had instilled new life—artistic and commercial—in a show that, though revered by its fans, had long been counted among Steve's flops. That I could do this for him and for a show I had always loved was among the project's biggest satisfactions for me.

I had no idea, at the time, that that collaboration had just ended.

During the casting process for *Follies in Concert*, I had a brilliant idea. What about Linda Lavin as Phyllis, the role created in the original Broadway production by Alexis Smith? Linda was (and is) an exceptionally gifted performer. In 1985 she was just coming off a nine-year run as the star of the hit sitcom *Alice*; she'd earned a Tony nomination for Neil Simon's *Last of the Red Hot Lovers* (1969) and was soon to win a Tony as Best Actress for another Simon play, *Broadway Bound* (1987). Nor was she a stranger to Steve, due to her starring role in *The Mad Show* back in the mid-1960s.

Linda has a real flair for the kind of sharp, sarcastic material that Phyllis specializes in, and I was sure Steve would agree with me that she was perfect for the part. I was so sure, in fact, that I made a grievous error: I asked her to be in the show before I'd talked it over with Steve.

Every actress in New York wanted to be in *Follies in Concert*, and Linda was no exception. She immediately agreed to play Phyllis, and I hung up the phone with her and almost immediately called Steve. I was sure he'd as enthusiastic about the news as I was.

That wasn't what happened. As soon as I told him about Linda and how happy and honored she was to be involved, an icy chill crept into Steve's voice, and I knew I'd made a big mistake.

"Who told you that you could do that?" he said, his anger obvious, even over the phone.

What I hadn't known was that Steve already had asked Lee Remick, one of his closest friends, to play Phyllis.

"Fix this," he hissed at me and hung up the phone.

Naturally, I did so without delay. My second conversation with Linda wasn't an easy one for me, but I did what had to be done. I told her that unbeknown to me, he'd already offered the part to somebody else, so I would have to withdraw my offer to her. She was understandably disappointed, and I think upset, though she was polite about it.

I felt terrible, both because of Linda and because of Steve. I should emphasize that I thought then and think now that Linda would have been better in the part, but that wasn't the point. The point was Steve had been involved in every step of the planning for the concert and was emotionally invested in every aspect of it, including the casting, even when he had left much of it to me. *Follies* was his show, and I had thoughtlessly exceeded my role.

That said, I had immediately done as he demanded and "fixed it." Steve got the Phyllis he wanted, and the concert was an overwhelming artistic and commercial success. At the time I assumed the Phyllis fiasco, like Steve's anger with me when it briefly seemed as if RCA wouldn't actually participate in the project, was in the past, just one of the inevitable bumps in the course of a project this ambitious and involving so many different aspects, personalities, and moving parts. I assumed my mistake was water under the bridge.

It wasn't. Nine years later a public spat between us led me to write Steve a personal letter in which I asked him what really lay behind what seemed to me too trivial a matter to spur the venom he'd publicly directed toward me. He wrote back and concluded his four-paragraph letter with, "I have just two words to say to you: Linda Lavin."

I have produced several hundred recordings, only eleven of which have involved Stephen Sondheim; I have twelve Grammy Awards, only four of which were for recordings of Sondheim shows. Nonetheless I realize that when my obituary is published, my collaboration with Steve will take pride of place over all the other work I've done. When people think of me, they think of Sondheim recordings. When I do lecture programs and take audience questions, most of the questions I'm asked include his name.

But I realize my association with him is part of what I am as an artist, and both of us benefited from it, however Steve may have felt about it at the end. Recording his shows challenged me on every level, forced me to raise my game, and made me what I am as a producer. On the other hand, what I am as a producer helped make Steve who he was, because my recordings permanently preserved the original productions of his shows, allowing generations of fans to enjoy them.

Steve wrote the complete scores for thirteen Broadway shows, of which I recorded six original-cast albums. I also recorded two Sondheim revues and two live concerts and compiled *A Collector's Sondheim*. Certainly no one has recorded as many Sondheim shows as I have or worked so closely with him in the recording studio for so long. Those years of joint work have shaped my opinions of Steve, as a man and as an artist.

The lyrics for *West Side Story* and *Gypsy* are brilliant. Because these two shows were the first taste that we had of Steve's talent, however, and because they remain the two that are performed and seen on film or television the most, they have skewed some people's sense of Steve as an artist. Early in his career, too many people who loved those shows but not his subsequent ones dismissed him as a lyricist who later took up writing music—almost as if his composition was nothing more than a hobby. Aside from the stubbornly unenlightened, however, Steve has long since been recognized as a uniquely gifted composer.

A Funny Thing Happened on the Way to the Forum, which was Steve's first and most successful show as a composer/lyricist, is often brushed off as nothing more than a showcase for comedians, as though anybody could have made a good show with that cast. I emphatically disagree. When I recorded *A Stephen Sondheim Evening*, Bob Gunton sang "Pretty Little Picture," one of the songs sung by Zero Mostel in the original production, and a personal favorite of mine. Both music and lyrics perfectly capture what's going on in the show, as Pseudolus is, for reasons of his own, trying to talk Hero and Philia into eloping. It's a delightful song by a guy who isn't just a brilliant lyricist, but also a brilliant songwriter.

I think *Forum* gets overlooked because it's a broad comedy, and its characters are archetypes. Steve's later shows tended to be much darker and more dramatic, with very complicated characters. But that he could write such perfect music for this wholly different kind of show speaks to his gifts as a composer.

In his later shows, in which Steve edged closer to opera, he made it very clear that when the story and situation called for it, he could let the music do the speaking—not to be a vehicle to move things along, but to highlight and create an emotion that is different from anything you can create with words alone. There are moments in his music that make me almost weep for joy or for sadness because they're so beautiful.

There are any number of other examples I could cite. Everyone thinks of Steve as a stage composer, but on the movie screen he also wrote the score for *Stavisky* (1974), contributed to the score for *Reds* (1981), and wrote the songs for *Dick Tracy* (1990), all three very successful.

Steve could write songs that would break your heart. "With So Little to Be Sure Of," from *Anyone Can Whistle*, brings tears to my eyes whenever I hear it and may be my favorite of all his songs. If not that, my favorite might be "In Buddy's Eyes," from *Follies*, which is another heartbreaker.

And Steve could be hilarious. He wrote any number of lines that never grow old. In *A Little Night Music*, for instance, I just fall off my chair for "she'll save the cigar butt"/ "Bizarre, but/you're joking."

His vocabulary was huge, but he worked very hard to make his lyrics comprehensible. He didn't care for the old-fashioned practice of inverting sentences—"with you I'm in love" and that sort of thing. He was attentive to rhythms: he criticized Gilbert's line "when you're lying awake/with a dismal headache" because it required an accent on the second syllable, "head-ACHE," and that's not the way the word is pronounced. He tried to make his lyrics conversational (albeit the conversation of educated, sophisticated people, for the most part).

After *A Funny Thing Happened on the Way to the Forum*, Steve developed something of a specialty in songs whose lyrics vivisected his characters, who were complicated people with streaks of cruelty, envy, lust, or hatred. He liked writing for characters where you have to look under the rock, where you have to hear not only what they say, but what they don't say. He was a twentieth-century, post-Freudian songwriter.

And his bad guys aren't cardboard villains. Just when you least expect it, they say or do something that makes you feel a bit of sympathy and understanding. Sweeney Todd is a serial killer, a ruthless man who kills innocent bystanders again and again in pursuit of his personal vengeance, and yet it's a hard-hearted audience member who doesn't weep for him.

Steve was essentially a composer, and that's why so much of his work consists of beautiful songs that don't really work outside of the shows for which they were written. Porter's songs or Berlin's songs work as well in a cabaret act as they do in the original show. Steve was different: you could sing "Losing My Mind" in a cabaret, sure, but stripped of the context of *Follies*, the character who sings it and the story that brings her to that point, it's only half the song it was meant to be, if that. But of course, *Follies* presents a very unusual context for any of its songs.

Steve had grown up in the tradition of Rodgers & Hammerstein, with Oscar Hammerstein II as his mentor and father figure, but to the songwriters of their generation and earlier, there was a certain type of property that was considered "right" for a musical—most often a straightforward, realistic story about a morally uncomplicated hero or heroine who faces all kinds of odds, ideally in some exotic surroundings, but triumphs and finds happiness (and usually, true love) through being unafraid and able to grow and change. Rodgers and Hammerstein's huge success with variations on this type of story in *Oklahoma!* and *Carousel* made most Broadway songwriters leap to imitate them in terms of structure and tone.

This general agreement on the right way to tell a story, and what kind of story to tell, was starting to change by the late 1950s, however, and Steve was in on the ground floor: love across ethnic lines amid street violence and the struggle of a stripper to escape from the shadow of her controlling mother weren't so obviously "right" for a Broadway show, but Sondheim, Laurents, Robbins, and Bernstein on *West Side Story* and Styne on *Gypsy*, made them into blockbusters.

By the time he emerged as a major composer/lyricist in the 1970s, Steve had embraced the idea that almost anything could be "right" for a musical. Gunboat diplomacy in nineteenth-century Japan? A murderous Victorian barber? An obsessive painter? Presidential assassins?

In one key respect Steve rejected the legacy of Rodgers & Hammerstein. They wrote for a wide audience, including children: whether it's *The King and I*, *Cinderella*, or *The Sound of Music*, you can take your kids and your grandchildren to their shows, and everybody can have a good time. Steve never emulated them in that. He wrote for sophisticated adults and didn't write his shows to please the biggest possible audience. Even in *Into the Woods*, which is a fairy-tale adaptation, Steve is writing from a viewpoint that's both wise and cynical, not to mention very judgmental at times—he lectures in his songs. "Children Will Listen" wants to entertain the audience only incidentally; mostly it wants to teach them, and its audience is adults, not kids. This is characteristic of later Sondheim. As the years passed, his writing became increasingly preachy and judgmental.

Steve wrote for an older audience, and—unlike any number of other Broadway songwriters—he wasn't writing about a wonderful world. His shows open a lot of doors, but what's behind those doors isn't always pretty. Whether it was the contemporary world of *Company* or the period settings of his subsequent shows, there wasn't a bright, golden haze on the meadow, and the hills weren't alive with the sound of music. In his musicals "there's a hole in the world like a great black pit, and it's filled with people who are filled with shit." You didn't bring your grandchildren.

Steve came from money—his father was a successful dress manufacturer, and his mother was chief designer for the Herbert Sondheim label. Both remained wealthy even after splitting when their son was ten—so he had the advantage (as Alan Jay Lerner and Cole Porter had before him) of never having to worry about paying his bills.

One of the most admirable things about Steve was that no two of his shows were alike. He had not only the courage, but also the intellectual curiosity, to turn the page after his most successful shows and his greatest failures alike, and to look for something new. Even if the radical experiment *Follies* lost money, he didn't retreat to conservative choices for his next couple of shows: a sophisticated European not-quite-operetta based on an Ingmar Bergman film, and a Kabuki-style history lesson with an all-male, all-Asian cast, certainly weren't guaranteed hits.

(His aversion to repeating himself extended to within the shows: a hallmark of the Rodgers & Hammerstein style was the artful use of reprises to hammer home the big songs and make sure the audience left humming the tunes. Steve never liked the idea of reprises.)

He was careful in his selection of collaborators and worked with the same people again and again, though he never settled into anything like a permanent partnership, except perhaps briefly with James Lapine. He preferred to change off from show to show: Hugh Wheeler wrote the books for *A Little Night Music* and *Sweeney Todd*, as well as the *Candide* revival. James Goldman did both *Follies* and the television musical *Evening Primrose*. For *Pacific Overtures*, *Assassins*, and *Road Show*, Steve worked with John Weidman, who was very gifted and super-smart, and came up with a different, tougher kind of show.

Steve's collaboration with James Lapine on *Sunday in the Park with George* sent him off in a new direction, as I discussed in Chapter 27. From that time forward, Steve's shows became looser in structure, with songs that were kind of strung together without the classic, accessible Broadway beginnings and payoffs. This led to a mixed record for him: it was an approach that audiences loved in *Sunday* and *Into the Woods* but responded to less well in the difficult shows *Assassins* and *Passion*.

There are many ways to approach a recording, no one necessarily better than any other, but I think each of us who has reveled in this trade has his own feelings about it, and fortunately this was one area in which Steve and I agreed magnificently.

He looked at making a recording of one of his shows the same way he looked at making a movie of one: instead of wanting to be as faithful as possible to what had been done onstage, he wanted the recording to have the same kind of artistic cohesion it would have had if he'd originally set out to make a recording, not a play. He was willing, sometimes even eager. to change things up, to rework songs or scenes to function better in their new medium. He wanted that recording to be a self-contained work of art.

Once we began working together, we quickly found common ground. As the years went by, we became more and more comfortable with the idea of re-envisioning his shows for recordings. There was a certain comfort level between us, a mutual sense of purpose.

Many years later, when I was making the recording of the 2012 revival of *Annie*, which Jim Lapine had directed, he joked with me about how much of the dialogue I was including on the recording, which was more than he would have preferred. He said, "You know, you and Steve, you like to have all that dialogue." What could I say? He was right.

Steve did keep writing into his old age, but I think he felt his audience was not the people who were going to the theater today. This is the age of movie adaptations and jukebox musicals, and Steve had always written for a more enlightened audience who didn't come in looking for more of the same—for people who were willing to work to appreciate something unfamiliar, something new and different.

Ironically, this is also the age of the big revival, and Steve's legacy has benefited from that. The pandemic aside, it seems like there isn't a year that goes by without two or three major Sondheim revivals in New York. Some of them are fairly conventional, others are gender-flipped or stripped-down or accompanied by the actors as their own orchestra, but they're still drawing audiences—in the case of *Follies* and *Merrily We Roll Along*, bigger audiences than they did in their original runs.

The Man Behind the Music

Not all the questions I'm asked about Sondheim concern his work. Often people want to know, "What was Sondheim like?" What kind of man, in short, could be responsible for such amazing works of musical theater?

I can't entirely answer that question because I was never one of Steve's intimates, the people—a handful at most—who may really have understood him if anybody did. I looked at Steve more from the outside.

Nonetheless, I did have access to the man and his work for a long time and saw him in several circumstances that nobody else did. Not everything I have to say about him is complimentary, but it's based on uncounted hours spent with Steve, sometimes alone but mostly with other people, so while my opinions are nothing but opinions, they are at least informed opinions.

The Linda Lavin episode was neither the first nor the last time I disappointed Steve, or he disappointed me.

In retrospect, I think the beginning of the end came not during *Follies in Concert* but back in 1981, when Steve, Hal, and George Furth were making some last-minute changes to *Merrily We Roll Along*, changes that I thought were hurting more than helping. I spoke my mind too freely, and while Hal didn't seem to mind, Steve obviously resented it. That was characteristic: Hal could smile and look you in the eye, while Steve would respond with a wry, one-sided twist of his mouth and avoid eye contact.

When I left RCA, a year after *Follies in Concert*, and moved to MCA, I wasn't surprised that Steve stuck with RCA. Jay Saks was still at RCA, and Steve had always gotten along well with Jay. It was Jay's time.

I was more upset—not on my behalf, but rather on Jay's and RCA's—in 1994, when I learned that after Jay had produced brilliant recordings of *Into the Woods* and *Assassins*, Steve was making a deal for Angel Records to record *Passion*.

I made the mistake of mentioning my feelings to writer Herb Scher, who was interviewing me for a profile in the magazine *Show Music*. In a lengthy story covering more than seven pages, Steve's name came up several times, and I made clear how much I loved his work and had enjoyed our projects together. On the last page, however, I spoke more freely than I should have. In discussing several incidents in which I'd had to stick to my guns on artistic matters—in going ahead with *Merrily We Roll Along* despite its punishing reviews, in making *Carousel* even after the Rodgers & Hammerstein Organization expressed its displeasure, and in refusing to let David Merrick sabotage the recording of *42nd Street*—I veered off topic and said two sentences that would come back to haunt me.

"I really went to bat for Sondheim," I said, "and in the end no good deed goes unpunished. He's even now left RCA because he got more money from EMI Angel for *Passion*, which upsets me because Jay Saks was such a loyal and devoted producer, just as I was."

The next issue of *Show Music* featured a long letter to the editor from Sondheim in which he not only challenged my account of the *Passion* deal (on the nonsensical grounds that the extra money went not to him, but to "promoting the show," as if promoting the show weren't likely to put money in his pocket) but also broadened his response to my two sentences into a wide-ranging, ad-hominem attack that depicted our entire professional relationship as a constant stream of abuse and humiliation suffered by him at my hands.

"If I were to reply to all of Tom's self-justifications, errors, distortions, and misstatements about the history of the records we did together, this letter would occupy the entire issue," Steve wrote. "The plain and simple fact is that I always dreaded the recording sessions with Tom—the combination of bluster and egomania made them tense and unpleasant experiences. . . . Tom Shepard has never gone to bat for anyone but Tom Shepard, and if he's ever done a good deed for anyone else, it's news to me. He is high-handed and self-important to a degree rarely encountered in the theatre or the recording industry, which is why there are so many people who, like me, don't want to work with him again."

I was stunned, almost literally, by the sheer disproportionality of Steve's venom, and I wasn't alone: the next few weeks brought a series of telephone calls and letters from people who had worked with me through the years, expressing their astonishment at Steve's letter and offering their reassurance that he didn't speak for them.

My instinctive response was to fire back, but the editor of *Show Music* didn't want to be in the middle of a prolonged back-and-forth, and in retrospect I think he was probably right. For Steve and me to repeatedly tear each other down in public wouldn't have done either of us any good.

All the same, I couldn't help feeling Steve's letter to the editor bordered on being unhinged. His account of his terrible experiences with me flew in the face of the actual historical record of our work together. After our first collaboration, on *Company*, he and Hal had actively urged Goddard to involve me in the sessions for *A Little Night Music*, even though Goddard was producing the show himself. Steve had agreed to come to RCA, knowing he'd be working with me, and had chosen to do so repeatedly for the next decade. If it was such an ordeal to work with me, he could have stopped at any moment. Yet for fifteen years he never did.

It was some time before I fully processed these experiences—my premature offer to Linda Lavin for *Follies in Concert*, my criticisms of *Merrily*, and the comments I made in *Show Music*—and realized that essentially they were three instances of the same phenomenon: I overstepped the boundaries of my relationship with Steve, impulsively speaking the truth as I saw it, and he reacted with an anger that clearly never really dissipated.

(I also think my quarrel with the Rodgers & Hammerstein Organization offended him. Steve and Mary Rodgers had been friends for most of their lives, as had Steve and James Hammerstein, and Oscar Hammerstein had been a surrogate father to him. Given these ties, it was probably to be expected that he'd respond to the *Carousel* episode, in which he himself wasn't involved, by siding with them.)

There may also have been a clearing-the-decks aspect to it. During the same couple of years he was cutting ties with me, Steve also broke off with Hal Prince and started working exclusively with James Lapine. He and Hal remained friends and saw each other quite a bit, but it was more than twenty-five years before they worked together again. In that same span he also changed publishers, moving from Tommy Valando, who had been his publisher for decades, to Frank Military at Warner Chappell, and parted ways with Patricia Sinnott, who had been his secretary for many years. So he dispensed with all of us, maybe just to prove he didn't really need us. And he nevertheless survived and prevailed, so I guess he didn't.

Many great artists have a self-esteem that borders on megalomania. They have to, if they're going to have the dogged persistence and determination it takes to overcome all the obstacles that usually face those who aspire to greatness.

If Steve had that sort of mindset—and I believe that he did—it's understandable. I'm sure many people in the theater community envied and resented this rich kid who was lucky enough to have Oscar Hammerstein in his corner, and who achieved such a stunning breakthrough with his very first professional show, *West Side Story*.

Even with that initial success, however, Steve still had to fight for his place in the theater. Initially it was the battle to win acceptance as a composer, not simply a lyricist. I've already told the story of his reluctance to work as lyricist on *Gypsy*, for which he'd have written both music and lyrics had Ethel Merman not objected. *Gypsy* was a triumph, of course, but Steve didn't want any more such triumphs. He wanted to write scores on his own.

It's to his credit he never stopped pushing for what he really wanted. He could have accepted the way other people saw him and had the career of a Sheldon Harnick, or an Oscar Hammerstein for that matter. But Steve had a relentless confidence in himself, and he didn't settle for what came easily. He fought for what he wanted, and he ended up remaking Broadway in his own image: many of today's conventions of even mainstream Broadway are lifted from Sondheim shows.

When he finally got his chance as a composer and scored a resounding hit with *A Funny Thing Happened on the Way to the Forum*, Steve seemed to be on top of the world—but quickly slipped into eight years of frustration and failure, with an ambitious flop, a disappointing collaboration with Richard Rodgers, and two projects that didn't even make it to Broadway. By the time he finally scored another success with *Company*, the glory days of *West Side Story*, *Gypsy*, and *Forum* must have seemed a long way in the past.

It wasn't until the 1990s, as his career was winding down, that Steve became widely appreciated. The next generation of musical-theater songwriters were overwhelmingly Sondheim fans, and he was warm and generous in his support of their work. Shows of his that had once seemed avant-garde and incomprehensible were revived and found new audiences that saw them as bold and original. I saw more pictures of Steve smiling in his last twenty years than I'd seen in the fifty previous years combined.

If he mellowed, though, it wasn't toward me. I'd burned my bridges, and while we still had occasional interactions related to recordings we'd made together previously, they were never more than formal. In the late 2010s, I wrote him a letter in which I suggested we both let bygones be bygones, that we were two old men who no longer had anything left to fight about. He responded with a brief note saying he appreciated my gesture, but that at his age he wasn't looking for new friends. It was the last time we ever communicated.

Steve may not have thought of Irene and me as friends by 1994, but in the 1970s and 1980s he invited us over to his home many times. It was an easy trip because he lived on 49th Street and we lived on 54th Street, well within walking distance.

We met interesting people at Steve's house, mostly show-business folks but not always. I remember talking with Michael Stewart there, who had written the book for *George M!* and initially disliked my recording, and another time with playwright Peter Shaffer.

It was always fascinating to be at Steve's house because it was full of games and puzzles. Some of them were old-fashioned games, antiques that were probably worth a lot of money, and others were newer ones—board games, mechanical games, and puzzles of all kinds. Steve was intrigued by that sort of thing, and his house was a treasury of games. And drugs—I remember a big bowl of what, in somebody else's house, would have been M&Ms or peppermints, except at Steve's house it was pot.

So we had once socialized, and Steve was always very gracious to Irene and to Elizabeth, our daughter. He was also a great gift-giver, and for some years I got wonderful Christmas presents from him, very thoughtful and sometimes very expensive. The one I remember most was a copy of *Essays of Clive James*, the great Australian critic and journalist; Steve had read them, admired James's work, and wanted me to read them.

But the year after *Merrily We Roll Along*, I think it was, the presents suddenly got very modest—there was nothing personal in them, they were obviously the same kind of routine gifts he was buying for members of his casts or whatever. Looking back, it was a sign things were no longer going well between us.

But when I think of Steve now, more often than not, it's mostly the good memories that come back to me. In 1975, after we'd made the recording of the London production of *A Little Night Music*, Steve and I flew back to New York together. We rode out to the airport in a taxi, and Steve was agitated and was smoking a joint. That wasn't unusual because he didn't like to fly. I don't know what the driver did after he let us out at Heathrow, because that car just reeked of marijuana.

It was an interesting flight back. I'm not a puzzle fanatic like Steve, but I do enjoy crosswords. At that time, though, I wasn't familiar with the kind of complicated, cryptic crosswords the English are so famous for. Steve loved them, though, and on the flight back he spent a lot of time going over the latest *London Times* crossword and explaining to me how he derived the answers from the clues.

He was so smart. I read an article recently where he talked about meeting Humphrey Bogart back in the 1950s. He and Bogart were able to play chess without a board, envisioning the moves in their heads. A mutual friend told me once that Steve did the *New York Times* double-crostics in his head, without needing to fill them in. I almost don't doubt it!

It took me years, after our blow-up in 1994, to get back to seeing my relationship with Steve in anything like an objective light. The *Show Music* letter was such a surprise, and it hurt so much, it colored everything else about me and him.

As the years have gone by, and maybe especially since his death, I've come to see things in a more balanced way. Yes, Steve could be casually hurtful, and he sometimes lacked any sense of proportion, but for most of the fifteen years we worked together he was a friend, a gifted colleague, and a fascinating man whose talent was breathtaking. Have I missed him since he died? Yes, but I'd been missing him for thirty-five years before that.

When I think of him now, I think of sharing a trans-Atlantic flight, talking about crossword puzzles for hours as the ocean went by below us. I remember sitting at Hal Prince's house and watching him and Hal act out a new show that clearly enraptured them, a strange new piece called *Sweeney Todd*. I think of the day, a year or two later, when I brought Steve the *Sweeney Todd* masters, after he'd had his heart attack, and the look of unabashed happiness on his face. I think of sitting with him on one show after another, taking apart the pieces of a great show and putting them back together in the shape of a great recording.

I don't pretend to understand exactly what made Steve Sondheim tick, but I shared some of our best years with him, and together we made some records that will outlive us both.

30

Interlude: *Song and Dance*

Song and Dance (1985)

Song and Dance is exactly that—*song and dance*: the first act is all songs, the second act is all dance. It featured a uniquely beautiful Lloyd Webber score.

The two halves of the show had different origins, and it was producer Cameron Mackintosh who came up with the idea of weaving them together. He also came up with the title and billed the show as "a concert for the theater."

The dance portion was based closely on *Variations*, an album-length instrumental piece for rock band and cello, which Andrew had written in 1977 for his brother, cellist Julian Lloyd Webber. The piece consists entirely of variations on Paganini's 24th caprice. It was first recorded in 1978 as a rock album, and it was a hit in Britain.

The song portion was originally a one-act musical called *Tell Me on a Sunday*, a romantic story about a young, unnamed Englishwoman who starts out in New York, goes to Hollywood with a man, and ends up back in New York, sadder, wiser, and happier on her own. It was written by Andrew and lyricist Don Black for Marti Webb, a protégée of Black's who had become a favorite of Andrew's when she understudied and then replaced Elaine Paige in *Evita* (1978). She performed it as a song cycle in 1979 and then originated the role in the London production of *Song and Dance* in 1982.

When the show opened on Broadway on September 18, 1985 (less than two weeks after *Follies in Concert*), the song portion had been adapted by Richard Maltby for American audiences and now starred my old friend Bernadette Peters as the woman, now called Emma. (She went on to win the Tony Award as Best Actress in a Musical.) Peter Martins choreographed the second act, which tells the story of a young man whom Emma meets in New York. It was danced by Christopher d'Amboise.

I freely confess that I came to the project with less than my usual unbridled enthusiasm. I was still basking in the afterglow of *Follies in Concert*, and I was still terribly busy with work on that recording when I had to take time out to record *Song and Dance*. The decision to make the recording should have been up to me, but that wasn't what happened. And I'll admit, it still stung that I'd been all but forced to agree to do my work on both recordings for less money and less royalty for some reason that I still don't understand.

On the plus side, I really liked the material as well as another chance to work with Bernadette. (And it looked like an easy enough recording to make—how hard could it be to record what was essentially a one-woman show followed by an orchestral suite?)

As it turned out, however, *Song and Dance* was a cursed recording. One thing after another went wrong, and it remains a session I don't look back on with pleasure.

To start out with, for the *Dance* portion, a great many of the orchestra players (and even conductor John Mauceri) wanted to record with headphones. We hadn't anticipated this, and it was difficult to suddenly get ahold of enough headsets to go around, and more trouble getting them adjusted properly.

The cellist, Clay Ruede, had particular trouble with it, and the result was it took us at least four hours to record the cello piece alone, by which time I had already decided it wasn't worth the effort.

So when it was all over and I was talking to Bob Summer, I said, "Look, I don't think we should spend all this money and time on editing and mixing the dance part. Why don't we just call it 'Song and Dance,' but subtitle it 'The Songs'?" He agreed, and even on the *Song* LP I had to make certain technical compromises, because one side of the disk ended up being 35 minutes long, which is stretching an LP to its maximum.

Bernadette wasn't in her best voice, but she did a beautiful job. There were nineteen songs on the album, counting three reprises and one song ("Married Man") from the London production that wasn't sung on Broadway, and she had to do every single one. It was a very long day for Bernadette.

It's a wonderful score, one of the best things Andrew has ever done. Andrew is a terrific theater composer. He idolizes Richard Rodgers, and he writes a big, sweeping, romantic music similar to the kind that Rodgers wrote.

So that was *Song and Dance*, a fine score that was recorded under difficult circumstances and an album that probably never got the attention it deserved. I was all the sorrier about that because it turned out to be the last show I recorded for RCA.

PART IV
MCA (1986–1989)

31

Parting Ways with RCA

FOLLIES IN CONCERT WAS A HIGH POINT of my tenure at RCA, which was rapidly drawing to an end. The waves of applause, the salutes from my fellow RCA executives (José Menéndez notably excepted, of course), and the plaudits from Bob Summer and Thornton Bradshaw didn't fool me. I had scored a resounding triumph, snatching victory from the proverbial jaws of defeat, but I knew better than to think all my RCA problems were in the past. Things would only get harder from here on.

José was assuming more and more authority at RCA, and he wasn't the kind to turn the page on a grudge just because his first attempt to shoot me down had failed. As long as both of us were with RCA, he'd always be lurking in the background, waiting for his chance to pay me back for his embarrassment over *Follies in Concert*. Even Bob Summer, while clearly in my corner, wouldn't be able to protect me if the going were to get tough again—as it certainly would.

After twelve good years at RCA, I knew it was time to leave. And as when I'd left Columbia for RCA, I was again lucky enough to have someplace else I wanted to go.

RCA's longtime head of legal affairs, Myron Roth, had recently been recruited by Irving Azoff to run MCA Records. Like Ken Glancy when he moved from Columbia to RCA, when Myron turned his attention to the classical and Broadway side of MCA, he thought of me.

When I had moved from Columbia to RCA, I had moved from one major player in the classical and Broadway fields to another. Columbia's Masterworks and RCA's Red Seal were longtime rivals, each with a formidable stable of exclusively contracted artists and a long history of classical excellence.

This was not the case with MCA. Myron wanted to increase MCA's presence on the classical scene, but he had no illusions of competing with Masterworks or Red Seal. One of the first things he told me was, "I don't want to spend a lot of money on classical."

However, MCA had acquired several companies with substantial classical catalogs, including Westminster Records, Decca Classical, and the English company Pickwick Records. He wanted me to build a new label, MCA Classics, which would draw on these libraries of classical recordings with a judicious smattering of newly recorded material. And as Ken Glancy had done for me at RCA, he agreed to follow Goddard Lieberson's Columbia model and place Broadway under the aegis of MCA Classics.

So Myron wasn't bringing me in to take the reins of a storied record label. He wanted me to build MCA Classics pretty much from scratch, using a strong back catalog, my knowledge of the marketplace, and a scrambling, seat-of-the-pants style to carve a place for us in the realms of classical and Broadway.

I'd report only to him, and he had no wish to tell me how to do my job. After a quarter-century walking between the raindrops, this was music to my ears.

Myron didn't want to spend a lot of money on signing famous musicians, but he wasn't averse to spending money in general. I had a very good contract at MCA—actually, two contracts: one as executive vice president for classical and Broadway, and the other as a producer of recordings. Besides paying me a sizable amount of money, the company also provided me with a beautiful automobile and the other thing I asked for, a grand piano in my office. I also brought along Sandy Smyth, my assistant through my last years at RCA and an invaluable collaborator in my new undertaking.

I was running a smaller operation at MCA, with a bare-bones staff. The person I most missed was, of course, Jay Saks. He was very well off where he was, taking over my position at Red Seal, where he would remain for the next decade. I knew he'd flourish in his new role, and he did.

With the smaller budgets now at my disposal, it wasn't realistic to expect to compete with Columbia or RCA for the biggest shows, for the work of Jerry Herman, Kander & Ebb, or Stephen Sondheim. I did have the resources to pursue some of the smaller, more interesting shows, but during my years at MCA, many of my most appealing projects would be ones I had initiated myself.

The biggest Broadway recording of my tenure at MCA was already in the works before I arrived: Andrew Lloyd Webber's *Starlight Express*. With my recording of Andrew's *Song and Dance* still fresh in my mind, and with my increasing esteem for his music, I would have loved to record *Starlight Express*, but the album had already been committed to MCA's pop department, and there was nothing I could do about it. Ultimately, they chose not to release a Broadway-cast album at all but rather a concept album called *Music and Songs from "Starlight Express"*, released to coincide with the show's Broadway opening but featuring different singers and omitting a great deal of the music.

This was a great opportunity missed, as far as I was concerned, but it did mean MCA had a relationship with Andrew, which I would cultivate as I settled in at my new company. And in the meantime, I had plenty to keep me busy.

Me and My Girl (1986)

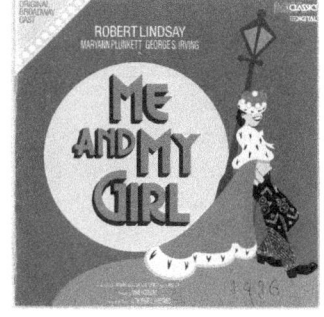

Me and My Girl was a classic example of Broadway's love of period pieces. Featuring a sparkling score by Noel Gay and a libretto by Douglas Furber and L. Arthur Rose, it had been a sensation in London in 1937, running for 1,646 performances and later being made into a movie and revived three times during the 1940s. The simple, humorous story of a cockney bloke named Bill Snibson, not necessarily always on the straight and narrow, who unexpectedly inherits the title and fortune of the Earl of Hareford was funny and relatable, charming audiences during the Depression, the Blitz, and the postwar era alike.

A 1984 London revival, featuring a revised script by Stephen Fry and director Michael Ockrent, proved to be even more popular, running more than twice as long and launching the careers of writer Stephen Fry, Robert Lindsay (Bill), and Emma Thompson (Sally, Bill's cockney girlfriend). The Broadway production, starring Lindsay and Maryann Plunkett, opened in 1986 and ran for more than three years, winning Tony Awards for Lindsay and Plunkett, as well as for choreographer Cillian Gregory.

I first heard about the show from Barry Reiss, a Broadway fan who was business-affairs director of MCA Records. He knew how successful it had been in London, and we both thought it was worth pursuing aggressively well before it opened on Broadway. When we landed it, I was very pleased.

It was a challenging show to record, though, because it had always been a star vehicle for a dancing comedian, originally Lupino Lane, and now Robert Lindsay.

The Furber/Rose/Gay score was a wonderful one, featuring two irresistible hits, "Leaning on a Lamppost" and "The Lambeth Walk," plus a good many other charming songs. It particularly appealed to me for the obvious influence of Gilbert & Sullivan on such songs as "The Family Solicitor" and "An English Gentleman." A scene in Act II is lifted lock, stock, and barrel from Gilbert & Sullivan's *Ruddigore*, as the family portraits of Bill's illustrious ancestors come to life and admonish him for letting down the family. For the recording, even without Lindsay's pratfalls, sleight-of-hand, and hilarious dancing, there was a lot to work with, and we got an excellent recording out of it.

Lindsay was awfully gifted, and I had only one note to give him. He used an intentionally harsh voice, along with the cockney accent, to communicate that Bill was a fish out of water in the earl's palatial estate, and part of that harshness was an occasional noise, an unpleasant nasal, edgy, whiny sound mixed in with that cockney. It was fine on the stage, when it was part of a big, physical performance, but I knew on a recording it would get annoying.

I told him what the problem was, and he said, "Yeah, I know what you mean. I'll try and take care of it." He did try, and he did pretty well. It wasn't gone completely, but it was considerably reduced.

That said, Lindsay was someone I couldn't get close to. He was very professional, but he shielded himself, in a way, and came across as somehow guarded. I never really felt there was any underlying reciprocal good will.

And there was one point on which we simply couldn't agree. There was a line of dialogue, one joke I wanted to add to the recording, and he absolutely refused to do it. I explained to him that we did this all the time, that it was standard procedure, but he was adamant.

"There are people who are going to see the show after they've bought the album," he said, "and they're not going to laugh."

What could I do? If he wasn't going to do it, wasting time arguing about it wouldn't get us anywhere. So it's not on the album.

I've run into this from time to time with actors worried about giving away jokes. It's an understandable worry, but it's short-sighted. Many people who listen to the recording will never see the show—this is the only version of your performance they'll ever experience, so why wouldn't you want it to be as good as it can be? The ones who do see the show will usually buy the album afterward, not before, and will appreciate being reminded of that funny line when they hear it on the record.

Lindsay was a magnetic performer onstage; you couldn't take your eyes off him. But I think, as a singer, he's better on the recording than he was onstage because he took the singing more seriously and focused on it. Onstage he had so many other things to think about. Just the ability to breathe naturally, instead of bouncing all over the stage and then singing, made a big difference.

The cast was good from top to bottom. Maryann Plunkett was very sweet. There was something unusual about her eyes. They were sky-blue and very wide, and I think she blinked more slowly than most people.

My good friend Tim Jerome played the lawyer, Herbert Parchester, and even had a big solo on "The Family Solicitor," a tongue-twisting patter song, which he rattled off very well. It's fun when you're doing something with a friend. We also had Jane Connell, a tiny little woman less than five feet tall who was very, very funny. She'd played Agnes Gooch in the stage and film versions of *Mame*, and I'd known her since she played one of the three crazy ladies in *Dear World*, back in 1969. This time she played the Duchess and got a Tony nomination as Best Featured Actress.

Another face from my past was George S. Irving, a wonderful actor with whom I'd worked on *Irene*. He played Sir John, and he and Jane Connell had a charming duet, "If Only You Had Cared for Me," late in the second act. George was a lovely person, and his wife, Maria Karnilova, was a Broadway performer and ballet teacher who, many years earlier, had been Irene's first dance teacher. It's a small world.

The recording session went smoothly, and it wasn't until afterward that the show started to look cursed. We made our recording in October, and a week or so later the conductor, Stanley Lebowsky, died of a heart attack. He was only fifty-nine. I hadn't worked with him before, but he was a talented musician who had conducted many Broadway shows.

Then in November Richard Armitage, who was the son of Noel Gay and had produced the revival of *Me and My Girl*, died of a heart attack in London. He was fifty-eight. There was a *New York Times* reporter at the session, and in Stanley's obituary she quoted him as telling the performers, "Ladies and gentlemen, I want you to dig into it. I want you to have fun with it." He instructed them, "We need to sound a little more amorous, It sounds a little uptight. Watch the smiles—it tends to change the whole timbre."

There was a strange postscript to my recording of *Me and My Girl*. It was released in October 1986, which—because of the Recording Academy's unusual calendar, which begins each eligibility year on October 1 of the preceding year—made it a 1987 release. It was duly nominated for a Grammy as Best Musical Cast Show Album, and on March 2, 1988, Irene and I were at Radio City Music Hall for the ceremony, where we heard presenter Liza Minnelli announce that the nominees included "*Me and My Girl*, produced by Thomas Two Shepard."

She was reading from a Teleprompter, I assume, and the Z in my name must have looked like a 2. Even so, I'd expect better from the brilliant performer whose famous television special was called *Liza with a Z*.

We lost to *Les Misérables*, and for some years afterward a few of my friends kept calling me "Two."

Carousel (1987)

Carousel, which premiered in 1945, was the show that made Rodgers & Hammerstein an institution. *Oklahoma!* was still running merrily when *Carousel* opened two years later, but *Carousel* made clear that Rodgers & Hammerstein were going to revolutionize Broadway. When you talk about Broadway history, it divides into before R & H and after R & H.

A lifelong devotee of Rodgers & Hammerstein, I'd relished my previous work on *Oklahoma!* and *The King and I*, and I hoped to someday record *Carousel*.

I began to plan a new studio-cast recording, but when I informed the Rodgers & Hammerstein office of my plans, they tried to stop me. They'd had a big success with a studio-cast version of *South Pacific* on Sony Classical (a recording that suffered from the casting of Kiri Te Kanawa and José Carreras, great artists but ill-suited for their parts, in the lead roles), and apparently, they were thinking of a *Carousel* along the same lines.

I talked to Ted Chapin and Mary Rodgers, both friends of mine, and they laid it on the line: "We don't want you to do it. We're doing a *Carousel*, very likely with Mandy Patinkin, and we were so successful with *South Pacific*."

I didn't see any problem with that. "Well, go ahead," I said. "You make yours; I'll make mine."

But to my surprise, they said, "No." They wanted theirs to be the only *Carousel* out there, but they didn't have the legal authority to prevent me from going forward. If I'd wanted to do a new *South Pacific* or *The Sound of Music*, I'd need to have the consent of the R & H office, but *Carousel* was different: the recording rights to this show didn't rest with the Rodgers & Hammerstein Organization.

Richard Rodgers and Oscar Hammerstein weren't simply the most successful creative team in Broadway history. They were also brilliant businessmen who controlled their own work better than anyone else, before or since. They produced most of their own shows, and some other creators' work as well, under the aegis of what is now the Rodgers & Hammerstein Organization, and they published their music through their own company, Williamson Music (so called because Hammerstein and Rodgers were both the sons of men named William).

All of this added up to enormous profits, and still does. According to a 2021 *Forbes* article, their song catalog alone is worth $350 million, third in the world behind the Beatles and Michael Jackson. Add theatrical-presentation rights and movie and television rights, and the Rodgers & Hammerstein legacy is unmatched in the history of Broadway.

For reasons that have never been clear to me, however, the recording rights to *Carousel* were, as late as 1987, outside of the control of Williamson Music.

Whatever the reason, the recording rights to *Carousel* rested with T. B. Harms. Harms had already granted me permission. I went ahead with my plans. I signed Paul Gemignani to conduct. We would record the show in London with the Royal Philharmonic.

From the start I'd wanted to cast Barbara Cook as Julie. She'd starred in two *Carousel* revivals at City Center, playing Carrie in 1954 and Julie in 1957, but had never gotten a chance to record the show. I built the rest of the cast around her.

For the leading man, the brutish carnival barker, Billy Bigelow, I asked Metropolitan Opera star Samuel Ramey.

I wanted Sarah Brightman for the key role of Carrie Pipperedge, Julie's foil and best friend. She was based in London, where we'd be recording. And she could sell records: after breaking through as Jemima in *Cats*, she had scored a No. 3 pop hit with the "Pie Jesu" from Andrew's *Requiem Mass*.

Actually, Barbara would have preferred to sing both parts on the recording. Her manager, Jerry Kravetz, was almost embarrassed when he told me this. When I said, "Not a chance," he laughed.

Barbara never raised the issue again. During the recording session in England, when Sarah was a little unsure of a couple of spots in "(When I Marry) Mister Snow," I said to Barbara, "Maybe you could coach her a little on this." Which Barbara did, and which Sarah took very nicely.

During the recording sessions in London, Barbara stayed at the Savoy, and she loved the shower heads there. She loved them so much, she went to the Savoy management and asked if she could buy some of them. They sold her maybe half a dozen, and when we got back to New York, she gave them to me, to Paul, to Sam.

I didn't know who I was going to use for Mr. Snow, but several of my London colleagues recommended David Rendall. I didn't know who he was, but I trusted the people who recommended him, and he did a terrific job. Both he and Sarah managed very credible American accents.

We brought Maureen Forrester down from Canada to play Nettie. She was an overdub, recording separately from everybody else, and she was wonderful, most especially when she sang "You'll Never Walk Alone."

Through all of this, though, the Rodgers & Hammerstein office kept throwing stumbling blocks in our path. As usual, I wanted to incorporate some bits of dialogue into the show, especially from the bench scene between Billy and Julie, a lengthy exchange with beautiful musical underscoring that wraps around the classic song "If I Loved You." It's more than twelve minutes long, and I wanted to record the whole thing.

Now, that took us into a strange, sticky corner of the recording world. We speak of "recording rights to a show," but actually there are two kinds of rights—grand rights and small or simple rights. Grand rights involve the right to perform a show, complete with sets, costumes, and lights, while small rights are limited to use of the songs in concerts or recordings. There's a quote from Oscar Hammerstein that sums it up pretty well: "Anyone can record 'Oh, What a Beautiful Mornin'. That's simple rights. But if he's wearing a cowboy hat and he's sitting on a horse, that's grand rights."

The tricky part is how to define that distinction from a legal point of view. The gray area of "how much dialogue can you add without turning it into a performance?" had over the years been largely a matter of working things out in practice, rather than arguing in court. By this time I'd been recording shows for many years, and when I added a few spoken lines before, during, or after a song, I'd never gotten into any trouble. Now, I learned that the only lines I was officially entitled to were the ones that appeared in the published piano/vocal score.

This shouldn't have been an issue at all, but Mary and Ted were angry with me, and they asked us for a crazy amount of money. Our lawyers talked to their lawyers and their lawyers talked to our lawyers, and finally we were able to do it basically the way I wanted to, but it ran into a lot of extra money.

The Rodgers & Hammerstein office also refused to rent us the original orchestrations, but there was nothing to prevent us from reorchestrating the songs, so that's what we did. I hired a team of three British orchestrators, and they did a wonderful job.

And even then, the Rodgers & Hammerstein office forced me to put a big headline across the top of the record cover saying, "Newly Orchestrated," in type as big as the words "Rodgers & Hammerstein's." Somehow, they thought that that would hurt its sales. If anything, as far as I was concerned, "newly orchestrated" was a plus, not a minus.

Where they did hurt me was with the ballet in *Carousel*. It's a beautiful piece, it runs about eight minutes, and I recorded it. But it had never been recorded before, and for that reason the R & H office had the right to withhold consent.

We had a beautiful party for the launch of the album, held at Gimbels, where there was an actual carousel. Sarah couldn't make it because she was busy somewhere else, but she sent a personal representative: her husband.

Andrew had come to one of the recording sessions in London, and to the people there—the engineers, the crew, and I think even the orchestra—he was a bigger star than Barbara or Sam. He didn't interfere with the session, just sat and watched and seemed to be enjoying himself. He was a great Richard Rodgers fan and told me later he was particularly pleased I had included the reprise of "(When I Marry) Mister Snow."

That party was a memorable night. Nobody from the Rodgers & Hammerstein office came, though. By then, Sony Classical had canceled its plans to record *Carousel*, but there was still a lot of bad feeling.

About six months later Joe Dash, the head of Columbia Records, invited me to lunch and also invited Ted Chapin—he'd decided it was time we all should make peace. Which was very, very sweet of him. We sat downstairs at a small table in Trump Tower, and Ted and I shook hands.

Many years later I attended an event at the Frederick Loewe Auditorium at New York University, something having to do with Broadway, but not with Rodgers & Hammerstein at all. In the audience I noticed the attorney who had represented the Rodgers & Hammerstein Organization in the *Carousel* affair.

He and I had never had any meaningful interaction because the business-affairs department at MCA handled all the negotiations. But I had met him. So, when the NYU event was over, I walked out with him and his wife. We said hello, and I said, "I haven't seen you since the *Carousel* days." And his wife said, "Oh, what a beautiful recording!"

That made my day. It really did.

Romance/Romance (1988)

Sometimes a show that seems too small for Broadway makes it there anyway, simply because it's so good. That had been the case with *Side by Side by Sondheim*, and it happened again with *Romance/Romance*, an even-less-likely long shot because its creative team, author/lyricist/director Barry Harman and composer Keith Hermann, lacked Stephen Sondheim's fan base on Broadway.

Romance/Romance was originally presented at the tiny Actor's Outlet Theatre, which was not even Off-Broadway but Off-Off-Broadway. (The distinction is not about location, but about seating capacity, with a Broadway house typically seating 500 people or more, an Off-Broadway house 100 to 499 people, and an Off-Off-Broadway house 99 or fewer.) It had a cast of four and a very modest orchestra, but its book was clever and the music was wonderful. It drew glowing reviews. Six months later it opened at the Helen Hayes Theatre and enjoyed a respectable (for its size and cost) Broadway run of 297 performances. It was nominated for five Tony Awards, including Best Musical, Best Book, and Best Score.

Aside from one overlapping song, the show is two separate one-acts. The first is adapted from "The Little Comedy," an 1893 short story by Arthur Schnitzler, and is set in nineteenth-century Vienna. It's a classic romantic-comedy plot in which Alfred, a millionaire playboy bored with his affluent-but-empty life, disguises himself as a struggling young poet and falls in love with a working-class girl named Josefine, who turns out to be a glamorous courtesan bored with her affluent-but-empty life. Having disguised themselves in a quest for "authenticity," the question is whether they can find something real amid their assumed poverty.

The second act is adapted from Jules Renard's 1898 play *Le Pain de Ménage*, which has been updated to the Hamptons in the 1980s. The same two actors return in different roles, joined by two new ones in a story about two couples (Sam and Barb, Lenny and Monica) sharing a summer house as their marriage vows start to fray, with Sam and Monica enjoying a flirtation that seems like it might turn into something more.

Barry Reiss, head of business affairs at MCA, was a friend of Barry Harman's, and I think it was on his advice I went to see the show, which I found totally charming. And even though the creators and the cast were new to me, I did know some people involved in the production, including music director Kathy Summer and orchestrator Michael Starobin. I immediately wanted to record the show.

Three of the original four cast members made the transfer to Broadway, led by Alison Fraser, who was terrific both as Josefine and as Monica, along with Deborah Graham (Barb) and Robert Hoshour (Lenny), who in Act I are entirely silent, harlequin figures hovering around the edges of the story. The sole newcomer, as both Albert and

Sam, was a relative newcomer named Scott Bakula, still a year away from breaking through on television as the star of *Quantum Leap* (1989–1993).

I don't have any particular memories of the session, except asking Scott to change one line reading. I said, "Scott, can you read it as though you were examining your fingernails?" That was maybe a little cryptic, but he knew exactly what I meant and gave me what I needed.

Otherwise it was just a very pleasant day spent with a handful of terrific young actors, recording a show I enjoyed as much as they did.

32

Parting Ways with MCA

LATE IN THE MORNING ON A WARM DAY in August 1988, I arrived at MCA's New York headquarters at Broadway and West 55th Street. I walked into the office and could tell immediately something was up. It was abnormally quiet, and everybody looked tense and troubled. The place felt like a memorial service.

I asked somebody, "What's going on?" And they said, "There's going to be a whole round of firings later today."

That was it. The word had gotten out, and nobody knew who was safe and who wasn't. There was little if any work done for the next several hours until, in the early afternoon, a company-wide memo came through, listing the positions or people who were being terminated.

My name was on the list.

In retrospect I should have seen it coming because the pattern was a familiar one. I'd been left very much alone at MCA, but not because MCA was a warmer, more humane place to work than RCA or Columbia Records. It was because my boss, Myron Roth, supported what I was doing, and his boss, Irving Azoff, supported what he was doing. Myron was my Ken Glancy, my Goddard Lieberson at MCA, and as long as he was the president of MCA Records and Irving was the president of MCA's Music Entertainment Group, I was on solid ground.

The trouble was, Myron wasn't there anymore. He'd been forced out a couple months before, taking the fall for a messy scandal that had rocked MCA in the spring.

In March 1988 a reputed organized-crime figure named Salvatore Pisello went on trial in Los Angeles on federal tax-evasion charges. He was charged with having concealed as much as six hundred thousand dollars in income from shady business deals involving the record industry—deals that involved people at MCA Records.

The whole affair had to do with what are known in the record business as "cutouts." The name comes from the actual cut made in the edge of the cardboard record jacket, or the box if it's a boxed set. A record becomes a cutout when it's discontinued by the company that released it and is dropped from the company's catalogue. When this happens, however, the company almost always has some of these unsold records still on hand. To clear inventory space for newer, hopefully more popular titles, these leftovers are sold to discount operators to be resold in retail stores at rock-bottom prices. (The artists typically receive no royalties for cutouts; this is one reason they can be sold so cheaply.) To make the package more salable, the companies usually add a small number of what are called "sweeteners"—non-discontinued records by popular stars.

Pisello's racket, apparently, was to buy cutouts by the truckload and then counterfeit the sweeteners. He'd then sell those counterfeit records at a huge markup, eventually racking up as much as $8 million. Because he had legitimately purchased a handful of sweeteners, any given record could be claimed to be legitimate. Anyone who got suspicious would have to track down every one of them to prove more records had been sold than the sellers had bought in the first place.

The case against Pisello alleged MCA executives had been aware of the scam and presumably had received kickbacks to turn a blind eye to it. Those allegations were never proved; they were incidental to the tax-evasion case, and the executives named were never charged with anything. It looked bad, though—and among the executives allegedly involved were Irving Azoff and Myron Roth.

I don't have any idea what went on in this affair, but I don't believe that Myron did anything wrong. He wasn't that kind of guy. But somebody had to take the hit, and it wasn't going to be Irving. Pisello was convicted on April 8, and Myron was pushed out not long afterward. (He landed on his feet—in November he was named senior vice president and general manager at CBS Records.)

I did not initially realize, however, how bad things might get for me or how quickly.

To replace Myron, Irving brought in Al Teller, former president of CBS Records. I knew Al slightly—he'd gotten his start as an assistant to Clive Davis at Columbia, back in 1968—and he was a bright guy. But he didn't look at the record business the way I did, or the way Ken Glancy or Goddard Lieberson did. He had an MBA from Harvard Business School, and he looked at the record business as a business, first and foremost.

Within weeks of getting into the company, Al decided certain areas were nothing but a drain on the company's energy, not making enough money to warrant keeping them. MCA Classics was one such area—and Al shared none of Myron's sense that a major record company ought to have a classical-and-Broadway department. To Al it was all about the profits. By his own lights Al was doing the right thing, and it paid off for him. In 1989 he took over for Irving as chairman and CEO of the Music Entertainment Group, and during his six-year reign, MCA made a lot of money. I'm sure he has no regrets.

My biggest grudge against Al isn't that he fired me and a lot of other people I knew at MCA. It's that he didn't have the balls to fire any of us face to face. I've fired a few people in my time, and it's never been something I enjoyed doing, but I did it face to face. That's only just; it's only fair. I'd have been ashamed to do it any other way.

So my name was on the list, and to make matters worse and even more humiliating, they wanted us out of the building that very day. My head was spinning—it was the first time I'd ever been fired from anything—but I flatly refused to be kicked out of the building like they'd caught me stealing. I called Irving, and I said, "Look, if I have to be let go, I have to be let go, but I've got a lot of stuff here, and it's going to take me time to sort through it." And Irving said, "It's OK, Tom. Take whatever time you need. Nobody's going to hassle you."

I told him I had an office full of audio and video equipment, and I'd like to take that with me. And Irving said, "OK, go ahead and take it." (I later thought I should have asked for the piano, but at the time it didn't occur to me.)

So Irving and I never had a harsh word for one another, even then, but we both knew he wasn't going to give me or MCA Classics a reprieve. Once he'd turned over the day-to-day running of the label to Al Teller, that was it. Irving was not going to second-guess Al's decisions.

I called Irene and told her what had happened, and she took it very matter-of-factly and practically. She said, "We're going to gather all your stuff and drive out to the house and put it away," and that's what we did. In the end, I was out of MCA within forty-eight hours of being fired.

I've been using the word "fired," but that's technically not what happened, because I had a three-year contract that still had a year to run. They let me go but still paid me for the third year, without my having to come into the office or do anything for the money.

Worse, my contract had a noncompete clause that prevented me from taking a full-time job at any other record label until the contract expired, which wouldn't be for a year.

My father, being an attorney, was upset about this. He felt the whole thing should have been contested and instead of giving me an extra year for doing nothing, they should have simply fired me, given me a decent severance package, and let me go on to the next thing. He was very aggravated I was not better protected.

I might have been, if it weren't for an unfortunate coincidence that hadn't bothered me in 1986 but came back to haunt me in 1988. My lawyer was Allen Grubman, an entertainment attorney whose client roster also included Irving Azoff, who was also a friend of his. He'd been my lawyer before I ever thought of going to MCA, and on the front end the relationship between him and Azoff made the contract negotiations easy. On the back end, though, it was a problem.

I should have gotten another lawyer to look at my situation, but at that moment it didn't cross my mind. As I said, it was the first time I'd been fired, and it hit me hard. I'd gone into the office that morning thinking about the projects I had lined up for the fall, and by the time I went home those projects had evaporated.

The hardest thing, for me, was to adjust to a nonstructured life. I hadn't had time on my hands since January 1960. I'd gone straight from Columbia to RCA and then straight from RCA to MCA. Within the first few days after being laid off, I actually had a manicure, something I would never even have thought of doing in other times. Right down the block from our apartment, there was a salon, and as I walked past it, I thought, "Why not? What else do I have to do?"

By the time I was legally able to look for full-time work, I was more than ready to start my next phase. I talked with people at all the other record companies, and several of them seemed to be on the verge of offering me full-time jobs but none ever came through.

Irene thinks it's because they were afraid of me, that with my track record they thought I'd want to come in and run the place, but I don't think that was it. I think it was that I was fifty years old, and in the record business, unless you're at the highest levels, a fifty-year-old is an old man. I'd been codirector of Masterworks when I was thirty-five and the head of Red Seal when I was thirty-seven; at that time fifty had seemed very old to me, too. There's no doubt that in 1986, it seemed old to some of the people considering me for jobs at other companies.

The thing was, I was never interested in corporate politics. I'd risen through the hierarchy at Columbia and been a vice president at RCA and then at MCA, but I'd climbed as far as I ever wanted to.

Whatever the reason, when I walked out of MCA that August, the day after being fired, I left behind my last full-time staff position at a record company.

But when you're running a department, you also must decide which recordings are going to be made, whether you'll produce them yourself or not, and you have a considerable amount of logistical material to deal with: sales estimates, production schedules, artwork, liner notes, sales reports, and an endless number of meetings. You hire people, manage people, assign people, and yes, fire people. I've seldom regretted leaving those aspects of the job behind.

On the other hand, I really like calling the shots. To some extent at Columbia, to a greater extent at RCA, and even more so at MCA, I had the ability to initiate my own projects, to have a fresh creative idea and then to marshal the resources necessary to bring it to fruition.

PART V
Free Agent (1989–Present)

33

Hired Gun

WHEN I EMERGED FROM THE LEGAL CONSTRAINTS of my MCA contract, I found there were many opportunities for me as a producer, even as a composer.

John Williams Conducts John Williams: The Star Wars Trilogy (1990)

One of the first people to reach out to me after I'd left MCA was John Williams, the film composer, and at the time, conductor of the Boston Pops.

I would do six albums with John and the Pops over the next three years, but also one other recording that didn't involve the Pops and was an altogether new experience.

John wanted to do a recording conducting his own music for the *Star Wars* movies, of which at the time there were only three, and he wanted it to be the first symphonic project created at George Lucas's Skywalker Ranch, a place that for *Star Wars* fans is a world apart, a cross between the Magic Kingdom and a high-tech Promised Land.

So in late 1990 engineer Buddy Graham and I flew to San Francisco, and from there we were driven to Marin County, California, where George Lucas had built his own private world, spending a stunning amount of money developing 25 acres of a much larger property, including installing an artificial body of water (Ewok Lake) and bringing in enormous adult trees.

The main buildings included a three-hundred-seat theater, an observatory, the ranch's own fire department, and most relevant to us, an enormous soundstage big enough for a symphony orchestra. To get from one place to another, there were bicycles everywhere, and you'd just pick up whichever bike was nearest to you and pedal off.

George was a quiet man. He was self-contained and had very little small talk.

The recording sessions went smoothly. It was credited to the "Skywalker Symphony" was a pickup orchestra of area musicians—most of them recruited from the San Francisco Symphony. There were several sessions over three or four days, and no significant problems arose. When we weren't rehearsing or recording, we explored the ranch, which had many attractions to offer, including Francis Ford Coppola's amazing collection of classic cars and a tour of Industrial Light & Magic, the special-effects house for Lucas's films and many others.

And then we went home and I went to work editing and mixing the recording.

Kismet (1991)

In the 1990s I wound up spending a lot of time at my old home, Columbia Records, which by then had become a division of Sony. I worked periodically throughout the decade remastering old cast albums (mine and those by other producers), and had an office there for a while as a part-time Broadway consultant. Additionally, they were receptive to my ideas for creating studio-cast recordings with all-star performers.

I recommended several titles, especially *Kismet* because it's a Broadway/classical crossover. Robert Wright and George Forrest wrote the lyrics and some original music, and arranged and adapted the bulk of the score, including its biggest hits, from the works of nineteenth-century Russian composer Alexander Borodin.

A little background: the show dates from 1953 and features a book by Charles Lederer and Luther Davis, adapted from a 1911 play by Edward Knoblock that was clearly inspired by the classic *Tales of the Arabian Nights*. It originally starred Alfred Drake as Hajj, a conniving poet who wins the heart of the chief wife of the Wazir of Police.

Borodin's music is ravishing, and Wright & Forrest's musical adaptation and delightful lyrics very deftly turn it from classical music into a lush and romantic Broadway score. *Kismet* ran for nearly two years, won the Tony Award as Best Musical, and was turned into a successful film in 1955.

At Sony, I was already working on a studio-cast album of *Man of La Mancha*, and the two recordings share several contributors: For both I was the producer and Paul Gemignani was the conductor, and Jerry Hadley, Julia Migenes, Mandy Patinkin, and Samuel Ramey were on both recordings.

Sam Ramey, with whom I'd worked on *Carousel*, was excellent as Hajj, filling Alfred Drake's shoes with distinction.

I hadn't decided whom I would ask to play Marsinah, the lyric soprano, the ingenue. I contacted Matthew Epstein, the highly respected vocal-concert manager at Columbia Artists Management. He suggested that the perfect person would be Ruth Ann Swenson. She was about to make her debut at the Metropolitan Opera, and this would be her recording debut.

There was a lovely song, "My Magic Lamp," which had been cut from the show before it opened. I included this song for Ruth Ann. It needed a new orchestration, and I asked Bill Brohn to do it for us.

I knew whom I wanted to play the Wazir, a comic villain. Dom DeLuise was a very big, big man with an equally sized sense of humor. He lived on the West Coast, but I managed to get his home telephone number. His son answered and said, "Dad's in the pool." Once DeLuise had come ashore and dried off, we had a brief conversation, and he said that he would be interested.

Fast forward to several months later: On the way to the recording session, I picked up Dom DeLuise at his hotel in Manhattan, driving my beautiful white Cadillac

Sedan DeVille with red leather upholstery. Dom got into the car, and it actually sank. I thought the springs would never recover. At the studio he was so heavy, he had to be brought up in the freight elevator with two men who supported him on both sides. He came in, sat down very heavily, and said, "Lunch!"

DeLuise was great fun to work with. Every time he made a mistake, he'd chastise himself by saying, "Ah, your mother's ass!"

He and I actually made two recordings that day. While he was there, I got a call from an executive at Music Masters Classics, a small label that was doing a recording of Prokofiev's *Peter and the Wolf* with DeLuise as the narrator. He asked if, since I had DeLuise in the studio, would I mind producing that for them. I've always loved *Peter and the Wolf* and was having a great time with DeLuise, so I said, "Sure."

Julia Migenes was perfect as Lalume. She was a wonderful character actress. She was particularly good on "Bored," which had been omitted from the original-cast album—a very funny song sung by a neglected wife.

Mandy Patinkin is also on this recording. He plays the Marriage Arranger, an Arab woman who sings a single song, "Zubbediya," an eccentric nonsense song in a very high, ululating falsetto. A few weeks before the recording sessions began, I ran into Mandy at the Sony studios, where he was working on another recording project. I stopped to say hello, and when I told him about the recording, he was intrigued by the prospect of playing an Arab woman.

As I mentioned, *Kismet* is as much classical music as it is show tunes, and Paul Gemignani and I wanted to have a really substantial orchestra for the recording. We got one of the best in the world: the London Symphony.

None of our soloists went with us to London. They all overdubbed their material in New York, but the chorus was in London—mostly. John McCarthy's Ambrosian Singers were a very busy chorus, and unfortunately there was a mix-up in scheduling. Somehow or other we got our signals crossed on the date and time of one of our recording sessions. The upshot was that for one London session where I expected to have a chorus, I didn't. As a result, I had to overdub some chorus material when we returned to New York.

Robert Wright and George Forrest were disappointed that they hadn't been invited to any of our recording session, but the fact is that Gemignani and I preferred to make studio albums without the songwriters being present.

Man of La Mancha (1996)

The idea of a studio-cast recording of *Man of La Mancha* starring Plácido Domingo seemed almost inevitable, in retrospect. After all, the show was based on Spain's most acclaimed novel, and Domingo is the most celebrated Spanish singer of his era.

There were obstacles, though. Most obviously, Domingo is a tenor, and the title role in the musical was written for Richard Kiley, a baritone.

The idea appealed to me, though. I'd worked with him on several classical projects during my years at RCA and Columbia, so there was already a very easy relationship between us. I'd also had a penchant, throughout my years of making studio-cast albums, for mixing and matching stars of Broadway and stars of opera.

Domingo prefers to make his recordings only after the orchestra has been recorded. I supply him with a rough mix of the orchestral tracks for rehearsal purposes, and then he comes in scrupulously prepared. This approach also suits his preference for recording late at night, into the wee hours of the morning.

Man of La Mancha never had a traditional Broadway orchestration, however. It had debuted Off-Broadway in 1965 at the ANTA Theater, playing there for two-and-a-half years before being transferred to Broadway. Like most Off-Broadway shows, it had only a small orchestra—sixteen pieces, consisting almost entirely of woodwinds and brass, with the only strings an upright bass and two flamenco guitars—and it had retained those orchestrations for Broadway as well.

A curious thing about *Man of La Mancha* is the printed score stipulates exactly how the orchestra should be arranged, with certain instruments placed on one side of the stage and the rest on the other side. The score offers no explanation for this—but I was careful to reproduce that positioning on the recording.

It was only afterward that my friend Neil Warner, the show's original orchestrator and conductor, revealed the truth to me: "The only reason it was arranged that way," he said, "was to keep the guys in the orchestra from having a poker game between songs."

I had liked Julia Migenes so much as Lalume on *Kismet* that I asked her to play Aldonza/Dulcinea on *Man of La Mancha*. Aldonza is a cynic who is dragged into Quixote's idealism, kicking and screaming the whole way . . . perfect for Julia.

For the pivotal role of Sancho Panza, I had originally cast Buddy Hackett. I was very pleased when he accepted the part. I sent him the material, and it was the last I thought about it until we got together for the recording session in New York, and to my dismay, Hackett was largely unprepared.

Sancho has two big solos, "I Like Him" and "A Little Gossip"; the title song is a duet for him and Don Quixote, and he sings as well in several ensembles. Hackett knew only "I Like Him" and the opening duet. He hadn't prepared the rest.

His suggestion was for me to teach him each phrase line by line, but I wasn't willing to do that.

Hackett himself became frustrated and then very angry. He snatched the microphone he was using, pulled it off its stand, and smashed it to the floor, destroying a piece of equipment worth several thousand dollars. I got in touch with his lawyer and said that we would not go forward with Hackett. We agreed to split the difference: we didn't charge him for the microphone, but we didn't pay him either. So, all of a sudden, I didn't have a Sancho Panza.

And then, for the second time in a row, I ran into Mandy Patinkin at the Columbia editing studios. He asked me how things were going, and I said, "I've got a problem, I just lost Buddy Hackett." And without thinking twice, he said, "I'll do it." Just like that, one problem less.

Mandy had very little time to work on the part, but he came into the session thoroughly prepared—a welcome contrast to Buddy Hackett! He had clearly thought a lot about how to play Sancho and he came up with a new spin on the character I'd never have thought of.

Having recruited Julia and Mandy from my *Kismet* cast, it was natural to tap the "repertory company" for two of the smaller male roles in *Man of La Mancha*. Jerry Hadley had played the Caliph in *Kismet,* so I brought him in as the Padre, who sings two songs, the wistful "To Each His Dulcinea" in Act I and the mournful "The Psalm" to mark Quixote's death. Sam Ramey, who had starred in our *Kismet*, was kind enough to accept the small role of the Innkeeper and to deliver a beautiful rendition of "Knight of the Woeful Countenance."

This was really a festival of tenors. Besides Plácido, we had Jerry Hadley and Mandy Patinkin, as well as Robert White as the Barber.

Domingo suggested that his sons, Alvaro and Plácido Jr., might sing "Little Bird, Little Bird," and they did it very nicely.

This was an excellent recording, but for a long time very few people knew that. Composer Mitch Leigh blocked its release for five years and might have blocked it longer if it weren't for the fact that in 1996 lyricist Joe Darion was on his deathbed and said, "For God's sakes, Mitch, let the album come out." And so Mitch relented.

He never said what it was he didn't like about the album. It can't have been Plácido, because apparently Mitch had pushed the idea of the recording with Domingo years before it came to pass. I've been told he had no problem at all with the recording; what he didn't like was that he hadn't been consulted or invited to the session.

Predictably the five-year lapse between the time it was recorded and the time it was released had led several smart-alecky critics to say things along the lines of, "It must be a terrible album for Sony to have suppressed it for so long." When it came out it got generally great reviews.

Catch Me If I Fall (1995)

This Off-Broadway show was the brainchild of the talented Barbara Schottenfeld, who wrote the book, the lyrics, and the music. Barbara was a very attractive and gifted woman, around thirty years old. She was a protégé of Jule Styne, but it was her publisher, Frank Military of Warner Chappell, who approached me about the recording.

In the normal order of things, this show—which was about a sculptor-turned-corporate-headhunter (James Judy) who is juggling three women in his life—wouldn't have been recorded. The reviews hadn't been especially good, and the show's limited run of sixteen performances at the Promenade Theatre had already ended by the time we were in the studio in Astoria to make the recording. But Barbara was newly signed with Warner Chappell, they expected great things of her, and so they underwrote the recording.

The recording was made in early 1991 but not released until 1995, on a label called Painted Smiles, and I assume it was a very limited release.

The Secret Garden (1991)

Frances Hodgson Burnett's famous young-adult novel *The Secret Garden* has been charming readers, especially girls, ever since it came out in 1911; it's never been out of print. The novel tells the story of Mary Lennox, an English child in India. When her parents die during a cholera outbreak, she is sent back to England to live in a remote country house with her uncle, a strange, tormented widower who keeps his distance from her and from his ailing son.

The book has been made into five movies and six television series through the years. I wasn't aware it had been made into a Broadway musical, though, until late 1991, when I received a telephone call from Lucy Simon. There was plenty of talent in the Simon family: Lucy was a composer; her sisters Carly and Joanna were, respectively, a pop singer/songwriter and an opera singer; and their brother Peter was a photographer. I knew Joanna but had never met Lucy. She phoned me because she couldn't find a record label willing to produce the original-cast album for *The Secret Garden*, which she had written with Marsha Norman (book and lyrics). She was hoping I might help.

I was happy to pursue this. I told her I'd do the best I could. I began by going to see the show, which was in previews, and I was utterly charmed by it. I came away determined to do everything I could to see that it got recorded. Already I could see that it had the makings of a great recording.

I was doing a lot of work for Sony at this point, so I started there. The company had no dedicated Broadway department, however, so I went to Mel Ilberman, the company's second in command.

Mel went to see the show himself, and he loved it. Mel had recently lost his wife of many years, and I think something in the story of Archibald Craven, the bereaved widower who can't get past his grief, hit home for him. He decided that, yes, Columbia would record it.

It wasn't an easy recording to make, because it's a long show with a tremendous amount of music. I wanted very much to tell its story because it's such a powerful one.

I had a lot of meetings with the conductor named Michael Kosarin and his assistant, who was also the dance arranger. (She subsequently got divorced, resumed her maiden name, and became famous as Jeanine Tesori, composer of *Twelfth Night*; *Caroline, or Change*; *Shrek: The Musical*; *Fun Home*; and *Kimberly Akimbo*—the last two of which won Tony Awards for Best Score.) We came out of that process with a fairly detailed plan of what this recording was going to be.

And then, a few days before the session, I had the startling realization I hadn't done a good enough job. I called Jeanine and Michael, and said to them, "We have to go back to square one."

I was asking everybody to do a lot of extra work at the last minute. I wanted to change a significant amount of the dialogue we'd decided to include, and—because so much of the dialogue in the show has underscoring—this meant a lot of extra work for orchestrator Bill Brohn. For each snatch of dialogue, we had to work out exactly how many seconds of underscoring would be needed. Then each of those bits would need to be rewritten, recopied and gotten onto the stands of the musicians by the time the session took place, which was only a few days later.

All show recordings are custom-made to one degree or another, but this one was especially so, with lots of material abridged, juggled, and then re-juggled in the service of telling the story. Meanwhile, I needed to come up with any number of sound effects, from the chugging of a train to the sound of a falling key hitting the ground.

In addition, there were questions of sound quality to be sorted out. I love shows like *Kiss of the Spider Woman* or *Lady in the Dark*, in which you're dealing with ghosts, fantasies or dreams, and you have a chance to play with sound to convey the idea that not everything is front and center, that some things are coming to you from far, far away, and that was certainly true of *The Secret Garden*. Right from the beginning, with Lily (Rebecca Luker) singing about the garden, the show needed to have an other-worldly feel. Lily isn't really there; she's a benevolent ghost, a good fairy. This sense of Misselthwaite Manor, with its hundred rooms and hidden garden, as a place of mysterious secrets is reinforced throughout the show.

It was worth the planning and the extra work during and after the recording session. In the end I think we did justice to Marsha and Lucy's musical, and to Burnett's story. It's probably my ultimate radio-play recording.

The cast was superb. Archibald Craven was a real stretch for Mandy, who normally plays big, flamboyant characters whose emotions are all over the place, whereas Archibald is a crippled man whose emotions are deeply repressed—every word, every note that comes out of him reflects anguish locked within him and gnawing at his insides. And Mandy did a wonderful job with the part.

Daisy Eagan was only eleven and she really had to carry the show, which is seen through Mary's eyes, and she was just wonderful. She won a Tony Award as Best Featured Actress for her performance—the youngest person ever to win a Tony.

The other young star of the show was John Babcock, who played Archibald's ailing son, Colin. The problem was his voice was changing, and he could no longer easily hit the high notes in his songs. They let him go on in the theater, because he acted the part very well and could still put over the songs, but Lucy didn't want to compromise the recording. John's standby, Joel E. Chaiken, was there for the session, and he could hit all the notes, so Lucy said, "Well, we won't use the kid, we'll use the standby."

Well, it made me very unhappy. I mean, John was a good actor, and he'd come to the session planning to do the recording, and he was only eleven years old and maybe this was the only Broadway recording he'd ever be on. So I suggested to Lucy that we record each song twice, once with each of the boys, and use John's voice except for those problematic high notes, where I would substitute Joel's voice instead. It would add more time to the recording session, but Lucy agreed. (On one song, "Come to My Garden/Lift Me Up," which has the most high notes in Colin's part, we used Joel throughout, and he's credited as the singer.)

One of the nicest moments for me came at the end of the session: John came up to me and he said, "Thank you."

I have only two regrets about this recording, one of which didn't really have anything to do with me. At the time Columbia was very strict about recording length. They were concerned that the current CD players might not successfully play a disk longer than 77 minutes. Like it or not, I had to adhere to this maximum length, and *The Secret Garden* was coming in a minute or so over that limit.

Rather than drop one of the songs altogether, we had to shorten one. Our choice fell on "Come Spirit, Come Charm"; the shorter version still makes sense, but for me, it loses some of its charm. Lucy was very unhappy about it, as was I, but she understood we really had no choice.

My other regret is more personal. There's a mistake on the recording, one I missed—an oversight that still bothers me to this day.

In the number "Lily's Eyes," a duet for Archibald and his brother (Mandy and Robert Westenberg), Mandy makes a tiny mistake just before the key change at the end. The words are "She has her eyes," and what's supposed to happen is Robert comes in first and then Mandy comes in, with the same words. On this particular take, Mandy began to come in a beat earlier than he's supposed to. It's not glaring—he instantly realizes what he's done and shifts to his own line—but the mistake is there and somehow, I can't imagine how, I didn't catch it when I put the pieces together during the editing process. We did multiple takes of the song, and I'm sure Mandy had that entrance right in all the others. Mea maxima culpa.

I believe that *The Secret Garden* is one of the best recordings I've ever made. It will always hold a special place in my heart.

Love in Two Countries (1991)

This project doesn't really belong in this book, which is about my career as a producer of Broadway recordings, because it wasn't on Broadway, and no commercial recording resulted from it. But this book is also about my life, and *Love in Two Countries* certainly loomed large in my life in 1991.

My old friend Sheldon Harnick and I had often talked about writing something together. In the late 1980s that came to fruition. We first wrote the one-act *That Pig of a Molette*, based on an 1882 French short story by Guy de Maupassant. We later wrote *A Question of Faith* based on the 1882 Russian short story, *A Slight Error*, by Nicolai Leskow. *Molette* had been workshopped at the O'Neill Theater Center in Waterford, Connecticut, in August 1989, followed in September by a staged reading at the John Houseman Theatre in Manhattan. In April 1991, Musical Theatre Works presented both shows for a six-week run at St. Peter's Church in Manhattan. On this occasion the two comic operas were presented as a double bill under the umbrella title *Love in Two Countries*.

I was there for many performances, and the audiences seemed to find both shows very entertaining. Some of the reviews were less than kind, however, and the operas haven't been performed since then that I know of. My music emerged from the critics largely unscathed—in fact, virtually unmentioned.

The point the critics seem to have missed—understandably, perhaps, given Sheldon's longtime mastery of the Broadway musical—was that we weren't trying to write the next *Fiddler on the Roof* or, indeed, a Broadway musical of any kind. *That Pig of a Molette* and *A Question of Faith* are comic operas, funny in a satiric, nineteenth-century-European kind of way. We wrote them the way we did because it was what we wanted to write.

34

A Jukebox, a Revamp, a Sequel, and a Revival

AS A FREELANCE PRODUCER I'VE HAD TO ACCEPT certain realities of life. One is that the highest-profile original-cast albums may not always be within my grasp.

All the same, the 1990s were among my most rewarding periods as a producer. Not all the best shows on Broadway are high-profile originals. In the next five years I would find overlooked gems amid the jukebox musicals, revivals, revamps, and even replacement casts—and now and then, a blockbuster.

Jelly's Last Jam (1992)

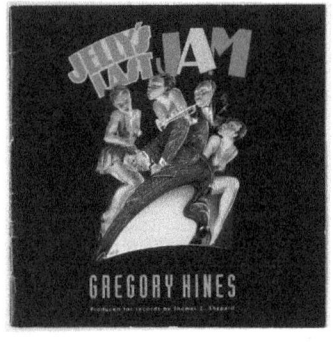

Jelly Roll Morton (1890?–1941), born into a wealthy, mixed-race family in New Orleans as Ferdinand Joseph Lemott, was an important early jazz pianist, bandleader, and composer. Although his claim to have invented jazz is pure hyperbole, he helped turn jazz music from an improvisatory style into a recognized musical genre of its own. He wrote and recorded many instrumental pieces that are still heard today, including "Jelly Roll Blues" (1915), "King Porter Stomp" (1923), "Wolverine Blues" (1923), "Black Bottom Stomp" (1926), and "I Thought I Heard Buddy Bolden Say" (1939).

For *Jelly's Last Jam*, author/director George C. Wolfe used Morton's story to explore the roots of jazz and the Black music of the early twentieth century, with lyricist Susan Birkenhead setting words to Morton's existing tunes. Gregory Hines played the adult Morton, who is first seen in the afterlife, looking back and trying to make sense of a life lived on the borders between races and between musical forms such as ragtime, blues, and jazz. Hines's tap-dancing protégé Savion Glover, at the time only nineteen, portrayed Morton's younger self.

The orchestrator of the show was my old friend Luther Henderson, and I think it was Luther who recommended me to Lisa Cortés, an executive at Mercury Records. Mercury didn't do a lot of cast albums, but Lisa was very interested in Black music and its history, and she wanted this one for Mercury. Lisa brought me onto the project, but only a week or two before the recording session was to take place, she told me some people on the production team—she didn't say who—were not convinced I was the right person to make this particular recording, and they wanted to sit down with me and talk about it.

So we met uptown—me, Lisa, George, Susan and Luther. Now, if I was on the carpet, I decided the best approach was to ignore that fact, assume it was a *fait accompli* that I would produce the recording, and talk them through the way I planned to do so. By the time I was done, it was all settled: there were some questions about details, but nothing about whether I was the right guy for the job. After we left, Lisa said, "You really did that well!"

George Wolfe is a very bright man, and his book for *Jelly's Last Jam* was a strong one. It was certainly about Morton's life as a Black musician in a segregated America, but it also explored universal themes of the alienation of artists and the conflicts between art and commerce (like most Black artists, Morton was badly exploited by any number of promoters, club owners, managers, and record labels). It rarely got preachy, and it was always entertaining. With great music and wonderfully varied tap choreography by Greg Hines and Ted L. Levy, and other choreography by Hope Clarke, it was an exhilarating show to watch.

Before we went into the studio, I sat down with George for a long meeting at Joe Papp's Public Theater, where he was the artistic director. We went over the whole show together, working out what dialogue we'd want for purposes of continuity. Because he was both the author and the director, this was an easier process than usual.

It's a tough job setting lyrics to music that people already know. There have been some great successes at this, notably *Carmen Jones* (1943), for which Oscar Hammerstein crafted a contemporary American libretto for the score to Bizet's *Carmen*, and *Kismet*, with Wright & Forrest's comic and romantic lyrics for a potpourri of melodies by Borodin, but it's hard to do well. Susan Birkenhead was a wonderful lyricist, though, a very talented woman whose lyrics fit Morton's music like a glove. (Coincidentally, she was married to Jerold Couture, who was my lawyer at the time, but I had never met her before.)

The orchestra was conducted by a woman, which was unusual on Broadway. The one thing I remember about Linda Twine is she asked me to use one mike for each of Luther's three trumpets, which I did.

I basically loved the entire creative team on *Jelly's Last Jam*, especially Luther Henderson. We were really close friends, of course, but we were also a mutual-admiration society. He was an endlessly inventive arranger/orchestrator, and he liked the way I produced records as much as I liked the way he arranged music.

That wasn't the case with everybody in the cast. I've already described how arrogant Greg Hines could be when we recorded *Sophisticated Ladies*. This was more than a decade later, but I'm sorry to say nothing had changed.

I'd seen *Jelly's Last Jam* several times in preparing for the session, and each time I was more impressed with Greg's work in the show. *Sophisticated Ladies* had proved he was a fine singer and an amazing dancer, but that show was a revue and didn't really require him to act. In *Jelly's Last Jam* he was playing a complex character who was far from admirable in his treatment of people, and Greg turned out to be as good an actor as he was a singer or dancer. It was a very impressive performance.

Even so, he aggravated me from the moment he came into the studio for the session. This was a tap show, so of course all the dancers had brought their tap shoes—except for Greg, who tapped more than anybody else in the show. His explanation was that I hadn't told him to bring them. I hadn't thought that that was necessary—everybody else had brought their shoes without being told.

So if you listen to that recording, you'll hear Greg singing, Greg talking, and Greg's tap choreography—but you won't hear Greg's feet. The taps for the recording were supplied by Savion Glover, who brought his shoes.

There's a song in the show I thought was very important. It's called "Lonely Boy," and in a show where Jelly Roll does a lot of strutting, preening, and self-promoting, it's one of the few introspective, sad moments. It was just Greg half-talking, half-singing, accompanied by the orchestra. But I wondered, "Do we even need the orchestra?"

I took Luther and George aside and suggested, "Supposing we make this number really lonely? Let's remove all accompaniment. We'll have Greg start out from one side of the floor and walk across, timing it so he's on the other side of the floor by the end of it." Well, they both liked the idea—and maybe they also understood why I thought George, who got along well with Greg, should be the one to explain it to him.

So on the recording session Greg sang the song with George standing next to him and walking across a designated area of the studio floor from one side to the other with Greg following him, setting a pace that would time out to be exactly how long it took to move from hard left to hard right on the recording. It took only one take, and it's very effective, particularly on a recording that's very noisy, with all the trumpets and taps, to have this moment that's so intimate and quiet. I'm very happy with how it turned out.

Savion was a good singer and actor, and a phenomenal dancer—it was hard to believe that somebody so young could be so dynamic. He was this gangly teenager, all arms and legs, sitting in the studio just draped over a chair, and then he'd get up and start dancing, and it was like magic, the energy, precision, and creativity. Greg was Savion's mentor and didn't seem threatened at all, just enormously fond and proud of him.

I really enjoyed working on *Jelly's Last Jam*, my issues with Greg notwithstanding. It was such an unusual and ambitious show.

Crazy for You (1992)

Some shows are built around an idea, some around a story, some around a joke. Some are built to showcase their star's performances or their creators' brilliance. *Crazy for You* was built around a feeling.

Coming out of the 1980s, in which Broadway was dominated by the dark romanticism of Andrew Lloyd Webber, the brittle complexity of Stephen Sondheim, and the blues-tinged edginess of Kander & Ebb, the creators of *Crazy for You* wanted something altogether different: the exuberance and exhilaration of pre–Rodgers & Hammerstein Broadway, when characters were silly, plots were ridiculous, songs were brilliant, and the whole thing was wrapped up in a glittering cloud of dance.

Producers Roger Horchow and Elizabeth Williams originally planned to revive the Gershwin musical *Girl Crazy* (1930), which had famously made a star of the young Ginger Rogers. Their idea was to have the Guy Bolton/John McGowan book revised by Ken Ludwig to complement the classic score by George and Ira Gershwin, which included such songs as "Bidin' My Time," "But Not for Me," "Embraceable You," and "I Got Rhythm."

This tactic of creating a new book for a classic musical was a time-tested one, with previous hits including the Cole Porter musical *Anything Goes* (1934), revised under the same name in 1962 and again in 1987, and the Gershwins' *Funny Face* (1927), revised as *My One and Only* in 1983. In all three cases the goal was to retain the light-hearted spirit of the original book while pruning it of dated references and/or gender and racial stereotypes that were offensive to contemporary ears.

However, as Ken, director Mike Ockrent, and choreographer Susan Stroman got into the project, they increasingly found the original book too dated to simply be revised. Ultimately, they cut away everything except for the basic skeleton of *Girl Crazy*, and rechristened it as a new musical, *Crazy for You*. This also gave them license to jettison all but six of the original songs, which were supplemented by fourteen Gershwin songs from assorted other shows and movies.

Crazy for You opened to rave reviews, which especially praised the classic score and Stroman's inventive choreography. Frank Rich called it "a riotously entertaining show [that] uncorked the American musical's classic blend of music, laughter, dancing, sentiment and showmanship with a freshness and confidence rarely seen during the *Cats* decade."

The show won two Tony Awards, as Best Musical and for Best Choreographer. It ended up running for more than four years on Broadway and almost three in London, where it opened in 1993.

I loved the idea of recording a Gershwin show and was very grateful to music director Paul Gemignani, who convinced Mike and Susan (who married during the run of the show) to tell Angel Records that they wanted me as the producer. The head of Angel, Steve Murphy, was really generous in one respect: "I don't care how long the recording takes to make," he said. "You know we're going to make it back on sales."

The only previous Gershwin recordings I'd made had been *Porgy and Bess*, which of course I love, and the abbreviated television production of *Of Thee I Sing*, but Gershwin was best known as a Broadway songwriter, and this was the first time I'd gotten my hands on a Gershwin show, packed with wonderful tunes from the 1920s and 1930s. And of course I've always loved tap dancing, so I wanted to include as much of the dance music as possible.

One of the things that struck me about Susan's choreography was the way she had all her dancers jump from one surface to another, tapping the whole time, with each surface giving off a different sound. I thought, "Wouldn't that be fun, and an original touch, on the recording?" I couldn't replicate the exact sounds from the stage (since I couldn't bring the set into the studio), but I set up a variety of different surfaces and had the dancers move from one to another as they danced, so we had the contrast and the feeling that these dancers were constantly traveling from one platform to another.

It turned out very well, but it was extremely time-consuming, pushing the session to two days—so Murphy's generosity turned out to be a good thing. As I had in recording *42nd Street* and several other shows with chorus tapping, I couldn't simply have the whole chorus dance their routines in the studio. Like any other choreographer, Susan loves precision and crispness. So she selected eight dancers, whom I recorded and overdubbed two more times, creating the sound of twenty-four dancers. But even with only eight dancers—all of them wonderful—precision is a tough thing to get, so it took a lot longer than it took to record the songs, which, like most 1930s songs, were relatively simple and easy to get down.

Not long ago I played this recording for myself in the car after not listening to it for a good many years. It's very entertaining, and it moves at a wonderful pace.

Annie Warbucks (1993)

Movie audiences love sequels. Book series like the Tarzan books, the James Bond books, the Narnia books, and the Harry Potter books have been big business for the past century or more. Spinoffs and reboots are a staple of television. Nothing succeeds like more of the same. Except on Broadway. The history of sequels to Broadway hits has been uniformly disastrous.

I've already mentioned *Let 'Em Eat Cake*, the failed follow-up to the popular, Pulitzer Prize-winning hit *Of Thee I Sing*. *Let 'Em Eat Cake*'s 89-performance run was good by Broadway-sequel standards! *The Best Little Whorehouse in Texas* had been good for 1,584 performances in 1978, but *The Best Little Whorehouse Goes Public* (1994) lasted only 16 performances. *Divorce Me, Darling* (1964), Sandy Wilson's sequel to *The Boy Friend*, never made it to Broadway, nor did Andrew Lloyd Webber's *Phantom of the Opera* sequel, *Love Never Dies* (2010), despite following in the footsteps of the longest-running show in the history of Broadway.

The all-time champion of this dubious pursuit is composer Charles Strouse. With author Michael Stewart and lyricist Lee Adams, he wrote both *Bye Bye Birdie* (1960, 607 performances) and *Bring Back Birdie* (1971, four performances). With author Thomas Meehan and lyricist Martin Charnin, he wrote *Annie* (1977), which ran for 2,377 performances, and *Annie 2: Miss Hannigan's Revenge* (1989), which closed out of town after a chaotic run in Washington, DC.

Refusing to say die, Strouse, Charnin, and Meehan started over and in 1992 launched *Annie Warbucks*, another sequel that was universally agreed to be superior to *Miss Hannigan's Revenge*. After touring the West Coast and Houston, it opened Off-Broadway at the Variety Arts Theatre on Third Avenue, with its eyes clearly set on Broadway. It drew strong reviews and ran for two hundred performances there, but in the end a Broadway move never came to pass. By the time that decision was made, however, I'd already produced the original-cast album.

I really enjoyed *Annie Warbucks*. It had a great cast with really good songs, but no big hits came out of it; it couldn't stack up against the original *Annie*, which is one of the all-time greats. That's the potential problem with any sequel: it comes with built-in comparisons to something that had to have been awfully good to deserve a sequel.

Of all the cast albums I've done, this is probably the most different from the show as it was seen onstage. At the beginning and ending, as a matter of fact, it's completely different.

There was no real overture to the show, but Charles wanted one for the recording, and wrote it practically overnight. We managed to get the parts extracted and copied just in time for the session. It's an interesting piece, far richer and a little more dissonant than a typical musical-theater overture. Charles is a very sophisticated composer who studied with, among other people, Nadia Boulanger.

The album is much better for the new overture. Besides the caliber of the music itself, it also gives the recording a fresh beginning, as opposed to starting cold with the first song, which is "A New Deal for Christmas," the last song in *Annie* (the sequel picks up from the very moment the original ends).

Things were unsettled at the other end of the show, as well. Angel Records planned to release this as an illustrated storybook album, one that tells the story of the play with dialogue excerpts, sound effects, and so on.

But when we sat down to look at the show, we realized that the finale, a song called "The Day They Say 'I Do,'" wouldn't work for a storybook. It wasn't a weak song, but it wasn't clear, with sound alone, what was happening in the play, and it would have ended the recording on a weak note. So Martin Charnin, who was also the director, sat down and virtually improvised a finale, picking up various materials from the show and using various cast members. He did a brilliant job of it.

Our leading lady was nine-year-old Kathryn Zaremba, who played Annie with great panache. She had played Duffy on the road but took over the lead role for New York and did very well. (She retired at thirteen and is now an illustrator and textile designer.) Harve Presnell played Daddy Warbucks, a role he had played as a replacement in the original *Annie,* and brought a nice humorous touch to it. Raymond Thorne, who had played Franklin Delano Roosevelt in the original, returned for *Annie Warbucks* and did a devastating impersonation of FDR.

I particularly liked Donna McKechnie as Sheila Kelly, one of the villains. Donna is best known as a dancer, courtesy of *A Chorus Line,* but she had a major singing role in this show: "But You Go On," all about how rotten Sheila's life has been and the terrible experiences that made her what she is—and then you learn, when the song is over, that she made the whole thing up. It was so convincing, so seemingly heartfelt, that I often wondered whether it had originally been written as a serious song, before Tom, Charles, and Martin decided to put this unexpected spin on it.

The real pleasure of the project, though, was working with Martin and Charles. I had never made an album with Charles, but we went back a long way. The *Bye Bye Birdie* recording session, back in 1960, was the first Lieberson session I ever attended, and Irene and I used to play poker with Charles and his wife, Barbara Simon, way back when.

Charles is a very gifted man, one of the most musically educated of Broadway composers. He was a graduate of the Eastman School of Music, just as Goddard was, and was friends with Schuyler Chapin, whom he had met at Tanglewood in the

1950s. I think, in fact, it was Schuyler who originally recommended *Bye Bye Birdie* to Columbia because he knew Charles. I would work with him again, later, when I produced the recording of the *Annie* revival in 2013.

Damn Yankees (1994)

I've never had much interest in sports, but I make an exception for *Damn Yankees*, unquestionably the best Broadway musical ever made about sports.

Written by George Abbott and Douglass Wallop (based on Wallop's novel, *The Year the Yankees Lost the Pennant*), with songs by Richard Adler and Jerry Ross, who chose to be jointly credited for both words and music, the show is a comic take on *Faust*. The Devil—known here as "Mr. Applegate"—offers long-suffering Washington Senators fan Joe Hardy a chance to become the power hitter his team needs to dethrone the mighty New York Yankees—at the price, naturally, of his soul.

The original production debuted in 1955, with Robert Shafer as Joe, Ray Walston as Mr. Applegate, Gwen Verdon as the seductive Lola (who has sold her own soul to Applegate in exchange for beauty, and now is his tool to control Joe), and Shannon Bolin as Joe's deserted wife, Meg. It enjoyed a healthy run of 1,019 performances. (It also ran for 258 performances in London, despite England's lack of a baseball tradition; presumably long-suffering soccer fans could identify with Joe's plight.)

While in some senses dated—the Yankees are no longer the eternally dominant team that they were in the 1950s, and the Senators decamped for Minnesota (where they became the Twins) in 1960—*Damn Yankees* is still very entertaining today, with a funny book and terrific songs from beginning to end. Though it didn't have a full-fledged Broadway revival until 1994, it was made into a successful film in 1958 (almost uniquely, the film featured almost the entire original Broadway cast, except that Robert Shafer was replaced by Tab Hunter). It's long been a staple of regional and community theater and is regularly staged in schools across the United States.

The 1994 Broadway revival was directed by Jack O'Brien, who was also credited with revisions to the book. Jarrod Emick played Joe and Victor Garber was Mr. Applegate, with Bebe Neuwirth as Lola and Linda Stephens as Meg. It ran for 519 performances and was a great deal of fun.

I was signed to produce the revival-cast album before it was certain there would ever be one. The people at Mercury Records told me there was some question about whether the cast members—especially Bebe Neuwirth—would consent to the recording. Nobody knew exactly what the problem was, so I was sent out to the West Coast, where the show was playing, to find out what was going on.

On arrival I saw the show and then attended a meeting with the whole cast after the performance. Cast members are almost never reluctant to make a recording, but Bebe was certainly not happy. I never found out exactly what her concerns were, but I sat with the cast and explained what we were going to do, answered their questions as best I could, and then went back to New York. I guess my answers were the right ones because soon afterward I heard the recording was on.

I came into the session with a little more trepidation than usual because I had reason to think that between Bebe and Jack—with whom, as I described earlier, I had clashed during the making of *Porgy and Bess* over my wish to incorporate the line "Bess, Bess, Porgy will take you"—this might be a rocky couple of days. As it turned out, though, it was a lot of fun, with only one minor impediment to my enjoyment.

Surprisingly, it wasn't Jack! He was there for the entire recording session, but he didn't interfere at all, and in fact, seemed to like everything I was doing with the show. As he ought to have, because I did my best to capture the charm of his particular production, which included some spoof radio commercials in the style of the 1950s. These things delighted me, and I included all of them. I wanted all the elements that reflected the era the show was depicting—the commercials, the sound of the games being broadcast on a small radio, everything that captured the feel of the show, which as Jack staged it was very much a period piece.

(I should note that I was careful to see to it that all the major dialogue portions were banded separately on the CD. If a listener doesn't want to hear them, he or she can easily skip over them. The CD insert even includes a list of the band numbers to be programmed for a song-only listening experience, if that's what the listener desires.)

As for Bebe, once the recording was actually happening, we got along wonderfully. There was an unusually long break between sessions, and during that time, she and I got to talking, and it turned out she came from New Jersey, just like I did. She'd grown up in Princeton, but her maternal grandparents owned Yudin's Paint Shop in East Orange, and I actually vaguely knew her father, Lee Neuwirth, who was the president of the high-school fraternity Mu Sigma, of which some of my friends were members. And then we discovered she had studied ballet with Alfredo Corvino, who had been Irene's teacher for many years.

I knew things with her would go all right, even before that conversation, though, because early on I overheard somebody ask her how the session was going, and she answered, "Well, the producer knows what he's doing."

The only fly in the ointment was Richard Adler. Jerry Ross, his partner, had died suddenly back in 1955, only a few months after the show opened, but Adler was very much alive, and he came to the session. I've mentioned before that I prefer not to have the songwriters present on studio-cast or revival sessions because there's simply no role for them to play and they can really get in the way. I certainly would have enjoyed this session more if Adler hadn't been there.

He and his wife sat in the back of the control room the whole time, and he made no secret of the fact that he didn't care at all for what I was doing. I think what he didn't like was everything Jack did like—the commercials, the bits of dialogue, and so forth. Adler was old-school, and I think, as far as he was concerned, *Damn Yankees* was all about the songs, period; all the other things I was doing were nothing but a series of distractions, a waste of time. But he didn't interfere. He just sat there and radiated disapproval, this dour presence sitting silently in the back of the room.

This show was so well cast. With a revival there's always a danger that because the show was a hit before, everyone will take it for granted that it will be a hit again.

That definitely wasn't the case here. Jack's staging was modern and imaginative, with lots of nice details, and all the actors brought fresh energy and commitment to the production.

Victor Garber played the Devil in this recording, and he was great. I knew him as Anthony in *Sweeney Todd*, of course, but Anthony is an ingenue, an innocent swept up in a world of chaos and corruption. Mr. Applegate is the opposite extreme—all corruption and no innocence—but it's a droll, roguish kind of corruption. Applegate is a fast-talking song-and-dance man, a con artist instead of a fire-breathing Biblical demon, and Victor showed how funny he could be. "Those Were the Good Old Days" and his duet with Bebe, "Two Lost Souls," brought the house down onstage, and they're among the highlights of the recording as well.

Bebe was terrific as Lola, which was to be expected. It's primarily a dancing part, and she's a wonderful dancer—but she can also sing with the best of them. Her sense of humor was her best tool as Lola; the character is outrageously sexy, but it's a tongue-in-cheek sexiness, consciously over the top, and Bebe found exactly the right balance in the part.

Joe Hardy is a difficult part to play because at different times in the show he's the funny guy, the straight man, and the romantic lead. Jarrod Emick hit all the marks and earned a Tony Award for his efforts.

Linda Stephens had scored her career breakthrough the year before as the star of the cult-favorite Off-Broadway show *Wings*, in which she was phenomenal. That performance had helped her land the role of Joe's wife, Meg, and she was an outstanding Meg. *Damn Yankees* is a funny show, but as its most famous song says, "You gotta have heart," and the heart in *Damn Yankees* comes from Meg. Linda is a wonderful actress, and she made "Near to You" and "A Man Doesn't Know" really moving—which didn't keep her from making "Six Months out of Every Year" hilarious.

Dick Latessa, who played the manager of the Senators, had only one real number, but it was the solo part in "Heart," and he nailed it.

And this recording was great preparation for my next show—which for me would be a trip into the future, and for Linda Stephens would be a trip into her past.

35

A Solo, a Replacement, a Revue, and Julie

Wings (1995)

I hold a special affection for *Wings*, which was a truly remarkable project, a powerful story built around a powerful performance. The journey from stage show to cast album was a long one, but it resulted in a highly unusual cast album.

Wings is based on Arthur Kopit's 1978 play of the same name, and its subject matter is unusual and autobiographical: Kopit began work on it shortly after his father suffered a devastating stroke and had to rebuild his ability to think, move, and especially to speak virtually from scratch. Emily, the protagonist of the play, is a former daredevil aviatrix incapacitated by a stroke; she's based on a woman Kopit got to know at his father's rehab center.

Wings premiered as a radio play in 1976 and two years later opened in a fully staged production on Broadway. The play was gripping and deeply moving, earning three Tony nominations, including one as Best Play, but it wasn't easy going. Emily is trapped inside her own malfunctioning brain, and her struggle to rebuild her identity is the core of the play. She spends much of the play angry, frustrated, and despairing. It didn't have "musical" written all over it.

Nonetheless Arthur Perlman (book and lyrics) and Jeff Lunden (composer) set out to adapt Kopit's play as a musical, and what they came up with was virtually a one-woman show, with vivid, kaleidoscopic projections and unearthly sound effects conveying the experience of a stroke as seen from the patient's point of view. Lunden (like me an Oberlin graduate) based his music on the way certain kinds of stroke victims experience the world, with musical motifs scrambling, combining, and recombining in disturbing, unpredictable ways. He also did his own orchestrations, which is very unusual for a musical-theater composer.

The show was no box-office hit, playing only a six-week limited run at the Public Theater in 1993. But these guys had created something wonderful; it moved and inspired many people, and by 1995, some of them had put enough money together to make a recording.

I didn't see the show, and I don't remember if I was even aware of it. Certainly it wasn't anywhere on my radar until Ted Chapin sent it my way.

Besides Ted and the Rodgers & Hammerstein Organization, there was a substantial grant from the Sandra Gilman & Celso Gonzalez-Falla Theatre Foundation. Sandra and her husband were very generous supporters of New York's nonprofit theaters, and I believe they paid for most of this recording. Warner Chappell was in on it, and so was BMG/RCA, which ultimately released the recording. I accepted far less than my usual fee because this was a labor-of-love project for everyone involved—the show put its audience through far too much of an emotional wringer to be likely to ever make a profit—and I was happy to be a part of it.

It's a very touching story. Emily is a very physically active, dynamic person until the stroke hits in her fifties. We meet her in a wheelchair, unable to form a coherent sentence, let alone sing or dance; and over the course of the show we watch her trying to recover her mental and physical abilities. Very gradually she seems to get better and better, to have more clarity on what's going on, only to have a second, fatal stroke. It's horrible, and yet it's so beautifully told. Jeff Lunden and Arthur Perlman did a fantastic job with a subject matter more suited to opera than to Broadway.

They built the whole thing around Emily (Linda Stephens), who is at the center of every scene and virtually every song. Linda, whose work I'd admired so much on *Damn Yankees,* brought the house down in a remarkable performance, which certainly comes through on the recording.

Linda wasn't the only person in the cast—there were four others, playing doctors, caregivers, and so on—but they were virtual walk-ons and walk-offs.

As for me, this recording was right up my alley, which may be why Ted thought of me in the first place. I love stories that involve altered reality, like *Lady in the Dark* or *Kiss of the Spider Woman,* and *Wings* was all about distorted perceptions of reality. I couldn't have been more challenged because the sound effects and the atmospheric manipulation of sound were not incidental detailing, but integral to the whole story. We had the sound-effects recordings they'd used in the theater, and between what they already had and the way the piece sparked my imagination, it was an exciting project.

Kiss of the Spider Woman (1995)

As I've noted, many revivals don't get cast albums. Even rarer, however, are replacement-cast albums. There are several reasons for this. The main one is that most revivals are produced by people other than the original producers and are released years after the original production has closed, offering reasonable expectations that if the revival is a hit, the album will be profitable for the new producers. By contrast, a replacement-cast album by definition will be made during the original run, following close on the heels of the original-cast album. Since the same producers control the recording rights, they have an understandable reluctance to spend more money to compete with themselves.

In addition, there is a general assumption that the replacement cast is made up of performers who couldn't make the cut for the original cast and therefore is the B team. Ticket sales often slump after the original stars leave a show, and the idea of releasing a second album with the next cast seems silly. Who would buy a cast album featuring the understudies of the original stars?

Finally, it's assumed that many people buy a cast album for the songs, not the performers. Once they have one recording of the songs, why would they buy another, with the same arrangements and different singers?

These arguments aren't entirely wrong, but they aren't always right. For one thing, the replacement leads are usually new to the show. Sometimes they're major stars; one example is Liza Minnelli, who replaced Gwen Verdon in the original production of *Chicago*. (And sometimes understudies are actually better than the originals.)

And of course, a replacement-cast album might be made in a different way than the original, offering advantages of its own. That was certainly the case in 1994, when I was hired to produce the replacement-cast album of *Kiss of the Spider Woman*, a year and a half after the show had opened on Broadway.

That it had a replacement-cast album was only one of many unusual aspects of *Kiss of the Spider Woman*, a brilliant but challenging show that, despite the participation of some of American theater's biggest names, had a long, circuitous route to Broadway through three different countries and barely made it at all.

The idea of making a musical out of Manuel Puig's 1976 novel *El beso de la mujer araña* (which had been adapted into a 1985 Hollywood movie as *Kiss of the Spider Woman*) was an unlikely one because the subject matter was problematic at best. Set in an Argentinian prison, the novel is about the relationship of two prisoners sharing a cell: Molina, a movie-crazed gay man serving a long sentence for corrupting a minor, and Valentín, a homophobic Marxist revolutionary. The title refers to the movie-derived fantasies that get Molina through his days in prison, and specifically Aurora, a movie diva whose signature character is the Spider Woman, whose kiss is deadly. In the course of the story, Valentín is repeatedly tortured, both men are poisoned, and the story ends with Valentín still in prison and Molina shot dead.

If it was going to be adapted into a musical, though, John Kander and Fred Ebb were the obvious people to write the songs, and Harold Prince was the obvious choice to direct it. In *Cabaret* and *Chicago* John and Fred had proven they weren't afraid of dark themes and downbeat stories; and as I've discussed, Hal had shown a positive attraction to musicals that arguably had no business getting made in the first place.

In 1990, with a book by Terrence McNally, the show was workshopped out of town, at SUNY/Purchase in Westchester County, which proved to be too close to Broadway: the New York critics were asked not to review the show in its developmental phase, but they did so anyway, and their reviews were negative. The sponsoring organization, New Musicals, went broke, and for a couple years nothing was heard of the show.

Eventually, however, Canadian producer Garth Drabinsky got behind *Kiss of the Spider Woman* and backed a Toronto production that opened in June 1992 with Brent Carver as Molina, Anthony Crivello as Valentín, and Chita Rivera as Spider Woman/Aurora. That production was clearly meant for Broadway, but its next stop was London, where it opened in October 1992 and scored a hit. It was during the London run that the original-cast album was recorded.

Kiss of the Spider Woman finally made it to Broadway on May 3, 1993, with the same principal performers and proved to be worth the wait. The New York reviews were much better (even Frank Rich, whose 1990 review had been particularly scathing, found some good things to say about the show), and Carver, Crivello, and Rivera all won Tony Awards, as did McNally's book and Kander & Ebb's score. The show ultimately ran for more than two years.

So far it was a classic Broadway story about The Little Show That Could, but the surprises weren't finished. By the end of June 1994, the three Tony-winning stars had all departed, but their replacements, Howard McGillin as Molina, Brian Mitchell (later Brian Stokes Mitchell) as Valentín, and Vanessa Williams as Spider Woman/Aurora, proved to be so good that many critics reported the show, already an acclaimed hit, was actually better with the new cast.

Apparently Drabinsky agreed, because in the fall of 1994 he asked me to produce a replacement-cast album, and on December 4 we went into the studio. (We returned on December 11 for some more work—one advantage of a replacement-cast album is less-pressing deadlines.)

I deliberately didn't listen to the original-cast album before setting to work on my own recording. I was certainly curious about it—I'm a big Chita Rivera fan, I love Kander & Ebb, and plenty of people had told me how great the show was—but that wasn't the show I had been hired to record, and I didn't want that album to color my decisions in making my own recording.

It was almost thirty years before I finally listened to the original, out of simple curiosity. I knew the record had been both produced and engineered by Martin Levan, an Englishman primarily known as an innovative theatrical sound designer. He had a few previous credits as a producer, mostly on Andrew Lloyd Webber shows—notably the Broadway original-cast album of *Cats* (1982)—but that was his only other Broadway credit. Most of the others were London-cast recordings, and I don't know that I'd ever heard his work before.

Listening to the recording, all those years later, I tried to be as objective as I could, but I have to say I didn't think much of it. It struck me as a great opportunity missed.

The three leads give very strong performances, and the recording is clear and well balanced; but that's the best I can say for it.

The problem is that Levan had simply put the singers in front of a microphone and let them sing. In my opinion he didn't make much effort to tell the story of the show, or to capture the unique atmosphere that defines *Kiss of the Spider Woman* as a one-of-a-kind musical (as most Kander & Ebb shows are) that lives or dies by its bruising story, its tormented characters, and its darkly romantic tone, none of which comes across in the original-cast album.

The differences are most pronounced when it comes to Chita. As always, she sings beautifully, but her songs are different in kind from the ones sung by Carver and Crivello as Molina and Valentín, because in the context of the play they don't actually happen—they're Molina's fantasies. They're snippets from movies he's seen featuring the actress Aurora and at face value don't have anything to do with the story. When Levan recorded her simply standing in front of a microphone, he didn't capture sonically the essence of the character. She is not real. She is a figment of Molina's fantasies.

It's rare for me to get a chance to sit back, listen, and find out what somebody else brought to a project that I came in late for. The only previous time I'd had that experience had been with *A Little Night Music*; in the end I preferred Goddard's recording, mostly because I liked the American cast better than the British cast—but it was also a beautifully produced recording.

As for *Spider Woman*, in my opinion, I think this revival had the better cast!

As Brian Stokes Mitchell, Brian Mitchell would later become one of Broadway's biggest stars, with three Tony nominations as Best Actor in a Musical and one as Best Actor in a Play between 1999 and 2003, including a win for his performance in *Kiss Me, Kate* (2000). Brian was not particularly well known in 1995, but he was on his way up, having previously replaced Greg Hines in *Jelly's Last Jam*. Valentín is another demanding role because he's so angry and bigoted that it can be hard for an audience to take to him. But Brian's performance was absolutely brilliant. He did a wonderful job tracing Valentín's arc from his hostile, tough-as-nails earlier scenes to the more human, more vulnerable man he is by the end of the show.

As for Vanessa, she was making her Broadway debut. She'd majored in musical theater at Syracuse University but had left in 1983 before completing her degree (she ultimately got it in 2008). She had gotten nice reviews for her work in two professional productions in 1985 and 1989, but Broadway was definitely a big step up.

The year before joining *Kiss of the Spider Woman*, she'd had her first No. 1 single with "Save the Best for Last," which she sang live at the 1993 Grammy Awards. (I was there, nominated three times for *Crazy for You*, *Jelly's Last Jam*, and *The Secret Garden*, though I lost to Jay Saks and *Guys and Dolls*.)

John Kander was there the whole day, smiling all the way through the sessions. He and David Krane, who orchestrated and arranged the dance music, were the only two of the creative team who came back to the studio for the replacement-cast sessions.

The editing and mixing were a lot of fun because the recording is full of sound effects and unusual acoustic textures—prisoners screaming in the distance, sirens going off, dream sequences, etc. We brought Vanessa's vocals in and out as if in Molina's dreams.

One of my fondest memories of this recording is that the sessions were at a studio in New York and were going very, very well—we were actually on schedule! So when the singers and the orchestra musicians went out for dinner, John Kander and I opted not to go with them. We'd been there for nine hours, so we were tired but happy, and we just sat there in the studio where we had paper cups and where we sipped from a bottle of scotch.

It wasn't me who brought the bottle; it was either John or somebody else, but there it was. It was a most enjoyable time.

Swinging on a Star (1996)

One of the ironies of the songwriting trade is that there's more money to be made in Hollywood than on Broadway, but far more fame to be achieved on Broadway than in Hollywood. A few top names used to move back and forth, including Irving Berlin, the Gershwins, and Cole Porter, who had all made their names on Broadway before cashing in at the movies, but most Hollywood songwriters labored in relative obscurity. On Broadway the songwriters' names would often be above the title; on the big screen Judy Garland, Fred Astaire, or Bing Crosby would have the starring slot, with most songwriters consigned to the small print—I think only Berlin was routinely listed above the title.

One of those songwriters was Johnny Burke (1908–1964), a lyricist whose most frequent partner was composer Jimmy Van Heusen. If you weren't in the business, Burke's name wouldn't ring a bell—but millions of people know his songs, including "Going My Way," "I've Got a Pocketful of Dreams," "Misty," "Moonlight Becomes You," "Pennies from Heaven," "The Road to Morocco," "Scatterbrain," and the Oscar-winning "Swinging on a Star."

Burke took one shot at Broadway, with *Donnybrook!* (1961), for which he wrote both music and lyrics, but it was a disappointment, lasting only eight weeks. Three years later he died suddenly of a heart attack at fifty-five. As rock 'n' roll took over the airwaves, Burke was largely forgotten.

There were people who remembered him and his music, though, notably his widow, Mary Burke Kramer, whose stage name had been Marissa Mason. She'd been a replacement Liesl in *The Sound of Music*, and she and Burke had met when she was in the ensemble of *Donnybrook!* She was the impetus behind *Swinging on a Star*, the Broadway revue of Burke's songs that opened on October 22, 1995, and ran for ninety-six performances.

Frank Military, head of Warner Chappell, got me involved in this one. Warner Chappell controlled the rights to Burke's songs, and Frank felt that a cast recording would boost the value of the Burke catalog. It was on a tiny label, After 9 Records, so I don't know that it got a lot of distribution, but it was a good project with very good material.

The show was an intimate revue, presented in the Music Box Theatre, a small house well suited to this sort of production. It featured a young, enthusiastic cast of seven; Terry Burrell and Lewis Cleale stand out in my memory, many years later, but the whole cast was excellent. Michael McGrath turned out to be the biggest name of the seven, in retrospect; he would go on to earn two Tony nominations, winning for *Nice Work If You Can Get It* (2012).

The show had no plot. It was a series of seven scenes in which Burke's songs were performed very effectively in period settings—a 1920s speakeasy, a 1940s USO show, a 1950s supper club, and so forth. It made for a very enjoyable evening at the theater.

Next to recording a live event, recording a jukebox revue may be the easiest thing for me to do. These shows deal in nostalgia, so you want to capture the feel of the period from which the music comes. Barry Levitt's orchestrations and vocal arrangements were very good, with a nice ear for the sound of the period.

So this was an easy show to handle. I cut in a little bit of dialogue to establish each of the seven settings, but basically the hard work had already been done for me by

Barry (who was also the conductor), by the cast, and of course, by Johnny Burke and his various collaborators.

My favorite memories of this project include meeting Mary Burke Kramer, who was very pleased that her late husband was getting the attention he deserved.

Victor/Victoria (1995)

Since movies learned to talk, one of the favorite pastimes on Broadway has been bemoaning the great stars whom Hollywood has lured away from Broadway, never to return. Fans of the dramatic stage mourn the departures of Marlon Brando, Paul Newman, and Meryl Streep; lovers of the Broadway musical bewail the loss of Fred Astaire, Dick Van Dyke, and Barbra Streisand.

In the early 1990s, however, the buzz began, first mutedly and then triumphantly. One of musical theater's most iconic lost stars was returning: Julie Andrews was on her way back to Broadway.

A child star in her native England, Andrews was blessed with a silvery voice that seemed appropriate for everything from Christmas carols to show tunes to folk songs to risqué music-hall numbers. She got her start singing for the troops in World War II and after the war proved herself in pantomimes, musical-hall revues, radio, and television. At thirteen she sang a solo before the King and Queen of England at the London Palladium. Andrews was only eighteen when she debuted on Broadway playing Polly Browne in Sandy Wilson's *The Boy Friend* (1954), which had been a hit (starring Anne Rogers) on London's West End the previous year.

From there Andrews went on to a career-making performance in Lerner & Loewe's *My Fair Lady* (1956), the most successful Broadway show of its era. Rodgers & Hammerstein wrote the television musical *Cinderella* (1957) especially for her, and she reteamed with Lerner & Loewe for a second hit, creating the role of Guinevere in *Camelot* (1960).

The lure of Hollywood was too much to resist, however. Broadway fans breathed a sigh of relief when they heard Warner Bros. had rejected Andrews as the star of the big-screen adaptation of *My Fair Lady* (1964), in favor of the more bankable Audrey Hepburn; it seemed as if more Broadway shows still lay in her future—but their relief was premature. Walt Disney snapped up Andrews to make her film debut in *Mary Poppins* (1964), a performance for which she won an Oscar as Best Actress. When the film of Rodgers & Hammerstein's *The Sound of Music* (1965), starring Andrews as Maria von Trapp, became the year's highest-grossing film, it was only too clear that Julie Andrews was a movie star now and wouldn't be coming back to Broadway.

And for thirty years she didn't. Occasionally there were rumors attaching her to various upcoming shows, but none of them ever panned out. Settled in Hollywood with her family (her second husband was filmmaker Blake Edwards), Andrews seemed to have no second thoughts about having left Broadway behind.

In the early 1990s, however, rumors began to circulate that Edwards, along with his favorite screen composer, Henry Mancini, and lyricist Leslie Bricusse, was working on a Broadway adaptation of their hit screen musical, *Victor/Victoria*. Andrews had starred in the 1982 movie, and the word spread with increasing confidence that when *Victor/Victoria* came to Broadway, Andrews would come with it.

When in 1993 Andrews appeared in the Off-Broadway Sondheim revue *Putting It Together*, it was an open secret that she was there to regain her stage legs. *Victor/Victoria* previewed in the summer and fall of 1995, first in Minneapolis and then in Chicago, and on October 25, 1995, it opened at the Marquis Theatre in New York. Julie Andrews was back on Broadway, and the whole world welcomed her home.

Unfortunately, the welcome for *Victor/Victoria* didn't match the welcome for its star. Mancini had died in 1994, leaving the score for the show unfinished; Frank Wildhorn was brought in to provide the rest of the songs, but the consensus was that the new songs in the musical didn't live up to the Mancini/Bricusse songs from the movie. The book was still being substantially rewritten up to and even after opening night, but the reviews were glowing for Andrews and good enough for the show to run—if she stayed in it.

That message came through loud and clear when the show received only one Tony nomination, for Andrews. Although she was considered a shoo-in, she declined the nomination because she felt the rest of the cast and crew had been "egregiously overlooked." She also refused an invitation to perform on the Tony Awards broadcast.

Despite Andrews's own belief in the show, it was clear her presence was the only thing keeping it open. When she took a four-week vacation in early 1997, she was replaced by another iconic star, Liza Minnelli—and ticket sales plummeted, picking up only when Andrews returned. When she left the show for good in June 1997, plagued with vocal problems, she was replaced by another big-name star, Raquel Welch, and nonetheless the show closed in July, after a good-but-not-great run of 734 performances.

That I got to record this show was due only to happenstance. It was originally going to be done by Jay Saks, who had produced at least two previous recordings with Julie (including the original-cast album for *Putting It Together*) and was a big favorite of hers. For some reason he couldn't do it, however, so he turned it over to me.

This was another one on which I had very little lead time. I saw the show only a couple times before the session, but I could see that the recording would have its challenges. The score was uneven; I particularly disliked "Paris Makes Me Horny," which struck me as simply vulgar. The bones of the story were good, and I could see some opportunities to shape the recording into a dramatic experience.

The biggest asset of the show was, of course, Julie herself. She brought so much charm and personality to the role of Victoria/Victor that she pulled it off. I decided I'd have to build my recording around her performance, the same way the show had been built.

Right away, Julie got what I was trying to do. She hadn't made a recording of a book musical since 1960, but I explained the idea of making the story and characters discernible from the recording, and she was excited about it. I remember her saying, during one scene, "Tom, should I turn my back, so it sounds like I'm coming from further away on this one?" I said, "Yes, that would be a good idea," and it was—but what I really liked about it was she was thinking the same way I was. She was completely into this as a project, she really enjoyed trying to serve the story and not just the songs. She was as easy to work with as anyone I've ever known.

There was one unusual aspect of the recording, as far as Julie was concerned. She sang very well and didn't need a great number of takes, but she took some extra editing because apparently, when she sang in the movies, the editors would remove the sound of her breathing. This had left Julie very conscious of it, and she wanted each inhalation taken out.

This wasn't at all difficult to do in the mixing process but it was time-consuming. She took a lot of breaths.

Robert Preston was, of course, Julie's costar in the movie, playing the warm-hearted gay cabaret singer who talks Victoria into disguising herself as the female impersonator "Victor," a great performance that earned him an Oscar nomination. He'd died in 1987, and the role was taken in the musical by Tony Roberts. Tony is a good actor, but his delivery was a little pompous for my taste; he didn't get the big-brother vibe that Preston had in the movie.

Michael Nouri played the romantic lead, the mob boss played by James Garner in the movie, and he was very good.

The biggest problem I had on this session didn't involve people, but the room we were in. For whatever reason I can't remember, we were unable to book a recording studio that was large enough for the size of the cast and orchestra. We ended up in a studio in the Edison Hotel that was simply too small. There was a little corridor that led from the control room to the actual studio, and I wound up setting up mikes in that corridor and putting the chorus there.

James Nichols, a wonderful engineer, worked the recording session. There were some technical problems on the session, but they didn't involve Jim. It was the people who worked at the studio, and it got to the point where I had to call a time out and tell the technicians I wouldn't start up again until they'd gotten things straightened out. They were trying to fix it on the fly, while we were recording, and it just wasn't working. Once we shut things down, it didn't take them long to identity and resolve the problems, but it was aggravating.

The conductor was Ian Fraser, who also did the vocal arrangements. I had worked with him twenty-five years earlier, when he was the music director for the film *Scrooge*. This time he drove me crazy by insisting we make a video of him conducting each take. Julie wanted to allow for the possibility of overdubbing if she couldn't get what she wanted during the session, and I think Ian was worried he might not be there for that and wanted her to be able to watch him on the screen. This made no sense to me because once the material was edited, Ian's video would no longer match the audio. I told him we couldn't do it, and he eventually agreed, but having that conversation also cost time.

Blake Edwards was there for the recording session in his capacity as director but didn't participate in it much at all. He was in bad shape, confined to a wheelchair by chronic fatigue syndrome. When it came time to approve the final mix, it wasn't Blake who came out to Master Sound in Astoria to listen to it for the final blessing but his producing partner, Tony Adams.

36

Trips to Chicago and Alaska

Chicago (1998)

If things continue as they are, *Chicago* will surpass *The Phantom of the Opera* and become the longest-running show in Broadway history sometime in 2031. This may not happen—that's seven years from this writing, and seven years is a long time—but it may well. And I think I can safely say that back when the show opened in 1975, or even when the current revival opened in 1996, nobody saw that coming.

The story of *Chicago* dates back almost a century to Chicago itself. It's based on the separate 1924 murder trials of Beulah Annan and Belva Gaertner, each of whom was charged with shooting her lover. The cases were heavily sensationalized in the press. The two were acquitted within two weeks of each other.

Maurine Dallas Watkins of *The Chicago Tribune* immediately recognized the lurid story, reeking of liquor, sex, and violence, as a potential play, and in 1926 *Chicago* became a Broadway hit. The fame-obsessed characters Roxie Hart and Velma Kelly were thinly disguised versions of Annan and Gaertner, and several other prominent figures in the trials also were fictionalized.

Two film versions followed: Cecil B. DeMille's silent *Chicago* (1927) and William Wellman's *Roxie Hart* (1942), starring Ginger Rogers. The play had been extravagantly hard-nosed and cynical, but Hollywood studios were expected to be moral and uplifting (particularly after the adoption of the Production Code in 1934), so the movies were softer in tone: DeMille's Roxie is punished for her crime, and Wellman's is unjustly accused.

The idea of making the play into a musical originated with actress/dancer Gwen Verdon, who suggested it to her husband, Bob Fosse, in the early 1960s. When Fosse made Watkins an offer for the rights, however, she turned him down; with the passage of time, her heirs proved more amenable, and Fosse teamed with Kander & Ebb to create the show.

As director, choreographer, and (with Fred Ebb) coauthor of the book, Fosse was the show's guiding spirit, and he had no interest in being moral or uplifting. He,

Kander, and Ebb went straight for the seamy side, creating a show that was as much about sex and celebrity as it was about crime—and crucially, they chose to tell the story in a highly stylized form, modeling the songs on vaudeville numbers and frequently breaking the fourth wall to talk directly to the audience.

Chicago: A Musical Vaudeville opened on Broadway on June 3, 1975, with Verdon as Roxie, Chita Rivera as Velma, and Jerry Orbach as celebrity attorney Billy Flynn. The critics were ambivalent, typically praising the songs and Fosse's flamboyant choreography but finding the story and characters unsettling, even off-putting. The show was nominated for most of the important Tony Awards but—in a busy Broadway year dominated by *A Chorus Line*—it won none.

Nonetheless the show was a solid hit, running for more than two years and touring the United States. After it closed, there were sporadic professional productions in locations as far-flung as Sydney, London, and Los Angeles—but not New York.

But by 1996 *Chicago* could fairly be described as one of "the rarely heard works of America's most important composers and lyricists"—to quote the mission statement of the Encores! series at New York's City Center, which every year presents three semi-staged productions of overlooked musicals from Broadway's past. In 1996, its third season, the chosen shows were Cole Porter's *DuBarry Was a Lady* (1939), Kurt Weill and Ogden Nash's *One Touch of Venus* (1943), and Kander & Ebb's *Chicago*.

The four principal roles in *Chicago* were played by established Tony- and Oscar-winning stars: Ann Reinking (Roxie), Bebe Neuwirth (Velma), Joel Grey (Amos, Roxie's sad-sack husband), and James Naughton (Billy). Reinking, a Fosse protégé re-created the choreography "in the style of Bob Fosse."

The Encores! production opened on May 2, 1996, and was a hit with critics and audiences alike. The show reopened on Broadway on November 14 and became a sensation. The cynicism, coldness, and obsession with fame that critics had complained about in 1975 seemed timely in the age of O.J. Simpson and reality television, and the stripped-down production focused the show and gave it a compelling intimacy. *Chicago* won five major Tony Awards and settled into a Broadway run that, as of this writing, has lasted for more than twenty-seven years.

I was very familiar with *Chicago* when, in 1998, I was asked to produce the cast album for its London production, which had opened in late 1997. Back in 1975 I'd seen the show during its Philadelphia tryouts; Mike Berniker and I went down to Philadelphia to evaluate the show for Columbia, and frankly neither of us was all that impressed. I appreciated the quality of the score, of course, and the choreography was dazzling, but I found it cold.

A sidebar: In 1988, while I was with MCA, I had worked with the classical-music radio station WQXR-FM on *The WQXR/MCA Classics Listener's Guide*, a series of music-appreciation recordings that I wrote, produced, and narrated as a joint project with the station. In doing this I got to know Warren Bodow, longtime president of WQXR, and eight years later he asked me if I'd be interested in producing a few programs with Bob Jones, who hosted a show called *WQXR on Broadway*. Each program would focus on a single Broadway show.

Well, I had some free time, and having established myself as a record producer and a concert producer, I thought it might be fun to be a radio producer for a little while.

So I did five or six of these programs with Bob. One was focused on *Chicago* and was timed to coincide with the opening of the revival on Broadway.

I prepared for these programs very thoroughly: I looked up some 1924 newspaper accounts of the original, real-life story, I watched *Roxie Hart*, and I tried to weave together the documented history with its later musicalization. I even put together some audio clips from the movie to go with the songs from the show, but the station wouldn't let me use the movie material because it might pose legal issues. Even so, it was a good radio program, and I got to know the show even better, which, unexpectedly, turned out to be useful a decade or so later.

It was Bill Rosenfield, vice president of A&R for RCA, who called me about doing the London-cast recording of the show. That was surprising, of course, because at the time Jay Saks produced nearly all of RCA's cast recordings. I don't recall why Jay was unavailable.

Whatever the reason, I liked the idea. I'd had a considerable history with Kander & Ebb but almost always around the edges. At that time, the only original-cast album of theirs I'd ever recorded was *70, Girls, 70,* back in 1971.

After I went through the script, I came away feeling there was a lot more good stuff in *Chicago* not in Jay's recording that should be on ours. Bill Rosenfield was skeptical. He didn't think John Kander would buy it.

So I ran it all by Kander. We had a very nice visit. He enthusiastically understood and approved of everything I wanted to do.

That meant I could make the album I wanted to make, which included a lot of additional material for Roxie. I added some great bits of dialogue that hadn't been recorded before—the most famous one being, "I gotta pee"—but the biggest addition was her spoken introduction to her song, "Roxie." It's a great song, which onstage is prefaced by a long monologue about her life, her dreams of fame, and her relationships with men. Roxie delivers the speech straight to the audience, backed only by a simple orchestral vamp. It's three minutes long and it's fabulous.

This is an American show, set in the American past, but I think the British, with their predatory tabloid press and their own celebrity culture, had no problem understanding it. Certainly the London cast understood it. What amazed me most about them was that none of them had English (or, in the case of Ute Lemper's Velma, German) accents. They all did some variety of American English. They'd be talking like themselves between takes, but the moment the tape rolled, they spoke like Americans.

Ruthie Henshall (Roxie) was making her first American recording. Her American accent was kind of Southern, more like Tennessee than Chicago, but she definitely sounded American.

Ute had lived in New York for many years, and after playing Velma in London (and winning an Olivier Award, the English equivalent of a Tony, for her work) went on to play the same role in New York. Her Velma has a decadent, louche quality that I liked very much.

I wasn't previously familiar with Henry Goodman, but he was wonderful as Billy, with a seductive, sleazy air that fit the part of a celebrity lawyer very well. There's a lazy, unhurried quality to his crooning that really stands out.

We recorded *Chicago* at what was formerly CBS Studios, a great studio on Whitfield Street in London where I'd done a lot of work over the years. The facility has passed through various hands since I first worked there in the 1960s, including stints under the Hit Factory and Sony Music, and these days it's called Whitfield Street Studios; whatever the name on the front of the building, it's still a great place to record.

The American producer of the Broadway show, Barry Weissler, came over to England for the sessions. I knew Barry and Francine, his wife and production partner, because they'd also been the producers of the *Zorba* revival. I had a very pleasant relationship with them both.

John Kander did not come over for the sessions but instead sent somebody, kind of a roving music director, to serve as his emissary and make sure everything went all right musically. Fortunately the guy never interfered, but I still didn't like having anybody looking over my shoulder. Nothing bad happened, but the lingering sense that something might happen wasn't pleasant.

It was one of the best orchestras I've ever encountered, and the musicians had that 1920s, jazz-swing idiom down cold.

We had a high-caliber team on that session. The engineer was a highly regarded man named Mike Ross-Trevor. We had worked together before. Mary Jo Little from RCA's London office volunteered to take all my notes for me. She sat next to me and took down virtually every word I spoke, mumbled, or murmured, so later, when I went to edit and mix it, all those comments were there.

I edited and mixed the recording at Master Sound, in Astoria, where the mastering engineer was Ben Rizzi, who has since died. His assistant was David Merrill, with whom I continue to work to this day. David is the most inspired engineer I've ever worked with, and I've worked with some great ones. Lately he's doing more and more of his own producing as well.

Possibly the world wasn't ready for this show in 1975. I wasn't enthusiastic when I saw it for the first time. But when I saw the revival, I realized at once what it could be for a new recording, and I think the album we ended up with captured the tone of the show just about perfectly.

King Island Christmas (1999)

King Island is a volcanic outcropping about forty miles off the western coast of Alaska, not far from the maritime border with Russia. It's uninhabited today, but back in the 1950s it was still home to several hundred Ugiuvaŋmiut natives who lived in houses built on stilts because the island terrain was so steep. The island has no port, and in those days was accessible only by massive, walrus-skin native boats called oomiaks. When freighters arrived with passengers and cargo, they would ride at anchor as the oomiaks, manned by locals, went out to meet them.

In December 1951 the last freighter of the season, before the Bering Sea froze and rendered the island unapproachable, anchored off the island, but the oomiaks were unable to cast off due to a storm. Aboard the ship was the island's only clergyman, Father Carroll; if the ship was forced to turn back, he would turn back too, and there would be no Christmas services on the island that year. The ship sailed around to the calmer waters on the lee side of the island, where an oomiak could pick up Father Carroll—but the only way for the oomiak to reach those calmer waters was for it to be carried over the island's central mountain, an arduous, dangerous journey, even without the burden of a boat weighing tons. Ultimately the whole village banded together to carry the oomiak over the mountain. Father Carroll was brought ashore, and Christmas went on as scheduled.

I don't tell this story out of my own knowledge of Alaskan local history, of which I have none! I know it only because author Jean Rogers retold the story as a children's book called *King Island Christmas* (1985), and playwright/lyricist Deborah Brevoort (who knew the story from years of living in Alaska) teamed with composer David Friedman to turn it into what its creators called "an oratorio for the stage." It had its world premiere at Juneau's Perseverance Theater in 1997.

I didn't know Jean Rogers or Deborah Brevoort, but David Friedman was a longtime conductor and arranger, both on Broadway and at Disney Studios in Hollywood. He'd contributed to several big Disney projects, including *Beauty and the Beast* and *Aladdin*. There were several producers involved in this show, which they were hoping to bring to Broadway after concert readings under the aegis of New Dramatists in 1997 and 1998. It was Lee Moskov who got in touch with me—possibly at the suggestion of orchestrator Peter Matz, whom I knew from *Harold Sings Arlen (with Friends)* and *Of Thee I Sing*—but she had a number of partners, including Anne Strickland Squadron and Jessica Levy. Their idea was to record a concept album, a sort of demonstration recording to promote the show to prospective investors, and to do it with top Broadway talent.

That they certainly did. The leading roles were played by Chuck Cooper (a Tony winner for Cy Coleman's *The Life*) and Marin Mazzie, the original Clara in Sondheim's *Passion* and at the time a Tony nominee as Best Leading Actress for her performance in *Ragtime*. The narrator was Paolo Montalban, a very talented Filipino-American who had just starred as the prince in the 1997 television movie *Rodgers & Hammerstein's Cinderella*. Future Oscar winner J. K. Simmons played the ship's captain.

Friedman wrote some very good music for this show, but he'd have been better served with somebody else conducting it. He was very literal in his conducting, insisting that every passing syncopation be played not loosely, as is usually the case, but meticulously accurately in terms of rhythm. I thought it took some of the spontaneity out of the music. But he was the composer, and he knew what he wanted.

He also kicked up a big fuss about Peter's orchestrations. I knew Peter was an excellent arranger, and I didn't see anything wrong with the orchestrations. Nevertheless, not very long before the first session, David decided he didn't like them and wanted them all rewritten.

Now, this was a pretty good show, but it wasn't *The Phantom of the Opera*, it wasn't playing on Broadway or anywhere else, and the whole recording was basically a loss leader—money being spent with no hope of immediate return. Lee Moskov and her partners had paid Peter something like seventy thousand dollars for the existing orchestrations, and she didn't like the idea of telling their backers they were throwing away seventy thousand dollars' worth of orchestrations. So she took me aside and asked me to see what I could do.

I arranged a meeting with Peter and David, and I said, "Let's get it all out onto the table. David, what is it you're looking for that so far hasn't been communicated?" We spent several hours sitting there, with David and Peter talking while I listened. In the end, Peter only needed to make minor adjustments, David was sufficiently happy, and I'd saved the producers seventy thousand dollars.

King Island Christmas didn't make it to Broadway, but the recording is very good because the cast was excellent, especially Chuck (who shortly thereafter married Deborah Brevoort) and Marin. It had a good orchestra of forty-two players, more than you find on a typical cast album. The sessions took several days simply because there was so much music, but things went smoothly—Peter and David seemed to be on the same wavelength by this time. We recorded it at Master Sound, and it came out well, although I doubt many people have heard it.

37

Lerner & Loewe, Live

BY THE 2000S MY CAREER WAS WELL PAST THE HALF-CENTURY MARK, and I could point with pride to my work on shows by most of the titans of Broadway history. There was an obvious gap in my discography, however, when it came to Alan Jay Lerner and Frederick Loewe. In my entire career I'd recorded only one Lerner & Loewe song, when Thomas Hampson sang the title song from *Gigi* on a studio album I produced.

I admired their shows a great deal, but I'd never worked on a Lerner & Loewe show, and if you'd asked me in 2006 if I ever would, I'd have told you, "Probably not." If you'd told me that, two years later, I'd have worked on their two biggest hits, I'd have said you were crazy.

But then, one day in late 2006, my telephone rang.

My Fair Lady (2007)

I've talked about the widening ripples of impact created by *Follies in Concert*, in my career and in the wider world of American musical theater. One of them was that once Ted Chapin and I talked the New York Philharmonic into doing a musical, they were hooked.

By 2007 the Philharmonic's musicals program had become a finely honed machine, often steered by producer/director Lonny Price, whom I remembered as the original Charley in *Merrily We Roll Along*. He'd long since grown up, and his Philharmonic productions of *Sweeney Todd* (2000), *Candide* (2004), and *Passion* (2005) had been very well received.

For 2007, however, things were out of kilter. First a planned concert version of *Company*, to be directed by Lonny, had been canceled due to a Broadway revival of the show. They pivoted to *My Fair Lady,* only to have Lonny also become unavailable due to his commitment to direct a Broadway revival of Jones & Schmidt's *110 in the Shade*.

That call in late 2006 was an invitation to come in and meet with Zarin Mehta, president and executive director of the Philharmonic, and his vice president of artistic planning, Matías Tarnopolsky.

"We would like you to produce this concert," they said. "So far, we've got just two people, Kelsey Grammer to play Henry Higgins and Rob Fisher to conduct. Otherwise, we're leaving the casting and everything else in your hands."

So I had a star, a conductor, a budget, and an opening date—March 7, 2007, less than three months away. Everything else was up to me.

My Fair Lady has several juicy roles, but at its heart it's a teacher-student story, the tale of Professor Henry Higgins turning Eliza the flower girl into a lady, while at the same time she turns him into a human being. I had been given my Higgins, and now I needed my Eliza—and I had my eye on a perfect candidate.

At thirty, Kelli O'Hara was just breaking through into what would become a major Broadway career. She'd received Tony nominations for her performances in *The Light in the Piazza* (2005) and *The Pajama Game* (2006), and she was a gifted actress and singer. Equally important, she was a confident performer who seemed unlikely to crumble under the inevitable comparisons to Julie Andrews's legendary performance as the original Eliza. When Kelli signed on, we checked off a big item on our list.

Next on that list was a director. If *Follies in Concert* had taught me anything, it was how crucial it was to have the right person at the helm. Herb Ross had turned the cast of *Follies* from a chaotic bunch of strangers into a smoothly functioning company; Herb had died in 2001, though, so I needed to find a new Herb.

It was Rob Fisher who pointed me toward James Brennan, who had done *My Fair Lady* before and had also worked with Kelli previously. Most of all, he shared Herb's gift of instilling confidence in his cast, a nebulous but crucial ability to convince high-strung artists that it was all going to come together. I haven't gotten the chance to watch too many stage directors at work, but in Herb and Jim I think I've seen two of the best.

I could now turn my attention to filling out our cast. We couldn't entice actors with large fees—*My Fair Lady* involved at least two weeks of rehearsal and three performances, plus whatever time they had to invest in learning their parts, but the top fee for anyone on the project was five thousand dollars—and we needed people who were available on only one or two months' notice. Nonetheless, we lined up a top-flight cast to support Kelsey and Kelli.

Colonel Pickering is the Watson to Higgins's Sherlock Holmes, a bluff, good-natured former military officer whose warmth helps to offset Higgins's total lack of consideration for others. I thought my friend Charles Kimbrough—who had played Jim Dial on the hit series *Murphy Brown* from 1988 to 1998—would make a great Pickering, and he did. He and Kelsey were very funny together.

I'd never made a recording with Brian Dennehy, but I knew him better than just about anybody in the cast because he and I had been neighbors in West Gilgo Beach, New York, for many years. It's a small community, so we knew each other pretty well, and somehow, when I looked at him, I saw Alfred P. Doolittle, Eliza's hard-drinking, folk-philosophizing father. It wasn't an obvious choice—in the movies Brian usually played tough cops, often corrupt ones—but I went with my gut, and it worked out great.

The only issue with Brian was he was a big man who, at almost seventy, had problems with his legs. He was a great actor with a strong singing voice, but he wasn't going to be dancing. So our talented and resourceful choreographer, Peggy Hickey, came up with some great-looking dances for "With a Little Bit of Luck" and "Get Me to the Church on Time" that basically had Alfie's buddies dancing around him, not with him. If you looked for it, you could see that he wasn't moving much, but it still worked.

Marni Nixon occupies a special place in *My Fair Lady* lore because when Audrey Hepburn played Eliza on the big screen, it was Marni doing all her singing—as she also had for Deborah Kerr in *The King and I* (1956) and *An Affair to Remember* (1957), and for Natalie Wood in *West Side Story* (1961).

I'd known Marni ever since she turned up at my RCA office to pitch an album of Arnold Schoenberg's cabaret songs, which we did indeed release in 1975. We became friends, and in 1988, when Sheldon Harnick and I were working on *That Pig of a Molette* and we needed demos, Marni and another one of my friends, Tim Jerome, got together with me to rehearse the songs and record those demos for us.

It would have been poetic justice to have Marni sing Eliza, but she was in her seventies by then. I wanted to honor her association with the show, though, so I hired her as Mrs. Higgins, Henry's acerbic mother. It's a small part, but one with some great lines—she absolutely turns Higgins into her straight man—and Marni had a lot of fun with it.

Tim Jerome could have played any of the male parts, but I ended up asking him to play Zoltan Karpathy, the pompous Hungarian dialectician who incorrectly exposes Eliza as a Hungarian princess at the embassy ball. As usual, Tim was perfect in the part. The only problem I had with him is that he loves talking politics with anyone he runs into, and he's very far to the left. One day I overheard him starting up a political conversation with Kelsey, who I knew was a right-winger, and I had to steer Tim away and say, "Not with Kelsey, Tim. This guy's not on your side."

I wanted Doris Roberts for the relatively small role of Higgins's down-to-earth housekeeper, Mrs. Pearce. Doris was eighty-two at this point, but she had just finished her run on *Everybody Loves Raymond* (1996–2005), and she really was a star. Her son was negotiating on her behalf, however, and he wanted more than we could offer—a lot more. So much as I liked her for the part, we had to move on. It worked out well, though. Somebody in the cast suggested Meg Bussert, and she was perfect.

The one role I didn't have to cast was the one that would have been the hardest. Henry Higgins is an iconic role and a very large, very difficult part; the character must be likable despite being (particularly to contemporary eyes) rude, contemptuous, and abusive to everybody, and especially to Eliza.

Kelsey did very well, though. He took direction readily, worked terribly hard, and was immaculately prepared. His performance was very much in the vein of Rex Harrison's original. He thought Harrison was perfect in the role, and he never aspired to bring something new or revealing to the part. He did Higgins the way Harrison had done it, and he was terrific. And beyond question, he was a better singer than Harrison.

Kelsey probably took the role in part because of the chance to perform with the New York Philharmonic. He'd spent a good part of his youth in New Jersey and was a big fan of classical music, and one day when he and I were shooting the breeze, he told me he loved classical music so much because his mother used to take him to Leonard Bernstein's Young People's Concerts in the 1960s.

I don't think he ever knew my name. "Sir," he would say, and I'd answer, "Yes, Kelsey?" I don't think he ever called me "Tom" or "Mr. Shepard" or anything but "Sir." He was extremely friendly, though, very good-natured.

From beginning to end, *My Fair Lady* was an unalloyed pleasure. Everybody got along with each other, everybody loved the material, and everybody worked their hardest because they loved working for Jim and Rob. It was a wonderful experience, and it carried over to the audience. The show just blew people away, with the audience enjoying it as much as we did.

And for once, because we weren't making a recording, I wasn't out in a truck around the corner! I sat in the house with the audience and enjoyed the show as much as they did.

When I say we weren't making a recording, I should add "not officially." We were indeed making a recording. The stage was very carefully miked for the performances, and afterward I sat with engineer Larry Rock, a very talented man who worked for the Philharmonic, and spent hours and hours choosing takes, editing the thing and mixing it.

It came out beautifully, and I had high hopes for a commercial release when I took it to CBS, which still controls the rights to *My Fair Lady*. That's when things got difficult.

The official explanation was that there was a movie remake in the works. The CBS executives were afraid our recording might cut into their sales of the soundtrack, so they declined to allow it to be released. That never made sense to me, since any royalties they lost from the soundtrack sales would be more than made up by the royalties from our sales. And seventeen years later, the movie still hasn't materialized.

Kelsey told me the real reason was that Les Moonves, who was running CBS in 2007, was fighting with him over large sums of money involved in the syndication of *Frasier* (which had been on NBC, but it was independently produced, and CBS was handling the syndication). The fighting got very personal, the story goes, and Moonves was ready to do anything that would tick Kelsey off, so he blocked our recording. Maybe that's true and maybe it isn't, but it makes more sense to me than the movie story.

Whatever their reason, I wish they'd rethink it. If they let the recording be released, even today, it would be worth a lot of money to them. It's a wonderful recording of a production that deserves to be preserved.

Camelot (2008)

The main problem with *Camelot* (1960) was, and remains to this day, the book. Alan Jay Lerner's libretto has been undergoing tweaks and revisions ever since that first production, with Lerner himself repeatedly revisiting it during the final twenty-six years of his life. When the book of a musical is revised, it's usually because of issues of cultural stereotyping; that's not the case with *Camelot*, a show whose book has been revised again and again simply because it doesn't quite come together.

All the same, through the decades *Camelot* has proven a popular and beloved show—particularly for its score. That fact, combined with the success of our *My Fair Lady*, inspired us to choose *Camelot* as the Philharmonic's next Broadway-musical-in-concert.

But as the original *Camelot* had failed to live up to the expectations generated by the extravagant success of the original *My Fair Lady*, so did our *Camelot* fall short of expectations after our *My Fair Lady* had been such a hit.

Lonny Price was back for 2008, and probably the Philharmonic ought to have thanked me profusely for an inspired rescue and then sent me on my way so that Lonny could get back to work unimpeded. Instead, presumably out of gratitude for how well I'd done my job, they came up with a dual monarchy—me as producer, Lonny as director—and that didn't really satisfy either of us.

Lonny and I got along reasonably well, but we were each used to running the show: Lonny, having already produced and directed several shows for the New York Philharmonic, expected to have a lot more input than Jim Brennan or Herb Ross had had. On paper I had the same job that I'd had the year before, but instead of the director handling the directing and me handling everything else, I kept turning around and bumping into Lonny.

Lonny and I got the job done, and the results were far from bad. Some of the problems we had were intrinsic to the project, since the book of *Camelot* is a puzzle that has never yet been solved.

It didn't help that we were immediately confronted with a casting problem that never quite got fixed. Casting King Arthur is virtually impossible because the part calls for a strong singing actor who must start out young, confused, and callow, then grow in stature, displaying by turns courage, gravitas, and moral substance, love, hatred, and anger, all in quick succession. Richard Burton had won a Tony Award as the original Arthur, but Richard Burtons are rare, and alas, we couldn't find one.

For a while it looked like Liam Neeson would be our Arthur, and I thought he could do the part very creditably, but suddenly he was no longer available. Lonny had other ideas, some of which appealed to me, but one by one they turned us down. Time was passing, Lonny wasn't getting anywhere, and I had to step in.

There was at the time an HBO show called *In Treatment*, about a therapist (Gabriel Byrne) working one-on-one with a number of different patients. I thought Byrne was very good, and it occurred to me that he might make a good King Arthur. So I pitched him to Lonny and the Philharmonic, and we all agreed—not with wild enthusiasm but more with a sense of relief.

I understood their reservations because Gabriel wasn't the obvious choice to carry a major musical. He acted extremely well, and his nuanced, ambivalent style was appropriate to Arthur, who's struggling to come to terms with who and what he is—but Gabriel couldn't sing. Music director Paul Gemignani had to work out a kind of talk-singing for Gabriel, not unlike what Rex Harrison had done in *My Fair Lady*, but without Harrison's brio.

Our initial choice for Guenevere was Audra MacDonald, and initially she was excited about the project—but she had committed to a television show, a *Grey's Anatomy* spinoff called *Private Practice*, which suddenly needed her sooner than she had anticipated. Audra would have been perfect for the role, but she was gone the way of Liam Neeson.

Once again, I came up with the answer—the only other contribution I made to the casting—but this time it didn't represent a compromise, and everybody was on board. I had been awed by Marin Mazzie on *King Island Christmas*; I knew she was an excellent singer, a wonderful actress, and a competent dancer, and I was sure she could act the part with grace, humor, and conviction. And indeed she gave us a wonderful performance, even in the duets where she was forced to rein in her vocal power to match what Gabriel could do.

She brought a tone all her own to the character. Marin was a very earthy, direct woman, with a kind of straightforward humor that played very well onstage. There was a primness, a coyness to Julie Andrews's Guenevere, and Marin didn't have that. When she sang about "the lusty month of May," you believed her.

The rest of the casting came from Lonny, and I thought most of his choices were terrific. Fran Drescher was an offbeat choice for the seductive sorceress Morgan le Fey, but her comic spin on the character was fresh and interesting. Christopher Lloyd brought goofy charm to Pellinore, and Stacy Keach had plenty of authority as Merlin. Neither Lonny nor I chose Metropolitan Opera veteran Nathan Gunn as Lancelot, as I recall—he came via the Philharmonic—but I've always liked combining operatic and theatrical voices in recordings, so why not onstage? Nathan's strong baritone was well suited to Lancelot's heroic and romantic music, and he acted the part well beyond our expectations. The scenes with him and Marin were among the best in the show.

But despite my happiness with the cast, this was a show that just never quite felt right. For one thing, while Lonny and I had both agreed, right away, that *Camelot* was the show we wanted to do, the Philharmonic was less happy about it. They didn't tell us we couldn't do it, but for some reason Zarin never was enthusiastic about it. Something about the plot of *Camelot* disturbed him. We had a small cast party after the final night, and Zarin didn't come.

For my part, I was uneasy about our trimmed-down dialogue, which I felt did not convey the story as effectively as it should. A musical really is always about the book, even in a concert version. The songs may be wonderful—most of the ones in *Camelot* are—but the book has to provide the skeleton. As I have said before, if the book doesn't work, the show won't work.

And our book only sort of worked.

There was so much in this show that did work. Except for Gabriel, the singing was wonderful, and of course Paul and the Philharmonic were at the top of their game. Marin was terrific, and Gabriel was very moving in the emotional scenes, very true. The supporting cast was excellent, and the audience clearly enjoyed the show. But it wasn't the runaway sensation *My Fair Lady* had been, and we all knew it.

The Philharmonic didn't ask me back for 2009, and I wasn't surprised. I think we all knew this two-headed leadership wasn't working, and they had a much longer relationship with Lonny than they had with me. He finally got to do his *Company* with them in 2011, with Neil Patrick Harris as Bobby, and it was very well received.

38

Yesterday, Today, and "Tomorrow"

MY PHONE WASN'T RINGING AS OFTEN in the 2000s as it had in the 1990s. It may be that my advancing age had something to do with it, but the primary reason was that fewer and fewer of my connections on Broadway and within the record industry were still at their posts. The people who had known and respected the work I'd done in the past were being replaced by younger people who didn't know me or didn't realize I was still available.

As I've said, I was never a great self-promoter. If I had been, I'd probably have recorded more shows in the 2000s. As things were, though, when my phone rang in 2013, with an offer to record a new revival of *Annie*, even I was surprised to realize it was my first Broadway show recording in eighteen years.

I had been far from idle in those years, of course. I'd made many recordings that weren't Broadway shows or cast albums, and I'd produced a couple of major concert stagings for the New York Philharmonic. Even so, I'd had more free time on my hands, and it had given me the opportunity to explore some of the unchosen pathways of my life, getting in touch with things that had been big parts of my life before I got into the record business.

Beauty and the Beast (2007)/ *The Little Mermaid* (2008)

I hadn't played the piano professionally since the summer of 1959, but in 2007 and 2008 I found myself doing just that—this time in the pit of a Broadway theater.

I was paid for my efforts, of course, but my primary motivation was simple curiosity. I'd worked with scores of Broadway orchestras, but always on my turf, always as a record producer, never as a player.

Sitting in the theater and watching or listening to the orchestra, I'd always wondered what things were like for them in their native habitat, in the darkened pit below the lip of the stage where they earned their living. With time on my hands in the mid-2000s, I decided to find out.

Apart from a Barbara Cook album of Disney songs that I'd produced, I'd had little dealings with Disney, but live stage versions of their popular animated features had become a defining feature of Broadway. As it happened, I knew somebody who was an assistant musical director on the Disney musicals, and I asked her about the possibility of my playing keyboards as a substitute in one of their orchestras. She was a little skeptical, I think, given that my last professional experience had been almost a half-century before, but I was able to demonstrate the proficiency to handle it.

So that's how one night in 2007 I found myself in the orchestra pit at the Lunt-Fontanne Theatre, waiting to begin the overture to *Beauty and the Beast*.

Lyricist/producer Howard Ashman and composer Alan Menken had been integral to the 1990s renaissance of Disney's animated features after a period of stagnation and box-office mediocrity. The studio's resurgence was driven by Ashman's belief that classic fairy tales retold as old-school Broadway musicals (a la Rodgers & Hammerstein's 1957 television musical, *Cinderella*) would appeal to audiences of all ages. Their delightful scores, as well as the Broadway-style structuring of the stories they told, made *The Little Mermaid* (1989), *Beauty and the Beast* (1991), and *Aladdin* (1992) blockbuster hits and created a formula that continues to sustain Walt Disney Pictures to the present day.

I was fortunate, therefore, to be working on *Beauty and the Beast* (and later, *The Little Mermaid* at the same theater) because their scores were in a musical language with which I was thoroughly familiar. (If it had been a rock score, forget it!)

And it was very much a challenge, despite my stylistic affinity for the music. The experience of playing the trumpet or the cello in a Broadway pit today is fundamentally the same as it was in the 1920s, but that isn't true of playing the keyboard.

To begin with, until the 1970s, the keyboard player in a Broadway orchestra would almost invariably be at a piano. Around that time, the synthesizer—an early type of electronic keyboard, which could generate the sound of many instruments or combinations of instruments—began to replace the piano in the pit. Electronic keyboards, which continue to evolve and grow ever more sophisticated, play a highly varied and very important role: as the size of Broadway orchestras has shrunk, the electronic keyboard has picked up the slack, being called on to produce dozens of different sounds over the course of a show. The keyboard can be used to beef up the string section, supply the sounds of winds and brass when the production couldn't afford to hire enough players, or reproduce the sound of an acoustic keyboard instrument like a harpsichord or a piano.

The various sounds that emanate from an orchestra keyboard are all pre-set by the orchestrator. The player follows a score the indicates all volume levels and all changes of sound. It is all very precisely worked out and it can raise havoc if, for instance, the next programmed sound is supposed to be a flute, but the keyboard player may not have caught the cue in time. When what you think is going to come out sounding like a flute instead comes out sounding like a tuba, you know you're in trouble.

Even the volume levels are tightly predetermined. Each volume level is assigned a number, which is notated in the score; you push the foot pedal down farther or less far, watching your screen, landing on that number. To add to my challenge: as a pianist, I rarely played under a conductor. As an orchestral player, all choices of tempo and interpretation are his.

Before my first performance, I spent three shows sitting in the pit next to the regular keyboard player so as to learn the routine and familiarize myself with the dangers. This is common practice among substitute show musicians because, without that preparation, playing the show means navigating many unexpected pitfalls on the fly. As things turned out, I was good enough at all this that, after three fill-in performances of *Beauty and the Beast*, I was invited back for three more on *The Little Mermaid* the following year. I was "good enough," however, not great, and it demanded a level of concentration I was not accustomed to. The closest I can come to explaining my anxieties is to think back to my final exams in college. Maybe more because during finals you can only ruin your own chances, but in a pit orchestra you can mess things up for the orchestra, the singers, and even the audience.

So it was a very good experience for me to demonstrate to myself and to others that, even in my first-ever stint in a Broadway pit, I could hold my own with top professional musicians who were all quite a bit younger than me. It gave me an even greater appreciation for the skills and professionalism of pit musicians, and especially, keyboard players!

Thespis (2008)

I've made no secret of my love for the operas of Gilbert & Sullivan, which were a pervasive element of my childhood, and especially, my Oberlin years, during which the college's Gilbert & Sullivan Players was a mainstay of my campus life. After my graduation, however, the Savoy operas took a back seat in my life—I amassed a substantial collection of G&S recordings, including many rarities, and I bonded with various fellow Savoyards who crossed my path, notably Sheldon Harnick and John Kander. But I didn't actually do any Gilbert & Sullivan for the next forty-five years, other than recording "The Buttercup Willow Affair," a symphonic medley on G&S themes that Luther Henderson put together for an instrumental album called *A Broadway Extravaganza* in 1987.

That changed in the 2000s, when I finally found the time to pursue a project I had toyed with for many years previously.

To a true Gilbert & Sullivan enthusiast there is no more tantalizing fantasy than the idea that, in some dusty attic or neglected file cabinet, someone may yet uncover the manuscript score to the opera *Thespis*, the first collaboration between W. S. Gilbert and Arthur Sullivan. It was a modest success in 1871, but the score was never published. We know Sullivan had the manuscript score with him in New York in 1879 because, in a rush to complete *The Pirates of Penzance*, he took one chorus from *Thespis* and literally pasted the pages into his score for the new opera. Since then, however, nothing has been heard of it. Gilbert published his libretto, so it survives intact, but—except for that chorus and a solo number called "Little Maid of Arcadee" that was published as sheet music, and some incidental ballet music that apparently

Sullivan later reused for a non-Gilbert project—the music for *Thespis* has vanished without a trace.

I am far from the first G&S-loving composer to have been tempted to step into Sullivan's shoes and write a new setting of Gilbert's libretto for *Thespis*, but the idea had always intrigued me, and in the mid-2000s I finally had the time to do it. It took a couple of years, but eventually I had a setting of *Thespis* that I thought was quite good. I hired four singers to perform some of my new music and auditioned it for the Manhattan-based amateur company, the Blue Hill Troupe. They were impressed, and on June 16, 2008, Blue Hill presented a semi-staged concert performance of my *Thespis*, with a two-piano accompaniment.

I really enjoyed that concert very much and was thrilled that so many people in the audience responded so enthusiastically. However, *Thespis* is a theatrical piece, and I definitely hoped to see it fully staged with a full orchestra. For some years after the concert, however, I didn't see how this might come about.

However, one of the benefits to doing new things is that it's a great way to meet new people, which in turn leads to doing other new things.

In promoting the *Thespis* concert, I'd appeared at a meeting of the Gilbert & Sullivan Society of New York, a group of G&S aficionados that meets once a month in Manhattan, and gotten to know Daniel Kravetz, who has handled the group's music for many years and often conducts shows by the various performing companies in the greater New York area.

Dan doesn't play the piano, however, and in 2011 he found himself in need of an accompanist for auditions for the Gilbert & Sullivan Light Opera Company of Long Island. Knowing I lived on Long Island, he called and asked if I might be available to help. Always interested in a chance to play Gilbert & Sullivan, I of course agreed.

That short-term job put me in contact with the company's president, David Groeger, who was intrigued when I mentioned *Thespis* in passing. Because of the missing music, *Thespis* was the only Gilbert & Sullivan opera that the company had never performed, and David thought that this might be an opportunity to remedy that. He convinced his board that the company should offer *Thespis* for its 2014 season—fully staged and with a full orchestra.

It was a great pleasure to see it staged by a group of talented amateurs, and to hear the music with my own orchestrations, the way I'd always heard it in my head. The company toured with the show around Long Island and Manhattan for the spring and summer of 2014, and I got a lot of terrific feedback from people who had seen it. I put together a CD of the production, which continues to be sold at the company's events and is still finding new listeners. I was particularly pleased when, in 2016, the music publisher G. Schirmer published a full score, orchestra parts, and a two-piano reduction.

An unexpected side benefit of this production has been my involvement with the Gilbert and Sullivan Light Opera Company of Long Island, which in various capacities continues to this day. I've music-directed a couple of touring revues, played as a fill-in pianist on several productions, served as an advisor to (and occasionally a member of) the company's board, and even found myself onstage once, as the Narrator in a 2014 production of *A Gilbert & Sullivan Christmas Carol*.

I can't say that my association with the company has been without its vexing moments, but it's been a very good experience overall. I've been able to immerse myself in Gilbert & Sullivan, which I still love as much as I did when I was six years old. I've also made a host of new friends, and it's gratifying to belong to a circle of people whose friendship has nothing to do with producing recordings, socializing with Broadway performers, producers or directors, or even winning Grammy Awards—aspects of my life of which many of the troupe are unaware.

One other ancillary benefit of my work on *Thespis* is this very book: my friend and coauthor, Gayden Wren, has been a mainstay of the Light Opera Company since the 1970s, and it was he who originally suggested that we might write a book together, so *Thespis* has proven to be a project that, fifteen years down the line, is still paying off.

Annie (2013)

Even in the 1930s heyday of child-centered movies, Broadway never had its own Shirley Temple. There were movies aplenty centered around children, but not Broadway shows. Singing kids, dancing kids, juggling kids, and Shakespeare-reciting kids were all over vaudeville, but any children who found themselves on Broadway stages were strictly window-dressing, walk-on parts in shows that were about adult stars. People loved the cute kids of *The King and I* and *The Sound of Music*, but everybody knew those shows were about Anna and the King, Maria and Captain Von Trapp. In the rare show in which the lead was a child, such as *Peter Pan (1954)* or *You're a Good Man, Charlie Brown* (1971), the alleged child was played by an adult. Even in *Oliver!* (1963), star Bruce Prochnik only looked like a lad—he was fifteen when the show opened on Broadway.

It would be more than a decade after *Oliver!* that composer Charles Strouse, lyricist Martin Charnin, and book author Thomas Meehan would come forward with *Annie*, a child-centered musical that opened a floodgate that hasn't closed to this day. Original star Andrea McArdle was only a year younger than Prochnik had been, but *Annie* became a perennial hit, with the lead role being passed to actresses as young as nine. Kids who wanted to be actors when they grew up suddenly didn't have to wait so long.

Annie ran for 2,377 performances, has been revived twice on Broadway, has been adapted into two theatrical movies and three television movies, and seems to be perennially on a national tour. It has been a mainstay of community theater and school shows for almost half a century. And by demonstrating that a musical about a kid could be a monster hit, it opened the door to such shows as *The Secret Garden*, *Wicked* (2003), *Billy Elliot* (2008), *Newsies* (2012), *Matilda* (2013), *School of Rock* (2015), and several of the Disney musicals. Since 1977 there has seldom if ever been a week in which Broadway didn't feature at least one child in a principal role.

When I was asked to produce the cast recording for the 2012 revival of *Annie*, I was of course intimately familiar with the show and its creators, having remastered the original-cast album and worked with Strouse, Charnin, and Meehan on *Annie Warbucks*.

One of the producers of *Annie Warbucks* was Dennis Grimaldi, and he and his partner, Douglas Denoff, were also involved in the revival of *Annie*. Grimaldi had liked my storybook recording of *Annie Warbucks*, and he asked me to produce the revival-cast album. They had a record label called Shout! Broadway, and this was their second release. (They had only five or six that I know of; the label didn't last long.)

This recording came out well, but I have to say that in certain respects this project was cursed. Everything took longer than it needed to take and turned out to be more difficult.

Doug and Dennis, for example, wanted me to make a storybook recording, but they decided they also wanted a conventional recording that was more or less the songs by themselves. Recording two different albums simultaneously involved a lot of extra work. Certain musical numbers, particularly the ones with President Roosevelt and his cabinet, had to be recorded in two different vocal versions, one that included interstitial dialogue between verses and another that didn't, because if you just cut the dialogue and jumped to the next verse, the underscoring wouldn't match up. Others needed alternate endings, based on whether they led to dialogue and a segue to the next song or simply jumped to the song. Accommodating the two formats didn't double the workload, but it certainly increased it.

And then, during the editing and mixing, when I had almost finished the storybook version, Dennis told me, "Put that aside, just finish the normal, straight-ahead version; we're not sure we're going to do the storybook version." I eventually finished both versions. I'd put too much work into the storybook version to simply scrap it; I still have it to this day, and it's very good, far better than the standard version, which is the only one that was released.

Martin Charnin's unhappiness with the revival was the true reason for the storybook album not coming out in 2013. The problem was that *Annie* was so much a part of Martin. He had not only written the lyrics, but also directed the original production and the 1997 revival. For some reason, however, James Lapine was hired to direct this second revival, but by the time we were making the recording Martin clearly wasn't happy.

The particular thing he objected to was that, because all the main characters in the show are from New York City, Lapine had decided to give the lead characters a New York accent—I'm tawking about a noo yawk accent, ya know? This didn't bother me, but Martin just hated it. I'm honestly not sure whether he actually hated the accents or if it wasn't also his frustration for his not having been the director, but either way the storybook version was loaded with accented dialogue, so Martin blocked it.

Martin's unhappiness colored the whole recording session. He didn't interfere—as a director himself, he understood this was Jim's show and there was nothing he could do about it—but he was clearly unhappy the whole time, and it wasn't something that you could miss.

It was a very strong cast. I thought Lilla Crawford (Annie) was awfully good. I've heard she wasn't everybody's first choice, and she had a difficult stage mother, but I had no problem with her mother, and I thought Lilla did an outstanding job. And she had a powerhouse of a voice!

The Australian actor Anthony Warlow was making his Broadway debut as Daddy Warbucks, and he was wonderful in the part. He was also very easy to work with—arguably too easy.

We recorded about half of the orchestra tracks ahead of time, without the singers, including Warlow's big ballad, "Something Was Missing." He was willing to have it done first by the orchestra, but he said that he'd like to come in early and be there when the track was being recorded, even though he wouldn't be singing. I had no problem with this, but technically it was against Equity regulations. You can't have an actor come to a session without paying him.

We rolled the dice and let him be there. I'm usually very meticulous with regard to union regulations, and I felt uncomfortable about the situation. But he came to the session with the orchestra, just to reassure himself that he and the conductor were on the same wavelength. And the next day, when we overdubbed him, he was completely at ease.

There was a separate "kid wrangler" to keep an eye on the little girls in the show, to make sure they were where they needed to be, when they needed to be, and so forth. I'm sure that was useful, but as far as I could see these kids would have been fine on their own. They were cute as hell, and they seemed very unspoiled and didn't act at all like stage brats. The wrangler must have had an easy day.

Katie Finneran, who played Miss Hannigan, was terrific in the show—and couldn't possibly have been further from the cold, scheming, ruthless character she played onstage.

A little background: We were making the recording later into the run than you'd normally do a cast album—the show opened in early November, but we didn't get into the studio until March—and the cast was already about to change. Katie was going to be leaving in May, to costar in a television show with Michael J. Fox. The TV star Jane Lynch was replacing her (as it turned out for only a couple of months). But just as I was finishing the final mix, Doug and Dennis decided we had to have Jane on the album, as well as Katie.

So this is the only original-cast album I ever heard of that includes bonus tracks in its original release. We went back into the studio to overdub Jane singing Miss Hannigan's three main songs, and we put them on the album as bonus material. Jane was fine, but Katie was better.

Jim Lapine was at the session and was helpful in working with the children, even though he wasn't that enthusiastic about the storybook version. Even the standard version probably had more dialogue than he'd have liked. The only time we'd worked together previously was on *Sunday in the Park with George*, which was also a very complex show to adapt as a recording. Jim remained very pleasant during the *Annie* sessions, but I remember him saying to me, in passing, that he preferred less dialogue.

I put a lot of effort into the storybook recording. I hadn't really gotten to know Tom Meehan during *Annie Warbucks*, but we got acquainted during *Annie*. Tom's book for the show is very skillful, sometimes very funny but definitely with a dark side—it's set in the Great Depression, and it's got poverty, hunger, child abuse, and lots of pretty dark stuff—so it was going to require a delicate touch in its adaptation. I went down to his beautiful house in Greenwich Village, where we sat at a table and went over the whole thing. I laid out what I had in mind, and generally he agreed. He suggested some changes and refinements, but basically we were in agreement all the way. By the time I left, we had it all worked out and I had a recording script that had his blessing.

The unsung hero there was Peter Lawrence, the stage manager at the Palace Theater, who took my script, assembled it into separate script pages for each of the actors, and made all the copies we needed, so that we could give them everything ahead of time and not throw it all at them at the beginning of the session. They came in knowing what they were doing, and that made a huge difference.

The people at Master Sound weren't nearly as prepared. The studio was in terrible shape. With my recording engineer, Charles Harbutt, we went in the night before we were going to record and checked everything out—all the mikes, all the patch cords, everything—and when we came back in the next morning, it was all a mess. Someone had clearly been in since we'd left, and there were mikes that didn't work or were out of place, patch cords which apparently had so much rust on them that they couldn't make firm connections.

It was particularly unfortunate because we already faced some significant technical obstacles due to when this recording was being made. The digital recording system Pro Tools—which today is the industry standard—had been around for a couple of decades in one form or another, but it was only in the late 2000s and early 2010s that it became the go-to choice for nearly all producers and engineers involved in new recordings. The assistant manager at Master Sound was not all adept at using Pro Tools.

Charles was and is an excellent engineer, and he came with a bonus: his wife is Grace Roe, a very smart woman with producing and engineering experience who used to work at Sony Classical (Irene and I were at their wedding). And for the recording of *Annie*, Grace volunteered to be my amanuensis and took copious, incredibly detailed notes of everything I said throughout the whole day—which was tremendously helpful, given the number of semi-disasters at the session.

It was a very stressful day, and one I remember very clearly. I can still see Tom, Charles, and Martin sitting side by side on a couch in the control room at Master Sound, practically under the loudspeakers, the three guys who'd created this wonderful show. Tom and Charles looking very pleased and not saying very much, Martin speaking the most but not talking about what was really bothering him.

I wasn't even aware, at that point, of a problem that would come back to haunt us in the editing. One of the important things about Pro Tools is how one assigns names and labels to each take. If you do it right, it makes life much easier on the back end; if you don't, it makes it difficult and time-consuming to figure out what you're dealing with and find what you're looking for. When Charles and I got to the editing, we discovered that the sound engineer at Master Sound had labeled each take in such a way that later, when Charles and I were doing the editing, it was very difficult to find what we were looking for. This made the editing process much slower and more cumbersome.

In the end this recording turned out well, but it was among the most frustrating recording, editing, and mixing processes that I have ever had to do. With the studio equipment being in a mess on our arrival, with the Pro Tools issues, and with Martin hating the direction of the show, plus the changing decisions regarding what kind of album we were making, this project was a real chore.

EPILOGUE

Still Putting Sound into Boxes

Anna Christie (2019)

Back in 1995 I happened to go to see an Off-Broadway show called *Ballad for a Firing Squad*, based on the story of the notorious World War I spy Mata Hari. Under its original title, *Mata Hari*, it had closed out of town in 1967. Revamped as *Ballad for a Firing Squad*, it had eked out seven performances Off-Broadway the following year, and now it was getting a revival. My old friend Martin Charnin was the lyricist, and the composer was a man named Edward Thomas, whom I had never met. I enjoyed the evening, and particularly, Thomas's music.

I didn't meet Ed Thomas on that occasion, but a few years later Sheldon Harnick called me and told me he had an extra ticket for a staged reading of *Desire Under the Elms*, a new opera based on the Eugene O'Neill play, with a libretto by Joe Masteroff and music by this same Edward Thomas. Would I like to go? "Sure," I said. It turned out to be a tremendous opera, and I was very impressed.

Sheldon and Ed were friends, so after the show we went backstage, and I met Ed. I told him how much I'd liked the opera and asked if it was being recorded. He said that it wasn't. I said that it should be. One thing led to another. Cut to 2000: I found myself producing a studio recording of *Desire Under the Elms*, which featured James Morris, Jerry Hadley, and Victoria Livengood. It was released on Naxos and was nominated for a Grammy as Best Opera Recording.

Ed and I became friends, and I subsequently recorded more of his music, which is how in February 2019 I found myself in a studio in Brooklyn, recording the original-cast album for Ed's new opera, *Anna Christie*, with a Joseph Masteroff libretto based on another classic Eugene O'Neill drama.

This wasn't a Broadway show. It was a chamber opera with a cast of five and an orchestra of thirteen. But it was musical theater, and I deployed my usual bag of tricks—positioning singers to reflect their stage positions, utilizing stereo to create movement and a sense of the stage in the listener's mind, interpolating sound effects, and so on. I told director Nancy Rhodes that this was what I'd be doing—"If there should be a foghorn, there will be a foghorn"—and she was very enthusiastic and provided valuable assistance in helping me understand the mood of individual songs and scenes as she saw them.

With David Merrill as my engineer, all the equipment worked flawlessly. Bunker Studio was small but up-to-date, and the people who ran it made sure everything went smoothly. The five cast members were terrific and very much excited about the project, and the recording itself turned out great. I had hoped it would also be Grammy-nominated; it deserved to be, but it wasn't.

Most of all, though, I enjoyed the experience of working with David, who plays Pro Tools the way Horowitz played the piano, and he even forgave me for my insisting on recording the singers working right next to each other as they had onstage. David would have rather had each singer sequestered in a different isolation booth, hearing each other and the orchestra via headphones. It would have made his job a little easier, but I wanted the performers to be able to look at each other, to feel each other's presence while they were performing.

After an extremely enjoyable session, David and I headed for my own home studio, where David set up everything we needed to do the editing and mixing with all the comforts of home. I dubbed our workspace "Shepard Sonic Laboratories."

This was when I really appreciated the freedom that comes with Pro Tools. Problems that would have been major obstacles in the 1960s or even in the 1990s were banished at the touch of a button. The pianist, for example, was occasionally out of sync with the rest of the orchestra, but David had placed a couple mikes inside the piano itself, achieving enough isolation that, thanks to Pro Tools, we could nudge the piano entrances a tiny bit earlier or later.

When we discovered I'd missed a three-note mistake by the vibraphonist, our editing and mixing session became a recording session: my Yamaha Clavinova had a vibraphone mode that was so convincing that, after David hooked the Yamaha up to his mixing console, I could play the correct three notes. Listening to our final mix, no one could tell that those notes did not come from the same vibraphone that was played on the recording session.

I was born into a world of hand-crank phonographs and have lived to see a world of iPods and streaming music, but to me they're all the same, simply the latest version of the best possible way to capture the evanescence of sound. And that's something I've always loved, and always will.

The tricks of the trade aren't what it's all about. In 1960 it was all about the music, and more than sixty years later, it still is.

Sound in a box. It still knocks me out.

APPENDIX

Discography

Note: Most of these recordings had more than one catalog number—in the 1960s for stereo and mono versions, in the 1970s for LP and cassette versions, in the 1980s for LP and CD versions, and for assorted foreign releases and subsequent reissues. The number listed here is the primary American one for each recording.

Show Boat (Studio album, Columbia Masterworks, 1962: OL 5820)
O Say Can You See! (Original-cast album, Grenville Company, 1962)
The Merry Widow (Studio album, Columbia Masterworks, 1962: PL 5880)
Lady in the Dark (Studio album, Columbia Masterworks, 1963: OS 2390)
Annie Get Your Gun (Studio album, Columbia Masterworks, 1963: OS 2360)
The Student Prince (Studio album, Columbia Masterworks, 1963: OS 2380)
The King and I (Studio album, Columbia Masterworks, 1964: OL 8040)
Harold Rome's Gallery (Studio album, Columbia Masterworks, 1964: KL 6091)
Oklahoma! (Studio album, Columbia Masterworks, 1964: OS 2610)
To Broadway with Love (Original-cast album, Columbia Masterworks, 1964: OS 2630)
The Secret Life of Walter Mitty (Original-cast album, Columbia Masterworks, 1964: OS 2720)
Bajour (Original-cast album, Columbia Masterworks, 1964: KOS 2700)
The Decline and Fall of the Entire World as Seen Through the Eyes of Cole Porter (Original-cast album, Columbia Masterworks, 1965: OS 2810)
The Zulu and the Zayda (Original-cast album, Columbia Masterworks, 1965: KOS 2880)
Harold Sings Arlen (with Friend) (Studio album, Columbia Masterworks, 1966: OS 2920)
The Megilla of Itzik Manger (Original-cast album, Columbia Masterworks, 1968: OS 3270).
George M! (Original-cast album, Columbia Masterworks, 1968: KOS 3200)
The Swimmer (Soundtrack album, Columbia Records, 1968: OS 3210)
I Ate the Baloney (Spoken comedy, Orson Bean, Columbia Records, 1968: CS 9743)
Dear World (Original-cast album, Columbia Masterworks, 1969: BOS 3260)
"I Don't Want to Know"/"One Person" (Single from *Dear World*, Columbia Records, 1969: 4-44787)

1776 (Original-cast album, Columbia Masterworks, 1969: BOS 3310)
Dames at Sea (Original-cast album, Columbia Masterworks, 1969: OS 3330)
The Reivers (Soundtrack album, Columbia Masterworks, 1969: OS 3510)
The Royal Hunt of the Sun (Soundtrack album, Columbia Masterworks, 1969: Number unknown)
Tell Me that You Love Me, Junie Moon (Soundtrack album, Columbia Masterworks, 1969: OS 3540)
Two by Two (Original-cast album, Columbia Masterworks, 1970: S 30338)
"Two by Two"/"You" (Single from *Two by Two*, Columbia Records, 1970: AE 35)
Bob and Ray: The Two and Only (Original-cast album, Columbia Masterworks, 1970: S 30412)
Scrooge (Soundtrack album, Columbia Masterworks, 1970: S 30258)
The Rothschilds (Original-cast album, Columbia Masterworks, 1970: S 30337)
"In My Own Lifetime/I'm in Love! I'm in Love!" (Single from *The Rothschilds*, Columbia Records, 1970: AE 31)
The Sesame Street Book and Record (Studio album, Columbia Masterworks, 1970: CS 1069)
The Year of Roosevelt Franklin (Studio album, Columbia Masterworks, 1970: C 30387)
"Mobity Mosely's Months"/"The Safety Boys Blues" (Single from *The Year of Roosevelt Franklin*, Columbia Records, 4-45378)
Company (Original-cast album, Columbia Masterworks, 1970: OS 3550)
"Another Hundred People"/"Company" (Single from *Company*, Columbia Records, 1970: AE 20)
M.A.S.H. (Soundtrack album, Columbia Masterworks, 1970: OS 3520)
"Suicide Is Painless" (Single from *M.A.S.H.*, Columbia Masterworks, 1970: 45-45130)
A Man Called Horse (Soundtrack album, Columbia Masterworks, 1970: OS 3530)
The Owl and the Pussycat (Soundtrack album, Columbia Masterworks, 1971: S 30401)
Little Big Man (Soundtrack album, Columbia Masterworks, 1971: C 30545)
No, No, Nanette (Revival-cast album, Columbia Masterworks, 1971: S 30563)
"I Want to be Happy"/"Tea for Two" (Single from *No, No, Nanette*, Columbia Records, 1971: 4-45335)
70, Girls, 70! (Original-cast album, Columbia Masterworks, 1971: S 30589)
Who Is Harry Kellerman and Why Is He Saying Those Terrible Things About Me (Soundtrack album, Columbia Masterworks, 1971: S 30791)
Le Mans (Soundtrack album, Columbia Masterworks, 1971: S 30891)
The Last Picture Show (Soundtrack album, Columbia Masterworks, 1971: S 31143)
Company (London-cast album, Columbia Masterworks, 1972: S 70108) (recorded in 1970)
Man of La Mancha (Studio album, Columbia Masterworks, 1972: S 31237)
Such Good Friends (Soundtrack, privately released, 1972: TS 79820)
"Suddenly It's All Tomorrow" (Single from *Such Good Friends*, Columbia Masterworks, 1972: 4-45591)
Of Thee I Sing (Television-cast album, Columbia Masterworks, 1972: S 31763)
No, No, Nanette (London revival-cast album, Sony West End, 1973: SMK 66173)
Sleuth (Soundtrack album, Columbia Masterworks, 1973: S 32154)

Irene (Revival-cast album, Columbia Masterworks, 1973: KS 32266)
Raisin (Original-cast album, Columbia Masterworks, 1973: KS 32754)
"Sweet Times"/"Sidewalk Tree" (Single from *Raisin*, Columbia Records, 1973: 4-45978)
Songs from Shelter (Original-cast single, Columbia Records, 1973: 4-45812)
Joel Grey Live (Concert recording, Columbia Records, 1973: KC 32252)
A Little Night Music (Original-cast album, Columbia Masterworks, 1973: KS 32265)
Dr. Selavy's Magic Theatre (Original-cast album, United Artists Records, 1974: UA-LA196-G)
Candide (Revival-cast album, Columbia Masterworks, 1974: S2X 32923)
A Little Night Music (London-cast album, RCA Red Seal, 1975: LRL 1 5050)
Goodtime Charley (Original-cast album, RCA Red Seal, 1975: 09026-68935-2)
Pacific Overtures (Original-cast album, RCA Red Seal, 1976: ARS1-1367)
Side by Side by Sondheim (Original-cast album, RCA Red Seal, 1976: CBL2-1851)
Rex (Original-cast album, RCA Red Seal, 1976: 09026-68933-2)
The King and I (Revival-cast album, RCA Red Seal, 1977: ABL1-2610)
Porgy and Bess (Revival-cast album, RCA Red Seal, 1977: ARL3-2109)
Sweeney Todd (Original-cast album, RCA Red Seal, 1979: CBL2 3379)
"The Ballad of Sweeney Todd"/"I Got My Eye on You (Love, Perfect Love)" (Single, RCA Red Seals, 1979: JD/PD-11687)
Ain't Misbehavin' (Original-cast album, RCA Red Seal, 1978: CBL2-2965)
Oklahoma! (Revival-cast album, RCA Red Seal, 1980: RL 13572)
42nd Street (Original-cast album, RCA Red Seal, 1980: CBL 1-3891)
Duke Ellington's Sophisticated Ladies (Original-cast album, RCA Red Seal, 1981: CBL2 4053)
Merrily We Roll Along (Original-cast album, RCA Red Seal, 1981: CBL1-4197)
Marry Me a Little (Original-cast album, RCA Red Seal, 1982: ABL1-4159)
Turned-On Broadway (Studio album, RCA Red Seal, 1982: AFL1-4327)
Turned-On Broadway, Vol. II (Studio album, RCA Red Seal, 1982: AFL1-4512)
A Stephen Sondheim Evening (Concert recording, RCA Red Seal, 1983: CBL2-4745)
Zorba (Revival-cast album, RCA Red Seal, 1983: ABL1-4732)
La Cage aux Folles (Original-cast album, RCA Red Seal, 1983: HBC1-4824)
Sunday in the Park with George (Original-cast album, RCA Red Seal, 1984: HBC1-5042)
A Collector's Sondheim (Compilation, RCA Red Seal, 1985: CRL4-5359)
Follies in Concert (Concert recording, RCA Red Seal, 1985: HBC2-7128)
Song and Dance: The Songs (Original-cast album, RCA Red Seal, 1985: HBC1-7162)
Me and My Girl (Original-cast album, MCA Classics, 1986: MCA 6196)
Carousel (Studio album, MCA Classics, 1987: MCA-6209)
A Digital Trip Down Broadway (Studio album, MCA Classics, 1987: MCAD-6220)
A Broadway Extravaganza (Studio album, MCA Classics, 1987: MCAD-6219)
Barbara Cook: The Disney Album (Studio album, MCA Classics, 1988: R 100854)
Sarah Brightman: The Songs that Got Away (Studio album, Decca Broadway, 1989: 422 839 116-2)
Romance/Romance (Original-cast album, MCA Classics, 1988: MCA-6252)

Symphonic Pictures: Jesus Christ Superstar/The Phantom of the Opera (Studio album, MCA Classics, 1988: MCAD-6230)
Music of the Night: Pops on Broadway 1990 (Studio album, Sony Classical, 1990: SK 45567)
John Williams Conducts John Williams: The Star Wars Trilogy (Studio album, Sony Classical, 1990: SK 45947)
Man of La Mancha (Studio Album, Sony Classical, 1996: SK 46436)
Kismet (Studio album, Sony Broadway, 1991: SK 46438)
Catch Me If I Fall (Original-cast album, Painted Smiles, 1992: PSCD-133)
The Secret Garden (Original-cast album, Columbia Records, 1991: CK 48817)
The Broadway I Love (Studio album, Atlantic, 1991: 82350-4)
"The Last Night of the World"/"Somewhere" (Single from *The Broadway I Love*, East-West, 1991: 9031-76193-2)
Jelly's Last Jam (Original-cast album, Mercury, 1992: 314 510 846-2)
Crazy for You (Original-cast album, Angel, 1992: CDC 7 54618 2)
Annie Warbucks (Original-cast album, Angel, 1993: CDQ 724355504029)
Damn Yankees (Revival-cast album, Mercury, 1994: 314 522 396-2)
Wings (Original-cast studio album, RCA Victor, 1996: 09026 68323-2)
Kiss of the Spider Woman (Replacement-cast album, Mercury, 1995: P2 26536)
Swinging on a Star (Original-cast album, After 9, 1996: 1004-2)
Victor/Victoria (Original-cast album, Philips, 1995: 446 919-2)
Leading Man: The Best of Broadway (Thomas Hampson, studio album, Angel Records, 1996: 7243 5 55239 2 8)
Betty Buckley: An Evening at Carnegie Hall (Concert recording, Sterling Records, 1996: S1012-4)
Chicago (London-cast album, RCA Victor-BMG Classics, 1998: 09026 63155-2)
To an Isle in the Water (Studio album, Patti Cohenour, Koch International, 1998: S1016-2)
King Island Christmas (Studio album, King Island Record Company, 1999: KIC 1001)
With a Song in My Heart: The Great Songs of Richard Rodgers (Studio album, Centaur Records, 2000: CRC 2501)
My Fair Lady (Concert recording, 2007: Unreleased)
Thespis (Original-cast album, Gilbert & Sullivan Light Opera Company of Long Island, 2014: Privately released)
Annie (Revival-cast album, Shout Factory, 2013: 826663-14208)
Anna Christie (Original-cast album, Broadway Records, 2019: BR-CD12519).

INDEX

Note: Photo insert images are indicated by *p1, p2, p3*, etc.

"Abbondanza," 239
Abbott, George, 292
ABC Stage 67, 124
"Ac-cen-tchu-ate the Positive," 90
Ackland, Joss, 165
Actor's Equity, 78, 170
Adams, Lee, 290
Adams, Tony, 303
Ader, Clément, 45
Adler, Bruce, 201
Adler, Richard, 292, 293
"After the Ball," 52
Ain't Misbehavin', 83, 95, 199–200
Albanese, Licia, 239–40
Albert, Donnie Rae, 182, 183
Aleichem, Sholom, 78
Alexander, Jason, 214, 231
Alic, Jim, 243–44
Alice, 251
Allen, Debbie, 152
Allen, Jay Presson, 220
Allen, Mana, 215
Allen, Woody, 106
"All Er Nuthin'," 69
Allers, Franz, 53–55, 57, 78
All in the Family, 147
Altman, Robert, 136
d'Amboise, Christopher, 261
An American in Paris, 96
Ames, Winthrop, 4
Anastasia, 215
"Anatole of Paris," 120
Andreas, Christine, 201
Andrews, Julie, 3, 71, 74; *Victor/Victoria* and, 301–3
Androcles and the Lion, 118
The Andy Griffith Show, 144
Angel Records, 257, 289, 291
Animal Crackers, 143
Anna and the King of Siam (Landon), 70
Anna Christie, 325–26

Annie, 122, 256, 290–91, 316, 320–24
Annie 2, 290
Annie Get Your Gun, 51, 56–58
Annie Warbucks, 290–92, 321, 323
Anyone Can Whistle, 124, 230, 238, 253
Anything Goes, 125, 289
"Anything You Can Do," 57
The Apple Tree, 115
A&R. *See* Artists & Repertoire, at Columbia Records
Arlen, Anya, 92
Arlen, Harold, 10, 87–89, 90–92, *p4*
Armitage, Richard, 267
Arms and the Girl, 102
Artists & Repertoire, at Columbia Records (A&R), 29, 33
Ashman, Howard, 317
Assassins, 169–70, 227, 257
Avery, Lawrence, 64
"Away from You," 174
Azito, Tony, 50
Azoff, Irving, 264, 273–75

Babcock, John, 284
"Bad, Bad Man," 57
The Badmen, 68–69
Bagley, Ben, 82–83
Baird, Bil, 115
Bajour, 80–82
Baker, David, 117
Bakula, Scott, 271–72
Ballad for a Firing Squad, 325
The Ballad of Sweeney Todd, 195, 196–97
The Barbra Streisand Album, 87
Barnes, Clive, 172
Barrie, Barbara, 129–30
Barry, Gene, 220, 221, 222, *p11*
Bartlett, D'Jamin, 165
Baskin, Richard, 244
Bates, Alan, 217
Beatty, Warren, 213

"Beautiful Girls," 239, 247, 248, 249
Beauty and the Beast, 215, 317–18
Beethoven, Ludwig van, 13, 235
"Being Alive," 126, 132
Bells Are Ringing, 24
Bender, David, 146
Bennett, Robert Russell, 19, 106
Bennett, Tony, 139
Berberian, Ara, 69
Berg, John, 156
Berkeley, Busby, 140–41
Berlin, Irving, 56, 100, 117–18, *p3*
Bernardi, Herschel, 39, 81, 217
Berniker, Mike, 90, 97, 305
Bernstein, Leonard, 35–38, 42–43, 123–25, 138, *p3*; *Candide* and, 153–55
Berry, Walter, *p3*
Beruh, Joseph, 101
The Best Little Whorehouse in Texas, 290
"The Best of Times," 100, 223
Between the Lions, 111
"Bewitched, Bothered and Bewildered," 67
"Beyond the Hills of Tomorrow," 211
Bikel, Theodore, 71–72, 175
Birkenhead, Susan, 286, 287
Black, Arnold, 117
Black, Don, 261
Blackton, Jay, 201
Blaming It on You, 146
"Blaming It on You," 122
"The Blue Danube," 9
BMI Theater Workshop, 152
Bob & Ray, 112–14
Bock, Jerry, 78, 114–16
Bodow, Warren, 305
The Body Beautiful, 115
"Le Boeuf Sur le Toit," 42
Bogart, Humphrey, 260
Bolin, Shannon, 292
Bond, Christopher, 188
Bookman, Leo, 68
"Bored," 280
Borodin, Alexander, 279
Boston Pops, 136, 278
Boulanger, Nadia, 31, 291
Boulez, Pierre, 28, 155
The Boy Friend, 171, 290, 301
The Boy from Oz, 95
"The Boy from Tacaremba," 171
The Boys from Syracuse, 125
Bradshaw, Thornton, 165, 235, 243, 264
Brancato, Rosemarie, 63
Brecht, Bertolt, 124
Brennan, James, 311
Brevoort, Deborah, 308
Brice, Carol, 183
Bricusse, Leslie, 301–2

Brightman, Sarah, 174, 269
Bring Back Birdie, 290
Brittan, Robert, 139, 152–53, *p6*
Broadway Bound, 251
Brooks, Harry, 199
Brooks Brothers, 4
Browing, Larry, 134
Browing, Susan, 134
Brown, Barry, 220
Browning, Susan, 167
Bruno, Frank, 35
"Brush Up Your Shakespeare," 86
Brynner, Yul, 70, 175, 177
Bucci, Mark, 138
Buckley, Betty, 103
Budapest String Quartet, 30
Buffalodians, 89
Burke, Johnny, 300–301
Burnett, Carol, 241, 247
Burnett, Frances Hodgson, 282
Burns, David, 143–44
Burr, Charles, 53–54, 92, 100, 101, 146, *p4*; *Dames at Sea* and, 105; *Such Good Friends* and, 138–39
Burrell, Terry, 300
Burton, Richard, 314
Bussert, Meg, 312
"Buy Bonds, Buster, Buy Bonds," 76
Bye Bye Birdie, 290–92
Byrne, Gabriel, 314, 315

Cabaret, 97
Cacoyannis, Michael, 217
La Cage aux Folles, 100, 109, 165, 219–20; original-cast recordings of, 221–24
Cagney, James, 97
Calamity Jane, 51
Callaway, Liz, 215, 239
Camelot, 53–54, 215, 301; New York Philharmonic and, 313–15
Candide, 35, 153–56
Cannon, Dyan, 138
"Can That Boy Foxtrot," 171
Capers, Virginia, 152–53
Capitol Records, 48, 143, 233
Capp, Al, 17
Capra, Frank, 80
"Capriccio Italien," 36
Cariou, Len, 190–91, *p8*
Carmen Jones, 81, 287
Caroline, or Change, 215
Carousel, 67, 268–72
Carr, Allan, 219–20
Carr, Leon, 79
Carter, Nell, 199, *p9*
Carter, Ralph, *p7*
Carver, Brent, 297–98

INDEX / 333

Cash, Johnny, 30
Cash, Rosalind, 112
Catch Me If I Fall, 282
Cats, 249–50, 298
Cavalieri, Deena, 55
Cavett, Dick, 27
CBS, 19, 23, 35, 96, 158, 164; *My Fair Lady* and, 25, 313
CBS Records, 159–60, 274
Cerf, Christopher, 111
Chaiken, Joel E., 284
Champion, Gower, 150, 203
Chanko, Toni, 13, 17
Chapin, Schuyler, 26, 43, 49, 55, 96, 157; *Bye Bye Birdie* and, 292; *Candide* and, 154; *Company* and, 132; *Lady in the Dark* and, 60; in Masterworks Department, 30–32; *O Say Can You See!* and, 76
Chapin, Ted, 231, 233–34, 236, 268, 295
Charlie Girl, 142
Charnin, Martin, 118–19, 121–22, 174, 290–91, 320–25
Chicago, 114, 304–7
"Children and Art," 227
Children's Television Workshop, 111
"Children Will Listen," 254
A Chorus Line, 291, 305
A Christmas Carol, 117
Cinderella, 118, 301
Cinema Center Films, 143
"Circus Dream," 60–61
"City on Fire," 195
Clark, Harry, 80, 86
Clark, Irene, 17, 109, 146, 153, 171, *p2*
Clarke, Hope, 287
Clayburgh, Jill, 116
Cleale, Lewis, 300
Clements, Otis, 150
Cleveland Orchestra, 182
Cleveland Pops Orchestra, 72
"Cocktail Counterpoint," 224
Cohan, George M., 66, 77
Cohen, Alexander, 101, 241
Cohen, Hannah, 116
Coke, Peter, 143
A Collector's Sondheim, 208, 216, 230–31, 252
Columbia Record Club, 29, 48–49; Kimbrough and, 227. *See also* studio cast albums
Columbia Records, 19, 20, 109, 157–58, 164, 279; A&R of, 29, 33; Lieberson at, 23–28, 30, 88, 94, 117; New York Philharmonic and, 234–35. *See also* Masterworks Department, at Columbia Records
Comden, Betty, 61, 241
"Comedy Tonight," 171, 231
"Come Rain or Come Shine," 88
"Come Spirit, Come Charm," 285

Company, 34, 58, 231, 315, *p5*; original-cast recordings of, 122, 125–33
Company: The London Cast Recording, 133–34
Conklin, Bob, 76
Connell, Jane, 101, 267
Conreid, Hans, 144
Cook, Barbara, 53, 71, 175, 239, 247, 269
Cooney, Joan Ganz, 111
Cooper, Chuck, 308
Copeland, Joan, 122
Copland, Aaron, 38, 110
Corigliano, John, 99
Cortés, Lisa, 286–87
Corvino, Alfredo, 293
"Cotton Blossom," 54, 62
The Court Jester, 120
Coward, Noel, 26
The Cradle Will Rock, 22
Crawford, Lilla, 322
Crazy for You, 288–90
Crivello, Anthony, 297–98
Crooks, Richard, 63
Cryer, Gretchen, 151–52
Cunningham, John, 217
Cyrano: The Musical, 174

Dale, Clamma, 182
Dames at Sea, 105–7
Damn Yankees, 292–94
Damon, Stuart, 118
Dandridge, Dorothy, 180
Daniels, Danny, 238
Daniels, William, 102, 103–4
Darian, Anita, 53, 64, 71, 138
Darion, Joe, 93, 282
Dash, Joe, 230, 235, 270
Da Silva, Howard, 84, 102, 103–4
Davis, Clive, 23, 85, 96–97, 117, 158; *A Little Night Music* and, 149; *Songs from Shelter* and, 151
Davis, Ivan, 43
Davis, Luther, 279
Davis, Ossie, 84
Davis, Sammy, Jr., 80, 182
Day, Doris, 51, 53, 56–57
Day, Edith, 150
"The Day They Say 'I Do,'" 291
Dearest Enemy, 102
Dear World, 99–100, 219, 221, 232, 267
The Decline and Fall of the Entire World as Seen Through the Eyes of Cole Porter, 82, 116
Della Casa, Lisa, 55
DeLuise, Dom, 279–80
DeMain, John, 180–81, 183
De Mille, Agnes, 23
DeMille, Cecil B., 304
Dennehy, Brian, 311–12
Denoff, Douglas, 321

De Paul, Gene, 17
Desire Under the Elms, 325
The Devil Wears Prada, 59
DeWitt, Fay, 54
Dick Tracy, 253
"Ding Dong, the Witch Is Dead," 90–91
Disney, 45, 317
Ditko, Steve, 77
Documentary Now!, 132–33
Do I Hear a Waltz?, 118, 124–25, 172, 238
"Doin' What Comes Naturally," 57
Domingo, Plácido, 280–81, 282
Donath, Ludwig, 92
Donnelly, Dorothy, 63
Donnybrook!, 300
"Doxey, Honey," 103
Drabinsky, Garth, 297, 298
Drake, Alfred, 67, 69, 241, 279
Drat! The Cat!, 188–89
Drescher, Fran, 315
"Drink! Drink! Drink!," 63
Dr. Selavy's Magic Theatre, 148, 182
Dubin, Al, 203
Duchin, Eddie, 89
Dussault, Nancy, 81
Dylan, Bob, 158

Eagan, Daisy, 284, *p14*
Eastman School of Music, 23
Eastronics, 93
Ebb, Fred, 106; Kander and, 114, 143, 217, 297–98, 304–5
Ebersole, Christine, 201
Edwards, Blake, 303
Edwards, Sherman, 102–3, *p4*
"The Egg," 103
Elephant Steps, 148
Elisabeth Irwin High School, 18
Elkins, Hillard, 115, 116
Ellington, Duke, 95, 200, 205–6
Ellington, Mercer, 205, 206
Elliot, Ramblin' Jack, 68–69
Elliott, Bob, 112–14
Elmore, Steve, 107, 128
Emick, Jarrod, 292, 294
Emmet, Daniel Decatur, 78
Encores! series, 250
Engel, Lehman, 59, 62, 72, 85, 152; *Bajour* and, 80, 81
"An English Gentleman," 266
Epstein, Danny, 110
Epstein, Matthew, 279
Epstein, Steven, 168
Erlichman, Marty, 90
Esposito, Giancarlo, 215
Essays of Clive James, 259
Evening Primrose, 124, 171, 237

Everhart, Rex, 104
"Everybody Loves Louis," 228
Everything Was Possible (Chapin, T.), 234
Evita, 261
The Exception and the Rule, 124, 125

"The Family Solicitor," 266, 267
Fanny, 68
Fantasia, 45
Farber, Mitch, 196–97
Faria, Arthur, 199
"The Farmer and the Cowhand," 200
Faust, 292
Feder, Richard "Winkie," 7
Ferber, Edna, 52
Ferren, Bran, 226
Ferro, Daniel, 72
Fiddler on the Roof, 78, 92, 114–15, 125
Fields, Dorothy, 56, 102
Fields, Herbert, 56
Fierstein, Harvey, 220, 222
Finneran, Katie, 322
Fiorello!, 115, 146
Fisher, Rob, 310, 311
Fisher, Todd, 150
"Flaming Star," 102
Florodora, 22
The Flowering Peach, 119
Foglesong, Jim, 44, 74, 83, 87, 157; Columbia Record Club and, 49; *Lady in the Dark* and, 60; *The Merry Widow* and, 55; RCA and, 65; *Show Boat* and, 54; *The Student Prince* and, 64; studio cast albums and, 49–50, 51, 234
Foh Shen, Freda, 169
Follies, 142–43, 191, 231–35, 250
Follies in Concert, 29, 239–41, 249–52, 264, 310; Goldman, J., and, 237–38; Menéndez and, 242–44; New York Philharmonic and, 235–36, 247–48; RCA and, 244–46
Ford, Nancy, 151–52
Foreman, Richard, 148
Forest Hills Tennis Club, 77
Forrest, George, 279, 280
Forrester, Maureen, 269
42nd Street, 116, 141, 202, 203–5, 218
Fosse, Bob, 304–5
Foster, Stephen, 78
Franke, Paul, 55
Frank H. Taylor & Son, 3
Franklin, Aretha, 30
Fraser, Allison, 271
Fraser, Ian, 303
Frasier, 171, 313
Frazee, Harry, 140
Freitag, Dorothea, 143
Friedman, David, 308–9
From A to Z, 106

Frost, Thomas, 32, 110, 156; at Masterworks Department, 139, 157, 159, 168
Fry, Stephen, 266
Funny Face, 289
Funny Girl, 87
A Funny Thing Happened on the Way to the Forum, 124, 187, 231, 253, 259
Furber, Douglas, 265
Furth, George, 125, 209

Gable, June, 155
Gallagher, Bill, 91, 159
Gallagher, Helen, 68, 141
Garber, Victor, 292, 294
Gardner, Ava, 15
Garfunkel, Art, 23, 77
Garland, Judy, 88, 90
Garner, James, 303
Gaslight, 101
Gavin, John, 175
Gay, Noel, 265
Gaynor, Charles, 150
Gemignani, Paul, 238–40, 248, *p7*, *p14*; *Camelot* and, 314; *Carousel* and, 269; *Crazy for You* and, 289; *Kismet* and, 279, 280
George M!, 96, 97–98, 108, 259
Gerhardt, Charles, 166
Gershwin, George, 19, 22, 89, 147, 179, 289
Gershwin, Ira, 18, 22, 147, 179, 289; *Lady in the Dark* and, 58, 60–61
"Getting Married Today," 128–29
"Getting to Know You," 72–73
The Ghosts of Versailles, 99
Gilbert & Sullivan, 4, 10, 318–20
A Gilbert & Sullivan Christmas Carol, 319
Gilbert & Sullivan Light Opera Company, 319–20
Gilford, Jack, 141–42, 146, 147
Gillette, Anita, *p3*
Gilman, Sandra, 295–96
Gingold, Hermione, 106, 165, 166
Girl Crazy, 289
Girl from the North Country, 95
"Girl of the Moment," 62
The Girls of Summer, 207
The Girls Upstairs, 124
"The Glamorous Life," 230
"Glamour Dream," 62
Glancy, Kenneth, 159–60, 165, 166, 173, 264, *p7*; *Side by Side by Sondheim* and, 170
Glover, Savion, 286, 288, *p14*
Goelet, Francis, 244
Gold, Jack, 144
Goldberry, Renee Elise, 133
Goldby, Derek, 116
Golden Rainbow, 80
"The Golden Ram," 121
Goldman, James, 124, 237–38, 246, 255

Goldman, Sherwin M., 180–82, 185–86
Goldmark, Peter, 25
gold records, 108–9
Gomer Pyle, U.S.M.C., 144–45
Gonzalez-Falla, Celso, 295–96
"Goodbye, Canavaro," 40
Goodman, Henry, 306
Goodman, Paul, 218, 249
Goodtime Charley, 99, 166–67, 232
Gordon, Ruth, 213
Gorme, Eydie, 80
Gossett, Louis, Jr., 84, 85
Gould, Morton, 102
Goulding, Ray, 112–14
Goulet, Robert, 56, 57
"Go Visit Your Grandmother," 143
Graham, Buddy, 35, 41–42, 157, 278
Graham, Deborah, 271
Grammer, Kelsey, 310, 312–13
Grammy Awards, *p12*; for *Candide*, 156; for *Follies in Concert*, 245; for *Porgy and Bess*, 182, 186; for *Raisin*, 153; for *The Sesame Street Book and Record*, 111; for *Sweeney Todd*, 196
The Grand Tour, 221
Gray, Margery, 171
Great Depression, 5
Green, Adolph, 61, 241
Green, Johnny, 118
Green, Stanley, 88–89
Greene, Michael, 111
Greene, Milton, *p5*
Gregory, André, 241, 247
Gregory, Cillian, 266
Grey, Joel, 97–99, 167, 305
Grimaldi, Dennis, 321
Groeger, David, 319
Groener, Harry, 201
Grossman, Cookie, 103
Grossman, Herb, 103
Grossman, Larry, 167
Grubman, Allen, 221, 275
Guettel, Adam, 176
Guettel, Mary Rodgers, 200, 246
Guittard, Laurence, 70, 165, 201
Gunn, Nathan, 315
Gunton, Bob, 253
Gypsy, 124, 252, 254, 258

Hackady, Hal, 167
Hackett, Buddy, 281
Hadley, Jerry, 282, *p14*
Haimsohn, George, 105
Haircut, 19
Hamilton, 102
Hamison, Judith, *p9*
Hammerstein, Oscar, II, 52, 114, 154, 174, 270; *Carmen Jones* and, 287; Rodgers, R., and,

66–67, 70, 118, 198; Sondheim and, 123, 254, 258
Hammerstein, William, 200
Hampson, Thomas, 310
Handler, Evan, 173
Hansberry, Lorraine, 152, 153
Harburg, Jim, 56–57
Harburg, Yip, 89
Harbutt, Charles, 323–24
Hardy, Joe, 114
Hariette Melissa Mills Teachers College, 3
Harman, Barry, 271
Harms, T. B., 269
Harnick, Sheldon, 11, 79, 109, 117, 285, 325; Bock and, 78, 114–16; Rodgers, R., and, 172, 174
Harold Rome's Gallery, 85, 86
Harold Sings Arlen (with Friend), 87, 91
Harper, Wally, 150
Harris, Charles K., 52
Harris, Neil Patrick, 315
Harrison, Rex, 74, 312, 314
Hart, Lorenz, 47, 66–67, 117
Hart, Moss, 18, 58, 59, 85
Hastings, Hal, *p5*
Hayward, Susan, 143
Hearn, George, 220–22, 239, *p11*
"Heart," 294
Hellman, Lillian, 153–54
"Hello, Dolly," 100
"Hello, Young Lovers," 71
Hello Dolly!, 99, 219
Henderson, Florence, 68
Henderson, Luther, 199, 205, 286, 288, 318
Hendry, Tom, 148
Henshall, Ruthie, 306
Henson, Jim, 110
Hepburn, Audrey, 301
"He Plays the Violin," 103
Herman, Jerry, 47, 99–100, 101, 106, *p11*; *La Cage aux Folles* and, 219, 220, 221, 223–24
Hermann, Bernard, 193
Hermann, Keith, 271
Heyward, DuBose, 22, 179
Hickey, Peggy, 311–12
Hines, Gregory, 206, 286, 287–88, 299, *p9*, *p14*
Hines, Maurice, 206
Hirschfeld, Al, 214
A Hole in the Head, 80
Holland, Bernard, 242–43
Holliday, Judy, 24
Holmes, Jack, 76
Holt, Fritz, 220, *p11*
Hooray for What!, 89
Horchow, Roger, 289
Horne, Lena, 139
Horne, Marilyn, 5, 145
Horowitz, Vladimir, 160

Horwitz, Murray, 199
Hoshour, Robert, 271
House of Flowers, 90
Houston Grand Opera, 179, 180, 185
Howard, Ken, 102
Howland, Beth, 127–29
Humor in Music, 42
Hunt, Peter, *p4*
Hurley, Laurel, 55
Husmann, Ron, 146
Hyman, Dick, 184

I, Don Quixote, 144
"I Am What I Am," 223
I Can Get It for You Wholesale, 87
I'd Rather Be Right, 97
"If I Loved You," 269
"If Only You Had Cared for Me," 267
"I Got Lost in His Arms," 57
I Hate Hamlet, 173
Ilberman, Mel, 283
"I Like Him," 281
I'll Cry Tomorrow, 143
I'm Getting My Act Together and Taking It on the Road, 151
"I'm Only Thinking of Him," 146
"The Impossible Dream," 144–45
"I'm Still Here," 247
"I'm the Girl Representing Brand X," 54
Inadmissible Evidence, 173
"In Buddy's Eyes," 253
"The Incomparable Mentalist," 18
"I Never Do Anything Twice," 171
"In the Shade of the New Apple Tree," 89, 92
Into the Woods, 227, 254, 257
I Remember Mama, 174, 202
"I Remember Sky," 171
Irene, 150–51
Irene O'Dare, 150
Irving, George S., 151, 267
"It's a Hit," 212, 231
"It's a Scandal, It's an Outrage," 200
It's a Wonderful Life, 109
"It's Hot Up Here," 229
"It Started Out Like a Song," 211
"I've Got to Be Me," 80
"I Want to Be Happy," 141

Jablonski, Edward, 91
Jacobson, Henrietta, 143
Jamison, Judith, 206
Jelly's Last Jam, 206, 215, 286–88, 299
Jerome, Tim, 115, 267, 312
Jerome Robbins' Broadway, 219
Jersey Boys, 95
Joan of Arc at the Stake, 27
Joel Grey Live 1973, 98–99

"Johanna," 192, 193
John McCarthy's Ambrosian Singers, 280
Johns, Glynis, 165
Johnson, Mary Lea, 187
The Jolson Story, 92
Jones, Bob, 305–6
Jones, Dean, 132, 134, *p5*
Jones, Dick, 233
Julliard School, 2, 11
Juster, Norman, 117
"Just We Two," 64

Kahn, Fred "Uncle Teddy," 5, 6, 7
Kahn, Louis (grandfather), 5, 9
Kahn, Madeline, 121, 146
Kahne, Harry, 18–19
Kander, John, 299, 306, 307, *p6*; Ebb and, 114, 143, 217, 297–98, 304–5
Kanin, Garson, 213
"Kansas City," 69
Kapp, Jack, 22
Karnilova, Maria, 217
Kasha, Lawrence, 80
Kaufman, George S., 85, 147
Kay, Hershy, 64, 154
Kaye, Danny, 58, 60–61, 120–21, *p5*
Kazantzakis, Nikos, 217
"Kazoo Concerto," 138
Keach, Stacy, 315
Kedrova, Lila, 40, 217, 218–19
Keeler, Ruby, 141–42, *p6*
Kelly, Patsy, 150, 151
Kern, Jerome, 52, 67, 89
Kernan, David, 165, 170
Kert, Larry, 132, 134
Kidd, Michael, 116
Kiley, Richard, 280
Kimball, Robert, 83–84, 182
Kimbrough, Charles, 127–28, 129–30, 227–28, 311
Kind, Richard, 133
Kindertotenlieder, 36, 40–42
The King and I, 69, 70–73, 175–77, 178
King Island Christmas, 307–9
Kings of Hearts, 171
Kirk, Lisa, 241
Kismet, 279–80
Kiss Me, Kate, 299
Kiss of the Spider Woman, 297–99
Kleban, Ed, 97
"Knight of the Woeful Countenance," 282
Knoblock, Edward, 279
Kopit, Arthur, 295
Kosarin, Michael, 283
Kosarin, Oscar, *p6*
Kotto, Yaphet, 84
Koussevitsky, Serge, 36
Kramer, Mary Burke, 300–301

Krane, David, 299
Krass, Ellen M., 246
Krauss, Susan, 185
Kravetz, Daniel, 319
Kravetz, Jerry, 269
Kreuger, Miles, 52–53
Kupferman, Meyer, 85

"The Ladies Who Lunch," 130–31
Lady in the Dark, 18, 58–63, 66, 75, 120
"The Lambeth Walk," 266
Landon, Margaret, 70
Lane, Louis, 72
Lane, Lupino, 266
Lane Theological Seminary, 14
Lang, Phil, 57, 70, 72
Langston, Diane, 165
Lansbury, Angela, 100–101, 124, 190–91, *p4*, *p8*
Lansbury, Edgar, 100–101
Lansky, Meyer, 6
Lapine, James, 225–27, 321, 322, *p12*; Sondheim and, 255, 256, 258
The Last of Sheila, 238
Last of the Red Hot Lovers, 251
The Last Resorts, 207
Latessa, Dick, 294
Laurents, Arthur, 123, 124, 220, 222, 223, *p11*
"Laurey Makes Up Her Mind," 23
Lavin, Linda, 171, 251–52, 256
Lawrence, Gertrude, 58, 59, 69, 70, 175
Lawrence, Jerome, 99–100
Lawrence, Peter, 323
Lawrence, Steve, 80
Layton, Joe, 97–98
Lazarus, Paul, 215, 238, 248
Leachman, Cloris, 112, 147
"Leaning on a Lamppost," 266
Lederer, Charles, 279
Lee, Eugene, 155
Lee, Michele, 147
Lee, Robert E., 99–100
Lee, Spike, 215
Lee, Stan, 77
"The Legacy Series," 68–69
LeGrand, Michel, 117
Lehman (teacher), 7
Leigh, Mitch, 144, 282
Leigh, Vivien, 71
Lemper, Ute, 306
Leon, Felix, 84
Leonard, Richard, 106
Leonardos, Urylee, 81
Lerner, Alan Jay, 310, 313
Leskow, Nicolai, 285
Let 'Em Eat Cake, 147, 290
"The Letter," 192
Levan, Martin, 298

Levin, Ira, 188
Levitt, Barry, 300–301
Levy, Jessica, 308
Levy, Ted L., 287
Lewis, Henry, 145
"Liaisons," 166
Lieberson, Goddard, 75, 82, 157, *p3*, *p6*; A&R and, 29; *Candide* and, 154; at Columbia Records, 23–28, 30, 88, 94, 117; Elkins and, 116; *Follies* and, 233; Glancy relation to, 160; *Harold Rome's Gallery* and, 86; "The Legacy Series" and, 68–69; *A Little Night Music* and, 149; Paley relation to, 96, 158; *Porgy and Bess* and, 23, 46, 129, 179, 182; Prince, H., and, 143, 233; Rodgers, R., and, 118–19, 172; *1776* and, 103
"Life Upon the Wicked Stage," 54
Lil' Abner, 17, 80
"Lily's Eyes," 285
Lincoln Center, 31, 96
Linden, Hal, 115, *p5*
Lindsay, Mort, 81
Lindsay, Robert, 266–67, *p13*
Little, Mary Jo, 307
"Little Bird, Little Bird," 282
"The Little Comedy," 271
"A Little Gossip," 281
"Little Maid of Arcadee," 318
The Little Mermaid, 317–18
A Little Night Music, 149, 165–66, 209–10, 230, 253, 299; original-cast recordings of, 161
"The Little Things You Do Together," 34, 129–30
Live from Lincoln Center, 156
Lloyd, Christopher, 315
Lloyd Webber, Andrew, 99, 245, 261, 265
Loewe, Frederick, 53, 310
Loewe, Fritz, 114
London Symphony, 27, 280
"Loneliness of the Evening," 118
"Lonely Boy," 288
"Lonely Room," 23, 69, 200
Long, Loretta, 110, 112
"Losing My Mind," 254
The Love Bug, 132
Love in Two Countries, 285
"Love Is in the Air," 171, 231
Love Never Dies, 290
The Love Parade, 143
Lubitsch, Ernst, 143
Lucas, Craig, 207
Lucas, George, 278
Luciano, Lucky, 6
Ludwig, Christa, *p3*
Ludwig, Ken, 289
Lunden, Jeff, 295, 296
Lundvall, Bruce, 113
Lynch, Jane, 322

Maas, Jon, 203, 204–5
Maazel, Lorin, 182
MacDonald, Audra, 314–15
Mack and Mabel, 221
Mackintosh, Cameron, 170, 249–50, 261
The Mad Show, 109, 111
The Madwoman of Chaillot, 99
Mahler, 36, 40–42
Mahler, Gustav, 130
Make Mine Mink, 143
Malle, Louis, 241
Maltby, Richard, Jr., 16, 199, 261, *p9*
"Mama Look Sharp," 103
Mame, 99, 219, 267
Mamma Mia!, 95
Mancini, Henry, 301–2
Mandel, Johnny, 136
Manger, Itzik, 93
The Man in the Moon, 115
Man of La Mancha, 144–46, 280–82
"The Man Who Owns Broadway," 97
"The Man with the Multiple Mind," 18
Marantz, Paul, 246
"March of the Siamese Children," 72
Marks, Walter, 80, 81
Marry Me a Little, 207–8
Marshall, Bob, 219
Marshall, Larry, 148, 182
Martin, Leila, 116
Martin, Mary, 30
Martin, Millicent, 170, 171
Martins, Peter, 261
Mary Poppins, 301
M.A.S.H., 136–37
Masteroff, Joseph, 325
Masterworks Department, at Columbia Records, 25, 30–32, 34–35, 43, 275–76; Columbia Record Club and, 49; Copland and, 110; Davis, C., relation to, 96; Frost at, 139, 157, 159, 168; *Harold Sings Arlen (with Friend)* and, 87
Mathews, Carmen, 101
Mathis, Johnny, 102
Matinee with Bob and Ray, 112
Mattos, Edward, 13–14
Matz, Peter, 90, 147–48, 308–9, *p4*
Mauceri, John, 262, *p7*
Maupassant, Guy de, 285
Mazzie, Marin, 308, 315
MCA Classics, 264–65, 274
McArdle, Andrea, 320
MCA Records, 264, 273–76
McCarthy, John, 280
McCarthy, Joseph, 150
McClure, John, 32, 34–35, 42, 43, 139, 157
McGavin, Darren, 71
McGillin, Howard, 239, 298, *p14*

McGrath, Bob, 110
McGrath, Michael, 300
McKechnie, Donna, 291
McKenzie, Julia, 170
McNally, Terrence, 297–98
McQueen, Armelia, *p9*
Meadows, Audrey, 112
Me and My Girl, 265–67
Meehan, Thomas, 290, 320, 323
The Megilla of Itzik Manger, 93–94, 97
Mehta, Zarin, 310, 315
Menéndez, José, 241–43, 249, 264
Menken, Alan, 317
Mercer, Johnny, 17
"Merci Bon Dieu," 167
Mercury Records, 286–87, 292
Merman, Ethel, 124, 223
Merrick, David, 93, 173, 202–3, 204–5, 257
Merrill, David, 307, 326
Merrily We Roll Along, 15, 209–15, 231–32, 256, *p10*, *p13*
The Merry Widow, 54–56
Metropolitan Opera, 185
Meyer, Helen, 6
Meyers, Seth, 132–33
Michaels, Sidney, 167
Migenes, Julia, 280, 281
A Mighty Man Is He, 102
Milhaud, Darius, 42
Military, Frank, 258, 282, 300
Miller, Bill, 76
Miller, Mitch, 30, 87
Miller, Robin, 105
"The Miller's Son," 165
Mills, Erie, 239–40
Minnelli, Liza, 267–68, 297, 302
Les Misérables, 249
Miss Saigon, 215
Miss Spectacular, 224
"(When I Marry) Mister Snow," 269, 270
Mitchell, Brian Stokes, 298, 299, *p14*
Mitchell, Joseph, 80
Moffo, Anna, 60, 164
"Molasses to Rum to Slaves," 104
Monk, Julius, 228
Monmouth-Evergreen Records, 88
Montalban, Paolo, 308
Montevecchi, Liliane, 241
Montgomery, James, 150
Moonves, Les, 313
Morley, Carol, 171
Morton, Jelly Roll, 286–88
Morton, Joe, 152, *p6*
Moskov, Lee, 308
Mosque Theater, 3
Mostel, Zero, 84, 92, 124, 253
The Most Happy Fella, 239

"Mostly Mozart," 96
"Move On," 227
Mozart, 30
Mrs. Santa Claus, 224
Mrs. Tisdale's Nursery School, 7
Mulaney, John, 132–33
Munderloh, Otts, 247
Murphy, Steve, 289–90
Musical Stages (Rodgers, R.), 120
Music and Songs from "Starlight Express", 265
Music Masters Classics, 280
The Music of Harold Arlen, 88, 89
"Must It be Love?," 81
My Dinner with André, 241
Myers, Paul, 71, 130
My Fair Lady, 25, 71, 74, 176, 301, 314; New York Philharmonic and, 310–13
"My Magic Lamp," 279
My Name Is Barbra, 87, 90

Nabors, Jim, 144–45, 146
Nash, S. Richard, 207
National Recording Registry, 196
Natwick, Mildred, 143
Naughton, James, 305
Neagle, Anna, 142
Nederlander Organization, 239
Nelson, Richard, 225
Nemiroff, Robert, 152, 153, *p6*
Neuwirth, Bebe, 292–93, 294, 305
Nevin, Mark, 11
"A New Deal for Christmas," 291
New England Music Camp, 13
Newman, Phyllis, 61, 68, 241
New York City Opera, 149, 156
New York Musical Theater Works, 117
New York Philharmonic, 35–37, 155, 182, 234, 250, 316; Bernstein and, 43; *Camelot* and, 313–15; *Follies in Concert* and, 235–36, 247–48; *My Fair Lady* and, 310–13
New York Times, 76
New York Times Magazine, 242–43
"Next," 169
Nice Work If You Can Get It, 300
Nichols, James, 303
Nichols, Mike, 220
Nichols, Red, 89
Nickel Plate Railroad train, 13
Night and Day, 95, 97
Nine, 241
Nixon, Marni, 71, 312
No, No, Nanette, 140–42, 146, 149–50
Norman, Marsha, 283
No Strings, 118, 172
"Not a Day Goes By," 212
Nouri, Michael, 303
"Now/Later/Soon," 166

Oberlin College, 13–14, 15, *p2*
"Oboe Quartet in F Major," 30
O'Brien, Jack, 180–81, 183, 185, 292–94
Ockrent, Michael, 266, 289
O'Connor, Carroll, 147
Odets, Clifford, 119
Of Thee Is Sing, 147–48
"Oh, I Can't Sit Down," 185
O'Hara, Kelli, 311
Oklahoma!, 22–23, 47, 74, 95, 177, 232; *Lady in the Dark* relation to, 58; studio cast albums of, 65–70, 200–202
"Old Friends," 216
Olivier, Laurence, 71
"Ol' Man River," 53
Olsen, Frank, 242
100 Years of the Metropolitan Opera and RCA Records, 240
O'Neill, Eugene, 325
One Minute, Please, 172
"One More Kiss," 240
102–40 67th Road, Forest Hills, 76–77
"Only a Moment Ago," 142
On the Town, 61, 146
On Your Toes, 27
"Opening Doors," 212, 214
Orbach, Jerry, 98, 204, 305, *p9*
Original Cast Album: Company, 126–27
Original Cast Album: Co-Op, 132–33
original-cast recordings. *See specific recordings*
O Say Can You See!, 76, 105
Ostrow, Stuart, 102
"Out of My Dreams," 201
Oz, Frank, 110
Ozawa, Seiji, 27

Pacific Overtures, 116, 161, 168–70
Paige, Elaine, 261
Le Pain de Ménage, 271
Paley, William S., 23, 25, 30, 96, 158, 164
Pal Joey, 66
Paris Electrical Exhibition, 45
"Paris Makes Me Horny," 302
"The Party's Over," 24
Pascal, Francine, 97
Pascal, John, 97
Passion, 257
Patinkin, Mandy, 61, 227, 229, 280, *p12*, *p14*; *Follies in Concert* and, 239; *Man of La Mancha* and, 281; *The Secret Garden* and, 284, 285
Patz, Peter, 89
"Peach on the Beach," 141–42
"The Pears of Anjou," 173
Peerce, Jan, 63–64
Péne Du Bois, Raoul, 140, 150
Pennebaker, D. A., 126–27, 131, 133, *p5*
People, 90

"People Will Say We're in Love," 200–201
Perlman, Arthur, 295, 296
Perón, Eva, 148
Peter and the Wolf, 36, 280
"Peter and the Wolf," 110
Peters, Bernadette, 98, 227, 228, 261–62, *p4*, *p13*; in *Dames at Sea*, 105, 107
Peters, Roberta, 63, 64
Phantom of the Opera, 290
The Phantom Tollbooth (Juster), 117
"Pie Jesu," 269
Pinkins, Tonya, 215
Pins and Needles, 84, 85
Pippin, Don, 222
The Pirates of Penzance, 50, 318
Pisello, Salvatore, 273–74
Pitt, George Dibdin, 188
Plaut, Fred, 35, 54, 82, 157, *p4*
Playwrights Horizons, 226–27
Plaza Music Company, 9
Plunkett, Maryann, 266, 267, *p13*
Poitier, Sidney, 180
"Poor Jud Is Dead," 69
"Poor Thing," 192
Porgy and Bess, 22, 28, 148, 180, 183–86, 195; Lieberson and, 23, 46, 129, 179, 182
Porter, Cole, 47, 82, 83–84, 97, 224, 289
Porter, Quincy, 16, 18
Prager, Stanley, 17
Preminger, Otto, 137–39, 180, *p6*
Presley, Elvis, 102
Presnell, Harve, 291
Preston, Robert, 303
"Pretty Lady," 169
"Pretty Little Picture," 124, 253
Previn, André, 3
Price, Lonny, 210, 213, 215, 310, 314–15
Prince, Charlie, 190
Prince, Daisy, 210, 241
Prince, Harold, 125, 127, 132, 148, 258, *p7*; *Candide* and, 154–55; *Follies in Concert* and, 238; *Kiss of the Spider Woman* and, 297; Lieberson and, 143, 233; *Merrily We Roll Along* and, 209, 212–13; RCA relation to, 161; *Rex* and, 172–73; *Side by Side by Sondheim* and, 170; *Something for Everyone* and, 143; *Sweeney Todd* and, 187, 260; *Zorba* and, 217
Prince, Judy, 165, 190, 210
Prochnik, Cruce, 320
Prokofiev, 36
Promises, Promises, 98, 106
Pro Tools, 323–24, 326
Prunczik, Karen, *p9*
Puffer, Merle, 55
Putting It Together, 302
"A Puzzlement," 175

Quantum Leap, 272
A Question of Faith, 117, 285
Quinn, Anthony, 40, 217, 218, *p11*

Raisin, 139, 152–53
Raitt, John, 53, 67
Ralston, Terry, 128
Ramey, Samuel, 269, 279, 282
Raposo, Joe, 109, 112
Razaff, Andy, 199
RCA, 19, 65, 86, 155–56, 159, 264; Columbia Records compared to, 164; *Follies in Concert* and, 244–46; *The King and I* and, 70–71; Menéndez at, 242; Merrick and, 93; Moffo and, 60; New York Philharmonic and, 235; *100 Years of the Metropolitan Opera and RCA Records*, 240; *Porgy and Bess* and, 28; Red Seal, 20, 160–61, 182, 197, 214, 236, 265, 275–76; *Rex* and, 172; Sondheim relation to, 160–61, 207–8, 230, 258; *Zorba* and, 39–40
Reams, Lee Roy, *p9*
Reardon, John, 55
Reds, 213, 253
Red Seal, RCA, 20, 160–61, 182, 214, 265, 275–76; *The Ballad of Sweeney Todd* and, 197; New York Philharmonic and, 236
Reimuller, Ross, 184
Reiner, Fritz, 183
Reinking, Ann, 167, 305
Reiss, Barry, 266, 271
The Reivers, 136
Remick, Lee, 230, 241, 251
Rendall, David, 269
René, Norman, 207
The Return of the Vagabond, 97
Rex, 172–74
Reynolds, Debbie, 150–51
Rhodes, Nancy, 325
Rich, Frank, 225–26, 289
Rigby, Harry, 140
"Ritual Fire Dance," 183
Rivera, Chita, 81, 297–98, 305, *p3*
Rizzi, Ben, 307
Robbins, Jerome, 123, 124, 219
Roberts, Doris, 312
Roberts, Howard, *p6*
Roberts, Tony, 303
Robertson, David, 19
Robinson, Jill Schary, 84–85
Robinson, Matt, 111–12
Rock, Larry, 313
rock 'n' roll, 96, 158
Rodd, Marcia, 151–52
Rodgers, Dorothy, 122, 203
Rodgers, Mary, 109, 268
Rodgers, Richard, 27, 174, 175–77, 202–3, 262, *p5*; Hammerstein, O., and, 66–67, 70, 118, 198; Hart, L., and, 47, 66–67, 117; Kaye and, 120–21; Lieberson and, 118–19, 172; Sondheim and, 118, 124–25
The Rodgers and Hammerstein Story (Green, S.), 88
Rodgers & Hammerstein Organization, 233, 258, 268–69
Roe, Grace, 323
Rogers, Anne, 142
Rogers, Ginger, 289, 304
Rogers, Jean, 308
Romance/Romance, 271–72
Romberg, Sigmund, 63
Rome, Harold, 84, 86
Roosevelt, Franklin Delano, 97
Rose, L. Arthur, 265
Rosen, David, 17, 106
Rosenfield, Bob, 306
Rosenstock, Milton, 176, 177
Ross, Herbert, 238, 246–47, 248, 311
Ross, Jerry, 292, 293
Ross-Trevor, Mike, 307
Roth, Lillian, 143
Roth, Myron, 264–65, 273–74
The Rothschilds, 115–17, 168
Roundabout Theatre Company, 226–27
Roxie Hart, 304, 306
Royal Philharmonic, 269
"Rubber Duckie," 111
Rubin, Arthur, 239, 247, 248, 249
Rubin, Cyma, 140, 149
Rubin, David, 11
Rubinstein, Arthur, 160
Ruede, Clay, 262
Running Scared, 206
Ryder, James Malcolm, 188
Ryskind, Morrie, 147

Saddler, Donald, 140–41
Saks, Jay David, 156, 168–69, 186, 194–95, 302, *p12*; *La Cage aux Folles* and, 224; *Follies in Concert* and, 249; at Red Seal, 265; Sondheim and, 257; *Sunday in the Park with George* and, 226
Salmon, Scott, 220
Salvatore, Tony, 190
Sandra Gilman & Celso Gonzalez-Fall Theatre Foundation, 295–96
Sarnoff, David, 164
Sarnoff, Robert, 159–60, 164
Saturday Night, 207, 231
Sauter, Eddie, 104
"Save the Best for Last," 299
Scavone, Joan, 5
Schafer, Milton, 188
Schary, Dore, 84
Scher, Herb, 257
Schlosser, Herb, 165, 243

Schnitzler, Arthur, 271
Schonberg, Harold, 31
Schottenfeld, Barbara, 282
Schroon Lake Camp, 13
Schulman, Alan, 19
Schumann Symphonic Etudes, 13–14
Schwartz, Jonathan, 91
Scianni, Joe, 32
Scott, Howard, 32, 34–35, 37–40, 44, 74, 157
Scovotti, Jeanette, 72
The Second Hurricane, 38
The Secret Garden, 73, 282–85
The Secret Life of Walter Mitty, 79
Selections from Oklahoma!, 23
Seltzer, Dov, 93
"Send in the Clowns," 216
"Serenade (Overhead the Moon Is Beaming)," 63
Serkin, Rudolf, 69
Sesame Street, 109
The Sesame Street Book and Record, 110–11
Seurat, Georges, 225
The Seven-Per-Cent Solution, 171
1776, 33–34, 102–4, 176, 222, 225
70, Girls, 70, 142–44, 306
Shafer, Robert, 292
Shaffer, Peter, 259
"Shall I Tell You What I Think of You," 71, 72
"Shall We Dance?," 176
Shapiro, Debbie, 219
Shaw, Artie, 15
She Loves Me, 92, 115
Shelter, 151–52
Shepard, Dorothy Kahn (mother), 3, 5, 6, *p1*
Shepard, Elizabeth (daughter), 122, 153, 195, 205
Shepard, Lewis (brother), 5, *p1*
Shepard, Seymour (father), 3, 4, *p1*
Shepard, Thomas Z., *p1, p2, p3, p4, p5, p6, p7, p8, p9, p10, p11, p12, p14*. *See also specific topics*
Sherin, Edwin, 173
Sherrin, Ned, 170
Shevelove, Burt, 142
Shimkin, Arthur, 109
Shinbone Alley, 144
Shire, David, 16
Shout! Broadway, 321
Show Boat, 52–54, 62, 66, 95, 125
Show Music (magazine), 257–58
Shuman, Earl, 79
Side by Side by Sondheim, 170–71, 271
Siegelstein, Irwin, 158–59
Silverman, Stanley, 148
Silverstein, Joseph, 43
Simmons, Jean, 165
Simmons, J. K., 308
Simon, Al, 73
Simon, Barbara, 291
Simon, Lucy, 283, 285

Simon, Paul, 23, 77
Simon, Richard, 73
Simon & Garfunkel, 158
Sing Along with Mitch, 30
Singin' in the Rain, 96
Sing Out the News, 85
Sinnott, Patricia, 258
Sister Act, 201
Skulnik, Menasha, 84, 85
Skywalker Ranch, 278
Slavin, Millie, 78
A Slight Error, 285
"Slow Talkers of America," 114
Smiling, the Boy Fell Dead, 117
Smith, Albert, 182
Smith, O. C., 139, *p6*
Smyth, Sandy, 265
Snappy Trio, 89
The Snow Queen, 53
"Soliloquy," 69
"Some Enchanted Evening," 214
Something for Everyone, 143
"Something Was Missing," 322
"Something Wonderful," 176
"Sonatas and Partitas for Solo Violin," 43
Sondheim, Stephen, *p5, p6, p7, p10, p12, p13*; *Candide* and, 155; *A Collector's Sondheim* and, 230–31; *Company* and, 34, 125–26, 128, 129–32, 134; *Follies* and, 142–43, 232–33, 235, 250; *Follies in Concert* and, 244, 246, 251–52; *A Funny Thing Happened on the Way to the Forum* and, 124, 253, 259; Goldman, J., relation to, 237; Hammerstein, O., and, 123, 254, 258; Lapine and, 255, 256, 258; *A Little Night Music* and, 149; *The Mad Show* and, 109; *Merrily We Roll Along* and, 15, 210–11, 213; *Pacific Overtures* and, 168, 169; RCA relation to, 160–61, 207–8, 230, 258; Rodgers, R., and, 118, 124–25; in *Show Music*, 257–58; *Side by Side by Sondheim* and, 170–71; *A Stephen Sondheim Evening* and, 215–16, 222, 253; *Sunday in the Park with George* and, 226–29; *Sweeney Todd* and, 187–89, 191–93, 195, 196, 260; Tunick and, 106; *West Side Story* and, 123, 124, 254
Song and Dance, 245, 250, 261–62
"Song of the King," 175
"Song on the Sand," 223
Songs from Shelter, 151–52
Songs of the Megillah, 93
Sony Classical, 268, 270
Sophisticated Ladies, 83, 95, 205–6, 287
The Sound of Music, 30, 71, 118, 172, 301
South Pacific, 69, 125, 198
Spinney, Caroll, 110
"The Spirit of 76," 104
Springer, Philip, 137–38

Squadron, Anne Strickland, 308
Stadlen, Lewis J., 155
Stafford, Jo, 145
Stage Delicatessen, 64
Stalag 17, 137
Starlight Express, 265
Starobin, Michael, 229, 271
Starr, S. Frederick, 15
Star Wars, 278
Stavisky, 230, 250, 253
Stein, Joseph, 150, 217
Steinway, Elizabeth, 31
Stelmach, Joseph, 197, 246
Stephens, Linda, 292, 294
A Stephen Sondheim Evening, 215–16, 222, 253
stereophonic sound, 44–46, 49, 54, 62, 64, 154; *Company* and, 128; *Sunday in the Park with George* and, 229; *Sweeney Todd* and, 194
Stern, Isaac, 11
Stevens, Risë, 59, 60, 71
Stewart, Michael, 97, 98, 259, 290
St. Louis Woman, 88
Stone, Peter, 102, 121, *p4*
Straiges, Tony, 225
Strayhorn, Billy, 205
Streep, Meryl, 59
A Streetcar Named Desire, 71
Streisand, Barbra, 84, 87, 90–91, *p4*
The String of Pearls (Ryder), 188
Stritch, Elaine, 126–27, 129, 130–31, 239
Stroman, Susan, 289–90
Strouse, Charles, 290–92, 320
The Student Prince, 63–64
studio cast albums. *See specific albums*
Styne, Jule, 124, 282
Subways Are for Sleeping, 61
Such Good Friends, 103, 110, 138–39, 152
"Suddenly It's All Tomorrow," 152
"Suicide is Painless," 136
Summer, Kathy, 271
Summer, Robert, 165, 188, 204–5, 217, 223, *p10*; *Follies in Concert* and, 242, 244–45, 249, 264; *Merrily We Roll Along* and, 209, 213–14; New York Philharmonic and, 236; *Song and Dance* and, 262
"Sunday," 229
A Sunday Afternoon on the Island of La Grande Jatte, 225
Sunday in the Park with George, 219, 225, 226–29, 231, 255
Surovy, Walter, 60
"Surrey with the Fringe on Top," 200
Susskind, David, 126
Sweeney Todd, 165, 187–96, 222, 260
Sweigert, Bill, 89
Swenson, Ruth Ann, 279, *p14*
Swift, Nancy, 191, 226

Swinging on a Star, 300–301
Switzer, Hester, 7–8

Tales of the Arabian Nights, 279
Tanglewood Music Center, 17
Taylor, Harry A., 3
Tchaikovsky, 36
"Tchaikovsky," 60–61, 120
Teller, Al, 274
Tell Me on a Sunday, 261
Tell Me that You Love Me, Junie Moon, 137
Tesori, Jeanine, 283
Tevye's Daughters (Aleichem), 78
Texas Pavilion, 77
Thaïs, 164
That Darn Cat!, 132
That Pig of a Molette, 117, 285
"There's a Boat that's Leavin' Soon for New York," 182
"There Won't Be Trumpets," 230
Thespis, 318–20
"They Go Wild, Simply Wild Over Me," 151
Thomas, Edward, 325
Thompson, David, 99–100
Thompson, Tazewell, 185
Thorne, Raymond, 291
"Those Were the Good Old Days," 294
"Three Little Fishies," 10
Three Little Words, 95, 97
Through Sick and Sin, 54
Thurber, James, 79
Time (magazine), 203
Time-Life, 109
To Broadway with Love, 73, 77–80, 115, 117, 182
"To Each His Dulcinea," 282
Tony and Lena Sing, 139
"Too Many Rings Around Rosie," 142
Toscanini, Arturo, 240
Tourel, Jennie, 35, 36, 40, 41
Towers, Constance, 175, *p8*
Townsend, Irving, 57
Tozzi, Giorgio, 64
Travesties, 202
Trial by Jury, 226
Trikonis, Gus, *p3*
Trumbull, John, 33–34, 104
Tucker, Richard, 92, 146
Tune, Tommy, 220
Tunick, Jonathan, 106, 128, 130, 169, 192; *Follies in Concert* and, 238–39, 248
Turner, Lana, 15
Twine, Linda, 287
Two by Two, 118–22, 172
"Two Lost Souls," 294
Tyler, Jim, 224

Union Prayer Book, 229
United Nations International School, 72–73

Valando, Tommy, 103, 134, 161, 244, 258
Vale, Jerry, 27
Van, Bobby, 141
Van Heusen, Jimmy, 300
Variations, 261
Verdon, Gwen, 292, 297, 304–5
Very Good, Eddie, 202
Vestoff, Virginia, 103, 106, 138
Victor/Victoria, 301–3
"Victor Victoria," 3
Vidnovic, Martin, 201
"Vilya, the Witch of the Wood," 55

"Waldstein" sonata (Beethoven), 13
Waller, Fats, 95, 199, 200
Wallop, Douglass, 292
Walston, Ray, 292
Walter, Bruno, 32
Walters, Susan, 93
Walton, Jim, 239
Warfield, William, 53
Warlow, Anthony, 322
Warner, Neil, 281
Warren, Harry, 203
Warrick, Ruth, 150
Washington, George, 102
Wasserman, Dale, 144
Watson, Susan, 142
Webb, Marti, 261
Webster, Albert Knickerbocker, 235–36
Weidman, John, 169–70, 255
Weill, Kurt, 18, 58, 60
Weissler, Barry, 307
Welch, Raquel, 302
Wellman, William, 304
Wells, Tony, 151–52
"We're Gonna Be All Right," 171
Westenberg, Robert, 219, 228, 285
"Western People Funny," 72
West Gilgo Beach, Long Island, 11
Weston, Paul, 145
West Side Story, 35, 42, 125, 176, 236, 252; Sondheim and, 123, 124, 254
"We Will Be Married on Sunday," 195
Wheeler, Hugh, 150, 154, 187–88, 189, 255, *p7*
White, Robert, 282
"White Christmas," 90–91
White Nights, 206
"A Whole Lotta Sunlight," 153

"Who's Gonna Investigate the Man Who Investigates Me?," 84
Wickes, Mary, 201
Wilcox, Herbert, 142
Wilder, Billy, 137
Wildhorn, Frank, 99, 302
Willard, Archibald, 104
Williams, Elizabeth, 289
Williams, John, 136, 278
Williams, Tennessee, 71
Williams, Vanessa, 298, 299, *p14*
Williamson, Nicol, 173
Williamson Music, 268–69
Wilson, Sandy, 290
Wings, 295–96
Wise, Jim, 105
"With So Little to Be Sure Of," 253
The Wizard of Oz, 89
Woldin, Judd, 152–53
Wolfe, George C., 286–87, 288
Wolf Trap Foundation, 14
"Wonderful! Wonderful!," 102
Woodard, Charlaine, *p9*
"The World Must Be Bigger Than an Avenue," 150
"The Worst Pies in London," 191
The WQXR/MCA Classics Listener's Guide, 305
WQXR on Broadway, 305–6
Wren, Gayden, 320
Wright, Robert, 279, 280

Yale Law School, 16–17
Yale Music School, 13, 16, 18
Yankee Doodle Dandy, 97
The Year of Roosevelt Franklin, 112
Yellen, Sherman, 173
Yeston, Maury, 220
Yoshida, Fusako, 169
"You Could Drive a Person Crazy," 130
"You'll Never Walk Alone," 269
Youngman, Henny, 64
"Young People's Concerts," 35, 42, 138

Zaremba, Kathryn, 291
Ziegfeld, Flo, 52, 77
Zorba, 39–40, 217–19
Zorina, Vera, 27
"Zubbediya," 280
The Zulu and the Zayda, 84–86
Zwillman, Abner "Longie," 6